WHILE SIX MILLION DIED

A Chronicle of American Apathy

ARTHUR D. MORSE

Hart Publishing Company, Inc.
New York City

PUBLISHED BY HART PUBLISHING COMPANY, INC., NEW YORK.

MANUFACTURED IN THE UNITED STATES OF AMERICA.

LIBRARY OF CONGRESS CATALOG CARD NUMBER: 67-22642
ISBN NO.: 0-8055-0170-3

FOR

Joan, Ann and Jon

Contents

Part III ▪ THE RESCUERS

Introduction

THE NAZI DESTRUCTION OF SIX MILLION Jews, as chronicled to date, is essentially a history of the killers and the killed. The rest of the world, with the notable exception of Pope Pius XII, has been unscarred by accusation as a mountain of literature rises above the nameless graves of the six million. It is as if there were no other world, as if two circling antagonists, one armed, the other unarmed, inhabited an otherwise vacant planet.

Many books have examined the administrative techniques and physical acts by which the Nazis accomplished the slaughter of the innocent. More recently, the historical focus has shifted to the response or, as some believe, the nonresponse of the Jews to their oppressors.

The following pages depart from these patterns. This volume concentrates on the bystanders rather than the killers or the killed. It attempts to answer two fundamental questions:

> What did the rest of the world and, in particular, the United States and Great Britain, know about Nazi plans for the annihilation of the Jews?
>
> What was their reaction to this knowledge?

To answer these questions, two types of information have been examined—materials published openly from 1933 to

1945 and, most important, government documents which were denied to the public. These official records are quoted extensively; many have never been published before. Their documentation, detailed in the Source Notes following page 386, may enable the reader to answer still another vital question:

> Could anything have been done to prevent the murder of six million men, women and children?

Some may wonder why this volume focuses on the plight of the Jews. After all, the total number of civilian victims of the Nazis was several times the estimated six million Jewish deaths. The Czechs of Lidice, the Yugoslav school children of Kragujevac, the Russians of countless villages, the Polish intellectuals, the gypsies, the Catholic priests imprisoned in Dachau, all these were equally precious and the loss of their lives is as significant an indictment of Germany as the death of the Jews.

But Jewish destruction was to be total. Hitler's indiscriminate attack began the moment he assumed power in 1933. The subsequent social and economic debasement of the Jews was unique and therefore the world's response was unique. In contrast to the selective murder of members of other ethnic, religious and racial groups, the Nazis' blatant announcement that they intended to destroy every Jew in Europe presented the United States and its allies with a clear-cut challenge. How this challenge was met is the subject of this report.

If genocide is to be prevented in the future, we must understand how it happened in the past—not only in terms of the killers and the killed but of the bystanders.

Arthur D. Morse
Scarsdale, New York
July 1, 1967

While Six Million Died

Part I

THE BYSTANDERS

■ I ■

A Plan for Murder

ON AUGUST 1, 1942, HISTORY THRUST A TERRIBLE burden upon Gerhart Riegner, the representative in Switzerland of the World Jewish Congress. On that day Riegner, who had himself fled from Nazi Germany, learned from a leading German industrialist that many months before, Hitler had ordered the extermination of all the Jews in Europe. The information, relayed in Lausanne at the risk of the German's life, even specified the instrument of murder—prussic acid, the lethal ingredient of Zyklon B gas.

Under any other circumstances Riegner might have dismissed the report as macabre exaggeration, but the evidence he had compiled at his listening post in Geneva forced him to take the German's revelation seriously. Riegner, like the governments of the United States and Great Britain, had been receiving a constant flow of information about the deportation of Jewish men, women and children to Poland. He knew, and they knew, about the mass executions of Jewish nationals in Poland and Russia; since the German invasion of the Soviet Union in June 1941, hundreds of thousands of Jews had been shot by the *Einsatzgruppen,* the mobile killing units which followed the Nazi armies for just that purpose. Their scale of murder was so massive that it could not be masked by the most elaborate security precautions. Detailed reports of their operations had reached the United States and its allies, and, in fact, had been published in daily newspapers.

But for all their awareness of the enormity of Nazi barbarism, and Hitler's repeated threats to destroy the Jews, neither the United States nor Great Britain had any knowledge in August 1942 of a specific order for the total extermination of the Jews. Riegner's informant, a high-ranking official of a firm employing more than thirty thousand war workers, had access to Hitler's headquarters. It was there, he claimed, that he had heard the order discussed.

Riegner realized that if the information he had received could be authenticated and transmitted to the United States and Britain, as well as to his colleagues of the World Jewish Congress, it might set programs of rescue in motion. At the very least it would awaken the leaders of the democracies who, until that moment, had been strangely apathetic about the plight of the Jews. In August 1942 the gas chambers for Zyklon B were still on the drawing board and the majority of European Jewry was still alive.

The thirty-year-old Riegner, fully aware that he had been forewarned of the greatest mass murder ever planned, nevertheless reacted with relative calm. Ironically, he could trace this to the influence of his law-school professors; before he left Germany in 1933, they had earmarked him for an eventual judgeship.

He had continued his studies in France and Switzerland, earning a doctorate in jurisprudence. In 1935–36 he attended Geneva's Graduate Institute of International Studies, where his talents came to the attention of Dr. Nahum Goldmann, a leading Zionist who was then visiting Switzerland.

The hard-driving Goldmann, a founder of the World Jewish Congress, was attempting to unify the divergent elements of

Judaism against the rising Nazi foe. He recognized immediately that the scholarly Riegner, a bachelor willing to work all hours, trained in the legal disciplines and with a command of four languages, was the perfect man to head the congress' Geneva office. Traditionally neutral Switzerland provided the best listening post in Europe.

As Goldmann had expected, Riegner was doing a superb job. He maintained contact with Jewish communities in Nazi-occupied Europe and relayed information to congress affiliates throughout the world, including the American Jewish Congress, which was headed by Rabbi Stephen S. Wise. In the process he had gained the friendship and trust of Paul Chapin Squire, the American consul in Geneva, who permitted him to send messages to the United States via State Department cable facilities. This ensured the security of the communications and kept State informed of Riegner's findings.

The more Riegner pondered the quickening tempo of Nazi anti-Semitism, the more he came to accept the credibility of his informant. On July 1, for example, the Polish government-in-exile had released a report from underground sources to the Allied governments and the press detailing the massacre of seven hundred thousand Jews since the German invasion in September 1939. It included a city-by-city roll call of death and revealed the first use of mobile gas vans, at Chelmno. Ninety Jews at a time had been packed into each van and asphyxiated by carbon monoxide. The death rate in this operation alone had reached one thousand a day.

In London the Polish report had been confirmed by Szmul (Samuel) Zygielbojm, a Polish Jew whose wife and two small children had been among the Nazis' victims. As a leader in the Jewish Socialist Bund, Zygielbojm had fought heroically in the defense of Warsaw before being captured by the Germans. Inflamed by a firsthand view of Nazi savagery, he had escaped to England, a feat which included a spectacular flight across the Third Reich. Now, as one of the two Jewish members of the

Polish National Council, the parliament of the exiled government, he had dedicated himself to the task of alerting the world to the systematic destruction of his people.

After testifying to the accuracy of the underground report, he had made a world-wide radio broadcast on the BBC. He asked his listeners "to ponder over the undiluted horror of the planned extermination of a whole nation by means of shot, shell, starvation and gas. It will really be a shame to live on, a shame to belong to the human race, if means are not found at once to put an end to the greatest crime in human history. The governments of Great Britain and America must be compelled to put an end to this mass murder. For if we do not try to find means of stopping it we shall bear part of the moral responsibility for what is happening."

At about the same time as the Polish document was issued, the World Jewish Congress had published its own compendium of Nazi crime, detailing the German establishment of a "vast slaughterhouse for Jews" in eastern Europe. According to information gathered from sources within occupied Europe, the congress estimated that more than a million Jews had been killed in less than three years.

Other events in July lent credence to the terrible news revealed to Riegner. On July 16 the Nazis had rounded up more than eighteen thousand Jews in Paris, separated the children from their parents and sent them off on their harsh journey eastward. Far from being a secret, the roundup had been announced on July 17 over the Berlin radio. The newscaster stated quite candidly that "all will be deported to the East, as previously announced."

On July 22 the Germans began the "resettlement" of the 380,000 Jews still in the Warsaw ghetto. "Resettlement" involved the shipment of some six thousand Jews each day by freight car to the nearby concentration camp of Treblinka, where they were asphyxiated by carbon monoxide. The Polish government-in-exile, whose couriers kept it informed of every new development, notified the United States and Great Britain that the Germans were now carrying out the annihilation of the remaining occupants of a ghetto whose population had once exceeded half a million. Besides the full information about all these developments, Riegner and the Allied world had received word in mid-July that deportation trains were removing Jews daily from Belgium, Holland and France.

In spite of this mounting evidence of an overall plan for mass murder, Riegner continued to seek additional confirmation. In the course of a one-week investigation he tried to check his German informant's credibility through the extraordinary channels open in neutral Geneva. He also enlisted the aid of a trusted friend, Professor Paul Guggenheim, a distinguished international lawyer on the faculty of the Graduate Institute of International Studies. As a result Riegner learned that the German industrialist had twice before transmitted secret information whose accuracy had been borne out by later events. Once he had revealed significant changes in the Nazi high command to the Allies long before they were aware of dissension. What was more remarkable, he had reported the precise date for the German invasion of the Soviet Union five weeks in advance.

Riegner now decided that he had sufficient justification to report his news to the United States government and to key officials of the World Jewish Congress. When he contacted the U.S. consulate he learned that his friend Paul Chapin Squire was on vacation, so on August 8 he met with the vice-consul, Howard Elting, Jr.

According to Elting's report of their conversation, Riegner "was in great agitation." He described the German informant's background and his past help to the Allies, and handed Elting the text of a cable to be sent to Rabbi Wise. At Guggenheim's insistence Riegner had ended the message on a note of caution:

> RECEIVED ALARMING REPORT THAT IN FÜHRER'S HEADQUARTERS PLAN DISCUSSED AND UNDER CONSIDERATION ACCORDING TO WHICH ALL JEWS IN COUNTRIES OCCUPIED OR CONTROLLED GERMANY NUMBERING 3½ FOUR MILLION [excluding Jews in the Soviet Union] SHOULD AFTER DEPORTATION AND CONCENTRATION IN EAST BE EXTERMINATED AT ONE BLOW TO RESOLVE ONCE FOR ALL THE JEWISH QUESTION IN EUROPE STOP ACTION REPORTED PLANNED FOR AUTUMN METHODS UNDER DISCUSSION INCLUDING PRUSSIC ACID STOP WE TRANSMIT INFORMATION WITH ALL NECESSARY RESERVATION AS EXACTITUDE CANNOT BE CONFIRMED STOP INFORMANT STATED TO HAVE CLOSE CONNECTIONS WITH HIGHEST GERMAN AUTHORITIES AND HIS REPORTS GENERALLY SPEAKING RELIABLE
>
> RIEGNER

In a covering memorandum to the State Department, which was mailed that same day, Elting wrote: "When I mentioned that this report seemed fantastic to me, Riegner said that it had struck him in the same way but that from the fact that mass deportations had been taking place since July 16 as confirmed by reports received by him from Paris, Holland, Berlin, Vienna and Prague, it was always conceivable that such a diabolical plan was actually being considered by Hitler."

Elting requested that Riegner's message be delivered to Rabbi Wise in New York, that the American and Allied governments be informed of its contents and that they attempt to seek confirmation through their intelligence sources. Elting closed with a strong endorsement of Riegner: "For what it is worth my personal opinion is that Riegner is a serious and balanced individual and that he would never have come to the Consulate with the above report if he had not had confidence in his informant's reliability and if he did not seriously consider that the report might well contain an element of truth. Again it is my opinion that the report should be passed on to the Department for what it is worth."

In order to inform his British colleagues, Riegner gave the same draft cable to the British consulate, adding as a precaution: "Inform and consult New York." It was addressed to Sydney Silverman, a Liverpool attorney, Member of Parliament and chairman of the British section of the World Jewish Congress. This telegram was also sent through diplomatic channels because of wartime censorship regulations and to ensure privacy.

When Riegner's cable and Elting's memorandum were received by the State Department's Division of European Affairs, they were circulated for comments and action. The reaction was one of universal disbelief. Paul Culbertson, assistant chief of the division, wrote: "I don't like the idea of sending this on to Wise but if the Rabbi hears later that we had the message and didn't let him in on it he might put up a kick."

Elbridge Durbrow, another member of the division, added: . . . it does not appear advisable in view of the . . . fantastic nature of the allegations and the impossibility of our being of any assistance if such action were taken, to transmit the information to Dr. Wise as suggested."

By general agreement, the cable was suppressed (it was the first of many similar decisions). On August 17 a telegram was sent to the senior U.S. diplomat in Switzerland, Leland Harrison, minister at the legation in Bern, informing him that Riegner's message had not been delivered to Rabbi Wise "in view of the apparently unsubstantiated nature of the information." On the same day the London branch of the World Jewish Congress received a copy of Riegner's cable from the British Foreign Office, which had *not* seen fit to suppress it. Acting on Riegner's instruction to "inform New York," the message was forwarded to Rabbi Wise. It did not reach him until August 28.

Wise immediately contacted Undersecretary of State Sumner Welles. Welles, usually sympathetic to the Jews, had in fact initialed the decision to suppress Riegner's cable. He now urged Wise to refrain from any public announcement of the extermination order until official confirmation could be obtained, and Wise agreed. Welles then informed Myron Taylor, President Roosevelt's personal representative at the Vatican, of the Riegner message and asked him to check its allegations with Vatican sources.

Meanwhile, in Geneva, Riegner was undergoing what he was to call "my great agony." After sixteen days of silence he was notified by the U.S. consulate that his message to Rabbi Wise had not been delivered because the facts had not yet been verified.

The State Department did not release Riegner's telegram despite the continuing flow of information from its own representatives abroad. On August 26 the U.S. ambassador to several governments-in-exile, Anthony J. Drexel Biddle, Jr., forwarded an eight-page single-spaced memorandum prepared by Ernest Frischer, a member of the Czechoslovak State Council. Biddle, a personal friend of President Roosevelt's, considered this document so significant that he sent a copy directly to the White House.

Describing the fate of the Jews of central Europe, Frischer wrote. "There is no precedent for such *organized wholesale dying* [italics his] in all Jewish history, nor indeed in the whole history of mankind."

The Czech exile stressed that the tragedy of the Jews was unique because they had been singled out for destruction by the Nazis. Their fate could not be compared to the hardships of the other captive peoples. The Allies must not respond as though this were a conventional discomfort of war. He illustrated his point with a chart of the weekly food rations in Poland as imposed by the Germans.

Frischer urged that the Allied blockade be eased so that relief supplies could reach occupied Europe, and proposed that the International Red Cross supply food parcels to ghettos and concentration camps as it did to prisoner-of-war camps. He asked that Jewish children be evacuated from German-occupied territories.

WEEKLY CONSUMPTION IN OUNCES

	Bread	*Meat*	*Sugar*	*Fats*
German	80	17½	8	9½
Pole	62	9	5½	2¼
Jew	14	4½	1¾	9/10

"This war is not being waged with bombs and guns alone," wrote Frischer, "nor will the nature of the coming world be determined only by the outcome of battles. The victory of morality is the issue in this war. Should we succeed in no more than mitigating the enemy's foul design against his most hated victim, it would amount to partial victory . . . once again we have arrived at a juncture when we are threatened by grave sins of omission . . . it is a case of putting a stop to boundless, unscrupulous destruction."

As this and similar reports filtered through the Washington bureaucracy which was still awaiting the Vatican's reply to Welles, another voice was heard—this time from France.

Dr. Donald A. Lowrie, an American representing the World Alliance of the Young Men's Christian Association, returned to Geneva from his assignment in unoccupied southern France, where he had observed the treatment of Jews in the concentration camps established by the Vichy government. He gave copies of his reports to the American consulate in Geneva, which forwarded them to the State Department. Among other things he described the first deportation of Jews from unoccupied France to Poland. In forwarding Lowrie's report, Vice-Consul Elting reminded his superiors that the information supported the allegations in Riegner's controversial cable.

On August 27 and 31 Consul Paul Chapin Squire forwarded additional Lowrie revelations to the State Department. The YMCA representative described the selection of Jews for deportation, "about the object of which no one had any illusions: falling into German hands meant either forced labor or slow extermination in the Jewish 'reservation in Poland.'" Parents being deported could either take their children with them to an unknown fate or leave them behind. Most parents chose the latter. "Eyewitnesses will never forget the moment when these truckloads of children left the camps, with parents trying in one last gaze to fix an image to last an eternity. . .

"In addition to the 3,500 Jews deported from the camps of nonoccupied France two weeks ago, new orders announce that between August 23 and mid-September, 15,000 others will meet the same fate . . . As it is the evident intention of the Nazis that their parents should not survive the treatment they are now undergoing, most of these thousands of children may already be considered orphans.

"The critical task," concluded Lowrie, "is to secure immigration permission from America."

Similar reports mounted higher and higher on Washington desks. One of the most dramatic was that of two non-Jewish escapees, one from Poland, who arrived in Geneva with details of the German liquidation of the Warsaw ghetto, the death of fifty thousand Jews of Lwów, and the German utilization of Jewish corpses for the manufacture of fertilizer. The United States took this report on the desecration of the dead seriously enough to communicate again with the Vatican. On September 26 Myron Taylor wrote to Cardinal Maglione, the Vatican Secretary of State, although he had not yet received a reply to his earlier communication asking for confirmation of German killings.

In his new note to the Holy See, Taylor repeated stories that Jews were being deported from Germany, Belgium, Holland, France and Slovakia in cattle cars to be butchered. "Lithuanian non-Jews are entrusted with fetching the candidates from the death ghetto in Warsaw . . . I would much appreciate it if Your Eminence could inform me whether the Vatican has any information that would tend to confirm the reports contained in this memorandum. If so, I should like to know whether the Holy Father has any suggestions as to any practical manner in which the forces of civilized public opinion could be utilized in order to prevent a continuation of these barbarities."

On the same day, U.S. minister Leland Harrison cabled from Bern that a Polish colleague had informed him that Jews in Warsaw were being collected in "lots" of 5,000–10,000 and shipped East, "their whereabouts and fate unknown." He supplemented this on October 6 with a firmer message: "Numerous reports which I have received and submitted from both Jewish and non-Jewish sources . . . indicate beyond doubt that Jews are being systematically evacuated from western European countries . . . ghettos of larger cities such as Warsaw are being cleared and that the Jews evacuated therefrom have been sent eastward to an unknown fate."

On October 10 Cardinal Maglione handed Myron Taylor's deputy, Harold Tittmann, an informal, unsigned response to Taylor's inquiries. The cardinal's note said that reports of severe measures against the Jews had also reached the Vatican but that it had not been possible to check their accuracy. Tittmann was dissatisfied with this reply, as he indicated to State: "I regret that Holy See could not have been more helpful, but it was evident from the attitude of the Cardinal that it has no practical suggestions to make."

The apathy of Pope Pius XII became the subject of numerous dispatches to Washington from Myron Taylor and Harold Tittmann. One dealt with an address by a Cardinal Salotti entitled *The Historical Mission of Pius XII*. The cardinal's assessment of the Pope included such sentiments as the following:

". . . . but at Rome there is a great Pope who, though navigating with extreme difficulty through the raging tempest, has given unmistakable proofs of a great and undiscriminating affection for all peoples and who has, moreover, in order to avoid the slightest appearance of partiality, imposed upon himself, in word and deed, the most delicate reserve."

Commenting on the cardinal's speech in a message to the State Department, Tittmann wrote: "His Eminence praises the Pope's spiritual qualities, his charitable acts and his powers of oratory; but one looks in vain in the address for the recording of any action on his part in recent months that could be construed as moral leadership or even as an exercise of that great moral authority that pertains to the Papacy and constitutes one of the infallible proofs of its universality. The self-imposition of 'the most delicate reserve' begins to look very much like abdication from this leadership. It is the continued silence of the Pope on the moral issues of the day, especially in the face of one notorious Nazi atrocity after another, that has alarmed many loyal Catholics and has led them to question whether the Holy See is not rapidly being reduced thereby to the status of a minor Italian state and the Pope's functions to those of an Italian patriarch."

In another dispatch Tittmann reported constant criticism of the Pope by the Allies: ". . . the Holy Father appears to be occupying himself exclusively with spiritual matters, charitable acts, and rhetoric, while adopting an ostrich-like policy toward these notorious atrocities . . . A long-term policy of appeasement based on the conviction that the Axis is destined to win the war is regarded by many as one of the chief reasons for the refusal of the Pope to speak out."

One of the more ambitious efforts to persuade the Pope to condemn Nazi atrocities had been undertaken early in September at the initiative of the Brazilian ambassador to the Holy See. The United States joined in this appeal, as did Great Britain, Uruguay, Cuba, Peru and representatives of the eight occupied nations of Europe. The British ambassador warned: "A policy of silence in regard to such offenses against the conscience of the world must necessarily involve a renunciation of moral leadership and a consequent atrophy of the influence and authority of the Vatican . . ."

But the Vatican decided to continue its silence, rejecting the appeal on the grounds that a denunciation of the Nazis by the Pope would result in more rather than fewer deaths. "Monsignor Montini [the present Pope Paul VI, then a Papal Undersecretary of State], however, stated to me," reported Harold Tittmann, "that the time may come when, in spite of such a grievous prospect, the Holy Father will feel himself obliged to speak out."

That time was never to come.

In Geneva, Gerhart Riegner renewed his attempt to substantiate the contents of his controversial cable about Hitler's order for the annihilation of the Jews. On September 28 he gave Consul Squire two sets of documents. The first was a report prepared by an anti-Nazi officer attached to the OKW (*Oberkommando der Wehrmacht*), the German High Command of the Armed Forces. An intermediary had turned it over to a Swiss university professor, who in turn had handed it to Riegner. According to the German informant, there were at least two factories processing Jewish corpses for the manufacture of soap, glue and lubricants. Scientific studies had established the value of one corpse at 50 reichsmarks.

Riegner's second submission to Squire consisted of two remarkable registered letters sent from a Swiss Jew in Warsaw to a friend in St. Gallen, Switzerland. The letters had been passed by German censorship, for they seemed innocent enough, their meaning concealed by the use of Hebrew and Yiddish words. The first letter bore Warsaw registry number 203, and the German stamp, a portrait of the Führer, had been cancelled September 4.

The letter included the following passage: "I spoke to Mr. Jäger. He told me that he will invite all relatives of the family

Achenu, with the exception of Miss Eisenzweig, from Warsaw to his countryside dwelling Kewer. I am alone here. I feel lonely. As to the citrus fruit I hope I shall receive them in time but I do not know whether I shall then find anybody of my acquaintance. I feel very weak. A week ago I spoke to Mr. Orleans. Mrs. Gefen telephones very often. Uncle Gerusch works also in Warsaw; he is a very capable worker. His friend Miso works together with him. Please pray for me."

The key words translate as follows: Mr. Jäger—Germans; family Achenu—our brethren, the Jews; Miss Eisenzweig—ironworkers; Kewer—tomb; citrus fruit—used toward the end of September in the Jewish feast of Sukkoth; Mr. Orleans—possibly the non-Jews; Mrs. Gefen—winetree; Gerusch—deportation; Miso—death.

The letter made it clear that all Jews of the Warsaw ghetto, with the exception of those working in German war industry (ironworkers) were being deported to their death in the countryside. By the end of September there might be no one left in the ghetto. The reference to Mrs. Gefen was not clear but could have meant that the pogroms were carried out by drunken soldiers and police.

The second letter, dated September 12, utilizing the same coding technique, revealed wholesale extermination.

In forwarding these letters to Secretary of State Cordell Hull, Squire added his own observation that an Aryan German source whom he regarded as trustworthy and whose reports had been reliable in the past, had "reconfirmed the extermination of the Polish people. High Party officials who have to do with Governor General Frank confirm this aim."

As if to resolve any doubts in the minds of the Allies, Hitler acknowledged these plans publicly in a speech at the Berlin Sports Palace on September 30, 1942. It was reported by both German press and radio.

"In my Reichstag speech of September 1, 1939, I have spoken of two things: first, that now that the war has been forced upon us, no array of weapons and no passage of time will bring us to defeat, and second, that if Jewry should plot another world war in order to exterminate the Aryan peoples of Europe, it would not be the Aryan peoples which would be exterminated, but Jewry . . . At one time the Jews of Germany laughed about my prophecies. I do not know whether they are still laughing or whether they have already lost all desire to laugh. But right now I can only repeat: they will stop laughing everywhere, and I shall be right also in that prophecy."

Undersecretary of State Summer Welles, troubled by the mounting volume of evidence tending to substantiate the Riegner revelations of August 8, and beleaguered by prominent Jews who requested clarification of similar reports in the American press, asked Minister Leland Harrison in Bern to submit any further material which might support the allegation that an extermination order existed. Welles said that Riegner and Richard Lichtheim, the representative in Geneva of the Jewish Agency for Palestine, would call on Harrison and that he was to telegraph any factual evidence they might submit.

The American minister met with Riegner and Lichtheim on October 22. Riegner, inwardly frantic after eleven weeks of U.S. inaction following his momentous message, handed the minister a three-page summary of the Nazi persecutions.

"Four million Jews," it began, "are on the verge of complete annihilation by a deliberate policy consisting of starvation, the ghetto system, slave labor, deportation under inhuman conditions and organized mass murder by shooting, poisoning and other methods. This policy of total destruction has been repeatedly proclaimed by Hitler and is now being carried out."

Riegner described the bedside interview he had had with a refugee from Latvia who told him about the massacre of the Jews in Riga, an event which the Nazis had concealed from the rest of the world for nine months.

The Riegner statement pleaded for urgent measures to save 1,300,000 Jews in Hungary, Italy, Rumania, Bulgaria and France, and asked for new approaches to the Vatican. It called for public denunciations of the Nazi acts, and warnings to the German satellites of future Allied retribution. Already half of the nine hundred thousand Jews of Rumania had been killed or deported to Transnistria (Trans-Dniestria), a barren waste of the Ukraine under Rumanian control.

Riegner had hoped to conceal the identity of his German informant, but the State Department's skepticism convinced him that he could no longer keep his secret, so he handed Harrison a sealed envelope containing the German's name and official title. To protect the German, Lichtheim was never told of his identity, and Riegner and Harrison guarded their secret from everyone but the Office of Strategic Services.

But Riegner's documentation was not exhausted, and now he revealed yet another piece of evidence: an unidentified high official of the International Red Cross had told Professor Paul Guggenheim that he too had heard of the existence of a German order dooming the Jews.

On October 24 Harrison, possibly suspecting an unsympathetic audience in the State Department's Division of European Affairs, incorporated the details of this meeting in personal correspondence with Sumner Welles. (This, together with a follow-up letter of October 31, was discovered in the unpublished private papers of Sumner Welles.)

Harrison's first letter informed Welles that the German industrialist, whose name he now knew, was indeed a member of the inner circle of advisers on the Nazi war economy. Furthermore, he verified Riegner's report that Professor Guggenheim had learned of the German order from a high Red Cross official. Harrison revealed that Consul Paul Chapin Squire had overheard a luncheon discussion between Guggenheim and a Swiss named Carl Burckhardt, during which the latter had mentioned the alleged order.

Burckhardt, a distinguished historian, biographer of Richelieu and colleague of Guggenheim's on the faculty of the Graduate Institute of International Studies, happened to be a key official of the International Red Cross as well. His credentials included service as the last League of Nations High Commissioner to Danzig. With this impressive background Burckhardt had become quite influential and had developed a far-reaching chain of personal acquaintances in both the Allied and Axis camps. He was regarded as a cautious, responsible source of information.

Harrison, determined to follow up these leads, assigned Consul Squire to take down a statement by Professor Guggenheim. This the consul did on October 29, in the form of a sworn affidavit.

In transmitting the affidavit to Minister Harrison, Squire wrote that he had known Professor Guggenheim for over a year and viewed him as "an intellectual possessed of integrity, reliability and sincerity." According to Squire, Guggenheim would not divulge the identity of his informant beyond saying that he was "an authoritative Swiss personality of Geneva international circles." (Within a week Squire would confirm that Carl Burckhardt was indeed the informant.)

The major points of Preofessor Guggenheim's affidavit were:

> 1. There exists an order of Hitler demanding the extermination (*Ausrottung*) of all Jews in Germany and in the occupied countries up to December 31, 1942.
>
> 2. Both Himmler and Frank (Governor of the General Government of Poland) opposed this order, not for humanitarian reasons, but for reasons of assuring the useful employment of Jews. Hitler, however, reiterated his order in September, 1942, because it had not been executed previously. Professor Guggenheim's informant is under the impression that the order is in the course of being executed.

Up to the month of September Professor Guggenheim's informant was enabled to make personal intervention in individual cases at the German Consulate General at Geneva, where he applied to the German official, Mr. Albrecht Van Kessel. Mr. Van Kessel begged Professor Guggenheim's informant to intervene no longer beginning with September since such steps were entirely useless and futile.

3. The existence of Hitler's order . . . has reached Professor Guggenheim's informant through two sources, each independent of the other, as follows:

a. An official of the German Ministry of Foreign Affairs at Berlin;

b. An official of the German Ministry of War at Berlin.

4. Professor Guggenheim's informant confirms all the bad news given by Dr. Gerhart Riegner, Secretary of the World Jewish Congress at Geneva, and Mr. Richard Lichtheim of the Jewish Agency for Palestine, at Geneva, concerning the Jewish situation in Latvia except that with respect to the details of the assassination of Jews as well as the number killed, there are numerous divergencies in the various reports.

5. The order of Hitler herein mentioned is also confirmed by a Swiss citizen with whom the informant is acquainted and who is at Belgrade, Yugoslavia, and who has always intervened in favor of the Jews. The German authorities told the same Swiss citizen that the Jewish question is one of high electrical tension (*Starkstrom*) and that it was not necessary for him to occupy himself with it. The Swiss acquaintance of the informant is convinced that there are no more Jews within the confines of Serbia proper.

On October 31 Minister Harrison enclosed a copy of Professor Guggenheim's affidavit with a personal letter to Sumner Welles. For some reason, neither the original nor an official copy was sent to the State Department.

On the same day that Consul Squire took the affidavit from Guggenheim, he recorded the sworn statement of a Latvian named Gabriel Zivian who substantiated the earlier materials about the fate of the Jews of Riga. Zivian had escaped from the ghetto on December 18, 1941, having lived through the machine-gunnings of November 30 and December 8 which claimed some twenty-five thousand of the thirty thousand Jews in Riga.

Zivian supplied many other details, some of which he had obtained from a talkative Latvian policeman. For example, he reported that vast piles of the clothes of the Jewish victims, adorned with the compulsory Star of David, had been returned from the execution area on the outskirts of Riga for shipment to Germany. There it is presumed the star was removed so its pure Aryan wearers would feel neither the embarrassment of identity nor the discomfiture of conscience.

Zivian had arrived in Geneva on September 22 after a harrowing nine-month odyssey, and Squire vouched for the accuracy of the affidavit.

Any doubts he might have had were dissipated on November 7 when he interviewed Carl Burckhardt himself. Reporting this interview to Harrison, Squire wrote that although Burckhardt had not personally seen the order, his information came independently from "two very well informed Germans." This contention supported Professor Guggenheim's sworn statement.

Burckhardt did not confirm the use of *Ausrottung,* the German word for "extermination," but used rather the phrase "must be *judenfrei*" (free of Jews).

"He then made it clear," wrote Squire, "that since there is no place to send these Jews and since the territory must be cleared of this race, it is obvious what the net result would be."

A convincing description of "the net result" was contained in yet another document received by the State Department later in November from a Vatican source. "The mass execution of Jews continues," said the paper, citing the locales of murder in Poland. "The number of Jews killed is numbered by the tens of thousands in the case of each of the towns in question . . . They are killed by poison gas in chambers especially prepared for that purpose . . . and by machine-gun fire, following which the dead and the dying are both covered with earth. There are frequent cases of collective suicide by Jewish families: Jewish mothers jump from high windows with their children. At Lublin the Germans themselves threw Jewish children onto the pavement. At Przewersk, a crowd of hard-pressed Jews assembled around a cross and invoked the pity of Christ. Convoys of Jews being led to their death are seen everywhere. Reports are being circulated to the effect that the Germans are making use of their corpses in plants manufacturing chemical products . . ."

Thus, in November 1942, an impressive collection of affidavits and personal testimony descended upon Cordell Hull and Sumner Welles in the State Department and Franklin D. Roosevelt in the White House.

Authoritative reports of anti-Jewish barbarity had begun to reach Washington soon after Hitler took power, but Riegner's revelation in 1942 and its subsequent documentation provided the United States with its first specific evidence of a German plan for the total extermination of the Jews.

During the weeks and weeks of skepticism that greeted the Riegner report, responsible officials in Washington were aware of bulging files reporting Nazi cruelties from every corner of Europe under Hitler's domination. Now that it was all so neatly documented, what would the United States and its allies do about it?

■ II ■

The Atrocity Stories

IN NOVEMBER 1942 SUMNER WELLES SUMmoned Rabbi Wise to Washington. The Undersecretary was grim as he showed the Rabbi the affidavits from Switzerland which supported the revelations of Gerhart Riegner.

"I regret to tell you, Dr. Wise," said Welles, "that these confirm and justify your deepest fears." He then released Wise from his promise not to publicize the German extermination order. Thus the rabbi, who commanded the respect of the nation's nearly five million Jews, was free to help mobilize a massive public and governmental response to the Nazi threat.

In spite of the stepped-up pace of Nazi killings, a great number of Europe's Jews was still alive. Surely a powerful demonstration of the Allies' outrage and of their determination to punish mass murder would force the Germans and their satellites to moderate their policies. The tide of war was beginning to turn. The Allies had landed in North Africa, and the Soviets, far from crumbling before Hitler's armored legions, had launched a massive counterattack.

Rabbi Wise realized that the world was still looking to the United States for moral leadership, and Franklin D. Roosevelt's reputation for humanitarianism had penetrated every corner of the earth. FDR and Rabbi Wise had met on many occasions and often exchanged warm letters. Roosevelt never failed to send cordial telegrams to be read at the frequent events honoring the eloquent Wise. For his part Wise, after an early disagreement about the need for local political reform, never lost an opportunity to support the President. The rabbi's admiration for the "Boss," as he called Roosevelt, was boundless. Surely an indignant Roosevelt would awaken the world to the crimes against the Jews.

Just a few weeks before the Welles-Wise meeting, the President had made an important announcement to the press. The United States would join Great Britain and the other Allies in establishing a War Crimes Commission. The commission would collect and record the acts of war criminals and prepare the judicial framework for postwar punishment. Rabbi Wise believed that the immediate exposure of these crimes and the threat of retribution were potentially powerful weapons for restraining the Nazis and their accomplices.

But what Rabbi Wise and the American public did not know was that the British had almost been forced to announce the formation of the commission without their American allies. Paradoxically, it was Roosevelt himself who had suggested the establishment of the commission during Mr. Churchill's visit to Washington in June 1942. The Prime Minister agreed enthusiastically and upon his return appointed a war crimes subcommittee of the War Cabinet which included Foreign Secretary Anthony Eden. The American ambassador to Britain, John G. Winant, attended a meeting of this subcommittee at which major points of policy were raised. Among them was a British proposal that armistice terms require the enemy to surrender war criminals. Winant was asked to submit these suggestions to the President.

On August 5, 1942, Winant wrote to the President requesting guidance. The subcommittee could not proceed until the United States position was clarified. Weeks passed without a response.

Meanwhile British public opinion became increasingly aroused by press reports of Nazi barbarities flowing from the European underground. More than two hundred British organizations, representing all segments of the public, had appealed to Winant, demanding strong counteraction in support of the Jews by the United States and Britain. As he waited for a reply from Washington, Ambassador Winant was also hard pressed by exiled officials of the occupied nations who had been receiving daily firsthand accounts of German mass executions.

Winant dispatched increasingly frantic telegrams on August 24, September 1 and September 20. In his third communication he reported that Eden had urged an immediate reply to the British questions, notably the proposal about the surrender of war criminals. On September 21 Winant finally received a short message from presidential aide Harry Hopkins. It stated simply that Winant's letter of August 5 had been mislaid but had just reappeared and that the matter had now been turned over to the State Department.

In desperation Winant cabled Secretary Hull directly, asking for his personal intervention "as nearly two months have gone by without my being able to give the authorities here an answer."

A few days later the harried Winant also reported to Washington that the British government had twice postponed debate in Parliament while awaiting an American response but that mounting public indignation at Nazi excesses was forcing governmental action.

On October 4 the ambassador, who must by now have sensed some disinterest on the part of his superiors, cabled the contents of a personal letter he had received from Eden. The

Foreign Secretary had warned: "This motion had now been put down again for the seventh October and we cannot avoid making a statement then . . . We much hope that we may receive their [the U.S. government's] views before the seventh October." This was recognized as an ultimatum. On October 5 Hull informed Winant that joint British and U.S. support of the War Crimes Commission could be announced.

There was one final irony for Winant. As far as he knew, the United States had not yet replied to the British proposal about armistice terms. He had to learn of the American approval from the British Foreign Office; Washington had neglected to notify its own ambassador.

But there was one point about which the State Department did not fail to brief Winant. President Roosevelt wished it emphasized that only the Nazi leadership would be punished by the War Crimes Commission. "The number of such ringleaders," the President had said, "would obviously be very small in relation to the total population of Germany." The official statement announcing the formation of the commission included the President's exemption from guilt of all but the Nazi leadership.

The page-one stories in the American newspapers of October 7, 1942, gave the clear impression that the new commission had been formed through American initiative. There was no hint of delay, no mention of the near-humiliation of a unilateral British statement.

Buttressed by the announcement of the War Crimes Commission and released from his pledge of silence, Rabbi Wise wrote to his friend the President of the United States, on December 2, 1942.

"Dear Boss," he began, "I do not wish to add an atom to the awful burden which you are bearing with magic and, as I believe, heaven-inspired strength at this time. But you do know that the most overwhelming disaster of Jewish history has befallen Jews in the form of the Hitler mass-massacres . . . and it is indisputable that as many as two million civilian Jews have been slain."

Wise asked if Roosevelt would meet a delegation of Jewish leaders representing organizations which had united to combat the Nazi threat, and he pointed out that the very day of his writing was being observed by Jewish people as a day of mourning all over the world.

One million Jews, doomed to die at Auschwitz from the effects of prussic acid, were among those who observed the day of mourning on December 2, 1942. The massive new crematoria installations ordered for Auschwitz were not yet ready, the efficient combination of hydrogen and cyanide in the amethyst-blue crystals had not yet been tossed into the "shower room," where naked men, women and children would fight for breath before the clawing, convulsive moment of suffocation.

The Nazi mask had been lifted. The euphemisms that had been used for extermination, words like "resettlement" and reassuring descriptions of "Jewish reservations," were no longer taken seriously in Europe. The Jews were bound for destruction, and the Allied press frequently published new evidence. On December 7, 1942, one year after the United States had entered the war, the London *Times* observed: "The question now arises whether the Allied Governments, even now, can do anything to prevent Hitler's threat of extermination from being literally carried out." The German-occupied countries were being given deadlines for the removal of Jews, said the *Times,* and "the dates are freely given on the Axis wireless or in reports from Berlin." German newspapers, the article continued, boasted that since the beginning of September, 185,000 Jews had been deported from Rumania to Transnistria. Virtually all the Jews of Croatia and Slovakia had been transported to eastern Poland.

"In all parts of Europe," the *Times* concluded, "the Germans are calling meetings, or issuing orders, to bring about what they call 'the final solution of the Jewish problem.' "

Members of the delegation that Stephen Wise led to the White House on December 8 had no illusions about the "final solution." They handed the President a twenty-page document entitled *Blue Print for Extermination*. It was a country-by-country analysis of annihilation. The President said that he was profoundly shocked to learn that two million Jews had already perished. He assured his visitors that the United States and its allies would take every step to end the crimes "and save those who may yet be saved." Roosevelt then added, "The mills of the gods grind slowly but they grind exceeding small. We are doing everything possible to ascertain who are personally guilty."

Wise emphasized that the tide of war had turned and that Jews everywhere recognized that an Allied victory would end the Nazi terror. The question, he said as the meeting ended, was whether any of them would be alive to see that great day.

In the months of U.S. and Allied apathy which lay ahead, Stephen Wise's question would be asked again and again. Those who opposed specific action argued that a swift Allied victory was the only way out and that any overt effort to save the Jews would somehow diminish the war effort. This placed those American Jews who wished to take direct action in an awkward position. If they fought for more vigorous U.S. policies toward their brethren, their own patriotism might be impugned.

The line of reasoning which led to the abandonment of the Jews had at its core the belief that rescue was incompatible with the Allies' principal war aims. The politicians, diplomats and military leaders who shared this view brushed aside the question that Wise and his colleagues had gently raised with the President: What would victory mean to the dead?

But beyond the issue of human survival lay other fundamental questions. What would the effect of Allied disinterest be on the captive peoples of Europe who might shelter the oppressed at the risk of their own lives . . . or on Axis troops weighing the commission of atrocities . . . or on churchmen in Nazi-occupied lands wrestling with their consciences . . . or on German commanders contemplating their own futures?

The United States, a nation founded and populated by the oppressed of all religions, of all lands, uniquely represented the aspirations of the beleaguered peoples of the earth. They clutched at news from America, listened at peril of death to Allied broadcasts, waited for the material power of the United States to free them from enslavement. Many would risk their lives to shelter countrymen who happened to be Jewish, but they knew that if the United States and its allies did not exploit rescue opportunities, the Jews would be doomed. In a moral and ethical sense the expectations of a continent in captivity would also be doomed.

But before December 8 the United States and its allies, far from engaging in rescue efforts, had not even used words as weapons in the battle to save the Jews. It was not until December 17, 1942, that Britain, the United States, the Soviet Union and the governments-in-exile issued their first joint statement directly condemning the Nazi extermination of the Jews. This, like the earlier announcement of the War Crimes Commission, was triggered by the indignation of the English and expedited by a committee of prominent Jews who had enlisted Foreign Secretary Eden's support. On the day that Rabbi Wise and his delegation visited the President, a first draft of this declaration, written by the British, arrived at the State Department. Secretary of State Hull gave the draft declaration his personal attention.

Hull was over seventy, a handsome, stooped Tennessean whom Roosevelt had selected for his political rather than diplomatic prowess. A former national chairman of the Democratic party, Hull had been first a congressman, then a senator, mastering the subtleties of political horse trading. As Secretary of State he was an effective bridge between Roosevelt and the conservative senators, whose support the President required. On the international scene Hull had focused on tariff reduction and international trade policy. Although ardently opposed to Nazi policies in the prewar period, the Secretary had mirrored his President's caution in dealing with Hitler, restricting himself largely to informal protests to German diplomats in Washington.

Hull had neither the time nor the conviction to go deeply into the refugee problem and, in fact, became short-tempered and rigid when faced with opportunities for rescue. For example, in 1940 a refugee ship carrying Jews who had escaped from France before the German occupation was turned away from Mexico. Mexican authorities ruled that the passengers' visas had been sold illegally, and the Jews were ordered to return to Europe—to certain doom.

When the ship made a brief stop for coal at Norfolk, Virginia, a delegation of American Jews, encouraged by Eleanor Roosevelt, visited Hull. Among them was one of Rabbi Wise's colleagues, Dr. Nahum Goldmann, the persuasive and tough-minded Zionist. Goldmann urged the Secretary to grant the refugees asylum, although they lacked U.S. immigration papers. Hull swung around in his chair and pointed to the American flag behind him. "Dr. Goldmann," he said, "I took an oath to protect that flag and obey the laws of my country and you are asking me to break those laws."

Goldmann reminded Hull that several weeks earlier a number of anti-Nazi German sailors had leaped overboard as their ship departed from New York. Since the United States was not yet at war with Germany, the Coast Guard had picked up the sailors and given them sanctuary on Ellis Island. Goldmann suggested that Hull might send a telegram to the refugees in Norfolk and ask them to jump overboard. "Surely they will not be allowed to drown," he said. "The Coast Guard will pick them up and they will be safe for the rest of the war."

"Dr. Goldmann," said Hull sharply, "you are the most cynical man I have ever met."

Unabashed, Goldmann replied, "I ask you, Mr. Secretary, who is the cynical one—I who wish to save these innocent people or you who are prepared to send them back to their death?"

Hull dismissed the delegation, refusing to shake Goldmann's hand; but in the end he yielded to Mrs. Roosevelt's intervention and the refugees were admitted.

Roosevelt usually ignored Hull in the shaping of foreign policy and did not invite him to the principal wartime conferences. To add to his problems, Hull felt that the President encouraged Undersecretary Sumner Welles to go over his head, and he admitted to associates that he spent sleepless nights worrying about this erosion of his prestige. But even those who considered Hull an intellectual liability found him a kind man. Anyone who mentioned the possibility that anti-Semitism might be at the root of his seeming indifference toward the Jews was told quietly that Mrs. Hull was a Jewess.

This, then, was the Secretary of State who examined the British draft of the proposed Allied declaration on war crimes:

"The attention of His Majesty's Government in the United Kingdom, of the Soviet Union and of the United States Government has been drawn to reports from Europe which leave no room for doubt that the German authorities, not content with denying to persons of Jewish origin in all the territories in Europe over which their barbarous rule has been extended, the most elementary human rights are now carrying into effect Hitler's oft repeated intention to exterminate the Jewish people in Europe."

The declaration described the deportation of Jews from the German-occupied countries to eastern Europe, adding; "None of those taken away are ever heard of again."

Secretary Hull made one change in the first paragraph. He deleted the phrase "leave no room for doubt" and inserted the word "numerous," so the sentence read: "The attention of His Majesty's Government . . . has been drawn to numerous reports from Europe that the German authorities . . ." This lessened the impact of the unqualified statement about German extermination of the Jews, but the remainder of the declaration left no doubt that the Allies were talking about wholesale murder.

When the draft was circulated in the State Department's Division of European Affairs, it underwent a more hostile scrutiny. The sharpest critic was a thirty-eight-year-old Foreign Service officer named Robert Borden Reams who was destined to play a minor but persistent role in the evolution of American policy.

Reams, a Pennsylvania farm boy, had attended Allegheny College for three years, then worked as a salesman and hotel manager before passing the Foreign Service examination. After experience at American consulates in France, South Africa, Denmark and Switzerland, he had joined the Division of European Affairs in 1942. His primary duties were as desk officer for South Africa and Greenland, but at some point during the year he added a new chore. He was put in charge of "Jewish questions" for the division. All communications dealing with such problems were channeled through him and he was frequently consulted on refugee matters, although he himself described specialists in refugee affairs as "people who live off the misery of others." (In recent years the man once in charge of "Jewish questions" has referred to his wartime role as that of "master sergeant," simply taking orders from higher authority.)

Secretary Hull delegated refugee and visa questions to Assistant Secretary of State Breckinridge Long, whose orders, as Reams knew, were to curb any special efforts on behalf of Jews, as these would create a diversion from the war effort. This restrictive approach, Reams believed, was not only Long's wish but also that of Long's good friend, the President of the United States.

When Reams was handed the British draft declaration of December 1942, he reacted much more negatively than Secretary Hull. He objected to its release, giving his reasons in a memorandum to his superior in the division:

"While the statement does not mention the soap, glue, oil and fertilizer factories, it will be taken as additional confirmation of these stories and will support Rabbi Wise's contention of official confirmation from State Department sources. The way will then be open for further pressure from interested groups for action which might affect the war effort."

Although Undersecretary Welles himself had confirmed the accuracy of information about the planned Naz massacre of the Jews, Reams blamed the spread of "atrocity stories" on Gerhart Riegner. In fact, Reams had initialed similar reports circulating within the State Department; they had been submitted by the Polish government-in-exile; by Anthony J. Drexel Biddle, Jr., the U.S. ambassador to six exiled governments; by representatives of the YMCA; and by numerous escapees of various religious faiths.

In another memorandum Reams described his meeting with a representative of the British embassy about the proposed Allied declaration on Nazi war crimes. He had told the Englishman that the primary sources of information about German inhumanity were Jewish. Reams also revealed a curious reservation about the suggested declaration. His memo warned that "the statement proposed by the British Government was extremely strong and definite. Its issuance would be accepted by the Jewish communities of the world as complete proof of the stories which are now being spread about. These people would undoubtedly be pleased that the Governments of the United Nations were taking an active interest in the fate of their fellows in Europe but in fact their fears would be increased by such a statement. In addition the various Governments of the United Nations would expose themselves to increased pressure from all sides to do something more specific in order to aid these people."

While the Allied declaration was being considered, Representative Hamilton Fish, Jr., of New York telephoned the State Department and inquired about reports of mass murder and whether State had any suggestions for thwarting the Nazis. Fish was an isolationist, but he had been moved by a letter to the *New York Times* from Pierre Van Paasen. Van Paasen, a journalist who had observed the Nazis at first hand, had written: "To be silent in this hour when thousands of unarmed, innocent Jewish human beings are murdered each day is not only a betrayal of elementary human solidarity, it is tantamount to giving the blood-thirsty Gestapo carte blanche to continue and speed its ghastly program of extermination."

Fish's call to the State Department was transferred to Reams. When asked about Van Paasen's statement, the man in charge of "Jewish questions" replied that the matter was under consideration and that the reports of Nazi killings were unconfirmed.

Two days later Reams's expertise on Nazi-Jewish matters was again utilized. The American minister to Costa Rica cabled that President Calderón wished to protest the Nazi order to exterminate the Jews if reports of that order were correct. Reams replied that the order had not been confirmed and he added: "For your confidential information the source of the reported order . . . was a Jewish leader in Geneva."

Reams's influence was insufficient to thwart the joint declaration, which was released on December 17, 1942, by the Belgian, Czechoslovak, Greek, Luxembourg, Netherlands, Norwegian, Polish, Soviet, United Kingdom, United States and Yugoslav governments and by the French National Committee.

The declaration, like the earlier announcement of the War Crimes Commission, was front-page news in the United States, but Congress responded with somewhat less emotion than did the Houses of Parliament.

In the House of Commons, Sydney Silverman, the Member from Liverpool who had received Riegner's information four months earlier, asked Foreign Secretary Eden whether it was true that the Germans planned to deport all Jews to eastern Europe and put them to death.

"Yes, sir," Eden replied, "I regret to have to inform the House that reliable reports have recently reached His Majesty's Government regarding the barbarous and inhuman treatment to which the Jews are being subjected in German-occupied Europe." Eden then read the joint declaration, after which a non-Jewish Member from London's East End asked whether the House might rise to express its grief. For two minutes the Members stood with heads bowed, the great chamber enveloped in silence. It was a gesture unprecedented in the long history of Parliament.

In the House of Lords, Sir Herbert Samuel asked whether some action could not be taken, particularly for the rescue of children. He reminded the peers: "This is not an occasion on which we are expressing sorrow and sympathy to sufferers from some terrible catastrophe, due unavoidably to flood or earthquake, or some other convulsion of nature. These dreadful events are an outcome of quite deliberate, planned, conscious cruelty of human beings. The only events even remotely parallel to this were the Armenian massacres of fifty years ago . . . they aroused the outspoken indignation of the whole of civilized mankind, and they were one of the causes of the downfall of the Turkish Empire."

Would the "outspoken indignation" of civilized mankind now be aroused? Within the next few months the United States organized the Bermuda Conference on Refugees, which was publicized as a massive Anglo-American effort. As secretary of the American delegation the State Department chose one of its experts on Jewish problems, Robert Borden Reams.

■ III ■

Bermuda and Warsaw

EARLY IN 1943 A NEW DETERMINATION TO halt the Nazi massacre of the Jews seemed to sweep the Allied world. In the wake of the first Allied condemnation of war crimes on December 17, 1942, suggestions for the rescue of the Jews poured into Washington and London. They took the following forms:

1. A direct appeal to the Axis powers via the neutrals for the release of the Jews, with an Allied guarantee to find them temporary havens until the end of the war.
2. The temporary suspension of American immigration quotas to expedite the flow of refugees, which had slowed to a trickle.
3. Relaxation of the Anglo-American blockade to permit the shipment of food, clothing, medical supplies and funds to Jews imprisoned in concentration camps.
4. A concerted Allied effort to convince the neutrals to open their frontiers to all escaping Jews. This would include American guarantees for the maintenance and support of refugees until permanent homes could be found after the war. Funds for this purpose had been pledged by American Jews

largely through the Joint Distribution Committee (JDC). Thus the American taxpayer would not be required to help support aliens and there could be no question of the diversion of funds for waging the war.

5. Pressure upon the International Red Cross to provide the same safeguards for imprisoned Jews as for prisoners of war or interned civilians. These had been denied because the Germans had declared the Jews to be "stateless," common criminals. The International Red Crosss had in effect accepted these German designations. Its infrequent and generally informal efforts to assuage the misery of the Jews in concentration camps were feeble and unconvincing.

6. Demands for the British to revoke their White Paper of 1939, which limited Jewish immigration to Palestine to a total of seventy-five thousand within a five-year period ending in March 1944. Palestine, the Jewish homeland pledged by Britain's Balfour Declaration in 1917, remained the one place in the world where Jewish escapees were welcome. Moreover, its Jewish residents wished to raise an army to fight side by side with Britain against the Nazis.

So in early 1943 these ideas with endless variations flooded the mails to Whitehall and Washington; inspired hundreds of thousands of signatures on petitions; flowed from churches of all faiths; and found their way in ever-increasing numbers to the United States Department of State.

The man most concerned with this deluge was Assistant Secretary of State Breckinridge Long, whose responsibilities encompassed refugee affairs. Long, a sixty-one-year-old Missourian, had been hand-picked by Franklin D. Roosevelt. A descendant of the politically active Breckinridges of Kentucky and Longs of Virginia, "Breck" Long had, in accordance with family tradition, graduated from Princeton. In the first of what would prove to be an unending series of misjudgments, he entitled his master's thesis *The Impossibility of India's Revolt from England.* He began a conventional law practice in St. Louis, but enhanced both his career and his family tree by marrying the wealthy granddaughter of Francis Preston Blair, the Democratic nominee for Vice-President in 1868.

Mrs. Long's wealth enabled "Breck" to contribute substantial funds to the presidential campaign of his former professor, Woodrow Wilson. In 1917 Wilson repaid this debt by appointing Long Third Assistant Secretary of State. Intensely conservative in most matters, Long nevertheless supported Wilson's internationalism and the League of Nations. His new State Department duties included supervision of Far Eastern affairs, and as he expressed it in his diary, "I am surprised how much can be done without any knowledge of it on my part."

Long resigned from the department in 1920 to run for senator from Missouri, campaigning in support of Wilsonian policies. A victim of the Republican landslide, he was defeated by more than 120,000 votes. He returned to the practice of law and moved East. But politics and his racing stable occupied more and more of his time, and Montpelier Hall, his country estate near Laurel, Maryland, became a social if not intellectual center. His frequent financial contributions to the Democratic National Committee (loans and gifts of $130,000 one year) included a generous offering to Franklin Roosevelt's campaign in 1932. As a floor manager at the Democratic National Convention he further ingratiated himself with the nominee. On April 20, 1933, Franklin D. Roosevelt appointed Breckinridge Long ambassador extraordinary and minister plenipotentiary to Italy.

The new ambassador was impressed by what he saw. He described Italy as ". . . the most interesting experiment in government to come above the horizon since the formulation of our Constitution 150 years ago."

As for Mussolini, Long rhapsodized: "The head of the Government is one of the most remarkable persons. And he is surrounded by interesting men. And they are doing a unique work in an original manner, so I am enjoying it all."

In a letter to Roosevelt in June 1933, he described improvements in Italian efficiency, cleanliness and morale: "Many men are in uniform. The Fascisti in their black shirts are apparent in every community. They are dapper and well dressed and stand up straight and lend an atmosphere of individuality and importance to their surroundings . . . The trains are punctual, well-equipped and fast. The running times have been decreased 20 per cent to 30 per cent and efficiency increased 100 per cent."

Several years later, Long's laudatory views were modified and he began to recognize the threat of Fascism. Nevertheless, as ambassador to Italy he cautioned against American economic measures to halt Mussolini's assault on Ethiopia. The League of Nations had branded Italy the aggressor but failed to enact sanctions forbidding the sale of coal, steel and oil to the invader. Long urged Roosevelt to emulate the League's weak stand and not to embargo the sale of U.S. oil to Italy. As he confessed in a letter to the President: "I expect I am a good deal of a cynic. Whether I am or not, I am unable to see any moral element in this whole war. To me it is not a holy war."

Although Long agreed that Italy deserved condemnation, he had also been quoted as calling victory in Ethiopia the "fruitful harvest of Mussolini's enterprise."

When he was recalled from Rome in 1936 (some said for his ulcers, others for his verbal indiscretions), the President wrote: "I do not need to tell you how proud I am of the splendid record you made in Rome in the midst of trying and difficult situations . . . You are a grand fellow—and you know my devotion to you."

In January 1940 Roosevelt kept his promise that Long would again be "part of the Administration." He was appointed Assistant Secretary of State with responsibility for no fewer than twenty-three of the department's forty-two divisions. These included the Visa Division, which served as overseer of foreigners entering the United States; and the Special Division, which acted as watchdog over transmission of U.S. funds overseas. Long's jurisdiction extended to prisoners of war and civilian internees.

Everything connected with possible relief for the Jews of Europe thus passed through divisions under Long's supervision—whether visas for visitors or immigrants; the dispatch of funds for food, clothing and medicine; or appeals to the International Red Cross for humane treatment of Jews comparable to that prescribed for prisoners of war or interned civilians.

Long had of course not originated United States immigration policy. He had inherited a law passed in 1924 which restricted immigration rigidly to some 150,000 aliens a year. Half of this quota was assigned to applicants from England or Ireland. The law had been buttressed with an incredible mosaic of regulations. These had been directed at nineteenth-century abuses but now kept out twentieth-century Jews.

With Long supervising the Visa Division, there would be no reform in the cumbersome procedures by which a Jew who escaped the Gestapo had to produce an official police record from his hometown in Germany attesting to his good character. On this issue, as we shall see, Roosevelt was ambivalent. Since he was afraid that the Jewish issue was a political liability, he helped to doom European Jewry by inaction even as he proclaimed America as the asylum for the oppressed. But if Roosevelt personally was sympathetic to the victims of Nazism, Long seemed untroubled by such considerations. In suppressing an influx of Jews, Breckinridge Long believed he was protecting the nation against an invasion by radicals and foreign agents. Through the years he persisted in his theories about enemy agents entering as refugees, although the record indicates that only one enemy agent entered the United States in the guise of a refugee. As it happened, the man was not Jewish.

Long's principal aides in handling refugee matters were George Brandt, his executive assistant; Howard K. Travers, chief of the Visa Division; and Robert Borden Reams, specialist in the Division of European Affairs. They shared Long's point of view and they were supported fully by the White House. Thus, at the beginning of 1943, as hopeful suggestions for the relief of the Jews poured into Washington, Breckinridge Long sat firmly in command under Cordell Hull, determined to protect the Republic from the foreigner seeking sanctuary from murder.

It was not easy. The wrath of Britain had been aroused by documentation of the Nazi crimes, aroused not quite enough to consider liberalization of its Palestine policy but enough to consider any other alternative. On January 20 the British proposed a new approach to the refugee problem. "The time for unilateral piecemeal action is past and practical measures must be taken," said His Majesty's Foreign Office. The British note called for international co-operation in settling the dispossessed. If such an international effort were undertaken, Britain and her colonies would examine the possibility of accepting more refugees in spite of the shortage of ships.

A month passed without an American response to the British suggestion. On February 20 Richard Kidston Law, the Parliamentary Undersecretary of State for Foreign Affairs, urged the American embassy in London to hasten a State Department reply. Mr. Law remarked that British public opinion on behalf of the Jews had risen to such a degree that the government "could no longer remain dead to it."

Law, who would later lead the British delegation to the Bermuda Conference on Refugees, pointed out that "the temper of the House of Commons was such that the government would be unable to postpone beyond the following week some reply to the persistent demands to know what it is going to do to help the Jews."

The threat that Britain would make some unilateral announcement regarding help to the Jews always struck terror into the heart of the State Department, for if it lagged in action, it wished to lead in announcements. This had been true during the birth of the War Crimes Commission in 1942, now it was true in 1943. Mr. Law's implied warning was effective. On February 25 Secretary Hull replied to the British suggestion of January 20, stating that intergovernmental action was obviously necessary. The note pointed out proudly that the United States had initiated the Evian Conference of 1938, which had in fact established an Intergovernmental Committee on Refugees.

Mr. Hull failed to add that the Evian Conference of thirty-two nations had simply confirmed the unwillingness of the world to accept Jews fleeing from the Nazis; nor did he point out that the Intergovernmental Committee was, for all practical purposes, defunct. Instead Hull suggested an Anglo-American meeting at Ottawa for a "preliminary exploration" of ways and means to help the refugees; its recommendations would be implemented by the aforementioned Intergovernmental Committee. But no matter what the recommendations might be, Hull wrote, the United States would be bound by its immigration laws. Stressing that the problem was not uniquely Jewish, he added another proviso: "The refugee problem should not be considered as being confined to persons of any particular race or faith."

On March 5, before the British had fully digested the U.S. reply, the State Department issued a press release outlining the contents of the American note. This brought Sir Ronald Campbell, of the British Embassy, to the State Department in a hurry. He told Acting Secretary Welles that the premature publication of the American reply embarrassed the British, since it made it appear "that the United States Government had taken the initiative in the matter, whereas it had been the British Government that had taken the initiative."

Sir Ronald was referring to the political discomfort of his Foreign Secretary. Mr. Eden, who appeared to spend much of his time waiting for delayed American responses to British initiatives, had been stalling for time in the House of Commons while awaiting the U.S. reply. Now its publication in advance of his own statement had cut the political ground from beneath him.

Sir Ronald's explanation of Mr. Eden's distress irritated Mr. Welles. The Acting Secretary replied icily that he regretted reaching the conclusion that the British government wanted to create the impression that it "was the great outstanding champion of the Jewish people and the sole defender of the rights of freedom of religion and of individual liberty, that it was being held back in its desire to undertake practical steps to protect the Jews in Europe and elsewhere and to safeguard individual rights and liberties by the reluctance of the United States Government and by the unwillingness of the United States itself to take any action for the relief of these unfortunate people other than words or gestures."

Sir Ronald, somewhat taken aback by Welles's vehemence, asked for documentation of this charge, but the Acting Secretary ignored this request, remarking that "it was a matter notorious to us that such a campaign of undermining United States foreign policy had been pursued by certain elements within the British Government for a long time past."

In this atmosphere of competitive humanitarianism, preparations began for the ill-fated conference, which was switched from Ottawa to Bermuda partly because someone had neglected to notify the Canadians.

During the two months before the opening of the conference there was scarcely any indication that the Allies had become more interested in aiding the Jews. On the contrary, there was an intensification of the American effort to stem the flow of information, and once again the irrepressible Gerhart Riegner was at the center of controversy.

On January 21, 1943, little more than a month after the Allied statement warning the Germans about mistreatment of the Jews, Riegner provided the American legation in Bern with a new and detailed description of Nazi atrocities. Minister Harrison forwarded it in the usual manner, that is, to Rabbi Wise via the State Department. His cable number 482 consisted of four pages of unbridled horror. It reported that the Germans were killing six thousand Jews each day in Poland.

The message described the particularly grave predicament of the 130,000 Rumanian Jews who had been deported to Transnistria in the fall of 1941. This remote area between the Dniester and Bug rivers in southwest Ukraine had come under the administration of the Rumanian dictator, Premier Ion Antonescu, on August 31, and had been designated a "reservation" for Jews. The Rumanians guarding their countrymen had robbed them of their possessions, literally stealing the clothes from their backs. Sixty thousand Jews had already perished and the remaining seventy thousand were slowly starving to death. These Jews in Transnistria, mentioned for the first time in this message, would figure importantly in the evolving chronicle of American policy.

Minister Harrison's cable number 482 was read by Sumner Welles, who passed it on to Rabbi Wise. His American Jewish Congress immediately began planning a mass meeting at New York's Madison Square Garden. But on February 10, before the meeting took place, Harrison received a strange communication from the State Department. Its file number was 354 and it began by referring to his most recent cable:

> YOUR 482, JANUARY 21. IT IS SUGGESTED THAT IN THE FUTURE, REPORTS SUBMITTED TO YOU FOR TRANSMISSION TO PRIVATE PERSONS IN THE UNITED STATES SHOULD NOT BE ACCEPTED UNLESS EXTRAORDINARY CIRCUMSTANCES

MAKE SUCH ACTION ADVISABLE. IT IS FELT THAT BY SENDING SUCH PRIVATE MESSAGES WHICH CIRCUMVENT NEUTRAL COUNTRIES' CENSORSHIP WE RISK THE POSSIBILITY THAT NEUTRAL COUNTRIES MIGHT FIND IT NECESSARY TO TAKE STEPS TO CURTAIL OR ABOLISH OUR OFFICIAL SECRET MEANS OF COMMUNICATION.

Harrison was astounded. The United States and Britain had publicly pledged to come to the aid of the Jews and to punish war criminals. To do that, both countries required continuing information about Nazi activities. Yet the United States was now instructing him to reject one of his most fertile sources of news from occupied Europe at a time when the war had distinctly turned to the Allies' advantage. With the surrender of the German Sixth Army at Stalingrad, a wave of optimism had swept across the Allied world.

Harrison would have been puzzled further had he known that the cable had been initialed by Sumner Welles. Later it would become clear that Welles had done so without realizing the implications.

In a somewhat apologetic note Harrison notified Riegner that new regulations would prohibit future private communications and said he would try to obtain clarification of the order.

But since Riegner's most recent catalogue of Nazi crimes had been delivered before the imposition of the ban, Rabbi Wise organized the "Stop Hitler Now" rally at Madison Square Garden on March 1. Police estimated that seventy-five thousand persons attempted to enter the Garden, which seated twenty-one thousand. More than ten thousand remained in the streets throughout the meeting as amplifiers carried the passionate appeals of speakers for governmental action.

"The world can no longer plead that the ghastly facts are unknown and unconfirmed," exhorted Dr. Chaim Weizmann, president of the Jewish Agency for Palestine. "At this moment expressions of sympathy without accompanying attempts to launch acts of rescue become a hollow mockery in the ears of the dying. The democracies have a clear duty before them. Let them negotiate with Germany through the neutral countries concerning the possible release of the Jews in the occupied countries. Let havens be designated in the vast territories of the United Nations which will give sanctuary to those fleeing from imminent murder. Let the gates of Palestine be opened . . . The Jewish community of Palestine will welcome with joy and thanksgiving all delivered from Nazi hands."

Prominent citizens of the nation which was closing the gates of Palestine also sent eloquent messages. Lord Halifax, Britain's ambassador to the United States, assured the audience that the Allied declaration "shall be followed by practical action." The Archbishop of Canterbury described the Nazi extermination of the Jews as "the most appalling horror in recorded history," and Cardinal Hinsley, the Roman Catholic Archbishop of Westminster, called for "cold deeds and speedy deeds" rather than words to save the oppressed.

An eloquent resolution was adopted: ". . . loyalty and racial self-respect impose the hard duty to register in this public assembly our solemn and reluctant protest against the continuing failure to act, against the strange indifference of the United Nations to the fate of five million human beings—members of an ancient race, bearers of an old religion that has given instructions to the religions of the world—who are captive in Nazi-occupied territories, who are unprotected by any code of human relations, who are unsponsored by any corporate state (neutral or belligerent) and who are doomed to planned, unhuman torture and death . . . thrown into the depths of unutterable despair and humiliation by the thought that they are merely the wastage of a cruel world, that they have no sponsors or protectors, that they are unclaimed and unwanted, and that there is no shadow of a hope for them to the East or West, to the North or South, in the air or under the ground."

Rabbi Wise forwarded the resolution to Secretary Hull. In a

covering letter he wrote ruefully: "It is a source of the deepest regret to me to have to underscore to you that despite the Declaration issued by the United Nations last December, little or nothing has been done to implement that Declaration and that the Nazi campaign of extermination has proceeded at an accelerated tempo . . . I ask you to take action which may aid in saving the Jewish people from utter extinction."

Far from Madison Square Garden the scientific genius of the Third Reich was moving closer to one of its greatest technical triumphs—the completion of the new equipment for Auschwitz. Engineer Pruefer of the firm of I. A. Topf & Sons, the oven builders of Erfurt who had constructed the Buchenwald crematorium, had tested the improved furnaces; they seemed to work very well. The underground gas chambers at Auschwitz, called *Leichenkeller* (corpse cellars), held two thousand people, tightly packed; the surface gas chambers, or *Badeanstalten* (bathhouses), were not quite as large. The prussic acid, referred to by Gerhart Riegner in August 1942, was solidified into pellets, which were tossed into the death chambers. Upon exposure to the damp air the pellets passed into a gaseous state, asphyxiating the victims within fifteen minutes. This was a distinct improvement over more primitive methods, such as the use of Diesel exhaust at the Belzec death camp described by SS Lieutenant Kurt Gerstein:*

"For a number of men there still flickers a lingering hope, sufficient to make them march without resistance to the death chambers. The majority know with certainty what is to be their

* Kurt Gerstein, a devoted worker for the Evangelical Church, had succeeded in penetrating the SS hierarchy to discover and reveal the truth about the death camps. His role in real life was much as it was portrayed in Rolf Hochhuth's play *The Deputy*. Gerstein attempted to inform the Vatican and the rest of the world of what he had seen but there is no evidence that anyone acted. Later Gerstein committed suicide but his description of the failure of the Diesel engines of Belzec has endured.

fate. The horrible, all-pervading stench reveals the truth. Then they climb some small steps and behold the reality. Silent mothers hold their babies to their breasts, naked; there are many children of all ages. They hesitate, but nevertheless proceed toward the death chambers, most of them without a word, pushed by those behind, chased by the whips of the SS men. A woman of about forty curses the chief of the murderers, crying that the blood of her children will be on his head. Wirth, an SS officer himself, strikes her across the face with five lashes of the whip and she disappears into the chamber. Many pray . . . The SS men squeeze people into the chambers. 'Fill them up well,' orders Wirth. The naked people stand on each other's feet. About seven to eight hundred people in an area of about a hundred square yards. The doors close, the rest of the transport stands waiting, naked . . . In the winter, too, they stand waiting, naked. But the Diesel engine is not functioning . . . fifty minutes pass by; seventy minutes. The people in the death chambers remain standing. Their weeping is heard. SS-Sturmbannführer Professor Dr. Pfannenstiel, lecturer in hygiene at Marburg University, remarks: 'Just like in a synagogue.' . . . Only after two hours and forty-nine minutes does the Diesel finally begin to work. Twenty-five minutes pass by. Many have already died, as can be seen through the small window. Twenty-eight minutes later a few are still alive. After thirty-two minutes all are dead . . . Jewish workers open the doors on the other side . . . The dead, having nowhere to fall, stand like pillars of basalt. Even in death, families may be seen standing pressed together, clutching hands. It is only with difficulty that the bodies are separated in order to clear the place for the next load. The blue corpses, covered with sweat and urine . . . babies and bodies of children, are thrown out. But there is no time! A couple of workers are busy with the mouths of the dead, opening them with iron pegs; 'With gold to the left—without gold to the right,' is the order. Others search in the private parts of the bodies for gold and diamonds . . . Wirth points to a full preserves tin and exclaims, 'Lift it up, and see how much gold there is.' "

The improved method at Auschwitz would spare the German executioners from the inconvenience of faulty equipment in the future. Sergeant Major Moll would shout, *"Na, gib ihnen schon zu fressen"* (Come on, let 'em eat it), and his subordinate would scatter the Zyklon B pellets down the shafts into the gas cellar. Twenty-five minutes after the sergeant major's order, the pumps would remove the poisoned air and the search of the dead would commence. German technology was incapable of refining this latter procedure, but it did provide Auschwitz with forty-six ovens capable of burning five hundred bodies per hour.

The first of Topf & Sons' improved crematoria was ready on March 13, 1943, as the United States and Britain were beginning the preliminary preparations for the Bermuda Conference.

Prior to the selection of the American delegation, Sir Ronald Campbell had visited Breckinridge Long with another British suggestion: since North Africa was now controlled by the Allies, the twenty thousand refugees in Spain could be evacuated immediately to that area. This would make it possible for the Spanish to receive other refugees of various nationalities, and thus a cycle of sanctuary could be established.

Long disagreed with this notion. North Africa, he pointed out, was a political entity controlled by the French and therefore the United States had no jurisdiction over such matters. At this point Long did not express his fear that the arrival of Jews might annoy North Africa's Moslem population, but later Roosevelt, Hull and Long would make it clear that this was their dominant consideration.

In his diary Long noted how difficult it had been to select a leader for the American delegation to Bermuda. Myron Taylor, who had tried vainly to persuade Pope Pius XII to condemn Nazi atrocities, had turned down the job. So had Supreme Court Justice Owen Roberts. After Charles Seymour, president of Yale, declined, Long and his colleagues offered the post to Dr. Harold Willis Dodds, president of Princeton University, and Dodds accepted. The other American delegates were Congressman Sol Bloom of New York, chairman of the House Foreign Affairs Committee, and Senator Scott Lucas of Illinois. Long's close friend Robert Borden Reams was appointed secretary of the delegation.

The selection of Congressman Bloom created consternation in the Jewish community. His intellectual resources in general and courage on the refugee issue in particular were notably deficient. His appointment, however, provided the Roosevelt Administration with a useful façade. When Rabbi Wise complained that Bloom was not an appropriate representative of American Jewry, Breckinridge Long replied that he was a representative of America, which indeed he was.

During the period before the Bermuda meeting, Long read many dispatches dealing with the destruction of European Jewry. One of the most significant messages, a cable from responsible Jewish sources in London, was forwarded to Long by Myron Taylor on March 26, 1943:

"Gravest possible news reaching London past week shows massacres now reaching catastrophic climax particularly Poland also deportations Bulgarian, Rumanian Jews already begun. European Jewry disappearing while no single organized rescue measure yet taken. Urge you energetically take advantage presence our visitor [Anthony Eden was then visiting the United States] solemnly impress British-American authorities duty responsibility convoke immediately . . . conference for action not exploration otherwise too late rescue single Jew. We doing all possible but effective action now rests

America." Details of the deportations of Jews from Berlin and Holland followed, the cable concluding with the words "exterminations reaching peak. Urge Allied relief action."

This and similar messages were ignored when the State Department drew up a memorandum for the guidance of the delegates to the Bermuda Conference. The Americans were instructed *not* to limit the discussion to Jewish refugees; *not* to raise questions of religious faith or race in appealing for public support or promising U.S. funds; *not* to make commitments regarding shipping space for refugees; *not* to expect naval escorts or safe-conducts for refugees; *not* to delay the wartime shipping program by suggesting that homeward-bound, empty transports pick up refugees en route; *not* to bring refugees across the ocean if any space for their settlement was available in Europe; *not* to pledge funds, since this was the prerogative of Congress and the President; *not* to expect any changes in the U.S. immigration laws; *not* to ignore the needs either of the war effort or of the American civilian population for food and money; and *not* to establish new agencies for the relief of refugees, since the Intergovernmental Committee already existed for that purpose.

On the positive side funds could be guaranteed to neutral nations for the support and evacuation of refugees. With this mandate for inaction, the American delegation left for the sunny sands of Bermuda.

The instructions to the Bermuda delegation took no cognizance of a groundswell of American public opinion on behalf of the victims of Nazism. One petition, signed by 282 leading scholars and scientists, called upon President Roosevelt to speak and to act:

"We appeal to you to find the means to let every German know what is being perpetrated by his rulers and to warn the German people that for generations this guilt will rest upon them unless the hands of the murderers are stayed . . . We appeal to you . . . to apply hitherto unused methods to save the millions of European Jews doomed to death by the enemy of civilization."

The Bermuda Conference opened on Monday, April 19, 1943. That day the *New York Times* editorialized that the conference "is important both as a symbol of future co-operation among the United Nations and as the first attempt at international collaboration to mitigate the appalling horror of Hitler's war of extermination since the outbreak of that war. In both aspects it appears to be pitifully inadequate . . . it would seem that even within the war effort, and perhaps even in aid of it, measures can be devised that go beyond palliatives which appear to be designed to assuage the conscience of the reluctant rescuers rather than to aid the victims."

The conference justified the *Times*'s prophecy. Even before it got under way the British delegation informed reporters that there was little possibility of immediate aid for the refugees. The Americans stressed in advance the critical shortage of shipping and reiterated Cordell Hull's theory that refugees should be sheltered near their homelands to simplify their eventual return. The victims, so it seemed, would be eager to return to the scene of the crime.

Only the texts of the opening speeches by Mr. Law and Dr. Dodds were released to the press. The remainder of the conference was shrouded in secrecy but the Law-Dodds statements were enough to cause dismay.

According to Law, victory in the war provided the only real solution of the refugee problem and the persecuted people "should not be betrayed . . . into a belief that aid is coming to them, when, in fact, we are unable to give them immediate succor."

Dodds reiterated this point and added: "The problem is too great for solution by the two governments here represented."

The Allied press responded sharply to this defeatism, British newspapers taking the lead. The London *Observer* commented: "Here are the leisurely beach hotels of the Atlantic luxury island, where well-dressed gentlemen assemble to assure each other in the best Geneva fashion that really nothing much can be done . . . The opening speeches of the conference have been widely noted in this country, and noted with dismay and anger. We have been told that this problem is beyond the resources of Britain and America combined . . . If Britain and America cannot help, who can? What is so terrible about these speeches is not only their utter insensitiveness to human suffering. It is the implied readiness of the two greatest powers on earth to humiliate themselves, to declare themselves bankrupt and impotent, in order to evade the slight discomfort of charity."

The *Manchester Guardian* noted that the conference had deliberately side-stepped the Jewish aspect of the refugee problem, ". . . but the Bermuda Conference has sprung from the horrors of the extermination of the Jews. It is a response to the demand that relief measures should be taken to abate those horrors . . . The facts remain, the extermination goes on."

Opening day in Bermuda was also upsetting to Breckinridge Long, though for another reason. His diary entry for April 20 reads:

"The 'Bermuda Conference' on Refugees has been born. It has taken a lot of nursing but is now in existence. One Jewish faction under the leadership of Rabbi Stephen Wise has been so assiduous in pushing their particular cause—in letters and telegrams to the President, the Secretary and Welles—in public meetings to arouse emotions—in full-page newspaper advertisements—in resolutions to be presented at the conference—that they are apt to produce a reaction against their interest. Many public men have signed their broadsides and [Senator Edwin C.] Johnson of Colorado introduced their resolution into the Senate.

"One danger in it all is that their activities may lend color to the charges of Hitler that we are fighting this war on account of and at the instigation and direction of our Jewish citizens, for it is only necessary for Nazi propaganda to republish in the press of neutral countries the resolution introduced in the United States Senate and broadsides bearing the names of high Government officials in order to substantiate their charges in the eyes of doubting neutrals. In Turkey the impression grows —and in Spain it is being circulated—and in Palestine's hinterland and in North Africa the Moslem population will be easy believers in such charges. It might easily be a definite detriment to our war effort."

With the exception of a brief press release, no report of the Bermuda Conference was ever published. The unpublished papers, however, shed light on its "deliberations."

According to these records the British chief delegate, Richard Kidston Law, added some "Don'ts" to the long list brought by his American friends. The British would not consider a direct appeal to the Germans, would not exchange prisoners for refugees or lift the blockade of Europe for the shipment of relief supplies. Mr. Law cited the danger of "dumping" large numbers of refugees on the Allies, some of whom might be Axis sympathizers masquerading as oppressed persons.

Sol Bloom, flattered to have been invited to a historical meeting but sensing suddenly that history was being delayed rather than made, spoke up. He suggested rather forcefully that the United States and Britain make an effort to admit refugees in large numbers. Finally President Dodds silenced him with the reminder that the delegates were bound by U.S. policy.

Robert Borden Reams contributed the observation that the State Department, like the Foreign Office, was opposed to any negotiations with the German government.

The potential exchange of refugees for war prisoners was dismissed without discussion, and it was agreed that questions relating to the Allied blockade of Europe were beyond the scope of the conference.

Shipping specialists attached to each delegation ruled out

the use of Allied ships to carry refugees, but a British expert made a positive suggestion. It occurred to him that there were Portuguese ships which might bring as many as fifteen thousand refugees to the Portuguese colony of Angola. Reams quickly countered this suggestion with the remark that the Portuguese government might not wish to have any refugees in Angola. Someone proposed that the State Department might negotiate this question with the Portuguese but President Dodds disagreed, recommending that this issue be handled by the Intergovernmental Committee. That took care of that matter—forever.

When Congressman Bloom, in a new burst of forcefulness, questioned Britain's closed-door policy in Palestine, Dodds cut off the discussion.

Although working sessions were closed to all but the delegates, the Americans held a special meeting for representatives of private organizations. George Backer, speaking for several Jewish groups, urged changes in the American quota system to increase the flow of refugees to the United States. Reams objected on the grounds that if one Nazi spy or saboteur entered the country in the guise of a refugee, it might end all immigration. Backer retorted that the number being admitted was so insignificant that a total cutoff would hardly be noticeable.

Organizations like the World Jewish Congress submitted carefully designed suggestions for rescue calling for liberalized immigration to the United States; appeals to the Germans; sanctuary in neutral or United Nations havens; shipment of food to captive Jews; liberalization of immigration regulations by Latin American nations; and opening the doors of Palestine. There is no indication that these proposals were studied or considered seriously.

Far from the diplomatic niceties of Bermuda, a harsh drama was being enacted. On the same day that the conference opened, the Germans launched their final assault on the Warsaw ghetto. Reinforced troops and police moved against the sixty thousand Jews remaining of the original half million inhabitants (more than three hundred thousand had already been deported and tens of thousands had perished from typhus, starvation and murder in the street).

While the United States and Great Britain were ruling out inconvenient methods of rescue at Bermuda, the ghetto fighters were simplifying the refugee problem by their heroic death. They fought against German armor with homemade bombs, a few light machine guns and a handful of revolvers and rifles. With the exception of one British airdrop of Joint Distribution Committee funds, the outside world contributed nothing to the resistance. The Jews appealed to the Polish underground army for weapons but few were delivered. In fact, the underground was itself so passionately anti-Semitic that its members killed several of the Jews who managed to escape through the sewers hoping to continue the fight outside the ghetto.

On the fifth day of fighting the citizens of the embattled ghetto addressed a desperate appeal to their Christian countrymen:

"This is a fight for your freedom as well as ours. Poles, citizens, soldiers of freedom! Above the din of German cannon . . . machine guns . . . through the smoke of the burning ghetto . . . we, the slaves of the ghetto, convey heartfelt greetings to you. We are aware that you have been witnessing our ordeal with horror and compassion . . . Every doorstep in the ghetto . . . shall remain a fortress until the end. All of us will perish in the fight but we will never surrender . . . This is a fight for your freedom as well as ours, for your dignity and honor, as well as ours. We shall avenge Oświęcim [Auschwitz], Treblinka, Belzec and Majdanek!

"Long live freedom!

"Death to the hangmen and murderers!

"Our struggle against the enemy must go on until the end."

On the ninth day of battle a message was sent from the ghetto fighters to their compatriots in London:

"Only the power of the Allied nations can offer immediate and active help now. On behalf of the millions of Jews burned and murdered and buried alive, on behalf of those fighting back and all of us condemned to die we call the whole world . . . Our closest allies must at last understand the degree of responsibility which arises from such apathy in face of an unparalleled crime committed by the Nazis against a whole nation, the tragic epilogue of which is now being enacted. The heroic rising, without precedent in history, of the doomed sons of the ghetto should at last awaken the world to deeds commensurate with the gravity of the hour."

It did not.

The Germans had planned to clear the ghetto in three days, but it took them four weeks. Their attacks were beaten back until they were forced to use heavy weapons to set the ghetto afire. Even so, resistance continued from the smoldering ruins long after the battle had presumably ended. The outside world heard radio reports and read newspaper articles about the defense of the ghetto—and remained silent.

Thus April 19, 1943, marked not merely the opening day of the Bermuda Conference but the beginning of the end of the Warsaw ghetto. It was also the eve of Passover, the holiday celebrating the exodus of the Jews from bondage in Egypt. In 1943 the events in Bermuda and Warsaw would not lead to a promised land. The Red Sea would not part.

The brief statement issued by the United States and Britain after the Bermuda Conference revealed no details of future action but stated that "the delegates were able to agree on a number of concrete recommendations which . . . will lead to the relief of a substantial number of refugees of all races and nationalities."

The vagueness of the statement was rationalized by the following paragraph: "Since the recommendations necessarily concern governments other than those represented at the Bermuda Conference, and involve military considerations, they must remain confidential."

The delegates' principal "confidential" recommendations proposed that the existing Intergovernmental Committee on Refugees be expanded; that paid administrators be hired; and that the committee's responsibilities be enlarged.

The Bermuda Conference authorized only one definite action on refugees: twenty-one thousand refugees in Spain would be removed to North Africa. Fourteen thousand were French nationals, mostly of military age, who had escaped the German occupation. Three thousand were Poles and Czechs of military age, and four to five thousand were Jews who were regarded as stateless or of enemy nationality. The British delegation pressed for their departure from Spain on the ground that "world opinion will be bitterly disappointed by the results of the conference if all future action is relegated to the Intergovernmental Committee."

Before the outbreak of the war the Intergovernmental Committee had accomplished virtually nothing. Its half-hearted search for areas of the world suitable for large-scale resettlement of refugees had ended in failure. German unwillingness to negotiate an orderly emigration of Jews had contributed to another major setback. Stultifying bureaucracy, the necessity to check every detail with every nation, and a less than vigorous leadership further doomed its good intentions. In August 1939, on the eve of the German invasion of Poland, the bank account of the committee, representing thirty-two nations and supposedly aiding tens of thousands of refugees, showed a balance of £2,400 (about $9,672).

The beginning of the war ended the committee's trickle of activity. It existed on paper, but that was about all. Robert Borden Reams, its acting secretary in 1942 and 1943, said recently that he does not remember sending or receiving one communication in its behalf.

This, then, was the principal achievement of the Bermuda Conference—the rejuvenation of a committee whose efforts epitomized failure.

Perhaps the most damning indictment of Bermuda was presented by Myron C. Taylor. After the conference he was asked to organize an immediate meeting of the Intergovernmental Committee in London. This time Taylor balked; he had led the American delegation to the earlier Evian Conference and had therefore been instrumental in founding the committee. In a hitherto unpublished memorandum to Hull, Welles and Breckinridge Long, he ignored the diplomatic niceties and demanded that the United States aid the settlement of refugees. The memorandum is dated April 30, 1943:

"Before any meeting is called, the position of our own Government with respect to the refugee situation must be clearly developed. The Bermuda Conference was wholly ineffective, as I view it, and we knew it would be. What the Intergovernmental Committee may be able to do, of course, is open to question, but with respect to anything that it may be able to do, it will require a commitment and large financial obligation if the plight of the refugees generally is to be relieved. The commitment also obligates this Government, if made, to find not only temporary places of refuge, but permanent places of settlement. It is my opinion, as it was before the Bermuda Conference, that the position of our government and of the British Government must be thoroughly clarified and clearly understood in advance and if nothing constructive can be assured, such a meeting will only be another failure."

A subsequent exchange of letters between Cordell Hull and Franklin D. Roosevelt helps to explain why Taylor's demands were never met. On May 7 Hull wrote to Roosevelt summarizing the Bermuda recommendations and adding his own comments for presidential consideration. Roosevelt replied a week later, commenting on each point in his Secretary of State's note.

Hull described the proposed movement of twenty-one thousand refugees from Spain to North Africa. General Giraud, the political leader of French North Africa, had agreed to accept the fourteen thousand Frenchmen in his territory. After they had been transported, wrote Hull, "so-called stateless central Europeans may be welcome to North Africa, where many of them may be able to contribute something to the common military effort."

Hull went on to say: "The unknown cost of moving an undetermined number of persons from an undisclosed place to an unknown destination, a scheme advocated by certain pressure groups, is, of course, out of the question." He added that "from time to time" the United States could share the cost of financing the migratory movements of specific people as determined by the Intergovernmental Committee.

Roosevelt agreed.

Hull then argued against bringing any refugees to the United States in excess of the immigration quota, since this "would be likely to result in throwing the whole refugee question into Congress, where there is a prevailing sentiment for even more dramatic curtailment of immigration into this country in time of war when our own citizens are going abroad to lay down their lives, if necessary, for their country . . . I cannot recommend that we open the question of relaxing the provisions of our immigration laws and run the risk of a prolonged and bitter controversy in Congress on the immigration question—considering the generous quantity of refugees we have already received."

The relationship between Americans fighting and possibly dying for their country and the arrival of the refugees was not explained. As for Hull's reference to "the generous quantity of refugees we have already received," official statistics reveal that between 1933 and 1943 there were more than four hundred thousand unfilled places *within* the U.S. immigration quotas of countries under Nazi domination.

Hull's note took cognizance of repeated suggestions that the United States might admit as temporary visitors those in immediate danger at the hands of the Nazis. Presumably this would reduce the red tape and controversy engulfing the full-fledged immigrants. To close this avenue of admission, Hull wrote in his letter to the President: "I cannot recommend that we bring in refugees as temporary visitors and thus lay ourselves open to possible charges of nullification or evasion of the national-origins principle embodied in the quota laws."

Roosevelt again agreed, and added: "We have already brought in a large number."

The Secretary of State asked whether the President approved of North Africa as a temporary depot for refugees. The President assented, but stressed that there could be no permanent residence in North Africa for the refugees without full approval "of all authorities," and added: "I know, in fact, that there is plenty of room for them in North Africa but I raise the question of sending large numbers of Jews there. That would be extremely unwise."

Fear of Moslem reaction in North Africa, Arab reaction in Palestine and, alas, Christian reaction in the United States—these were hallmarks of the American policy toward Jewish refugees. The policy was authorized at the highest level of government, the Presidency, then translated into action by the Secretary of State through instructions to the Assistant Secretary, who supervised those divisions of the department in direct contact with the problem. Finally it was transmitted to American consuls overseas who held life-and-death power in the granting of visas. These policies of exclusion were in effect long before the Bermuda Conference and will be treated in more detail later, but nowhere is Roosevelt more explicit in writing about them than in his exchange with Cordell Hull.

The Bermuda Conference has faded from memory, along

with other exercises in diplomatic futility. Even those who participated in it deplore its memory. Richard Kidston Law, who headed the British delegation, is now Lord Coleraine. In 1965 he was asked to recall the events at Bermuda.

"It was a conflict of self-justification," he said, "a façade for inaction. We said the results of the conference were confidential, but in fact there were no results that I can recall."

There was, however, one indirect result. The conference convinced one man that there was no hope for the Jews and no rescue in store for his countrymen. The man was Szmul Zygielbojm, the Polish labor leader who had escaped across Germany after the murder of his wife and two children.

Zygielbojm, a member of the Polish National Council in London, had pleaded tirelessly with the Allied governments to come to the rescue of the men and women he had left in the Warsaw ghetto, to force the Germans to realize that swift punishment awaited them for their barbarities. Zygielbojm pounded on the doors of embassies, sent cables to heads of state (including Roosevelt) and addressed public meetings. No audience was too small, for he was aflame with indignation. Desperate messages from his friends facing German guns in the battered ghetto consumed him with guilt.

On May 12, 1943, thirteen days after the adjournment of the Bermuda Conference, Szmul Zygielbojm, aged forty-eight, committed suicide in London. He left a farewell note addressed to the President and Prime Minister of the Polish government-in-exile.

"I cannot be silent," he wrote. "I cannot live while the remnants of the Jewish population of Poland, of whom I am a representative, are perishing. My friends in the Warsaw ghetto died with weapons in their hands in the last heroic battle. It was not my destiny to die together with them but I belong to them and in their mass graves.

"By my death I wish to make my final protest against the

passivity with which the world is looking on and permitting the extermination of the Jewish people.

"I know how little human life is worth today, but as I was unable to do anything during my life, perhaps by my death I shall contribute to breaking down the indifference of those who may now at the last moment rescue the few Polish Jews still alive . . . I bid farewell to everybody and to everything that was dear to me and that I have loved."

■ IV ■

The Reluctant Rescuers

COULD MANY JEWS HAVE BEEN SAVED FROM the Nazis during the war *without* diverting men, money or materials from the Allied effort? Unpublished State Department papers of 1943 reveal that many Jews *could* have been saved. And far from lessening the Allies' effort, the results might have strengthened their cause.

There were many avenues of rescue. Three of the most promising were

escape from Nazi-occupied Europe to a neutral nation;

concealment within an area controlled but not occupied by the Germans;

protection by Germany's allies, fearful of later punishment for war crimes.

During the year of the Bermuda Conference and of the uprising in the Warsaw ghetto, the United States and Britain were asked for specific co-operation in these rescue efforts. Each request was finally rejected.

The possibility of escape to a neutral nation was epitomized by a Swedish proposal. Sweden was prepared to request that Germany release twenty thousand Jewish children, who would be cared for in Sweden until the end of the war. The Swedish government inquired if the United States and Great Britain would share the cost of food and medicine for the children and if they would permit these supplies through the naval blockade. The Swedes, who had already admitted thirty-five thousand Jews, also requested that the United States and Britain agree to place the twenty thousand youngsters in Palestine or another haven after the war. On May 19, 1943, the British Foreign Office indicated its approval of the idea and transmitted the Swedish inquiry to the State Department.

On June 5 George Brandt, Breckinridge Long's executive assistant, wrote an internal memorandum stating that he, Long and Robert Borden Reams were agreed that no action on the Swedish proposal should be taken until an Anglo-American agreement had been reached regarding expenditures for refugees in general. They had also agreed that approval should be withheld, until President Roosevelt stipulated the fund from which payments for the children could be authorized. At this time, as the State Department well knew, Jewish philanthropies in the United States were prepared to pay the full costs of such rescue operations.

The State Department did not acknowledge the inquiry of May 19. On June 8 the British embassy reminded the State Department that the Foreign Office was pressing for a reply to its letter. The British stressed that food would be the principal item for the children and that shipment could be permitted through the blockade. For this there were such precedents as the Allies' feeding of the starving Greeks.

State delayed its response an additional two months. On August 12 it notified the British that the United States had not yet made a final decision as to the method of procedure.

Three more weeks passed. Washington remained silent. On September 4 the British embassy resumed the one-way correspondence. Its letter asked whether the United States was prepared to approve the expenditures for the Swedish relief action and if so whether it would instruct its representatives to the Intergovernmental Committee on Refugees to join with their British colleagues in recommending the plan.

There was still no reply. The British repeated their inquiries on September 21 and again on October 7. Finally, on October 11, the United States responded. After almost five months of consideration the State Department, with its curious logic, had concluded that limiting the rescue program to Jewish children, as suggested by Sweden, might antagonize the Germans. Further, the United States stipulated that the proposal be channeled through the Intergovernmental Committee.

In the meantime Sweden was busy providing sanctuary for the eight thousand Jews who had escaped from Denmark. State asked the British whether Sweden remained interested in the twenty thousand children in view of these new obligations. The British, still under heavy pressure to aid the Jews but trying to meet American objections, hastily revised the plan to include some non-Jewish Norwegian children. In accordance with American insistence, they resubmitted the idea through the creaky bureaucracy of the Intergovernmental Committee. In January 1944, by the time the plan reached the incredulous Swedes, eight months had elapsed, months in which many more than twenty thousand Jewish children had perished in the Nazi crematoria.

The Swedes were certain that the Germans, angered by Swedish hospitality to the Danish Jews, would now reject the proposal. They were also convinced that the United States and Great Britain were more interested in the propaganda than in the children. The idea was abandoned, the escape of twenty thousand children to a neutral haven was thwarted.

Escape by concealment within a Nazi-dominated area, a second possibility in 1943, was nowhere better illustrated than by events in southern France. Here heroic Catholic and Protestant clergymen and ordinary citizens had braved death and brutal reprisal to shelter the Jews. Thousands of children were hidden in the farms and homes of their Christian countrymen while the French clergy admitted the hunted youngsters to convents and children's institutions.

Twenty-five organizations, banded together as the Nîmes Committee, had been bringing relief to the Jews of Vichy France. Nineteen of the twenty-five organizations were non-Jewish, including Quaker, Unitarian and Catholic groups. The Nîmes Committee was chaired by Donald Lowrie, the American representative of the International YMCA in Geneva.

The principal Catholic and Protestant clergymen of France, far from pursuing the policy of silence which characterized so much of the ecclesiastical world, spoke out defiantly. When the Germans first rounded up Jews in the unoccupied, southern portion of France, protests had been written to the Nazi authorities by Cardinal Gerlier of Lyon; Dr. Marc Boegner, president of the Protestant Federation of France; and Archbishop Saliège of Toulouse, among others.

As a pro-Vichy newspaper put it: "Every Catholic family is sheltering a Jew. French authorities supply them with false identity cards and passports. Priests assist them to cross into Switzerland. Jewish children are hidden in Catholic schools. Catholic officials give advance notice to Jews scheduled for deportation, so that half of them escape."

Cardinal Gerlier's assistant, Abbé Glasberg, a converted Ukrainian Jew, was involved personally in the rescue of thousands. On one occasion he led a group of Catholics in German uniforms to a camp at Vénissieux and guided 108 Jewish children through the barbed wire to safety. A Capuchin priest, Father Marie Benoit, eluded the Gestapo as he smuggled Jews into Spain. Father Charles Devaux of the Pères de Notre Dame de Sion rescued at least one thousand Jews and there were many others, including Protestant youth groups, who were equally courageous.

As if the Germans did not have enough trouble with the

rebellious French clergy, they discovered opposition even among their Italian allies. In 1942 the Italian army had occupied eight districts of southeast France. Wherever the Italians took charge they protected the Jews and obstructed the Nazis. They released Jews from prisons in Grenoble and Annecy, ordered the Vichy police to behave humanely and surreptitiously transferred Jews from the German into the Italian zone of occupation.

Under this canopy of resistance to Nazi barbarism, the Jewish welfare organizations continued intensive operations underground. One of the most far-flung and significant of these groups was Oeuvre de Secours aux Enfants (OSE), the relief organization for children. Like virtually all rescue operations in France, it was financed by the American Jewish Joint Distribution Committee. The OSE funds came from America, but it could not have survived without the co-operation of the French Catholic and Protestant churches. For example, the OSE's regional director in Nice, Moussa Abadi, was sheltered at the home of Monsignor Rémond, Bishop of Nice. "My duty as a prelate and Christian is to offer you my hand," said the bishop. The OSE director remained at the bishop's house during the entire occupation, directing his organization's clandestine activities in the area. Thousands of children, sheltered by Christians, were linked to their parents by a courier service; none was betrayed. False ration cards, baptismal certificates and identity cards were prepared with the active assistance of the clergy.

This vast interfaith movement was handicapped by one shortage—funds. Jewish children, smuggled south from Paris at the time of the German occupation, brought no possessions but the clothes on their backs. The economic squeeze, and the shortage of food and clothing, were as dangerous as the Nazis and their collaborators.

The situation was described vividly in a telegram of September 11, 1943, from Donald Lowrie to the Joint Distribution

Committee via the State Department. Lowrie reported that all Jewish children in the Paris area had been registered by the Germans for deportation. Already the OSE was having great difficulty caring for thousands of children. "The financial situation is catastrophic, children perish for lack of the 2000 francs to pay fare to the provinces. Even the 3700 in hiding are threatened because 600 francs monthly pension is not guaranteed for the coming months. Thus the lack of relatively small funds constitutes a greater danger than the Gestapo."

Lowrie mentioned the heroism of the OSE-JDC workers. "Eugene is daily awaiting his own arrest but has taken necessary measures that his work may continue . . . regardless of this frightful situation all OSE personnel not personally sought by the police remain at their posts." Lowrie added that volunteers were risking their lives with "efforts foiled by lack of funds."

Before the United States severed relations with Vichy France, the Joint had had no difficulty sending funds to the unoccupied zone, but with the German occupation of all France in November 1942, the transmittal of money without a specific license would have violated the American law forbidding trade with an enemy nation. The economic hardships placed an added burden upon the Christian families who had agreed to shelter the Jewish youngsters.

The Joint's reputation in Europe was so high that some funds became available upon the mere promise of repayment after the war, but the needs were vastly greater than the amounts available.

Abbé Glasberg, who today is still active in Paris, has said that he and his colleagues could have saved virtually all of the sixty thousand Jewish victims of the Nazis in France if they had possessed two weapons—American visas and more money.

Thus the Jews of France and the non-Jews who sheltered them did not require American military intervention, the diversion of troops or equipment to support their rescue activities. They required financial aid for the purchase of food, medicine and clothing.

This was not a secret at the time.

In Rumania, an ally of Germany, there were at least seventy thousand Jews who could have been saved in 1943. The opportunity was rejected. This led to a governmental scandal in the United States and to a written accusation that forced Franklin Roosevelt to take drastic action. Before embarking on this incredible chronology, we must examine the situation in Rumania, a dictatorship with a sudden interest in the protection of its Jewish citizens.

During 1941 and 1942 the Fascist government of Marshal Ion Antonescu had deported 185,000 Rumanian Jews from their homes in the northern provinces of Bessarabia and Bukovina. On three hours' notice they were shipped like cattle to primitive camps in the Ukraine district called Transnistria, north of Odessa. The Soviets had formerly controlled the area but had been driven deep within their own territory by the Nazis, whose Rumanian allies now administered the region. The Rumanian army, emulating their German partners, had subjected their own Jewish citizens to the most extreme barbarities.

The Hungarian writer Eugene Levai obtained accounts of their agony from survivors. The possessions of the Jews had been confiscated and distributed among the army officers. The inmates of one camp, having sold their clothes for food, were completely naked. Parentless children wandered everywhere, and some Jews had become paralyzed from eating cattle feed. In one district, run by a Colonel Isopescu, Jews were herded into stables and shot. When the stables were filled with bodies they were set afire.

The overflow of victims who could not be accommodated in the stables were marched to a precipice above the Bug River.

As Levai describes it; "There they were stripped of all their belongings, and their ring fingers were chopped off if the rings could not easily be removed. Even their gold teeth were forcibly extracted. After that, standing stark naked in a temperature of 40 degrees below zero, they were shot. The corpses fell over the precipice into the river." During a nine-day orgy Colonel Isopescu's troops massacred forty-eight thousand Jews.

By early 1943, more than a hundred thousand of the Jews in Transnistria had perished. Then Marshal Antonescu underwent a sudden change of heart. The course of the war had been reversed and the marshal felt the first stirrings of an Allied victory: the Soviet armies were driving the Nazis back toward Transnistria; eventually the frustrated Germans would come upon the seventy thousand Rumanian Jews still in the camps between the Bug and the Dniester rivers, and the resulting slaughter would reflect upon the Antonescu government. The marshal, riddled with syphilis and false hopes, expected to avoid postwar punishment by moving the Jews to safety. Presumably he would not be held accountable for the more than hundred thousand who had already died. Since vast quantities of food and clothing would be needed by the survivors, the Antonescu government put out feelers for assistance to the Allies.

On February 12, 1943, the *New York Times* correspondent C.L. Sulzberger, in a dispatch from London, reported some of the details: "The Rumanian Government has communicated to United Nations officials that it is prepared to co-operate in transferring seventy thousand Rumanian Jews from Trans-Dniestria to any refuge selected by the Allies, according to neutral sources. This proposal, which was made in specific terms, suggests the refugees would be moved in Rumanian ships, which would be permitted to display the insignia of the Vatican to insure safe passage."

The article went on to describe the proposed mass movement to Bucharest, thence to Palestine, but pointed out that the Allies had made no decision on the plan because of the danger of spies infiltrating the ranks of the refugees. There was as yet no indication of the British reaction to a scheme which would enable seventy thousand Jews to enter Palestine. Later there would be.

During the ensuing weeks the Allies failed to respond to the Rumanian offer. Nothing happened until March 31, 1943. Then Rabbi Wise notified Undersecretary Welles that Gerhart Riegner had obtained information of importance for relay to the United States. Wise urged that Welles instruct Minister Harrison in Switzerland to meet with Riegner.

It will be remembered that Riegner's earlier attempt to forward information had resulted in the State Department's telegram number 354 of February 10, 1943, which banned future transmittal of messages from private persons. Nevertheless, Welles promptly cabled Wise's request to Harrison.

Harrison, now doubly confused, replied on April 20 that he would forward Riegner's information, but first he took advantage of this opportunity to state his own conviction: "May I suggest that messages of this character should not—repeat not—be subjected to the restriction imposed by your 354, February 10 and that I be permitted to transmit messages from Riegner more particularly in view of the helpful information which they may frequently contain."

Later that same day Harrison relayed Riegner's message. It concerned rescue in two areas, Rumania and France: "Wide rescue action possible for Rumania especially Transnistria provided necessary amounts available." Six hundred thousand dollars would be needed to clothe and feed the naked, starving Jews (about $8.50 per person). Riegner, aware of Allied fears that money might fall into the hands of the enemy, added: "Transfer of money to Rumania not necessary if definite guarantee be given that amount would be put at disposal Switzerland or America and paid after war."

The second part of Riegner's message requested funds for

France. The money would be used for the rescue of children in the concentration camps of the south and would expedite the departure of those in hiding to safety in Spain and North Africa. Safeguards for the protection of this currency would be carefully observed and the United States government would have to license its transmittal.

Riegner's message of April 20 thus proposed the possible rescue of almost a hundred thousand men, women and children poised between life and death. The State Department did not have to rely on Riegner's word alone, since it had been receiving continuing information from France. Donald Lowrie, for instance, saw to it that copies of each of his reports to the International YMCA were distributed to American diplomats.

State's reaction to Riegner's message was epitomized by Robert Borden Reams's memorandum of May 17 to Breckinridge Long: "I have certain definite doubts about the subject matter referred to in the telegram. In the first place, questions of this sort will properly fall within the competency of the Intergovernmental Committee."

That committee, stirred from its hibernation by the Bermuda Conference, had not yet been reconstituted and was incapable of action. Reams, having just returned from Bermuda, must have been aware of this.

He expressed additional doubts. The cable from Switzerland had not indicated where the French children in question were located, the manner in which they could be rescued or the method by which ships could be obtained for any evacuations. Thus Reams complicated the problem. As he should have known, the French required only food, medicine and clothing.

Riegner's message might have remained unanswered if it had not come to the attention of Dr. Herbert Feis, the department's adviser on economic affairs. Feis, a distinguished economist (and, later, a Pulitzer Prize-winning historian), appealed directly to Sumner Welles, suggesting that the State

Department obtain more details of the proposed rescue from Riegner. Such a cable, Feis pointed out, was merely a request for information and would not bind State to any action.

Thanks to Feis, a telegram was dispatched to Minister Harrison on May 25, asking a variety of questions to be answered by Riegner. On June 4 Riegner met with Daniel Reagan, the commercial attaché at the American legation in Bern, and explained the proposed arrangements for Rumania and France. The $600,000 for the support of the seventy thousand Jews of Transnistria would be raised by some wealthy Rumanian Jews who had survived the persecution and who would accept reimbursement *after the war*. The funds to repay the loan could be deposited in a blocked account in Switzerland or the United States, thus eliminating the possibility that the currency might fall into Axis hands.

The distribution of the relief supplies would be supervised by Dr. Wilhelm Fildermann, the acknowledged leader of Rumanian Jewry and a man whose reputation had been unmarred by any collaboration with the oppressors of his people.

On June 14 Harrison incorporated the substance of the Riegner-Reagan talk in a lengthy message to the State Department. In its coverage of the French situation it stressed that the French Jewish underground had exhausted its resources. Funds were needed to provide false papers for Jews in hiding and to help support Jewish children being sheltered by non-Jewish families. Financing could be accomplished by permitting persons in Switzerland with assets in France to release their French francs to the underground through intermediaries. U.S. funds, donated by Jewish organizations, would be converted to Swiss francs to repay the lenders within Switzerland. Harrison's description of the process stressed that "care would be taken that dollar or Swiss franc recipients are not working for or have any connection with Axis." Harrison forwarded Riegner's request that the World Jewish Congress forward him $10,000 immediately to begin the effort.

Riegner would have a long wait.

On July 3 Minister Harrison, attempting to stimulate interest in the Riegner proposals, notified the State Department that the International Red Cross had been informed by the Rumanian government that "there is nothing to prevent forwarding of financial relief and supplies to the Jews in Transnistria."

Three days later Riegner relayed similar information in a letter to commercial attaché Reagan. A Red Cross delegation had returned from Rumania and Bulgaria with news that the evacuation could take place "at once if the necessary funds were available." Riegner had visited the Red Cross and had been informed that there was new urgency for a decision by the United States. By coincidence, the permanent Red Cross delegate to Rumania would be coming to Geneva within the next few days and would require instructions prior to returning to Bucharest.

"It was also emphasized," Riegner explained in his letter, "that at the present moment the Rumanian authorities were disposed to admit an action of relief, but that possibly a delay of making use of this opportunity may render it problematic again."

On July 10 Harrison reminded the State Department that an anxious Riegner was still awaiting an answer to his proposals of June 14 regarding the arrangements for financing Rumanian and French relief. He reiterated the availability of the Red Cross delegate to expedite the Transnistrian project.

While the State Department continued to procrastinate, Cordell Hull received a somewhat embarrassing request. A group planning an Emergency Conference to Save the Jewish People of Europe requested that the Secretary send a greeting to delegates attending a five-day meeting in New York City. Participants would include Senator Guy M. Gillette of Iowa, William Randolph Hearst, Secretary of the Interior Harold Ickes, Van Wyck Brooks, Louis Bromfield, and other well-known citizens. The force behind the meeting was an extraordinary firebrand named Peter Bergson who had sparked a series of full-page advertisements in leading national newspapers calling attention to United States apathy in the face of the Nazi extermination program.

Bergson's zeal often proved disconcerting to his supporters, and his plans to organize a Hebrew army and set up an embassy in Washington representing the Jewish state diminished some of his effectiveness. But his attention-getting techniques were in dramatic contrast to those of the more conventional Jewish spokesmen.

A number of congressmen and senators supported Bergson's group, so Secretary Hull asked Robert Borden Reams to draft a message for his signature. Reams produced two letters, one of which said simply that it was against State Department policy to send messages to such meetings. The second reflected State's sensitivity to the criticism it had been receiving since the Bermuda Conference:

"The Conference at Bermuda, was not, as some sources have stated, a farce or a cruel mockery. It was a sincere attempt on the part of the two Governments concerned to rescue as many people as possible from the torture house of Europe . . . During the stresses and strains of a terrible war upon which depends the fate of civilization itself the needs of any particular individual, nation or race must be subordinated to the needs of the whole."

Hull vetoed both of Reams's drafts and contented himself with a bland statement to the Emergency Conference that rescue "is under constant examination by the State Department and any suggestions calculated to that end will be gladly considered. An intergovernmental agency has been created designed to deal with these problems."

Hull had developed a remarkable immunity to the documented tales of Nazi horror which were brought to his attention. While the exchange of cables with Harrison concerning rescue in Transnistria and France was going on, the ambassador of the Polish government-in-exile visited the Secretary. He was greatly agitated as he showed Hull a cable from his superiors in London.

"It is now confirmed," said the cable, "that the Germans are carrying out in the Lublin province the greatest mass murders that have ever occurred in the entire criminal history of the occupation of Poland." Then followed the names of eight districts whose populations were being exterminated. The Germans' intention, the cable continued, "is to remove the Polish population from a 100-kilometer zone passing through the eastern Polish territories and settle there the German element and thus assure the eastern zone ethnographic security." The cable described babies being kicked to death; men deported in sealed cars; children up to thirteen years of age, women, and persons over fifty being shipped to their death in the gas chambers of Majdanek.

In a memorandum prepared after the meeting, Hull noted his comments to the ambassador: "I said that this was something new and naturally of serious concern and that I would keep especially in mind all phases of the matter."

With this somewhat understated reaction to the Polish catastrophe it is not surprising that Hull did not press his subordinates for more speedy action on the Transnistrian and French rescue proposals. Actually his subordinates were pressing him to reject the suggestions on the grounds that if followed, they would violate the rules of economic warfare. In raising this argument, however, the State Department automatically brought Treasury into the controversy, for its approval was required for the licensing of financial transactions.

Treasury's Foreign Funds Control Division was charged with the responsibility of preventing American currency and supplies from reaching the Axis powers. On July 15, 1943, its representatives met with three members of the State Department to discuss the Riegner proposals. Randolph Paul, general counsel to the Treasury Department, also attended and reported State's objections to Secretary Henry Morgenthau, Jr.:

"Mr. Reams, Foreign Service officer, presently assigned to the European Division, and also assigned as State Department's refugee expert, threw cold water on the proposal on the grounds that it would be probably impossible to work out as a practical matter satisfactory arrangements with the Rumanian authorities and that the transportation of any persons evacuated could only be arranged with German consent which would not be forthcoming."

In spite of Reams's opposition, it took Treasury just one day to approve the arrangements. But the consent of both departments was required and State persisted in its refusal.

On July 22 Rabbi Wise visited the President and protested the inaction. Roosevelt, as usual, extended his deepest sympathies. The following day Wise wrote to the President reiterating their conversation: "It gives me deep satisfaction to find while with you yesterday that out of the depth of your understanding sympathy with Hitler's victims you welcome the proposal which is now before the State and Treasury Departments to permit funds to be forwarded to Switzerland by Jewish organizations from our country." Roosevelt sent copies of the letter to State and Treasury. A memorandum of August 2 written by Bernard Meltzer of the State Department reveals the dilemma this created:

"Treasury has informed me that Dr. Wise's letter has been referred to them for reply and that they propose to indicate that they will issue the required licenses. Accordingly, if the [State] Department should turn down the proposal it would have to face squarely the responsibility for overriding the Treasury Department which does not see any compelling economic warfare objection to the scheme."

Rabbi Wise's letter was read by Secretary of the Treasury Morgenthau, who had now become aware of the State Department's obvious dawdling. Morgenthau, although a member of a distinguished Jewish family, had taken no particular interest in religious matters. If anything, he had gone out of his way to avoid charges of favoritism or divided loyalty. It is one of the fascinating paradoxes of the era that it was necessary for the non-Jewish members of his staff to awaken him to the interminable delays in the rescue of the Jews, delays which State áscribed to its concern for economic warfare.

As a result of Rabbi Wise's letter, Morgenthau sent Hull a note reaffirming Treasury approval of the proposed arrangements. Hull accepted Treasury's reasoning and agreed that the enemy would be unable to acquire the blocked funds. Presumably this cleared up the question. Actually, it would be another two months before State instructed Leland Harrison to issue the license to Riegner.

Unfortunately for the Jews, the Nazis did not operate on so leisurely a timetable. In late August the Allies published an accounting of Axis war crimes in occupied Europe, accusing Germany and her allies of "carrying out with increasing tempo a deliberate program of wholesale theft, murder, torture and savagery unparalleled in world history."

A tabular summary of destruction detailed the magnitude of the tragedy. This is how it appeared in the *New York Times* of August 27, 1943:

BY EXTERMINATION

Countries	Total Number of Dead	Organized Murder	Deportation	Starvation Epidemics	Killed in Actual Warfare
Germany	110,000	15,000	75,000	20,000	—
Poland	1,600,000	1,000,000	—	500,000	100,000
U.S.S.R. Occupied	650,000	375,000	—	150,000	125,000
Lithuania	105,000	100,000	—	5,000	—
Latvia	65,000	62,000	—	3,000	—
Austria	19,500	1,500	10,500	7,500	—
Rumania	227,500	125,000	92,500	10,000	—
Yugoslavia	35,000	15,000	12,000	5,000	3,000

Countries	Total Dead	Organized Murder	Deportation	Starvation Epidemics	Killed in Warfare
Greece	18,500	2,000	8,500	6,000	2,000
Belgium	30,000	—	25,000	5,000	—
Holland	45,000	—	40,000	5,000	—
France	56,000	2,000	34,000	15,000	5,000
Czechoslovakia	64,500	2,000	47,500	15,000	—
(a) Protectorate	(27,000)	(2,000)	(15,000)	(10,000)	—
(b) Slovakia	(37,500)	—	(32,500)	(5,000)	—
Danzig	250	—	250	—	—
Estonia	3,000	3,000	—	—	—
Norway	800	—	600	200	—
Total	3,030,050	1,702,500	345,850	746,700	235,000

On September 28, 1943, Harrison was finally notified that he could issue Riegner the license for the relief actions in Rumania and France. John Pehle, director of the Treasury Department's Division of Foreign Funds Control, having wearied of State's dilatory tactics, drafted the cable himself and saw to it that it was forwarded by the State Department:

"The Treasury authorizes you . . . to issue an appropriate license to the World Jewish Congress and its agents to undertake transactions necessary for the purpose of evacuating Jewish refugees from Rumania and France subject to the conditions set forth in our cables . . ."

But Harrison faced yet another obstacle. His standing instructions were to refer any licensing matters to the British Ministry of Economic Warfare for its concurrence. On October 6 Harrison notified State that the commercial secretary of the British embassy "in absence of specific instructions from Ministry of Economic Warfare does not—repeat not—concur in issuance of license." Harrison then added the latest complication in the seven-month sequence. "Legation is uncertain," he cabled, "to exercise authority granted by the Treasury to issue licenses to implement Riegner plan in the absence of the Department's specific instructions."

Once again rescue was stalled.

State conferred with Treasury again and worded a message to Harrison in a manner calculated to make him realize that authorization for relief was being made at the insistence of Treasury rather than as a matter of State Department policy. There was a dispute within the department as to whether even this grudging co-operation with Treasury was necessary. Reams had written Breckinridge Long a memo protesting the dispatch of the cable:

"I do not believe that we can or should accede to the desire of Treasury and send this message as a joint message from Treasury and the Department . . . I feel that this proposal is objectionable from the Department's point of view." Then Reams placed the Jews seeking to escape the Nazis in a new category: "We are granting to a special group of enemy aliens relief measures which we have in the past denied to Allied peoples." Reams's final objection was that the proposed American action will "incense the British."

Long sought to soothe his colleague: "As a matter of probability," explained the Assistant Secretary of State, "these transactions will not be completed. There is no available, presently known method for the people for whom the funds are intended to leave the jurisdiction of the enemy." Thus Long acknowledged that his approval of the rescue plan was based in part on his realization that it probably would not succeed anyway.

He added in his note to Reams that there were precedents for the transmission of funds to enemy-held areas and that the President approved of the objectives. Long had learned about these precedents from John Pehle, the tough-minded Treasury specialist who was developing a mounting fury as he observed the daily torpor of the State Department. Pehle's staff began developing a detailed record of the stalled negotiations, for it was now clear to them that the economic-warfare argument was a blind for inaction.

At a meeting with Long, Pehle disabused the Assistant Secretary of the notion that everything had to be checked out with the British. Pehle reminded him that the agreement with the British was supposed to cover major transactions, that it was inconceivable that the relatively small amounts of currency for Riegner would affect the war effort. Furthermore, he told Long, the British had transferred £3,000 sterling to Guernsey to feed English children in the Channel Islands occupied by the Germans. The Ministry of Economic Warfare in London had notified Treasury of the transaction but had not requested United States permission to transfer the money. It was too small a matter on which to obtain U.S. concurrence. Anyway, there had been no American objections; everyone agreed that English children should be fed.

Pehle's illustration of the British transfer of funds finally convinced Long that the delayed joint message from Treasury and State could be sent to Minister Harrison in Switzerland, but even then it was worded in such a manner as to inhibit Harrison's action. State's cable number 2626 of October 26, 1943, notified him that the department had taken up the contents of his last message with Treasury "which requested the Department to send the following reply quote Considerations raised by you including those mentioned by your British colleague were all considered carefully in Washington . . . Instructions are given you herewith to issue appropriate license . . . to the World Jewish Congress and its agents unquote You should of course comply with the Treasury Department's desires."

Harrison reacted to the cable as expected. He was a representative of the State Department, not the Treasury, and he was perceptive enough to sense State's disenchantment with Treasury's interference.

So on November 14, 1943, almost three weeks after he was ordered to issue the license to Riegner, Harrison informed his superiors that the British Ministry of Economic Warfare had notified its representative in Bern that it "shared his objections" to the proposed licensing and had told him "to withhold consent meanwhile." As for Harrison, in spite of his previous orders, he now said he "should greatly appreciate specific instructions if I am expected to comply with desires Treasury Department."

At a Treasury staff meeting John Pehle summed up the attitude of the State Department: "This file is full of State Department cables which are full of little remarks like the Treasury wants this, the Treasury desires you to do this, and the Treasury this, and the Treasury that . . . Harrison, unless he is just a dumbbell, can see through that. State is, in effect, saying this is only what the Treasury wants you to do."

Secretary Morgenthau, who had assumed that his earlier exchange of friendly notes with Secretary Hull would end the delay, now drafted a new message to his fellow Cabinet member. His letter of November 24 began with "My dear Cordell," and reviewed the chain of events beginning with Treasury approval—he did not go all the way back to the first inquiries from Switzerland.

"I find the three and one-half months' delay which has ensued since Treasury first indicated its approval, and you concurred, most difficult to understand. I fully appreciate that some delays are inherent in handling these problems by cable. However, it is hard to understand the delays that have occurred in this case over the relatively simple matter of getting our Minister to Switzerland to issue a license at my direction and with your concurrence. Since programs of this character can be just as effectively vitiated by delay as they can by denial of the necessary licenses, your assistance is badly needed in order to expedite this matter."

This seemingly endless sequence now took a new turn. The

British government introduced the most callous argument that had yet been raised on the subject of rescue.

On December 15, 1943, the Ministry of Economic Warfare addressed a letter to Ambassador Winant in London, who immediately cabled its contents to Washington. The text, read in the light of what was *then* known of the Nazi extermination program, represented nothing less than a death sentence.

"We have now received the views of the Foreign Office on the proposal of the U.S. Treasury to license the remittance to Switzerland of $25,000* as a preliminary installment to be expended on the rescue of Jews from France and Rumania. The Foreign Office are concerned with the difficulties of disposing of any considerable number of Jews should they be rescued . . . They foresee that it is likely to prove almost if not quite impossible to deal with anything like the number of 70,000 refugees whose rescue is envisaged by the Riegner plan."

During 1943, when the Foreign Office was concerned "with the difficulties of disposing of any considerable number of Jews," Britain's 1939 White Paper on Palestine was choking off immigration to that haven. And in 1943 the United States, with an annual quota permitting the immigration of more than 150,000 persons, admitted a grand total of 23,725. Of these, only 4,705 were Jews fleeing from persecution.

On December 20 Henry Morgenthau and John Pehle visited Cordell Hull and Breckinridge Long. Hull had already drafted a strong reply to the British. He handed a copy to Morgenthau. The British message had been "read with astonishment," said the cable. The State Department was "unable to agree with the point of view set forth." The philosophy was "incompatible with the policy of the United States government and with previously expressed British policy as it has been understood by us."

Long then announced that on December 18 Harrison had

* Riegner had increased the suggested first installment from $10,000 to $25,000.

received orders to issue the license to Riegner. Hull seemed genuinely outraged by the delay. "Of course," he explained, "the people down the line get hold of these things. When I don't know about them, I just can't handle them. But down the line they just don't understand these things . . . you just sort of have to rip things out if you want to get them done."

On December 23, 1943, eight months after Riegner's first description of relief possibilities in Rumania and France, he was personally handed his license, and a few days later the first installment of $25,000 arrived.

But the episode had not ended. Henry Morgenthau and his colleagues at the Treasury Department were now convinced that rescue activities must be removed from direct State Department control. To prove their case, they began to prepare a documented résumé of State's ineptitude. They planned to take this directly to the President.

■ V ■

"Acquiescence of This Government . . ."

AS SECRETARY MORGENTHAU AND HIS COLleagues studied the State Department's eight-month delay in authorizing relief for the Jews of France and Rumania, they discovered the duplicity surrounding cable number 354. Before his recent death Morgenthau said that this message from Washington instructing Minister Harrison in Switzerland to cut off the flow of information about the desperate situation of the Jews shocked him more profoundly than anything else in the long chain of apathy.

Morgenthau was certain, however, that Sumner Welles had initialed cable number 354 without realizing its significance. Welles, unlike most of his associates, was consistently sympathetic to the victims of persecution, but he was burdened heavily by overwork and by the ineptitude of Cordell Hull. Each day Welles reviewed a mass of routine outgoing messages prepared by subordinates. Cable number 354, drafted as though it were a conventional administrative instruction, might easily have slipped by his scrutiny. On the surface, the State Department's refusal to let persons send private messages via its communication facilities seemed reasonable and justified. Nothing in the text indicated that it concerned the persecution of the Jews.

But the hidden meaning of cable number 354 was contained in its innocent introductory phrase, "Your 482, January 21." This referred Minister Harrison to his earlier message, which had detailed in the most precise manner the massacres in Poland and the ghettoization of survivors; the deportation of Rumanian Jews to Transnistria; and the deliberate starvation of the remaining Jews of Germany, Austria and Czechoslovakia. Unless Welles had checked the text of 482 before initialing 354 he could not have realized the nature of the earlier message.

Morgenthau himself never saw the cable of suppression, but a minor State Department official had leaked word of its contents and its cross reference to a friend in Treasury, who had informed the Secretary. At his meeting with Hull and Breckinridge Long on December 20, 1943, Morgenthau had casually requested the complete text of 354. When Long sent a copy to his office, Morgenthau was not surprised to find that the cross reference had been deleted.

The areas of deception were growing, and so was Morgenthau's indignation. He assigned the Treasury Department's general counsel, Randolph Paul, to check the original text of 354. Paul managed to get hold of an exact copy of the original, complete with its introductory cross reference. Now Morgenthau, convinced of State Department perfidy, instructed Paul to prepare a background paper documenting the eight-month delay. At the same time he scheduled a meeting with the President for January 16.

Paul turned the project over to his assistant general counsel, an intense young man named Josiah E. DuBois, Jr. DuBois became the principal architect of the paper, although he was given a major assist by John Pehle and the Foreign Funds Control Division.

This eighteen-page narrative, prepared by three Protestants.

was entitled *Report to the Secretary on the Acquiescence of This Government in the Murder of the Jews.* It was signed by Randolph Paul and has never before been published.

> [State Department officials] have not only failed to use the Governmental machinery at their disposal to rescue Jews from Hitler, but have even gone so far as to use this Governmental machinery to prevent the rescue of these Jews.
>
> They have not only failed to cooperate with private organizations in the efforts of these organizations to work out individual programs of their own, but have taken steps designed to prevent these programs from being put into effect.
>
> They not only have failed to facilitate the obtaining of information concerning Hitler's plans to exterminate the Jews of Europe but in their official capacity have gone so far as to surreptitiously attempt to stop the obtaining of information concerning the murder of the Jewish population of Europe.
>
> They have tried to cover up their guilt by:
>
> (a) concealment and misrepresentation;
>
> (b) the giving of false and misleading explanations for their failures to act and their attempts to prevent action; and
>
> (c) the issuance of false and misleading statements concerning the "action" which they have taken to date.

The report pointed out that over a year had elapsed from the time the United States and its Allies had publicly acknowledged and denounced the Nazi policy of extermination, and then went on to make an explicit accusation:

> While the State Department has been thus "exploring" the whole refugee problem, without distinguishing between those who are in imminent danger of death and those who are not, hundreds of thousands of Jews have been allowed to perish.

The Treasury document assailed the cumbersome procedures of obtaining visas to the United States and quoted from a speech by Congressman Emanuel Celler of New York, one of the few who had spoken out consistently in behalf of the refugees:

> According to Earl G. Harrison, Commissioner of the Immigration and Naturalization Service, not since 1862 have there been fewer aliens entering the United States. Frankly Breckinridge Long, in my humble opinion, is least sympathetic to refugees in all the State Department. I attribute to him the tragic bottleneck in the granting of visas . . . It takes months and months to grant the visa and then it usually applies to a corpse.

The draft report submitted to Morgenthau included a point-by-point chronology of State's listless response to rescue opportunities.

Morgenthau retitled the document *Personal Report to the President,* condensed it by half and changed some of the language, but it remained tough and uncompromising.

When Morgenthau, Paul and Pehle visited the White House on Sunday, January 16, 1944, the Secretary handed the President his *Personal Report.*

Roosevelt read it quickly in their presence. The new version began with a direct attack, its emotion compensating for its syntax:

> You are probably not as familiar as I am with the utter failure of certain officials in our State Department, who are charged with actually carrying out this policy, to take any effective action to prevent the extermination of the Jews in German-controlled Europe . . . Although they have used such devices as setting up intergovernmental organizations to survey the whole refugee problem, making it appear that positive action could be expected, in fact nothing has been accomplished . . . Whether one views this failure as being deliberate on the part of those

> officials handling the matter, or merely due to their incompetence, is not too important from my point of view. However, there is a growing number of responsible people and organizations today who have ceased to view our failure as the product of simple incompetence on the part of those officials in the State Department charged with handling this problem. They see plain anti-Semitism motivating the actions of these State Department officials and, rightly or wrongly, it will require little more in the way of proof for this suspicion to explode into a nasty scandal.

After detailing the delays in approval of the French-Rumanian rescue plan, the report described Morgenthau's confrontation with Secretary Hull on December 20. On that very day Long suddenly approved the license to transmit funds. He did this in the face of British protestations of "disposing of any considerable number of Jews" and in spite of Harrison's misgivings. Morgenthau's *Personal Report* attempted to explain Long's change of heart:

> Breckinridge Long, who is in charge of such matters at the State Department, knew that his position was so indefensible that he was unwilling even to try to defend it at my pending conference with Secretary Hull on December 20. Accordingly he took such action as he felt was necessary to cover up his previous position in this matter.

Morgenthau also pointed out how Sumner Welles had urged Minister Harrison in October 1942 to forward all information concerning the Nazi assault on the Jews, then had unaccountably reversed these instructions with cable number 354.

> The cable has the appearance of being a routine message which a busy official would sign without question. On its face it is most innocent and innocuous, yet when read together with the previous cables, is it anything less than an attempted suppression of information requested by this Government concerning the murder of Jews by Hitler?

The document ended on a fervent note:

> The facts I have detailed in this report, Mr. President, came to the Treasury's attention as a part of our routine investigation of the licensing of the financial phases of the proposal of the World Jewish Congress for the evacuation of Jews from France and Rumania. The facts may thus be said to have come to light through accident. How many others of the same character are buried in State Department files is a matter I would have no way of knowing . . . This much is certain, however. The matter of rescuing the Jews from extermination is a trust too great to remain in the hands of men who are indifferent, callous and perhaps even hostile. The task is filled with difficulties. Only a fervent will to accomplish, backed by persistent and untiring effort, can succeed where time is so precious.

Roosevelt reacted sympathetically to the *Report,* and to the comments of his visitors as they amplified their criticism of the State Department. John Pehle, as head of Foreign Funds Control, argued forcefully that the rescue of the Jews would in no way impede economic warfare against the Axis. The lean young man who stood before the President of the United States backed his arguments with an arsenal of facts. The President was clearly impressed.

Pehle, born in Minneapolis, had spent his youth in Sioux Falls, South Dakota, followed by three years at Creighton University in Omaha, Nebraska. It was at Yale University Law School, though, that he had received his intellectual stimulus. As a senior he won a Sterling Teaching Fellowship and following a year of graduate study he joined the Treasury Department.

In 1940, at the age of thirty-one, he was appointed a special assistant to Morgenthau as well as director of Foreign Funds Control, thus directing a Treasury division with thousands of employees supervising billions of dollars' worth of assets.

As Roosevelt listened to his exposition of the facts and fallacies of economic warfare he must have noted Pehle's obvious talents and filed them for future reference. Later this most political of Presidents would select the nonpolitical Pehle to direct an American rescue operation whose details will be revealed for the first time in this volume.

As the Treasury representatives dissected the obstructive tactics of the State Department, Roosevelt must have realized that his own failure to liberalize refugee policies bore much of the responsibility. Furthermore, Morgenthau's *Personal Report* contained political dynamite and Roosevelt knew it. If it were made public the damage to the prestige and good faith of his Administration would be incalculable.

Morgenthau had always admired Roosevelt uncritically, never doubting his sincerity or motivation. But the determined Secretary standing before the President on January 16, 1944, was not the same man who could usually be manipulated by Rooseveltian charm. This time he would not be won over by the affectionate nickname "Henny Penny," which the President invoked when smoothing over their occasional conflicts.

Morgenthau's *Report* aggravated an already serious situation. Only a few weeks earlier the secret testimony of Breckinridge Long on November 26 before the House Foreign Affairs Committee had been released, arousing wide public protest.

The committee had been considering a resolution "urging the creation by the President of a commission of diplomatic, economic and military experts to formulate and effectuate a plan of immediate action designed to save the surviving Jewish people of Europe from extinction at the hands of Nazi Germany."

In his testimony Long denied the need for such a commission on the ground that State was already aiding rescue work in the most effective manner. "I have been in supervisory control and direction of its movements," he exclaimed, describing the teamwork between himself, George Brandt, Robert Borden Reams and Howard Travers, chief of the Visa Division.

According to Long, the appointment of a presidential rescue commission would signify a repudiation of the State Department's efforts and would reflect unfavorably upon the work of the Intergovernmental Committee on Refugees.

This latter comment awakened the interest of Congressman Will Rogers, Jr., of California, a co-sponsor of the resolution. Rogers pointed out that the Intergovernmental Committee seemed to have no American office. "We have never known in the past exactly where to go," he told Long. "Is there any office of the Intergovernmental Committee any place other than London?"

"No," Long replied, "that is the seat of the committee."

"They have no branch office?" Rogers asked.

"They have not up to now," Long admitted, "but we have made that proposal to them."

The statement by Long which evoked the most bitter criticism, however, was his claim that "We have taken into this country since the beginning of the Hitler regime and the persecution of the Jews, until today, approximately 580,000 refugees."

This was an utter misrepresentation of the facts. The official annual reports of the Immigration and Naturalization Service revealed that of the total of 476,930 aliens of all religions from all countries who entered the United States between July 1, 1933, and June 30, 1943, 165,756 were Jews. Of these, about 138,000 had escaped persecution. During this ten-year period, United States immigration quotas could have permitted the entry of over 1,500,000 aliens. Thus the number of Jews entering the United States during this period approximated 10 percent of the total number of immigrants permissible under law.

The remainder of Long's testimony was almost as distorted as his immigration statistics. He claimed that the establishment of a rescue commission was unnecessary because everyone in the State Department had been "endeavoring to save the Jewish people from the terrorism of the Nazis."

Long and Congressman Karl E. Mundt agreed with each other that it was not the American way to single out one group for special consideration, the implication being that the proposed rescue commission might be considered as favoring the Jews. Here are two of their comments:

> MUNDT: As a general policy for this country it is not good practice for us to establish a precedent, or if the precedent is already established, to emphasize it, whereby we pass legislation which singles out groups of people by their religion or by their color or their faith, or their political affiliations, either for special consideration or for special penalty.

> LONG: . . . the State Department has maintained that attitude all through, but the situation has come to a state of publicity today where I think the Jewish interests have emphasized the fate of the Jews as such . . ."

Long described the continuing activity on behalf of the Jews. As an example he cited the fact that after the Bermuda Conference, seventeen additional nations had joined the thirty-two original members of the Intergovernmental Committee on Refugees. What's more, the committee was receiving new rescue proposals each day. This seemed to impress his congressional audience. Unfortunately, at another point in his testimony, he admitted that seven months after Bermuda, the United States and Britain were still working on the organization and responsibilities of the committee.

As for past rescue operations: "We did every legitimate thing we could and we observed the laws of the United States." According to Long there was one insurmountable obstacle—the shortage of ships. This, said the Assistant Secretary, presented the principal barrier to greater efforts by the United States.

This argument conflicted with the report by a study group on shipping and transportation which had met some months earlier and had reported its findings to the Emergency Conference to Save the Jews of Europe. According to the representative of the *Norwegian Journal of Commerce and Shipping*, there were sufficient vessels available to transfer at least fifty thousand Jews a month from the Balkans to Palestine or the Mediterranean ports. Furthermore, United States troop transports to Europe and Allied ships bearing food to Nazi-occupied Greece often returned empty.

A private study in Britain had come to similar conclusions. The British report included a reference to the fact that the Allies always managed to find shipping to transport thousands of Moslems on their annual pilgrimage to Jidda, while simultaneously denying the availability of ships for Jews in flight.

Long closed his testimony before the Foreign Affairs Committee by urging Congress to suspend any bills to set up a special presidential rescue commission for the Jews. "The point is," he said, "that the historic attitude of the United States as a haven for the oppressed has not changed. The Department of State has kept the door open. It has been carefully screened but the door is open and the demands for a wider opening cannot be justified for the time being because there just is not any transportation."

The repercussions of Breckinridge Long's testimony must have been on Franklin Roosevelt's mind as he listened to the Treasury Department's documented case against the State Department on January 16, 1944.

The criticism that had followed Long's appearance lent substance to the arguments for a presidential rescue commission. It was very late but not too late for a determined new effort. As the Secretary of the Treasury and his associates singled out opportunities offered and rejected, Franklin D. Roosevelt knew that he would have to take action—and quickly.

The Treasury men had been far-sighted enough to bring along the suggested draft of an executive order establishing a War Refugee Board. Roosevelt reacted to it enthusiastically and proposed that Secretary of War Henry Stimson join Morgenthau and Hull as its nominal heads. He urged Morgenthau to discuss the proposal with the new Undersecretary of State, Edward R. Stettinius, Jr.

That afternoon at five-thirty, Morgenthau, Paul and Pehle met with the handsome, silver-haired Stettinius and with Roosevelt's assistant and confidante, Sam Rosenman. Morgenthau told Stettinius bluntly that some State Department officials, particularly Long, had obstructed rescue. Once again Pehle described the repeated inaction which had led the Treasury officers to the White House. Though shocked by the Pehle outline, Stettinius said that he was not surprised by Long's performance, since the Assistant Secretary had also bungled a proposed exchange of prisoners.

Stettinius, who was planning an administrative reorganization of the State Department, said that Long would be assigned to congressional relations and removed from matters affecting refugees.

On January 22, 1944, only six days after the confrontation with the Treasury Department, Franklin D. Roosevelt announced the establishment of the War Refugee Board. John Pehle was named acting executive director.

Executive Order 9417 creating the board began by stating that "it is the policy of this government to take all measures within its power to rescue the victims of enemy oppression who are in imminent danger of death and otherwise to afford such victims all possible relief and assistance consistent with the successful prosecution of the war."

The order went on to define the administrative structure of

the board within the executive office of the President, responsible directly to the President. The board's function would include "without limitation, the development of plans and programs . . . for (a) the rescue, transportation, maintenance and relief of the victims of enemy oppression, and (b) the establishment of havens of temporary refuge for such victims." The board was given added sinews in its power to work with private organizations and foreign governments in achieving its objectives.

For the first time since Hitler's accession to power in 1933, United States policy called for the rescue of the innocent. Seventeen months had passed since Gerhart Riegner's revelation that Hitler was carrying out his threat to eliminate every Jew in Europe. At least four million had perished during the period of Allied apathy.

It was late, very late in the war. The German machinery of destruction was in full operation. Thousands of men, women and children were walking to their death each day. Lieutenant Colonel Adolf Eichmann was efficient and implacable, and he always managed to find cattle cars for his victims in spite of the wartime shortage of transport.

The complex problems of supplying Zyklon B gas, which deteriorated unless stored properly, had also been solved. When the Auschwitz administration received authorization "to pick up materials for the Jewish resettlement" (*Abholung von Materialen für die Judenumsiedlung*), it sent its trucks to Dessau where, at the Dessauer Werke für Zucker und Chemische Industrie, the supply of lethal gas was waiting. Among its other attributes, the sale of the gas was quite profitable.

In attempting to combat this mass slaughter, the War Refugee Board would work with a small staff, meager funds and in close contact with a State Department which had displayed a monumental disinterest in the problem. Could it accomplish anything? And why had it taken the United States so long to affirm principles as old as the nation itself?

Before we examine the board's record it is necessary to try to answer this latter question. In the years between 1933 and 1944 the American tradition of sanctuary for the oppressed was uprooted and despoiled. It was replaced by a combination of political expediency, diplomatic evasion, isolationism, indifference and raw bigotry which played directly into the hands of Adolf Hitler even as he set in motion the final plans for the greatest mass murder in history.

Part II

THE VICTIMS

VI

"Wenn das Judenblut vom Messer spritzt . . ."

ON JANUARY 30, 1933, THE FIFTY-FIRST birthday of Franklin D. Roosevelt, Adolf Hitler was appointed Chancellor of Germany. Little more than a month later, when Roosevelt took the oath of office as the thirty-second President of the United States, he faced a banking crisis, the specter of some twelve million unemployed, and a nation which had lost much of its faith in itself during the gravest economic depression in its history.

Unlike the American President, the German Chancellor had never won a majority of the votes of his nation. On March 5, the day after Roosevelt's inauguration, the Nazis polled 44 percent of the vote in national elections. This, combined with the right-wing Nationalist party's 8 percent, gave them a sixteen-seat majority in the Reichstag.

But the rumble of Nazi jackboots and the ominous announcement that Japan was withdrawing from the League of Nations did not divert the United States from its own immediate crisis. The attention of Americans was focused upon a more direct menace, one that threatened every family and shadowed every home. Herbert Feis, the economic adviser to the State Department, has described this preoccupation:

"To almost every American, man and woman, what counted most was whether the bank in which they had their savings was going to be allowed to reopen; whether they would be given a chance to postpone payments on their mortgage and so retain possession of their house or farm; whether the stocks they held would recover their value; whether the prices of wheat and corn and cotton and tobacco and hogs they raised would improve enough to maintain their family and pay their debts; and above all, whether factories would resume operations and they would again have paying jobs. These and other phases of the domestic situation were to the forefront of America's thoughts, the primary focus of activity on Capitol Hill and in every city, town and village in the country."

While the President and the people of the United States were turning their attention inward, Hitler clamped an iron grip on German life and institutions. On March 23 the Reichstag, by a vote of 441 to 84, handed over its power of legislation to Hitler and his Cabinet, making him the absolute master of Germany.

Prior to Hitler's assumption of power, his brown-shirted *Sturmabteilung* (SA) had engaged in countless acts of brutality, intimidation and sadism. With their leader now firmly in command, the storm troopers roamed the streets arresting, imprisoning and, in hundreds of cases, murdering opponents of the Nazis.

There were more Christians than Jews among the initial victims of Nazi terrorism. Socialists, Communists, trade union leaders and proponents of democratic government were brutalized without regard to religion. But from the very beginning of Hitler's reign, the more than five hundred thousand Jews of Germany were singled out for a special fate—social, political and economic extinction.

Their place in the new German sun was memorialized in two lines of the "Horst Wessel" song, which thundered from the ranks of every parade: *"Wenn das Judenblut vom Messer spritzt, dann geht's nochmal so gut"* (When Jewish blood flows from the knife, things will go much better).

"Horst Wessel" provided one indication that the Nazis might not be satisfied by the mere social, political and economic annihilation of the Jews. The shouted cadences of *"Judah verrecke"* (Perish Judea) provided another.

From the start the Nazi persecution of the Jews was unselective, beyond any test, genuine or spurious, of loyalty to the Fatherland. Stressing disproportionate Jewish eminence in the arts, sciences and professions, the Nazis ignored their equally disproportionate service to the Fatherland in the World War. Ninety-two thousand Jews had served in the German army, 78 percent at the front. Twelve thousand had been killed in action, and thirty-five thousand decorated for heroism. None of this mattered. All five hundred thousand Jews in a nation of sixty-five million were to be outcasts. Long before *Mein Kampf,* Hitler had spelled out his policies in the first program of the Nazi party, dated February 24, 1920: "None but members of the nation may be citizens of the state. None but those of German blood, whatever their creed, may be members of the nation. No Jew, therefore, may be a member of the nation."

As the Nazis launched their legislative and physical assault on the Jews, American diplomats and foreign correspondents reported the most minute details of the onslaught. Rereading the dispatches to the State Department and the newspaper articles of 1933, one is struck by the acuity of the observations.

On March 9 the U.S. ambassador to Germany, Frederic M. Sackett, wrote that "Democracy in Germany has received a blow from which it may never recover." He informed Washington that uniformed Nazis had forced the closing of Jewish-owned stores, and he added that any attempt on the life of a

Nazi official "may perfectly conceivably lead to sanguinary pogroms against Jews and wholesale massacre of political opponents."

Consul General George Messersmith in Berlin reported that Jews holding public office were being rapidly dismissed, that Jewish judges in Prussian criminal courts had already been displaced, that in Breslau only seventeen of seventy-two Jewish lawyers were allowed to appear in court, that Jewish musicians and conductors (including Bruno Walter) had been discharged. In one dispatch he described the boycotting of Jewish shops:

"The boycott proclamation and the advice which has been issued today to employers to discharge all Jewish employees are instances of a brutality and a directness of action which have not been excelled in the history of modern times since the declaration of unrestricted submarine warfare by Germany during the World War . . . One must appreciate that reason is in reality absent from the majority of the leaders of the National Socialist movement."

From Stuttgart, Consul General Leon Dominian reported that "Jews of the well-to-do classes are refusing to accept invitations for evening engagements because of their fear of being attacked in the streets . . ."

The number of beatings and murders became more frequent as a result of Reichsminister Hermann Göring's announcement to police that they would no longer be required to protect enemies of the Reich. The official encouragement of terror was symbolized by the appointment of Count Wolf von Helldorf as police commissioner of Potsdam. A former storm-troop leader, Von Helldorf had organized the early anti-Semitic rioting in Berlin and his career included a prison sentence for murder. Now he would preside over law and order in Potsdam. His appointment and his background were reported to the State Department, which was also informed on March 27 that Dr. Werner Best, the author of the notorious Boxheim Documents, had just been appointed head of the Hesse state police.

The Boxheim Documents, written in 1931, contained secret instructions for the Nazi overthrow of the state government of Hesse and the subsequent treatment of its population. One of Dr. Best's unique contributions was a plan for starving the Jews of Hesse by denying them ration cards.

Dr. Best's plans were revealed to police by a horrified ex-Nazi named Schaefer. The newspapers of Hesse published the Boxheim Documents as a warning to the public on the eve of a local election, whereupon the Nazis polled 46 percent of the votes and Herr Schaefer was shot and hurled to his death from a bridge fifty feet above the railroad tracks. His unknown assailants were never apprehended.

In the chaotic days after Hitler assumed power, the United States government refrained from any protest to the German government until storm troopers, roaming the streets in search of Jews, beat up several who happened to be American citizens. The U.S. embassy took immediate action, complaining vigorously to the German Foreign Office and police authorities. The incidents were described extensively in the American press.

The results of this exposure were reported fully by Consul General Messersmith: "I understand . . . that representations made by our Embassy to the Foreign Office and by this Consulate General to the Police . . . greatly disturbed the Government, and that this, coupled with the publicity in the American newspapers, brought about the decisive action taken towards the end of last week . . . It is only when things went too far and when the unfavorable repercussions from abroad were felt that Mr. Göring changed from his inflammatory tactics at Essen to the abovementioned orders to National Socialists to cease direct action . . ."

Although Messersmith had stressed that the Nazis were sensitive to unfavorable publicity in other countries, the United States restricted its protests to the molesting of those few American citizens.

The violence was, of course, more widespread, as foreign newspapers revealed. Correspondents assigned to Germany often filed their stories from other countries both to avoid Nazi censorship and to obtain eyewitness accounts from refugees who had fled from Germany. One of these stories, datelined Paris, March 19, 1933, was widely reprinted in the United States. This article denied that physical attacks had abated since Hitler's restraining order, and pointed out that "Violence is better cloaked and the outrages are better protected, but both are continuing, whether they are carried out in response to orders 'from above' or are a manifestation that Herr Hitler's young men have really got 'out of hand' . . . Particularly, returning Americans say, there is no longer any doubt that to be either of Jewish faith or of Jewish origin and to exist in Germany now constitutes a crime in the eyes of the ruling faction there."

Specific instances of brutality were detailed. Seven Jews had been brought to storm-troop barracks where, at the point of leveled revolvers, they were ordered to flog each other. A father and son were among those who lost consciousness.

Another episode concerned a German Jew and his American wife who were asleep when the doorbell rang. The wife answered and five armed Nazis broke into the apartment, beating the husband unconscious with clubs and chains and shouting "Death to the Jews!" The wife later fled from Germany, leaving her husband in the hospital.

The same article also revealed that bodies were frequently found in the woods surrounding Berlin. It concluded with the observation that "The feature of all this which most impresses Americans seems to be the comparative indifference displayed by the German people as a whole."

The English press was even more outspoken about Nazi

brutality, often mentioning the names of the victims. The London *Times* of March 13, 1933, for example, reported the death of Dr. Wilhelm Spieger of Kiel, a Jewish lawyer and Socialist candidate for municipal office. Dr. Spieger and his wife were awakened at 2 A.M. by the ringing of their doorbell and loud shouts of "Open for the police!"

Mrs. Spieger begged her husband not to answer and began to telephone the police but he said, "What has anyone got against me?" and opened the door. Two Nazis were waiting for him. While his wife was still on the telephone they shot Dr. Spieger and fled as he lay dying on the floor.

During the first weeks after Hitler became Chancellor, scores of American newspapers proclaimed that Germany was departing from the ranks of the civilized nations of the world.

Said the Syracuse *Post-Standard:* "The whole weight of world disapproval should be summoned to stop this tragic situation, to impress upon the present rulers of Germany that the world will not permit a return to the dark ages."

The Providence *Journal* agreed. "If there ever was a time in recent history for marshaling world public opinion against such brutality such a time is now."

The Daily *Oklahoman* observed: "Humanity, to say nothing of Christian duty, would call insistently for an American protest."

They were joined by a growing chorus, including the Charleston *News and Courier,* the Lancaster *Intelligencer-Journal,* the Tulsa *World,* the Sacramento *Bee,* the Lynchburg *News* and the Philadelphia *Inquirer.* It was not surprising that on March 20, 1933, representatives of the American Jewish Committee and the fraternal order of B'nai B'rith visited Secretary Hull and requested that the United States protest the persecution of the Jews in Germany. The Secretary, who had been reading both the diplomatic dispatches and the newspapers, said it would be necessary for him to ascertain the facts. His cable to Ambassador Sackett in Berlin, asking for more information about the persecution, noted somewhat surprisingly that "Telegrams thus far received from the embassy would not appear to bear out the gravity of the situation . . ."

On March 21, before Sackett's reply arrived, Hull held a press conference and informed reporters that the German ambassador in Washington had given the department a statement by Göring to the effect that law and order would be maintained. "He does not believe," Hull assured the press, "that much will be heard in future concerning unlawful acts in Germany."

A reporter inquired if the United States had made a formal protest to Germany, and Hull replied that he was attempting to learn the truth about the situation.

When the facts were supplied from Berlin, they indicated that the use of violence had lessened but that "Jews in administrative, executive, and even judicial positions in the Reich Government are being expelled from their positions in large numbers and the same is true in state, provincial and communal governments . . ."

Hull omitted much of this information when he wrote to the Jewish delegation on March 26: "A reply has now been received indicating that whereas there was for a short time considerable physical mistreatment of Jews, this phase may be considered virtually terminated . . . Meanwhile I shall continue to watch the situation closely with a sympathetic interest and with a desire to be helpful in whatever way possible."

The Secretary of State, not nearly as sanguine as he seemed, notified the American embassy in Berlin that public opinion in the United States was alarmed at press reports about the mistreatment of the Jews. The government was now under heavy pressure to make a formal protest to Germany. "I am of the opinion," wrote the Secretary, "that outside intercession has rarely produced the results desired and has frequently aggravated the situation."

With varying phrasing this was to be the central theme of American policy toward Nazi Germany for years to come.

On March 30, 1933, George Gordon, chargé d'affaires in Berlin, notified Washington that "reports have come to the Embassy from numberless sources which indicate that the situation is rapidly taking a turn for the worse."

Then Gordon, in spite of the Hull message revealing his reluctance to intercede in German affairs, proposed exactly that. Gordon reported that a German industrialist had suggested that if the United States indicated to Hitler "in a friendly way the serious concern with which developments in Germany were being viewed in our country . . . it might have a favorable effect . . . he had every reason to believe that Hitler would listen to such a message from this Embassy more readily than from any other mission here."

Hull did not encourage the idea.

The following day Consul General Messersmith renewed the warnings from Berlin: "It is now evident that the movement has reached an intensity and a diffusion of action which was not contemplated even by its most fanatic proponents and there is real reason to believe now that the movement is beyond control and may have a bloody climax."

The Germans had scheduled a nationwide boycott of Jewish shops for April 1. Jewish groups in the United States, in order to counteract this demonstration, were attempting to organize an American boycott of German goods. Hull, hoping to stop both events, suggested a compromise to the Germans: if they canceled their plans, he would issue a temporizing statement. But the Germans were intractable and went ahead with their scheme. Hull's statement was never released but it remains an interesting commentary on the official State Department attitude:

"Unfortunate incidents have indeed occurred and the whole world joins in regretting them. But without minimizing or condoning what has taken place, I have reason to believe that many of the accounts of acts of terror and atrocities which have reached this country have been exaggerated, and I fear that the continued dissemination of exaggerated reports may prejudice the friendly feelings between the peoples of the two countries and be of doubtful service to anyone."

Hull's stated belief that reports of terror were exaggerated was of course contradicted by virtually every diplomatic communication of the period. In fact, it was supported only by the American consul general in Hamburg. Writing on March 31, 1933, Consul General Kehl claimed that the foreign press had included "a considerable display of exaggerated news on events and conditions in Germany." He admitted that "beatings, isolated killings and house visitations by private individuals have taken place in the consular district, but not on an extensive scale."

According to Kehl, the revolution was "bloodless, well-organized and efficiently conducted. Many persons are still held in custody, largely in the interest of general order and the personal welfare of those detained . . . The welfare of the majority—those who sincerely have the interests of the country at heart—have apparently been well and satisfactorily served, while those, including Communists and Radical Socialists, whose interest in national welfare efforts may be seriously questioned, have not fared so well—a situation as it should be. It must be admitted that the National-Socialist organization before it came into power, and since then the Nazi-Nationalist Government, have rendered invaluable services to the world at large in crushing Communism in Germany, which may have a salutary effect in other countries inasfar as the erradication [*sic*] of the Communist plague is concerned."

Although Consul General Kehl was alone in this view among the men in the field, his beliefs were widely shared within the State Department. But the American public, informed of Nazi terrorism by their newspapers, was becoming aroused. Despite an understandable preoccupation with domestic problems, there was a restless stirring in intellectual circles and a growing sense of involvement by religious leaders.

Among the more than four million Jews in the United States there was of course great apprehension; there was also paralyzing disagreement about what to do. Sporadic rallies were held across the nation. The largest meeting of 1933 occurred at Madison Square Garden in New York. An audience of twenty thousand within the Garden and thirty-five thousand outside heard former Governor Alfred E. Smith and Senator Robert F. Wagner of New York excoriate the Nazis' racist policies. Bishop William T. Manning expressed Protestant indignation at the turn of events, and Bishop Francis J. McConnell spoke for the Catholics. In 1933, interreligious meetings were rare and the rally seemed to bode well for American unity against a common foe.

The White House maintained a discreet silence, neither applauding nor criticizing these expressions of public sentiment. But congressional opinion seemed in the main to support the views of Representative Hamilton Fish, Jr., of New York. Fish defended the right of Jewish groups to protest the violence done to American Jews in Germany but stressed that "It is of no concern to America what form of government is set up in Germany or in any other nation."

On April 7, 1933, Nazi Germany issued its Law for the Restoration of the Professional Civil Service. This innocent title concealed a tidal wave of discriminatory legislation that would pour forth in an endless stream to inundate Jews and tens of thousands of Christians of Jewish descent. A German careless enough to have one Jewish grandparent or parent was considered a non-Aryan. Later the search for Jewish blood would be carried back to the year 1800 before a certificate of purity was issued.

Hitler appointed a *Reichsstatthalter* in each of the eighteen

German states; they were all Nazis, with carte blanche to dissolve state parliaments, make state laws, and appoint or dismiss employees. Government officials, doctors, lawyers, workers in educational or cultural fields were now required to sign the following statement:

"I declare officially herewith: I do not know of any circumstance—despite careful scrutiny—that may justify the presumption that I am not of Aryan descent; in particular, none of my paternal or maternal parents, or grandparents, was at any time of the Jewish faith. I am fully aware of the fact that I expose myself to prosecution and dismissal if this declaration proves untrue."

The first non-Aryans to lose their jobs as a result of the law of April 7 were government employees on all levels: teachers in public educational institutions, members of judicial tribunals, employees of the Imperial Railway Administration and of municipal theaters, gas and electrical works, public banks and insurance companies.

Jewish and other non-Aryan employees of the postal service and of public welfare institutions were discharged. So were police officers and civilian employees of the army. The legal profession was closed to non-Aryans, and their right to practice medicine and dentistry, though not completely eliminated, was sharply curtailed.

Within a matter of months the fields of literature, the press, films, broadcasting, the theater, music and the plastic arts were also forbidden to the Jews. The Germans made no distinctions in driving their victims from the intellectual and cultural life of the nation. Eight of the thirty Germans who had won Nobel Prizes happened to be non-Aryan, and they were barred from their laboratories and universities in the same manner as the clerks and stenographers.

As the months passed, German industry, agriculture and commerce adopted similar regulations proscribing virtually all forms of employment for non-Aryans. Conversely, these restrictions opened up new opportunities for jobless Aryans.

The State Department was continually informed of the implementation of this legislation, and the following examples will serve to illustrate the emotional as well as factual commitment which characterized the reports from U.S. consulates throughout Germany:

April 10

"It is the undisguised intention of the National Socialist Party to get absolute control of all forms of German Government and of intellectual, professional, financial, business and cultural life . . . The forcing of the Jewish judges from the courts . . . are brought about by Party pressure and action . . . It is a question as to whether such direct ruthless and complete control of a civilized people has ever been achieved in so short a time by a minority."

May 4

"Not only careers, but whole families are being ruined and the moral and physical distress which has resulted out of this action against the Jews in the legal profession would be difficult to describe."

[Regarding book burning scheduled for May 10 at all universities]: "This ceremony which is to be given wide publicity seems to be as medieval in form as it seems in spirit . . . The state of mind of the Jews from the highest to the lowest in Germany is difficult to describe and I can only state that I have come in contact in the past few months here with moral suffering such as I have not seen anywhere and under any conditions heretofore."

May 12

"The campaign then is comprehensible, and like that of Torquemada for the saving of human souls, can give no quarter; for the stake is the soul of the German people already endangered by the cancerous infection of the Jewish plague which has got a dangerous hold upon present day German life. Believing this as the National Socialists do—God knows how they can, but they do, and they are serious men who never laugh—they can not hesitate, they must break the influence of the Jew, and if they can not literally and bodily get rid of him, at least rob him of all influence and position in the community."

June 30

"All potential sources of resistance to the Nazi regime—except the Reichswehr and the police—have now been either absorbed by the Nazis or largely, if not totally crushed . . . With the exception of the Evangelical Churches, which valiantly, though in vain, fought against the threatened Nazification, no group in Germany actually offered serious resistance."

July 8

"Consistently and relentlessly the Jews are being eliminated from practically all walks of life." Nazi doctors and lawyers are "conducting bitter, relentless boycott against their Jewish colleagues . . . Nazi leaders have repeatedly boasted in the past that one of the first acts of a Nazi regime would be to set up ghettoes in Germany . . . the outward and official manifestations of anti-Semitism in present-day Germany fail to reveal the real brutality and truculence of the Nazis toward the Jews, and that they are determined to make life for Jews in Germany well-nigh insufferable."

As the Nazi drive gained rather than lost momentum in 1933, there was an increasing demand on the part of the public that the United States communicate revulsion and horror of these excesses to the German government.

On April 19 Samuel Untermyer, one of the nation's leading lawyers, forwarded a resolution of protest passed by the Federal Bar Association of New York, New Jersey and Connecticut to the White House, asking presidential secretary Marvin

McIntyre to "please bring to the attention of the President, in the interest of his Administration and of the Party, the intense surprise, disappointment and hostile comment that one hears on all hands against the Party because of the silence of Congress at Germany's admittedly official disfranchisement and persecution of the Jews of Germany."

As if to stress the nonsectarian aspects of protest, a group of distinguished non-Jewish leaders of the New York Bar forwarded a message on May 20 to the State Department for transmission to the German government. Their statement emphasized the abandonment of civilized legal traditions in Germany as reflected in the removal of Jewish judges and prohibition of Jewish lawyers. The petition was signed by John W. Davis, Charles C. Burlingham, Samuel Seabury, Bainbridge Colby, Henry W. Taft, Elihu Root, Charles Evan Hughes, Jr., Joseph H. Choate, Jr., Paul D. Cravath, Robert T. Swaine, Grenville Clark and James W. Gerard, among others.

In reply, Undersecretary of State William Phillips noted that State Department policy forbade the transmission of messages from private individuals to foreign governments. However, Phillips agreed to call in the German ambassador and have him read the petition.

Secretary Hull, harassed by resolutions from such diverse quarters as Baptist churches in the rural South and Jewish temples in the North, decided to have a "friendly chat" with German ambassador Hans Luther. It was the first in a series of such meetings during which Hull would speak as an "individual" rather than as Secretary of State, and complain informally rather than protest officially.

The first of these talks took place on May 3. Later Hull wrote a memorandum describing the conversation. His account mirrors the attitude he adopted in his dialogues with representatives of the German dictatorship.

Hull said that he had invited Luther "in order that I might ascertain from him in person whether it would be agreeable for me to discuss with him in the most unofficial, personal and friendly manner the Jewish situation in Germany, and to make full and emphatic representations to him in this tone and manner of the state of sentiment in the United States, both among the Jews and the general public, relative to the reported atrocities and mistreatments of the Jews in Germany either by individual groups or by the Government, or both . . . I then called the attention of the Ambassador to the vast heaps of memorials, letters and other solemn and earnest protests by groups of American citizens of all religious denominations and racial persuasions earnestly protesting against the reported mistreatment of Jews in Germany and urging our government to take all possible steps to terminate such treatment, even to the extent of making very definite and more or less peremptory demands of the German government itself."

Ambassador Luther replied that Germany was in the midst of a revolution "in which the young Germans are undertaking to bring into control the best pure German element." He assured the Secretary that the German government itself was not a party to the antagonism toward the Jews. According to Herr Luther, the worst was over and the situation improving.

Two weeks after Secretary Hull's meeting with the ambassador, Assistant Secretary of State Wilbur Carr attempted to sum up United States policy regarding a formal protest to Germany.

"As I understand the matter," he wrote in a memorandum, "while in general it is recognized that strong anti-Jewish feeling exists in Germany and considerable persecution has occurred, there is nothing which the United States can do to alleviate the condition (1) Because that which is happening is an internal matter of the German Government; and (2) Even if the United States were to make representations to Germany on the ground of humanity, it is likely that instead of causing a more considerate treatment of the Jews, it would probably have the opposite effect and incite further activity against them."

Carr added significantly: " . . . admitting that the United States would be justified in making representations, the time when such representations could have been made with some effect has now passed."

In a later addendum he noted that he had discussed this question with Secretary Hull and Undersecretary Phillips on May 29 "and it was agreed that no representations on the part of this Government should be made."

In future meetings with Ambassador Luther and other German officials Hull, still remaining a friendly individual rather than a strong Secretary of State, would hedge in his characterization of the German onslaught while revealing the reluctance of the United States government to file a formal protest.

Ironically, the few protests that were made originated with the German government. On August 11, 1933, Rudolf Leitner, the German chargé d'affaires in Washington, called on Hull to complain about a Samuel Untermyer speech urging intensification of the privately organized boycott of German goods.

As Hull reported it: "I then proceeded, personally and unofficially, to recite to him the alleged mistreatment of Jews in Germany and the terrific demand of Jews and other leaders in this country for some action, or utterance at least, by the American Government, properly characterizing such conduct." In this conversation Hull suggested that if the Germans stopped persecuting the Jews, the United States would appeal for discontinuance of the boycott of German goods.

In September, Hull had another talk with the chargé, which he recorded as follows: "I stated to him that something clearly was going on in Germany in relation to Jews and Jewish conditions; that it was not my purpose to go into detail as to just what it was, except to say that to my knowledge an immense amount of news or information has been coming out of Germany to the effect that serious mistreatment of the Jews has taken place and is still being continued."

As for the public response, "we were being terrifically bombarded from week to week, over a period of many months back, in the way of demands for strong characterization of the acts of German officials in mistreating Jews in Germany."

Of course Hull could not originate a formal protest to Germany without the approval of the President and it was quite clear that Roosevelt did not consider this a proper move. He had made his position clear in a talk with William E. Dodd, prior to Dodd's taking up his new duties as ambassador to Germany in July 1933.

According to Dodd's diary entry for June 16, Roosevelt summed up the situation in these words: "The German authorities are treating the Jews shamefully, and the Jews in this country are greatly excited. But this is also not a government affair. We can do nothing except for American citizens who happen to be victims. We must protect them, and whatever we can do to moderate the general persecution by unofficial and personal influence ought to be done."

The same argument, expressed somewhat more vividly, had been made by Vice-President John Nance Garner at a Cabinet meeting early in 1933. Garner told his colleagues that the internal policies of Germany were no business of the United States and remarked that the hotter the Nazi excesses, the sooner they would burn out.

The silence of the United States government was made more conspicuous by the fact that the British Parliament had already debated and deplored Nazi inhumanity, and that the first reports about German concentration camps had been published in America. On April 22, 1933, a *New York Times* correspondent had written one of the earliest first-hand descriptions of Dachau. He reported that four thousand new inmates were expected to join the more than five hundred already hard at work in the camp. He noted that each hut was surrounded by a double fence of high-voltage wire, which would cause death at a touch. Storm troopers with rifles at the ready escorted work parties. The prisoners' heads were shaved and some, according to the reporter, appeared "long-starved and crippled." The week before his visit, four prisoners had been shot "while trying to escape."

The commandant informed the correspondent that the inmates were Communist leaders, although he admitted to a "sprinkling" of doctors, lawyers, students and former Reichstag deputies.

The existence of Dachau was not precisely a secret; the Nazis even published election returns from the camp. (In 1933 the Dachau prisoners cast 2231 votes for the government and 3 against. Nine ballots were declared invalid, no doubt due to technical irregularities.)

In the face of this and other revelations the demand soared for a strong U.S. statement. Dr. Jonah B. Wise, an officer of the Joint Distribution Committee, put it quite candidly at a meeting in Town Hall, New York:

"It is difficult for Americans—Jews and Gentiles alike—to understand the silence of President Roosevelt in the face of one of the great human disasters of our time. The tragic and needless sufferings of the Jews in Germany are such that it should have been impossible for the President of the United States not to have spoken a word of warning and condemnation to the German government. I am aware of the niceties of diplomatic procedure and the amenities of international life. But in a crisis such as exists in Germany today diplomatic discretion must yield to moral indignation."

One factor which enabled Roosevelt to maintain his discreet silence without losing political support was the disunity of

American Jewry. This was reflected most sharply in the conflict between the American Jewish Congress and the American Jewish Committee.

The congress was militant. It had played the principal role in organizing a nationwide boycott of German goods. The committee, a conservative group representing the wealthiest and most influential segment of the Jewish population, boycotted the boycott, opposed demonstrations and noisy scenes, and tried to exert its influence quietly. Dorothy Thompson, one of the most vivid chroniclers of the time, described the committee's timidity:

". . . The American Jewish Committee tried to soft-peddle things. It advised watchful waiting. It refused to participate in parades, demonstrations, protest meetings. It tried to get the government to do something, but very, very quietly. Hush-hush was the word. In short, while the stress of the situation demanded leadership, the American Jewish Committee offered restraint. It did nothing, most diplomatically."

The description was somewhat unfair. The committee's notion was to relate American action to the American tradition, to make the government realize that the Nazi persecution of the Jews was but another episode in the long history of human indignity. Since its founding, the United States government had ranged itself against such indignities, had in fact interceded in the internal affairs of other nations. This was to be the central theme of the committee's efforts.

The president of the American Jewish Committee was Dr. Cyrus Adler, a distinguished scholar who had taught Semitic languages at Johns Hopkins University, served first as librarian, then secretary, of the Smithsonian Institution, and later as president of the Jewish Theological Seminary. Dr. Adler was one of the members of the delegation who had urged Cordell Hull in March to file a formal protest with the German authorities.

On May 3, 1933, Dr. Adler had tried again. He wrote to

Hull, pointing out that the British, French and Australian governments had expressed their distaste with Nazi policies, and added: ". . . there are many people who think that some expression of feeling—and I use the word 'feeling' advisedly—ought to come from a great and liberal government like the United States . . . I have not tried in speech to be eloquent to you, dear Mr. Secretary, but I think you realize that this is not and should not be treated as an internal German question. If Germany says in effect that the Jews are not fit to be members in good standing of a modern State, that is an attack upon every Jew throughout the world."

Adler said he hoped that we would not limit our concern to American citizens, "but that we shall revert to our earlier and more liberal traditions that what is human concerns us and that we shall dare do as the mightiest country in the world what we freely did when the Republic was young and feeble."

Adler called Hull's attention to a memorandum prepared by his committee on the history of U.S. intercession. It detailed a whole series of U.S. "interferences" in the internal affairs of other nations. One such episode had occurred in 1840, when the medieval charge of ritual murder was brought against the Jews of Damascus. (This myth about the sacrifice of Christian children would later be resurrected by the Nazi leadership.) In the rioting which followed the accusation, many Jews were imprisoned, tortured and murdered. Needless to say, the Jews of Damascus were not American citizens, but President Martin Van Buren immediately directed Secretary of State John Forsyth to make strong representations to the Sultan of the Ottoman Empire, who then ruled the area.

As a result Forsyth wrote to David Porter, the U.S. minister in Constantinople: ". . . The President has learned, with profound feeling of surprise and pain, the atrocious cruelties which have been practised upon the Jews of Damascus and Rhodes, in consequence of charges extravagant and strikingly similar to those which, in less enlightened ages, were made pretexts for the persecution and spoliation of these unfortunate people . . . The President has directed me to instruct you to do everything in your power with the Government of his Imperial Highness, the Sultan, to prevent or mitigate these horrors—the bare recital of which has caused a shudder throughout the civilized world."

As a direct consequence of the American intercession, the Sultan of the Ottoman Empire issued an order to the judges of Constantinople directing them to release all Jews accused of ritual murder.

Another example of American intervention occurred in November 1857. Learning that Jews were excluded from certain Swiss cantons, President James Buchanan's Secretary of State, Lewis Cass, ordered the U.S. minister to Switzerland "to use all the means in your power to effect the removal of the odious restrictions complained of, which, it is understood, are contained in the laws of but four of the Swiss cantons."

Minister Theodore Fay responded affirmatively, noting that every oppression against the Jews "is as contrary to the spirit and letter of the Holy Scriptures as to the principles of civilization, and to the dignity of the United States and other free governments."

On his own initiative, Fay studied the structure of the twenty-four cantons. He concluded that seven were free from any restrictions, seven absolutely restrictive and ten essentially illiberal. The American minister then transmitted his findings to the Swiss government, and on October 25, 1859, Swiss President Furrer sent him a friendly note: "I have the satisfaction of transmitting a debate in the general council of Zurich, by which you will see that an immense majority of the Council is disposed to change the legislation respecting the Israelites, in the interest of humanity and progress."

In 1874 a new Swiss constitution was adopted, establishing without reservation the principle of religious liberty.

. . .

Even when the United States was torn by civil war and one might have expected its humanitarian instincts to be postponed to a more convenient time, it expressed itself clearly and forcefully.

Lincoln's Secretary of State, William H. Seward, was so concerned about the Jews of Tangier that on December 9, 1863, he authorized the U.S. consul "to exert all proper influence to prevent a repetition of the barbarous cruelties to which Israelites in the Moorish Empire have on account of their religion been subjected."

Fifteen years later Felix A. Mathews, then the American consul in Tangier, could write proudly to Secretary of State Evarts: "I am happy to state that my relations with the Government of Morocco are such that I can exercise my unofficial friendly offices on behalf of the Israelites in this country . . . as it has been the case lately when a Jewish family was murdered near Laraiche, another Israelite near Arzila, and the town itself menaced by the Kabyles, who were preparing to murder and plunder all the Israelites in the place . . . the murderers of the Jewish family are now in prison and the Minister for Foreign Affairs has assured me that their punishment will be such as to deter others from committing similar acts of violence in the future."

American intercession was not limited to the occurrence of discrimination in less powerful states. In one instance it led to the cancellation of the Treaty of 1832, which governed trade and commerce with Czarist Russia.

The incident stemmed from the events of Christmas Day 1881 in Warsaw, then a part of Russian Poland. A false fire alarm was blamed on the Jews, and in the ensuing pogrom more than one thousand shops were pillaged, leaving ten thousand people without a livelihood.

Secretary of State Frederick Frelinghuysen informed the chargé at the American legation in St. Petersburg that "The prejudice of race and creed having in our day given way to the claims of our common humanity, the people of the U.S. have heard, with great regret, the stories of the sufferings of the Jews in Russia."

The chargé was instructed to contact Czarist officials with the message that "the friendship the U.S. feels for Russia impels us to hope the Imperial Government will find means to cause the persecution of these unfortunate fellow-beings to cease."

But the Russian depredations continued and were climaxed by a pogrom in Kishinev in April 1903. The alleged cause of this outbreak was the discovery of the body of a young Russian boy. The rumor was spread that the boy had been the victim of Jewish ritual murder.

The Russians of that era were quite ready to accept the story, and by the time the real murderer had been located (he turned out to be a Gentile relative of the victim who had committed the crime for financial gain rather than ritual necessity), 2,750 Jewish families had been uprooted, forty-seven killed and over four hundred injured. Property damage amounted to 2,500,000 rubles.

When news of the pogrom reached the United States, seventy-seven public meetings were held in fifty communities of twenty-seven states. Thousands of distinguished citizens of all religions signed a Kishinev Massacre petition addressed to the Czar:

"The cruel outrages perpetrated at Kishinev during Easter of 1903 have excited horror and reprobation throughout the world . . . Religious persecution is more sinful and more fatuous than war . . . Far removed from Your Majesty's dominions, living under different conditions, and owing allegiance to another Government, your petitioners yet venture, in the name of civilization, to plead for religious liberty and tolerance. . . ."

President Theodore Roosevelt forwarded the petition to the

Russian Minister of Foreign Affairs, who refused to accept it. The President promptly published the cablegram, including the text of the petition.

Along with these protests, which concerned the Russian treatment of Russian citizens, the United States attempted to remove restrictions imposed by the imperial government upon American Jewish businessmen in Russia. American diplomats continued to warn the Russians that this discriminatory treatment violated the Treaty of 1832. Their complaints resulted in occasional but not consistent improvement; and a wave of new pogroms, clearly sanctioned by the Russian authorities, resulted in thousands of deaths.

An American consular official reported to Washington that on the night before the pogrom in Seidlitz, Russian troops had notified Christians to display devotional objects so they would not be harmed during the scheduled violence. Congress responded by passing a joint resolution on June 22, 1906:

"Resolved by the Senate and House of Representatives of the United States of America in Congress assembled, That the people of the United States are horrified by the report of the massacre of Hebrews in Russia on account of their race and religion, and that those bereaved thereby have the hearty sympathy of the people of this country."

On December 13, 1911, the House of Representatives voted 300 to 1 to terminate the Treaty of 1832. Formal abrogation took place as of January 1, 1913.

The Rumanian government, equally adept at using the political and economic expediencies of anti-Semitism, had also heard the clear, uncompromising voice of American indignation. At President Theodore Roosevelt's direction, Secretary of State John Hay in 1902 sent a stiff note to Rumania whose text has a prophetic ring:

"The political disabilities of the Jews in Rumania, their exclusion from the public service and the learned professions, the limitations of their civil rights and the imposition upon them of exceptional taxes, involving as they do wrongs repugnant to the moral sense of liberal modern peoples, are not so directly in point for my present purpose as the public acts which attack the inherent right of man as a breadwinner in the ways of agriculture and trade. The Jews are prohibited from owning land, or even from cultivating it as common laborers. They are debarred from residing in the rural districts. Many branches of petty trade and manual production are closed to them in the overcrowded cities, where they are forced to dwell and engage, against fearful odds, in the desperate struggle for existence. This government cannot be a tacit party to such an international wrong. It is constrained to protest against the treatment to which the Jews of Rumania are subjected, not alone because it has unimpeachable ground to remonstrate against the resultant injury to itself, but in the name of humanity."

So wrote Secretary of State John Hay, thirty-one years before Adolf Hitler came to power.

American protest was not restricted to the protection of the Jews. In 1915 the U.S. ambassador to Turkey, Henry Morgenthau, father of the future Secretary of the Treasury, described the persecution of the Armenians in a dispatch to the State Department: "Reports from widely scattered districts indicate systematic attempt to uproot peaceful Armenian populations and through arbitrary arrests, terrible tortures, wholesale expulsions and deportations from one end of the Empire to another accompanied by frequent instances of rape, pillage and murder, turning into massacre, to bring destruction and destitution on them."

As a result of Morgenthau's continuing reports, Secretary of State Robert Lansing informed him on October 4 that Turkish barbarities "have aroused a general and intense feeling of indignation among the American people. You are instructed to continue to use your good offices for the amelioration of the conditions of the Armenians, and to prevent the continuation of the persecution of the Armenians, informing the Turkish Government that this persecution is destroying the feeling of good will which the people of the United States have held towards Turkey."

Morgenthau carried out his instructions vigorously, and United States interest in the fate of the Armenians moderated the Turkish assault. Under the leadership of the Norwegian explorer-statesman Fridtjof Nansen, the League of Nations resettled three hundred thousand Armenians, as well as vast numbers of uprooted Russians after the First World War. The intervention of the United States and other nations prevented the annihilation of the Armenians.

The American Jewish Committee's attempt to refresh the memory of the United States government with these events of past history failed. The State Department's legal adviser said there was no analogy between past American intercessions and the plight of the Jews under Nazi rule.

Failure to protest was the first in a long series of refusals to respond *in any manner*. One might describe the American response to Nazi racism as an almost co-ordinated series of inactions. The moribund immigration policy of the United States, and America's failure to reassert its traditional defense of humanity, combined to produce total apathy. It was one thing to avoid interference in Germany's domestic policies, quite another to deny asylum to its victims.

■ VII ■

"Likely to Become a Public Charge"

MORE THAN 37,000,000 IMMIGRANTS ENTERED the United States between 1820, when such statistics were first recorded, and 1933, when Hitler came to power. During the first fifteen years of the twentieth century, an average of 900,000 immigrants a year sailed past the Statue of Liberty toward new personal, political and religious freedom.

In 1933, with the total U.S. immigration quota fixed at 153,774, only 23,068 newcomers arrived; of these, a mere 1,798 were Germans. In 1934, in spite of the intensity of the Nazi persecution, only 4,716 Germans entered the United States, and in 1935 the number increased slightly, to 5,117. Between 1933 and 1935, about one-third of the German immigrants were Jewish. From 1933 to 1936 more Germans departed from the United States than entered it. The total population of the United States remained quite constant during the years preceding World War II which many Americans associate with wide-scale immigration.

As a matter of fact, during the entire Hitler period the number of immigrants lagged far behind the total permitted under U.S. law. From 1933 to 1943, there were 1,244,858 unfilled places on U.S. immigration quotas. Of these vacancies, 341,-567 had been allotted to citizens of countries dominated or occupied by Germany or her allies. Each unfilled place represented a potential life exposed to annihilation.

What had happened to George Washington's admonition to his countrymen "humbly and fervently to beseech the kind Author of these blessings . . . to render this country more and more a safe and propitious asylum for the unfortunates of other countries"?

And what of the legacy of Thomas Jefferson, who, in 1801, had asked: "Shall we refuse the unhappy fugitives from distress that hospitality which the savages of the wilderness extended to our forefathers arriving in this land? Shall oppressed humanity find no asylum on this globe?"

The barriers that faced the refugees from Hitler were erected late in the nineteenth century. Before that time the image of America as a haven had gained luster as the refugees who fled the poverty, persecution and exploitation of the Old World were welcomed into the New. Until the 1890's the nations of western and northern Europe—Great Britain and Ireland; Germany; Norway, Sweden and Denmark—yielded the overwhelming majority of immigrants. These countries provided 72 percent of the new arrivals between 1881 and 1890, while only 18.3 percent came from southern and eastern Europe.

The northern and western Europeans were, for the most part, industrious farmers and skilled workers. The Irish tended to concentrate in the East, but there was a large westward movement of other immigrants. These were predominantly Protestant, with a high literacy rate, and they were easily assimilated into the existing population.

At the turn of the century the geographic pattern was reversed. Millions of immigrants poured in from the destitute countries of southern and eastern Europe. Between 1901 and 1910, more than 70 percent of the immigrants were Poles,

Russians, Austrians, Hungarians, Italians, Rumanians, Czechs, Slovaks, Serbs and Croats. Large-scale migration from the United Kingdom, Germany and Scandinavia had ended.

These new immigrants were mainly Catholic, Greek Orthodox or Jewish. They were desperately poor, and their proportion of illiteracy was higher than among their predecessors. Unlike most of the earlier immigrants, who had dispersed throughout the nation, they settled in the cities. They remained in identifiable groups, retained much of their language and customs, and became easy prey for exploitation by landlords and factory owners. Moreover, the large reservoir of unskilled workers alarmed the labor organizations, the burgeoning "foreign" slums appalled the city dwellers, and the cacophony of unfamiliar sounds disturbed the "earlier" Americans. The drive to restrict immigration gained momentum and was aided by laws passed in the late 1800's. The restrictions against immigrants likely to become public charges, a stipulation which would later be applied to large numbers of Jews fleeing Hitler, was first enunciated in 1882. The immigration act of that year excluded "any convict, lunatic, idiot or any other person unable to take care of himself or herself without becoming a public charge."

The Alien Contract Labor Law of 1885 would also be invoked in the Hitler era, although it was designed for an utterly different purpose—the prevention of such abuses as the importation of foreign labor to drive down wage rates, particularly in the coal fields. The act stipulated that it was unlawful to assist the entry of aliens under a prior contract for labor.

In the early 1900's, groups like the anti-Catholic, xenophobic American Protective Association sprang up in the Midwest. In Boston, Senator Henry Cabot Lodge helped to organize the Immigration Restriction League. The league pressed for a literacy test as an immigration requirement, a move which passed both houses of Congress and was defeated only by President Grover Cleveland's veto.

Scientifically hazy theories of the biological superiority and inferiority of various European races now began to dominate the formulation of immigration policy. In this atmosphere the United States government appointed a nine-man Immigration Commission in 1907. After three years of work by a staff of three hundred at a cost of $1,000,000, the commission published a forty-two-volume report. This massive work supported the notion that southern and eastern Europeans were racially inferior to northern and western Europeans.

As Professor Oscar Handlin documented extensively in *Race and Nationality in American Life,* the commission's work was utterly unscientific, its conclusions already formulated before the investigation began. It launched its work with the assumption that the new immigrants were far less capable of becoming Americanized than their predecessors. The commission never proved its thesis; it merely presented a kind of guilt by announcement. Thus, in its discussion of causes of emigration, the commission stated that "a large proportion of the emigration from southern and eastern Europe may be traced directly to the inability of the peasantry to gain an adequate livelihood in agricultural pursuits." As Professor Handlin pointed out: "The statement could just as well have been applied to the peasantry of northern and western Europe."

Comparable examples of bias appear throughout the key volumes. Findings which did not support the commission's predilections were omitted or glossed over so quickly as to be lost in the sheer bulk of data. The layman who found the forty-two-volume report somewhat formidable turned to Madison Grant's best seller, *The Passing of the Great Race,* published in 1916.

Grant, an anthropologist at the American Museum of Natural History, wrote that the glory of the old immigrants could be traced to their predominantly Nordic origins. By contrast, Grant said, "The new immigration contained a large and increasing number of the weak, the broken, and the mentally crippled of all races drawn from the lowest stratum of the Mediterranean basin and the Balkans, together with hordes of the wretched, submerged populations of the Polish ghettos. Our jails, insane asylums, and almshouses are filled with this human flotsam and the whole tone of American life, social, moral and political, has been lowered and vulgarized by them."

These notions were propounded at a psychologically propitious moment. With the end of the First World War the United States was ripe for a dogma which would shield it from intruders. The heightened distrust of foreigners, the fear by labor unions of an influx of cheap workers, and the hostility of "early Americans" to the later arrivals, bred a new kind of isolationism. In this atmosphere the demand grew for immigration controls based upon national origins. As an example of the intensity of national feeling, the House of Representatives voted in 1920 to suspend immigration altogether, a precedent which the Senate declined to follow.

The Quota Act of 1921 placed the first numerical restrictions on European immigration; it was slashed to 3 percent of the number of foreign-born of each European nationality residing in the United States *in 1910*. The census of 1910 was chosen in preference to that of 1920 in order to minimize the proportion of southern and eastern Europeans in the population. In addition, a maximum annual quota of 355,000 immigrants was established. The congressional debates which preceded the legislation were marked by flamboyant references to "alien floods," "barbarian hordes" and "foreign tides."

The Immigration Act of 1924 further reduced the entry of aliens, and in 1929 a maximum annual immigration quota of 153,774 was adopted. Thus immigration, which had averaged 900,000 a year at the beginning of the century, had been slashed by more than 80 percent. Under the new legislation, the acceptance of the immigrants by country would be based upon the ethnic backgrounds of the United States population in 1920.

From July 1, 1929, when the restriction went into effect, until the Administration of Lyndon Johnson approved a new law, the quota of 153,774 was dominated by the 83,575 assigned to Great Britain and Ireland. Thus more than half the available places had been allocated to nations which were known to provide relatively few applicants. By contrast, the countries with large numbers of potential immigrants were assigned small quotas: Germany, about 26,000; Poland, 6,000; Italy, 5,500; France, 3,000; Rumania, 300. Later these impersonal figures would doom Rumanian, Polish and French Jews seeking sanctuary while the English and Irish quotas lay unused.

Until September 1930 the provision denying admission to an immigrant "likely to become a public charge" had rarely been invoked; immigrants of good character and robust health, and with perhaps $100, were regarded as good risks in the expanding American economy. It was the massive unemployment in the wake of the 1929 crash and not refugees from Adolf Hitler which caused the "public charge" provision to be resurrected from the statute books, dusted off and utilized. And it was Herbert Hoover, not Franklin D. Roosevelt, who revived it.

President Hoover issued a White House statement on September 8, 1930, calling attention to the abnormal times and announcing that consular officers "will before issuing a visa have to pass judgment with particular care on whether the applicant may become a public charge, and if the applicant cannot convince the officer that it is not probable, the visa will be refused."

The President made it clear that if the consul believed that the applicant might become a public charge *at any time,* even long after his arrival, the consul must refuse the visa. The State Department obeyed these instructions diligently, and the number of aliens admitted to the United States fell from 241,700 in 1930 to 97,139 in 1931. Immigration further plummeted to 35,576 in 1932, the year before Hitler came to power.

The State Department publicly acknowledged but also defended the severe effects of the provision. In March 1933 Assistant Secretary of State Wilbur Carr, whose jurisdiction then included consular, passport and visa matters, testified before the House Committee on Immigration. Congressman Samuel Dickstein of New York, chairman of the committee, had introduced a resolution in an effort to revoke Hoover's 1930 order. Dickstein wanted to liberalize immigration, but was opposed by the majority of committee members.

Assistant Secretary Carr opposed the resolution, stating that the Hoover order had rightly kept 500,000 immigrants from entering the United States at a time when unemployment had leaped from 2,500,000 to 12,000,000. At first Carr denied any connection between the Jews of Germany and the Dickstein proposal, but in response to a question he admitted: "The public would look at it as opening the way to allow those there to come to the United States."

Representative Emanuel Celler of New York, unimpressed by Carr's testimony, charged at the hearing that the State Department was slapping Congress in the face. "When Congress passed immigration laws," said Celler, "the State Department has no right to reduce quotas ninety-two percent."

In preparing Assistant Secretary Carr for his appearance before the committee, A. Dana Hodgdon, chief of the State Department's Visa Division, had reminded him in writing that the reports of persecution of the Jews of Germany might be exaggerated and he included a thought which would occur again and again: "It may be added with regard to a possible increase in immigration from Germany in view of recent reported troubles in that country that it has been alleged that undesirable classes including Communists will wish to come to this country and will be encouraged to leave Germany."

The Dickstein resolution did not pass. The opposition of the State Department, "patriotic" societies and a majority of Dickstein's own committee prevailed. The judgment "likely to become a public charge" continued as one of the most effective barriers to immigration during the prewar and war years.

Another major obstacle to immigration for Jews fleeing from Hitler concerned Section 7 (c) of the Immigration Act of 1924, which required the applicant to furnish a police certificate of good character for the previous five years, together with a record of military service, two certified copies of a birth certificate and "two copies of all other available public records" kept by the authorities in the country from which he was departing. The law required these documents only "if available," but many American consuls insisted upon full dossiers—and the police certificate in particular.

Although the notion of a Jew dropping by police headquarters to receive a certificate of good character from his oppressors may strike the reader as a particularly sardonic touch of bureaucracy, State Department files refer repeatedly to this requirement and its importance.

Jewish organizations frequently protested the incongruity of this rule. In August 1933 the State Department's legal adviser, Green H. Hackworth, commented on these complaints: ". . . it is believed that the mere fact that a Jew has been driven out of Germany into another country, or has found it desirable to flee from Germany to escape persecution, does not in and of itself excuse him from producing the documents required by Section 7(c) if it is reasonably possible for him to obtain such documents upon applying therefor to the appropriate German authorities." Such pronouncements, divorced from the reality of life in Nazi Germany, were issued regularly by the legal adviser. Phrased with Olympian rectitude, they shattered many last hopes in a land where law had ceased to exist.

One wonders whether the State Department lawyers ever had an opportunity to read the dispatches from Germany describing police treatment of the Jews. In any case, the legal adviser had a firm position, which he expressed quite clearly. His objection to the waiver of documents, he wrote, lay "in the likelihood that numerous undesirable persons, including criminals and anarchists, would take advantage of the waiver."

At precisely the same time as the legal adviser was warning about criminals and anarchists from his office in Washington, Consul General Leon Dominian in Stuttgart was reporting to the State Department about the character of the prospective immigrants: "It is interesting to note that the Jewish applicants are uniformly of the better class. There are many young professional men and sons of wealthy families. Among the latter class are many students who desire to continue their studies in the United States but do not wish to return to Germany . . ."

The reluctance of State Department officials to accept such unsolicited testimonials to good character offered in behalf of the Jews of Germany represents a curious phenomenon. This suspicion was manifested not by American consuls in the localities where Jews had served as university professors, businessmen, doctors, lawyers and creative artists but thousands of miles from the scene, in Washington. It was as if the caricature of Jewry which Hitler had drawn to serve his own political and psychotic purposes had gained a measure of acceptance among American officials who would be called upon to judge the Jews' fitness for American citizenship and, in fact, for life itself.

The State Department's preoccupation with the police records of the Jews in Germany cropped up repeatedly in 1933 and 1934. In a report dealing with immigration from January to August 1934, the American consulate in Berlin analyzed the occupations of the 471 heads of families who had obtained visas. The breakdown showed 65 physicians; 63 lawyers or other professionals; 19 university professors; 32 independent businessmen; 156 salesmen, clerks or salaried employees in commercial enterprises; and 136 who listed other forms of conventional employment.

In the course of his long, detailed report the vice-consul noted, in connection with the immigrants' submission of documents, that German police departments habitually expunged records of minor crimes five or ten years after their occurrence. This prompted C. Paul Fletcher of the Visa Division in Washington to note: "The statement relative to the unavailability in Germany of complete police records strengthens the contention that the United States is being made the dumping ground for criminals."

Stringent quotas, the "public charge" provision and the necessity to provide police certificates "if available" were not the only barriers facing the potential immigrant. There was also the "contract labor" provision which made it impossible for workers to enter under employment contracts. Thus the prospective immigrant, attempting to meet the "public charge" provision, might assure himself of a job and then be barred because of his foresight.

The American consul in Rotterdam was one of the few who protested to the State Department about the application of this provision. He pointed out that in past years an immigrant who worked on his brother's farm in the United States would not have been considered a contract laborer. The new ruling would force an American farmer who wanted his brother to work with him to swear falsely that he would keep him in idleness. "Such a ruling," wrote the consul, "is a penalizing of honesty and a strong incitement to perjury."

As if the "public charge" provision, the necessity to supply police records and the complexities of the "contract labor" clause were not enough, a further restriction in the Immigration Act of 1917 called for the "exclusion of persons whose ticket or passage is paid for by any corporation, association or society, municipality or foreign government either directly or indirectly." The originators of this provision could not have foreseen the plight of the German Jews, who were stripped of all their possessions before being cast adrift on endless seas. They were expected to be self-sufficient though penniless, capable of supporting themselves though unemployed, and prepared to pay their passage without accepting help from friends.

But the Immigration Act was not revised. Everyone from the White House on down expressed fears that any attempts to reform it would bring down the wrath of the conservative Southerners, who dominated congressional committees and who would be just as happy to end immigration altogether as to simplify its procedures. Martin Dies of Texas, who led the restrictionists in the House of Representatives, put it simply: "We must ignore the tears of sobbing sentimentalists and internationalists, and we must permanently close, lock and bar the gates of our country to new immigration waves and then throw the keys away."

For their part, the "sobbing sentimentalists" tried to publicize the case against the State Department. An article entitled "German Refugees and American Bureaucrats" in the January 20, 1934 issue of *Today* magazine sharply criticized consuls for their arbitrary use of the "public charge" clause. The department sent copies of the article to several consuls and requested their comments.

In reply, the consul in Rotterdam summarized the disposition of visa requests during 1933 to document his fair treatment of applicants: 74 German refugees had applied to the Rotterdam consulate for visas; 16 were granted. All but one of the 58 refusals were based primarily on the "public charge" provision. The consul sent the following case histories to the State Department. Although the names of the applicants have been omitted, the text is virtually unchanged.

Case A

Twenty-one-year-old German merchant without any personal resources. He is being supported by the Jewish Aid Committee of Holland. He has an affidavit from a cousin in the United States guaranteeing his support. The cousin has savings of $3,200, owns $7,500 in property and is employed as a clerk. The report of his savings is substantiated by a letter from his bank. In addition the young man has a second affidavit guaranteeing him support from an uncle in the United States. The uncle has a savings account of $1,300, this amount substantiated by a bank statement.

Consul's Analysis

The young man has no personal resources. There is no direct obligation upon his cousin or uncle to support him. The resources claimed on the affidavits were not proved. The applicant has not seen his uncle or cousin. His passage is being paid by the Jewish Aid Committee.

Disposition of Case A

Visa refused on the grounds that he is likely to become a public charge and that he is an alien whose passage will be paid by an association, thus violating the law.

Case B

Thirty-three-year-old German physician and his thirty-one-year-old wife. They have 1,000 florins $[1,600] and three affidavits of support from a sister, cousin and friend in the United States. It is claimed that a second sister in the United States owns $70,000 worth of property and $12,000 in additional resources.

Consul's Analysis

1,000 florins is insufficient. The greater part of the resources as listed on the affidavits is unproved. The number of dependents of the cousin, sister and friend signing the affidavits is unstated. The cousin, sister and friend have no direct obligation to the physician.

Disposition of Case B

Visas refused on the grounds that the physician and his wife are likely to become public charges.

Case C

Twenty-five-year-old German merchant. Has 70 florins [$112] in personal resources. Has affidavit of support from sister in America who claims savings of $3,200 and a job paying $30 a week. A letter from her bank supports her savings claim and a letter from her employer vouches for her salary. In addition the applicant has an affidavit from his uncle, attesting to a $19,000 joint savings account and employment at $50 a week. A letter from his bank substantiates his savings. The young man has a third affidavit from friends claiming resources of $30,000, their statement supported by a bank letter.

Consul's Analysis

The young man has not proved that he has 70 florins, and in any case this would be insufficient. His passage to the United States will be paid for by his sister. There is no direct obligation on his sister, uncle or friends to support him. He has never seen his uncle. His sister is already caring for his mother and father, who have been admitted from Germany.

Disposition of Case C

Visa refused on grounds that applicant is likely to become a public charge.

Case D

Applicant is a twenty-eight-year-old Polish dentist who has come from Germany with $70 of personal resources. He has an affidavit from his sister in America with savings of $1,000 and what she regards as an adequate weekly salary.

Consul's Analysis

The $70 is insufficient. There is no direct obligation upon the sister to support her brother. The resources of the sister are inadequate to support two people. His passage is to be paid for by the sister.

Disposition of Case D

Visa refused on grounds that applicant is likely to become a public charge.

Case E

Twenty-one-year-old German electrician without any resources. His uncle in the United States provides affidavit claiming that his business is worth $25,000, that he owns real estate valued at $15,000 and has savings of $2,800, the latter substantiated by a bank letter.

Consul's Analysis

The applicant has no personal resources. There is no direct obligation on the part of the uncle to support his nephew.

Disposition of Case E

Visa is refused on grounds applicant is likely to become a public charge.

This was the way the U.S. consul in Rotterdam refuted the charges made by *Today* magazine against the State Department.

When a copy of the article was sent by State to its Hamburg consulate, Consul General Erhardt turned it over to Vice-Consul Burke. Burke had been in charge of administration of the immigration laws and regulations in Hamburg since 1924 and therefore was in a good position to assess the charges made in the article.

Burke's analysis was quite unorthodox. He happened to agree with the writer's argument against the current practice of declaring an applicant "likely to become a public charge" on the basis of vague criteria. The author of the *Today* article had suggested that instead the applicant's relative in America execute a bond in advance, thus demonstrating the sincerity of his promise to guarantee the immigrant's support. Burke added that resources of friends and relatives could best be investigated at the place where their assets were located and their income earned, i.e., in the United States.

"It must be freely conceded," Burke wrote, "that at the present time it is not an easy matter to handle the problem of 'public charge' in a satisfactory manner . . . The interpretation has not only varied somewhat as between one consular officer and another . . . but has varied strikingly from one year to another, even in the hands of the same officials."

Burke pointed out that applicants suppressed the fact that they had jobs awaiting them lest they be rejected as "contract labor." This of course prevented the examining officer from estimating the applicant's ability to support himself. "The immigrant, in other words," Burke commented, "is compelled to steer artfully between the rocks and the whirlpool."

Burke observed that at one time an immigrant with $100 had no problem gaining admission to the United States. After the Hoover order of 1930, however, "it became doubtful whether a man possessing $10,000—one hundred times the former amount—should be regarded as unlikely to become a public charge."

In spite of Vice-Consul Burke's candor and the continuing complaints of social agencies interested in assisting applicants, the State Department did not alter its consular procedures until 1937. These restrictions had a profound effect on U.S. immigration in general. In particular, only 6,514 of the 63,000 Jews who fled from Germany in 1933–34 entered the United States.

Consul General Messersmith referred to this surprisingly

low number in an early dispatch: ". . . the number asking for visas to the United States is comparatively small. This is due to the fact that the difficulties of securing visas for the United States are well known and the Jews without resources are obliged to remain in the country."

During the same period France, in spite of her own difficult economic and geographic position, respected the right of asylum and sheltered no fewer than thirty thousand Jewish refugees.

As Germany tightened the noose, the financial pressures against Jewish emigrants became more severe. At the beginning of Hitler's regime, Jews who left Germany were permitted to take out as much as $10,000, but soon this was reduced to $6,000. When it was lowered to $4,000, the American consul in Stuttgart reported that the reduction "will result in many immigrants to the United States from Germany encountering grave difficulty in showing that they are not excludable under the public charge clause."

But the Nazis had only started their campaign to plunder the Jews, and soon the maximum amount they could take with them dropped to $800. In October 1934 the Third Reich issued its most drastic currency restriction, limiting each emigrant to a total of 10 reichsmarks (about $4). The Jews were thus trapped by both German and American regulations.

The harshness of American immigration policy was not lost on Hitler, who turned each aspect of the world's apathy into a weapon for himself. A month after he had assumed power he issued a statement that American citizens had no right to protest his anti-Semitism in view of the United States' own racial discrimination in its immigration policies. "Through its immigration law," said Hitler, "America has inhibited the unwelcome influx of such races as it has been unable to tolerate in its midst. Nor is America now ready to open its doors to Jews fleeing from Germany."

For those who might have missed his remarks, which were widely reprinted in the press, he repeated the theme in an interview for *Collier's* magazine in June 1933.

In a similar vein the *Völkischer Beobachter* observed: ". . . we merely wish to state that the United States possesses rigorous immigration laws while Germany has absolutely none thus far. We further point to American relations with Negroes—social and political. And finally, certain American universities have long since excluded Jews."

There had been many attempts by prominent Americans to make the Roosevelt Administration relax the rigid implementation of the "public charge" and other restrictions which had reduced immigration to a trickle.

The American Civil Liberties Union made a determined effort on September 10, 1933, addressing an appeal to the President signed by thirty-six distinguished educators, lawyers and clergymen, including Reinhold Niebuhr, Professor Felix Frankfurter, the Reverend John Haynes Holmes, Oswald Garrison Villard, Professor Charles A. Beard and the Misses Jane Addams and Lillian Wald. They called for "revision of the immigration laws to admit religious and political refugees, particularly from Germany, in harmony with the American tradition of asylum for refugees escaping from foreign tyrannies."

Several specific recommendations were submitted to the President. The first one called for the posting of bonds by responsible citizens, as insurance that the immigrants would not become public charges. Next, they urged him to revise President Hoover's executive order of 1930 which, they said, "had the effect practically of stopping all immigration." Third, they suggested that consuls accept certificates of good character in behalf of the immigrants instead of requiring police certificates from the countries they were fleeing. Finally, they asked the President "to call to the attention of Consuls the special claims in law of political and religious refugees to asylum in the United States."

On the same day that the ACLU petition arrived, the President received a letter from William Green, president of the American Federation of Labor, protesting schemes to relax immigration regulations. The labor leader reminded the President that eleven million Americans were still unemployed.

Secretary Hull's advisers furnished reasons other than unemployment to justify the continuation of stringent policies. A revealing insight is furnished by legal adviser Green Hackworth in his commentary on a proposal made to the Secretary by Judge Joseph M. Proskauer of the American Jewish Committee.

Judge Proskauer was one of many prominent Americans who suggested that a bonding procedure be substituted for consular caprice as insurance to the government that an alien would not become a public charge. Under Section 21 of the Immigration Act of 1917, such a bond could be filed and approved by the Secretary of Labor, who would then inform the Secretary of State, who would then advise the consul to issue a visa if the applicant met all other requirements.

Lawyer Hackworth, trapped by this logic, turned to new arguments to justify the old system. In a memorandum to the Secretary he pointed out that the "public charge" provision embraced more than the mere possession of money. According to Hackworth, even an alien with a lot of money might be inadmissible as likely to become a public charge. "In many cases the Consul's finding would be based principally upon the peculiar mental or physical characteristics of the alien application, brought out upon a personal examination and interrogation of the latter, rather than upon a mere lack of money or of connections in the United States by which a living might be made or support found."

Hackworth compared this to the clause prohibiting the entry of aliens with criminal tendencies. Such a person might never have committed a crime, but a consul could deny him a visa, reaching his decision on the basis of "his physical and mental make-up and peculiar characteristics." According to the law, Hackworth argued, the consul must be the final judge of the immigrant's qualifications. The fallacy in the Proskauer plan was that "the issuance of a visa would not depend finally upon the exercise of a Consul's judgment and discretion."

Hackworth ended his brief with a quotation from the House Committee on Immigration, which, in recommending adoption of the Immigration Act of 1924, had stated: "This country thus serves notice that it can no longer be an asylum."

As the testimony of the consuls themselves has indicated, there was little uniformity in their decision-making process. Hackworth's new criteria further reduced objective evaluation. "Mental make-up," "peculiar physical charactristics"—what exactly did these phrases mean? Was this not, in fact, an invitation to reject applicants on the basis of the most narrow prejudice and the most rigid conformity?

There was but one significant response to complaints about the harsh implementation of the immigration law. Cordell Hull notified consuls to be lenient to applicants who might be endangered by efforts to obtain a police certificate.

Throughout the prewar and wartime years Franklin D. Roosevelt insisted on living up to the letter of the immigration law, maintaining that restrictionist elements in Congress would block any reform. But a change in the law would not have been necessary. As James McDonald, a specialist in international affairs who had been chairman of the Foreign Policy Association, observed: "Just as President Hoover, by administrative interpretation, in effect instructed the consuls to block immigration, so now President Roosevelt could, by relaxing further the requirements in the case of refugees, make easier the admission of a few thousand additional Germans a year."

But there would be no relaxation. In 1938 the Nazis burned

every synagogue in the nation, shattered the windows of every Jewish establishment, hauled twenty-five thousand innocent people to concentration camps, and fined the Jews 1,000,000,-000 marks for the damage.

Five days later, at a White House press conference, a reporter asked the President, "Would you recommend a relaxation of our immigration restrictions so that the Jewish refugees could be received in this country?"

"That is not in contemplation," replied the President. "We have the quota system."

The United States not only insisted upon its immigration law throughout the Nazi era, but administered it with severity and callousness.

In spite of unprecedented circumstances, the law was constricted so that even its narrow quotas were not met.

The lamp remained lifted beside the golden door, but the flame had been extinguished and the door was padlocked.

■ VIII ■

The New Germany

DURING THE "HUNDRED DAYS" WHICH FOLlowed the inauguration of Franklin D. Roosevelt in March 1933, the morale of the nation was transformed. Proposals designed to revive the economy flooded the Congress, and the President radiated confidence and courage as they were approved in record time.

Roosevelt surmounted the banking crisis, modified the Volstead Act so that citizens could enjoy wine and beer, aided farmers with the Agricultural Adjustment Act, established the Civilian Conservation Corps, inaugurated unemployment relief, created the Tennessee Valley Authority, stimulated legislation to prevent the foreclosure of small homes, and pushed through the National Industrial Recovery Act.

Most Americans, understandably immersed in their own problems, concentrated on these achievements and on the new national hero who had made them possible. Nevertheless, many Americans reading about Nazi terror in their daily newspapers roused themselves from purely personal considerations and demanded action in defense of Hitler's victims.

During all of 1933 they bombarded the State Department and the White House with resolutions condemning the cruelties and urging a sympathetic American response to the danger facing the Jews. The petitions and pleas came not only from all the major population centers, but also from such places as Douglas, Arizona; Savannah, Georgia; Butte, Montana; Racine, Wisconsin; New Haven, Connecticut; Pottstown, Pennsylvania; and Saratoga Springs, New York. The White House and the State Department acknowledged receipt of the sentiments and signatures, but their replies were couched in noncommittal language. They were clearly designed to blunt public indignation.

A Cincinnati physician addressed a letter to Cordell Hull asking whether it was true that Jewish doctors in Germany were banned from practicing their profession. "This information is so startling that in the opinion of many it smacks possibly of exaggeration or even of anti-German propaganda," wrote the physician.

Hull turned the letter over to Pierrepont Moffat, chief of what was then called the Division of Western European Affairs. At that time the division's files were filled with reports of Jewish physicians who had been ousted, but Moffat's reply avoided any confirmation. Instead, he suggested that the Cincinnati physician obtain exact information about the matter from the German consul in Chicago.

State Department and Administration attitudes of "wait and see" were based to a certain extent on the hope that Nazi excesses were a temporary by-product of the German "Revolution" and that they were bound to diminish as the government asserted its authority. The ruthless implementation of the Law for the Restoration of the Professional Civil Service of April 7, 1933, should have shattered any such hopes.

The Nazi technique for outlawing the Jews economically began with the destruction of the professional classes and worked its way down to the humblest citizen. Within three months after the law's enactment, more than 30,000 heads of families, representing 100,000 individuals, had been deprived of a living. These included 5,000 of 6,000 Jewish government employees; 1,200 of 2,800 lawyers; 3,500 of 7,000 physicians; 3,000 musicians, singers and actors; 1,000 dentists, pharmacists and related occupations; and 20,000 merchants, artisans and their employees. In some localities the economic destruction of the Jews was slowed down deliberately to lessen the hardship upon the rest of the community. These ominous facts were of course reported to the United States government. More alarming than these statistics were the startling details of German sadism.

From the advent of the Hitler onslaught, the actions taken against the Jews were carried out with the full knowledge of the German public. Communities vied with one another to proclaim restrictions against Jews; they competed for the honor of posting signs at town limits boasting that they excluded Jews, refused to sell them real estate or, most triumphant of all, were *judenfrei*. From the list of those Germans who knew nothing about such Nazi activities—a list which grows longer each year—one must therefore exclude the citizens of such forbidden areas as Ockenheim, Rommersheim, Udenheim, Schweisweiler, Königstatten, Dieburgstatten, Niederstein, Würzburg, Rotenburg, Hassfurt, Schotten, Frohnhofen, Adelshofen, Schriesheim, Asemissen, Greste, Bechterdissen, Bacharach, Bechtheim, Doddenheim, Bunzlau, Brilon, Delbrück, Kreis, Detmold, Frankenberg, Frankfurt on the Oder, Fraustadt, St. Goarhausen, Hangen-Weissheim, Neuss, Waldshut, Wallerstädten, Westhofen, Arnsheim, Schönebeck, Oppenheim, Teterow, Edenkoben, Coburg, Herborn, Freystadt, Osann, Hundsaugen, Pleutschbach, Weroth, Oberhausen, Wittlich, Bergzabern, Rosslau, Wimpffen and Breunigweiler. This is of course only a partial list. Other forbidden areas included the public baths of Leipzig, the beach at Wannsee, the park in Anhalt, and most seaside and holiday resorts including Misdroy, Arendsee, Swinemünde, Neustrelitz, Lychen, Heringsdorf, Norderney, Borkum and Sylt.

For those citizens of the Third Reich who missed these public notices of hostility or failed to observe the occasional disappearance of a Jewish neighbor, there were other opportunities to view Nazi anti-Semitism. These included numerous instances of public humiliation. On July 20, 1933, three hundred Jewish shopkeepers in Nuremberg were arrested, herded together and paraded through the city to the music of a storm-troop band. Old people who did not move fast enough were kicked by the Brown Shirts while the Nurembergers on the sidewalks jeered the Jews who were taken to storm-troop barracks for questioning, detention and more humiliation. Eventually they were released.

A similar incident occurred the same day in Stuttgart. At five o'clock in the morning, the homes of members of the Jewish Benevolent Association were searched and four hundred men, women and children ranging in age from twelve to eighty were rounded up. They were forced to lick the dirty pavement and to pull up grass with their hands while they were cursed and spat upon by their fellow townsmen. When an old man defended himself against a spectator trying to pull his beard, the crowd attacked and severely beat him. At the end of the day, sixty Jews were detained for further punishment. The *Manchester Guardian* and other British newspapers reported the incident. So did Ambassador Dodd and much of the American press.

On July 28, 1933, Dodd provided further information to his superiors in Washington. The Association of Blind University Men had called a general meeting in order to incorporate Aryan principles into its statutes. Dodd also mentioned that Jews were now prohibited from the municipal swimming pools and baths in Plauen and that the municipal council of Munich was considering a motion to exclude the ashes of cremated Jews from nonsectarian cemeteries.

The same municipal council had been involved in another related issue. Dr. James Loeb, a Jewish banker who had founded the Loeb Library of Classics, had also provided the principal support for the Munich Research Institute of Psychiatry. Dr. Loeb had died shortly before and his will included a bequest of $1,000,000 for the institute. Members of the Munich municipal council had been informed that they would not be allowed to attend Dr. Loeb's funeral in their official capacities or lay wreaths at his grave. Presumably they were permitted to accept the bequest.

Vice-Consul Gray in Stuttgart recounted the case of storekeeper Willy Stein, who had come to the consulate to inquire about immigration. The officer conducting the interview noticed that Stein walked with great difficulty and asked him about the disability, since it might affect his chances of obtaining a visa. Stein, a World War veteran without political leanings, assured the officer that he was in good health, though recovering from a beating. Stein explained that a customer whose mother had just died had come to his shop wearing a mourning band. The customer asked whether Stein would be kind enough to accompany him home. When Stein arrived he was seized and beaten, then taken to Nazi headquarters in Heilbronn and beaten again by seven Nazis armed with clubs. He had spent four weeks in the hospital and in a convalescent home. The nerves of the lower part of his back had been injured, his nose had been crushed, his lip cut severely and his fingers smashed.

Willy Stein reported the attack to the police but they advised him to forget the whole thing. If he took the case to court, they said, they would not be responsible for the consequences. It seemed to Willy Stein that the best thing to do was to leave

Germany. Gray's report did not reveal whether or not Stein had qualified for his American visa.

The fate of Jews like Willy Stein had been outlined in ponderous but ominous language by Dr. Achim Gercke, the expert on racial questions in the German Ministry of the Interior. Dr. Gercke's confidential memorandum of September 1933 fell into the hands of American officials in Berlin who, in turn, forwarded it to Washington:

"All propositions which intend to create a permanent condition or a permanent regulation for the Jews in Germany do not solve the Jewish question, as they do not detach the Jew from Germany . . . plans and programs must have a definite aim which leads into the future and which is not merely the regulation of a momentarily unpleasant situation. The organization of the Jews does not lead to a better future, but only a systematically attacked final solution of the Jewish question. We must build up our country without the Jews; they can only remain strangers without nationality and may not occupy any legal and legitimate permanent position within the structure of the country. Only in this way will Ahasuerus be forced to reach for his staff for the last time and exchange it for the axe and spade."

In the dispatch to Washington accompanying the confidential memorandum, Consul General Messersmith also described the murder of a prominent German Jew who had been wounded five times during the war and had insisted upon returning to the front. After being released from a concentration camp in 1933, he was requested to report to the police. They later telephoned his wife and asked her to come to the police station for "good news about your husband." When she arrived she was shown his lifeless body but was permitted to see only one side of his face.

As if expecting a skeptical response from his Washington readers, Consul General Messersmith added: "The facts in this case as above recited, horrible and unbelievable as they may seem, come to me from sources which are unimpeachable."

In a letter to Undersecretary Phillips a few weeks later, Messersmith commented again on his new and disturbing awareness of German sadism: "There is an element of brutality and hardness in the German character which I have never before believed was there, but which we must recognize as existing."

He then recounted the experience of the seventeen-year-old son of a German diplomat. When the boy was asked to join the Hitler Youth movement in his Bavarian school, he had replied that he would like to wait a few weeks before deciding. "That night five of his comrades in the school came to his room and submitted him to such mistreatment that it is believed his liver and kidneys are so seriously injured that he may not ever get well." The school punished the attackers by prohibiting them from participating in Hitler Youth activities for two weeks.

Messersmith closed his letter with a capsule description of Hitler; "I am thoroughly convinced that the man is mentally a pathological case and that it is impossible to foresee what he will do." The letter was dated October 28, 1933.

The German capability for mass destruction was sensed by many observers during the very first year of Hitler's rule. Frederick T. Birchall, writing to the *New York Times* from the site of the 1933 Nuremberg rally, said prophetically: "Aryanism is now the keystone of Nazi policy, as all along it has been the principal tenet of Adolf Hitler's faith. It is also in Germany the most popular of the Nazi principles, and of all the Nazi tendencies is the most warmly defended by the Germans. Its corollary is persecution even to extermination—the word is the Nazis' own—of the non-Aryans, if that can be established without too much world disturbance."

The concentration camp existed in Nazi Germany as early as 1933, and it was no secret to the world. As we have seen,

Dachau was publicized early in the Hitler regime. Most of the first prisoners were not Jews but leaders, or alleged leaders, of the opposition to Nazism. From the beginning the Jews were isolated from the others and required to do the most loathsome jobs, such as the hand cleaning of latrines.

In August 1933 the *Neuer Vorwärts,* a newspaper published by exiled German Socialists, estimated that there were eighty thousand prisoners in sixty-five camps. Correspondents permitted to visit camps were able to note scarred backs and other visible evidence of beatings, although their visits had been arranged so as to avoid such sights.

The most vivid description of a concentration camp in 1933 was provided by an eighteen-year-old inmate who was neither Jewish nor a member of an anti-Nazi organization. He had enrolled in an agricultural school at Wolzig which was founded by the Jewish Agricultural Committee. There were forty-three boys in the school; he was one of thirteen who were not Jewish. As the young man later reported; "Our ages ran between thirteen and eighteen. None of us cared about politics. We were only interested in animals and in making things grow."

In May 1933 storm troopers inspected the school and returned a month later to round up the students. They were beaten with cudgels and taken to Berlin. They were not permitted to keep any belongings. The boys were placed on public display for three hours in Berlin while their guards shouted at passers-by to look at them because their fathers had robbed Germany of all its money since the war. If a boy tried to reply he was beaten.

They were then taken to the Oranienburg concentration camp, near Berlin, where they were forced to stand at attention for three hours. They were given a cup of coffee and a piece of black bread, and told to join the twenty-five hundred Oranienburg inmates, who slept on thin straw in a large hall. The camp was illuminated by searchlight all night, and guards with machine guns covered the area from rooftop positions. A barbed-wire fence of eight strands, one of which was electrified, further guaranteed against escape.

They were awakened at five o'clock the next morning and handed two slices of black bread and coffee. Two hours of military drill was followed by heavy manual labor until noon. Their "lunch" was a cup of watery soup.

Prisoners were treated as criminals, their heads were shaven, and at the slightest pretext they were sent to solitary confinement. Some three hundred storm troopers, described by the boy as "common people of the lowest kind," divided up the prisoners' possessions at periodic intervals. The guards drank heavily after which they took savage pleasure in beating former Reichstag members, journalists, judges and scholars.

Captain Krüger, the commandant, selected the young non-Jewish prisoner as a typist in the camp office. This enabled the boy to learn the names of many of the inmates. He recognized several distinguished men among them, including Friedrich Ebert, son of the first President of the Weimar Republic. Ebert displayed remarkable courage and dignity in accepting his fate. Not so fortunate was Professor Neubeck, a leading musical director for radio and theater who had arrived with Ebert, but hanged himself the next day.

Another celebrity at Oranienburg was Herr Braun, a leading reporter for the German radio. He was beaten frequently by guards who abused him for having earned too much money as a broadcaster. One day the young man saw Herr Braun after his return from an "interrogation." He had been injured severely and both eyes were closed. The boy asked him if he would like some water to bathe his eyes and Braun replied that he was afraid the boy would be punished for his kindness. "In any case," Braun said, "I am finished with life."

The boy was finally released after signing two papers, one stating that living conditions had been good, another pledging that he would not work against "the new Germany." He fled from the country as soon as possible, and lengthy accounts of his experiences appeared in the London *Times* of September 19, 1933, and the *New York Times* of October 1. His narrative included the names of prisoners who had committed suicide in Oranienburg.

Another widely publicized story of the time concerned the death of Dr. Theodor Lessing, a professor of philosophy at Hanover University whose forebears had lived in Hanover for more than three hundred years. He had earned doctorates in medicine and philosophy and had written widely in many fields. His best-known books were *The Decline of the Spirit on Earth* and *The Symbolism of the Human Being*. Dr. Lessing and his wife had founded Hanover High School and Mrs. Lessing had devoted fourteen years to developing it into one of the finest secondary institutions in Germany.

But Lessing was a Social Democrat and a Jew. After twenty-six years of teaching and research he was dismissed from the university. Disaster followed upon disaster. At the age of sixty-two he lost his pension and the bank withheld his small life savings. When the Nazis took over Hanover High School, the Lessings fled to Marienbad in Czechoslovakia, ten miles from the German border. They took a house on a hill where he could continue his writing. But they were not left alone. The Nazi newspaper, *Völkischer Beobachter,* printed a virulent article about their departure and German authorities offered 80,000 marks to anyone who brought them back. A pair of Munich storm troopers, named Eckert and Zischka, decided to collect the reward. Eckert, twenty-one, had been a poacher in Czechoslovakia and knew all the local trails. On August 31, 1933, he led his companion to the Lessing home. Through the window they could see the scholar working at his desk. Apparently the target was too tempting; instead of kidnapping Lessing they shot him to death and slipped back across the border.

Two weeks before Lessing's death he had written to the *Manchester Guardian* about his situation. The closing lines of his letter were: "I am and shall remain a German; I am and shall remain a Jew; I am and shall remain a Socialist . . . I am now fighting for justice under my own name, against my own country, which I love."

As 1933 drew to a close, the reports of murder and molestation increased. Lord Marley, Deputy Speaker of the House of Lords, estimated that two thousand assassinations had occurred in Germany during the year. The House of Commons actually invited a German refugee who had been imprisoned in the Sonnenberg camp to recount his experiences. The man, who used the pseudonym "Lentz," described how murders were disguised as suicides; the beating of disabled prisoners with carbines; and the sight of men lying in the prison courtyard with flesh torn from their arms and legs.

James G. McDonald, who would later dedicate himself to the cause of the refugees, had visited Dachau in September. In a broadcast from London, McDonald stressed the clear intention of the camp officials to mislead him as to the treatment of inmates, but he had seen the look in the prisoners' eyes: "What I read there I shall not forget—fear, mounting fear, a sense of utter subjection to arbitrary, ruthless will."

On October 11, 1933, the League of Nations selected McDonald as "High Commissioner for Refugees (Jewish and Other) Coming from Germany." Since the League did not wish to antagonize Germany, which was still a member, the High Commission was established as an autonomous agency, largely removed from League jurisdiction and entirely removed from its financing. It was, in fact, virtually powerless and ran into trouble from the start.

Professor Joseph P. Chamberlain of Columbia University, a member of the High Commission's Governing Board, said at the first meeting that the United States would like to do its share to help the refugees but that difficult economic conditions complicated the problem of immigration.

Senator Henry Bérenger, the French delegate, replied tartly that hard times were universal. He reminded the commission that France had accepted nearly half of all the refugees and that the United States had taken very few. The French government had spent $500,000 for the care of the dispossessed and had placed forty German professors in French universities. The Dutch, Polish and Czech delegates then described their own hospitality to Germans in flight, but pointed out that they had neither the space nor the money to continue supporting this influx.

The South American countries, notorious for their restrictive immigration practices, behaved as expected. The Uruguayan delegate stated that his country was too small to receive refugees but he hoped that Argentina and Brazil, which did have the room, would lift their barriers. Unfortunately, the Argentinians and Brazilians who had been invited to the meeting failed to show up. The session ended with Britain's Lord Cecil stressing that Europe was already filled with refugees and that any hope for a solution must come from overseas.

In the United States, the most powerful, spacious and historically hospitable of the overseas countries, the drive to liberalize immigration centered on the children.

A group called German Jewish Children's Aid was organized in New York City for the sole purpose of bringing over children to be cared for in American homes. The executive secretary of this group was a redoubtable lady named Cecilia Razovsky. Born in St. Louis into a family of poor Jewish immigrants, she had worked in a factory as a child, sewing buttons on overalls at the rate of nine cents a dozen. After graduating from high school, she attended night school, taught American history and English to foreigners and trained as a social worker.

Appointed an inspector in the Child Labor Division of the Children's Bureau, she toured the cotton mills in the South from 1917 to 1920, combining her natural charm with a thunderous sense of righteousness. From 1920 to 1934 she worked for the Department of Immigrant Aid of the National Council of Jewish Women, where she learned all about public charge, contract laborer, potential criminal and other State Department synonyms for "refugee."

Then, as executive secretary of German Jewish Children's Aid she, along with her colleagues, launched a campaign for the temporary shelter in the United States of endangered German youngsters. Newspaper reports of Nazi persecution had inspired thousands of American families to volunteer sanctuary for these children, and Cecilia Razovsky worked out a plan for implementing these offers. The children would be cared for in American homes until danger subsided. There would be no question of formal adoption, since the children would eventually be reunited with their parents. This simplified the immigration procedure, as did the proviso requiring the American families to pledge that the children would not seek employment of any kind. With a well-organized screening procedure and uniform qualifications, the youngsters would, hopefully, be brought over in large groups rather than one at a time. This would require State Department approval but there could not possibly be any opposition to such a clearly humanitarian gesture.

Miss Razovsky had even worked out a solution to the thorny "public charge" problem. The Attorney General of the United States had ruled that in certain cases, advance bonds could be accepted by the Secretary of Labor as an alternative to a consular ruling on public charges. Miss Frances Perkins, the Secretary of Labor, approved of Miss Razovsky's proposal and had so notified Colonel Daniel W. MacCormack, the Labor Department's commissioner of immigration. The colonel, an overtly compassionate man, agreed to authorize a first contingent of two hundred and fifty youngsters under the age of sixteen. German Jewish Children's Aid would handle all the details and safeguards.

On April 9, 1934, Miss Razovsky met with John Farr Simmons, chief of the State Department's Visa Division, Colonel MacCormack and Professor Chamberlain of Columbia University, who was always in the forefront of every move to liberalize immigration. Miss Razovsky told the group that she hoped the children could be admitted within the next six months.

In reporting the meeting to Assistant Secretary of State Wilbur Carr, Simmons observed; "I gathered the impression that the Jewish groups had originally wanted a much larger number of German refugees admitted, but had, as a practical matter, realized that they had better make their demands very moderate for the present."

Three months later Miss Razovsky came to Washington to make final arrangements with Colonel MacCormack, but he had been called away and had asked a subordinate named Wixon to carry on the discussion. Wixon had not known about the proposed arrangements and was upset about the whole idea. In the words of John Farr Simmons, Wixon "studied it very hurriedly and came to the independent conclusion that the whole scheme was dangerous and impractical and should not be carried out in the form suggested and, incidentally, tentatively approved by Colonel MacCormack two months ago."

Wixon argued that the children would wish to remain in the United States indefinitely, would eventually add to the labor population and would want their parents and families to join them. Miss Razovsky was able to persuade him not to cancel the whole scheme, but Wixon later talked Colonel MacCormack into temporarily nullifying the bonding procedure. This reduced the responsibility of the Labor Department. Without the bonds, the principal burden of accepting the children would revert again to the consuls of the State Department.

Visa chief Simmons was alert to Wixon's ways. "The disadvantage," he wrote, "is that they are placing the whole responsibility for the admission of these children upon us."

Obviously a great deal had happened to the Republic which had admitted more than thirty-seven million immigrants and which was now so troubled by the problem of finding temporary sanctuary for two hundred and fifty children.

In the end Wixon's views were overruled by Colonel MacCormack. He drafted a letter for Secretary Perkins in which she accepted responsiblility for the youngsters under a provision of the law enabling her to admit unaccompanied children under sixteen if they were not likely to become public charges.

To keep the record clear, Simmons now wrote a memo for the files about the vast burden lifted from the State Department: "I thought that this is very important, since it puts the whole responsibility for the special action taken directly back upon the Department of Labor, whereas otherwise Colonel MacCormack had seemed to show a disposition to place the entire burden upon us. In this connection we must think of possible future criticism of this action on the part of patriotic and restrictionist groups . . ."

Although State had yielded some of its prerogatives to labor, it instructed the U.S. consul in Berlin to make sure that payment of the children's passage did not violate the clause in the immigration law excluding "persons whose ticket or passage is paid for by any corporation, association, society, municipality or foreign government either directly or indirectly." The Labor Department had already assured the State Department that transportation was being financed by individual subscription in a manner approved by law, but consuls were ordered to ascertain the method of payment in each case. That was on August 31, 1934.

Apparently Simmons had hoped that MacCormack would lose interest in the project and permit State to handle visa applications in its conventional leisurely manner. But the commissioner pressed vigorously for the children's admission. On

October 8 Simmons wrote another memo to Carr: "I regret very much that I was unable to dissuade Colonel MacCormack from taking action in these cases. He seemed determined to go as far as he could to help the Jewish group interested. He had apparently previously promised them to do all he could and felt obliged to keep his promise. I insisted also against the wishes of the Department of Labor and of Professor Chamberlain and Miss Razovsky that our consular officers must require that full evidence be submitted by each individual child in each case, the opinions of the Department of Labor merely being forwarded to assist in a general way in their consideration of such cases." Simmons wrote a similar note to Undersecretary Phillips but added a word of reassurance: "Summing up the situation, I believe that there was no possibility of effectively dissuading Colonel MacCormack from entering into some kind of a scheme with Professor Chamberlain . . . and that our record is such that we can defend ourselves against any criticism of restrictionist groups should it be known that any special arrangements were being made to bring Jewish children into this country."

The "patriotic" and restrictionist groups did not wait long to assert their views about the admission of two hundred and fifty Jewish children. The American Coalition of Patriotic, Civic and Fraternal Societies, led by Captain John B. Trevor and numbering such stalwarts as the Sons and Daughter of the American Revolution, Veterans of Foreign Wars and the American Legion Auxiliary, registered immediate objections. According to the coalition, the State and Labor departments were allowing "international sentimentality" to run riot.

Jewish organizations bristled at this comment, and Assistant Secretary Carr, commenting on this conflict, drew a parallel between the contending groups in another note to John Farr Simmons: "I am rather apprehensive that between the aggressiveness of our Jewish friends and that of Captain Trevor and his followers, a considerable commotion may be in the making in regard to immigration and the administration of the immigration laws."

Cecilia Razovsky and the German Jewish Children's Aid prevailed against bureaucratic opposition and brought their two hundred and fifty children safely to the United States; thereafter they could average little more than a hundred arrivals per year. Most of their energy was expended in surmounting the hazards of Washington.

The record of the United States in welcoming endangered children stands in sharp contrast to that of Britain. In one ten-month period before the outbreak of the war in September 1939, England welcomed more than nine thousand German children, nine-tenths of whom were Jewish. They were without parents or possessions and this was an England in imminent danger of attack, a nation undergoing economic hardship, an island which had never been able to grow enough food for its population. More than one thousand of these immigrants eventually served in the British armed forces, a record no doubt noted and approved by that nation's patriotic societies.

In the United States, John B. Trevor and his patriotic confederates opposed every move to liberalize immigration. Trevor also headed a Committee on Immigration and the Alien Insane under the unlikely auspices of the New York State Chamber of Commerce. In May 1934 a report prepared for that committee was mailed to all chamber members. Its recommendations included: no exceptional admission for Jews who are refugees from persecution in Germany; no admission for any immigrant "unless he has a definite country to which he may be deported, if occasion demands"; and no admission to immigrants whose ancestors were not "all members of the white or Caucasian race."

The study was directed by Dr. Harry Laughlin, a geneticist whose views played a prominent role in the framing of the immigration laws prejudicial to residents of southern and eastern Europe. In his report the geneticist touched upon a variety of nongenetic matters, praising, for example, President Hoover's executive order which had toughened the "public charge" provision. Dr. Laughlin proposed a 60 percent reduction in quotas and he outlined his philosophy about the role of the immigrant:

"If they who control immigration would look upon the incoming immigrants, not essentially as in offering asylum nor in securing cheap labor, but primarily as 'sons-in-law to marry their own daughters,' they would be looking at it in the light of the long-time truth. Immigrants are essentially breeding stock."

In Dr. Laughlin, Captain Trevor had found a geneticist who met the special requirements of the ladies of the D.A.R. and the gentlemen of the S.A.R.

The anti-immigration forces in the United States made it quite clear that they feared an influx of Jews, but in their zeal to keep them out they forgot that the Nazi assault was directed against the Catholic and Protestant churches as well. In fact, there were many Christian men and women opposed to the Nazis who also sought sanctuary in other lands; more than 10 percent of the would-be immigrants were non-Jewish. For them there was virtually no assistance in financing or organizing their exodus. Only the American Friends Service Committee (Quakers) and the Unitarians were consistently on the job; it was up to the hard-pressed Jewish organizations to provide relief for Hitler's Christian victims as well as their own constituents. James G. McDonald, as High Commissioner for Refugees, articulated this dilemma in speeches throughout the United States.

In July 1935 McDonald reported to the League of Nations that 15 to 20 percent of the fifty thousand German refugees remaining in Europe were non-Jews who had fled for reasons of conscience or politics. Many were gravely impoverished. "The position is particularly difficult for the non-Jews in these places," he wrote, "because of the failure of the Christian bodies hitherto, with the splendid exception of the Quakers, to raise funds for assistance."

Eventually McDonald's prodding resulted in the formation of a few Christian refugee organizations, but their activity and their contributions were slight in comparison to the need. This may seem somewhat surprising, since the degradation of the Protestant and Catholic churches in Germany was widely publicized. An ardent Nazi army chaplain named Ludwig Müller was imposed upon the more than forty million German Protestants as "Reich Bishop." With a few notable exceptions, such as Pastor Niemöller, the opposition was meager indeed. Müller's stupidity rather than his un-Christian doctrines led to his ultimate decline, but Protestant power had been broken—and broken easily.

As for the Catholics, Hitler had signed a concordat with the Vatican in 1933, which he violated within days of the agreement. Catholic youth groups and family organizations were dissolved and thousands of priests, nuns and lay functionaries arrested. Erich Klausener, the leader of Catholic Action, was murdered in the "Blood Purge" the next year and cremated by the Nazis. Only a few days before, he had made the closing address at the Berlin Catholic Congress, reaffirming the devotion of Catholics to their nation and their religion. Dr. Klausener's ashes were sent by registered parcel post to his wife. Dorothy Thompson envisioned the scene in the December 1934 issue of *Harper's Magazine:*

"I kept thinking how it must have been when the postman rang the bell. I could imagine the postman—a nice jolly sort of man.

" 'Good morning,' he would say. 'I have a package for you this morning.' "

"Probably she would put it under her arm while she signed. Then the postman would tip his hat. They are awfully polite in Germany."

The mistreatment of some Catholics by the Nazis did not

turn the Church against the regime to a significant degree. It was an inherently anti-Semitic institution, as Guenter Lewy has documented so impressively in *The Roman Catholic Church and the Third Reich.* Lewy, as have others, pointed out that any sympathy expressed by Church leaders toward the victims of Nazi racism was directed to Jewish converts to Catholicism rather than the practicing Jews. There were frequent efforts by the bishops to improve the lot of these converts and to isolate them from the Jews. The clergy found frequent occasions to emphasize to their Nazi masters that they sought to protect only those Germans of Jewish origin who had seen the theological light.

It should be stressed that this charge applies *only* to German Catholicism. The French, Dutch and Belgian bishops and their parishioners responded in an entirely different manner. They spoke out, sheltered the Nazis' would-be victims at the risk of their own lives, and defended the sanctity of their churches even while the German armed forces occupied their lands. They did this without encouragement from His Holiness, Pope Pius XII.

But if German Protestant and Catholic leadership was swept along by the Nazi tide, it is also true that several thousand individual priests, ministers and lay leaders were murdered, brutalized or imprisoned by the Nazis. Their American co-religionists did not speak out forcefully, did not express outrage at their treatment. Perhaps their lethargy can be traced to the same current of isolationism that flowed through the American people in 1934 and presumably paralyzed their efforts on behalf of the Jews.

In 1934, as America began its slow recovery from economic disaster, a committee of the United States Senate began its dramatic revelations of munitions profits during World War I. Day after day the nation shuddered at new exposés of the bankers and arms manufacturers, the so-called merchants of death. The hearings were skillfully conducted by an isolationist group led by Senator Eugene P. Nye of North Dakota. The propaganda drums, beaten most loudly by the Hearst newspapers, boomed that the war had been fought not "to save the world for democracy," as Woodrow Wilson had proclaimed, but to enrich the profiteers whose wealth rose in direct proportion to the maimed bodies of the battlefield.

With grim ranks of Nazi troops filling the newsreel screens and frightening headlines from Europe dominating the newspapers during 1934, the Nye hearings touched powerful chords of public response. Young people formed an organization called Veterans of Future Wars, housewives banded together for pacifism, and Americans in overwhelming number agreed that we would never again pull Europe's chestnuts out of the fire.

In the White House, Franklin D. Roosevelt, with detailed reports of Nazi atrocities before him, failed to use his immense influence to reverse the trend. As historian James MacGregor Burns described it:

"Gliding with the current of opinion favoring the probe, Roosevelt not only joined the chorus denouncing the arms trade but allowed Nye access to executive papers that were greatly to aid the senator's efforts to dramatize the skulduggery of bankers and diplomats. Even more, he tolerated—and to some extent encouraged—the Nye committee in its ambition to use intensifying disgust with arms makers as an anvil on which to beat out a rigid policy of isolationism for the United States.

"At this crucial juncture Roosevelt offered little leadership. It was not inevitable that popular hatred of arms makers and war profiteers should deepen popular feeling that America ought to isolate itself from foreign entanglements and thus from foreign wars. That hatred might as well have bolstered a public desire to work with other nations in order to stop war and hence end the grim accoutrements of battle, including merchants of death. But such a channeling of opinion demanded an active program of education—in short, leadership. Roosevelt only drifted."

The indifference which enveloped the American government and people toward the Jews of Europe punished Hitler's non-Jewish victims as well. James McDonald's plea for a Christian response would never be answered fully.

■ IX ■
The Olympic Spirit

THE NAZI DICTATORSHIP PRESENTED A VAriety of moral challenges to the United States. One of the most widely discussed was the issue of American participation in the 1936 Olympic games in Berlin. From 1933 onward this occupied the attention of diverse theologians, politicians and broad jumpers. It dominated the lives of the executives of amateur athletics, preachers of the gospel of fair play, who searched their souls to discover whether there would be anything immoral about co-operating with the Third Reich's re-creation of the games of ancient Greece.

The Olympic games were no casual matter to the government of Adolf Hitler. This was to be a vast spectacle enhancing the international prestige of the regime, and a unique opportunity to propagandize vast numbers of visitors. The refusal of the United States to participate, for example, would have dealt a massive blow to the Nazis. And there were indications that the United States might withdraw because of Germany's treatment of its Jews—or rather, of its Jewish athletes.

In November 1933 the Amateur Athletic Union of the United States voted almost unanimously to boycott the games unless the Nazis permitted the Jews equal opportunity in athletics. Although the AAU dominated American sports, the American Olympic Committee (AOC) was responsible for U.S. participation in the Olympic games. Membership on the AOC was socially prestigious, and the businessmen and retired generals who dominated it were not the sort to permit the cancellation of the Olympics by an irrelevancy like religious persecution. The AAU vote threatening to boycott the games thus annoyed these dignitaries.

The significance which the Nazis attached to U.S. participation was demonstrated within twenty-four hours of the AAU vote. The three German delegates to the International Olympic Committee cabled the AAU reiterating their pledge of nondiscrimination in the selection and treatment of athletes. In spite of these reassurances the AAU did not withdraw its threat. Its leaders were aware that athletic facilities had been denied to thirty thousand Jews belonging to sporting clubs, and they were also aware of the Nazis' treatment of Daniel Prenn.

Daniel Prenn was not only a Jew but, to make matters worse, an immigrant from eastern Europe. During his childhood in Berlin in the pre-Hitler era, he had demonstrated certain talents not generally associated with "inferior races." These included a highly developed backhand, forehand and serve. Prenn, the German national junior tennis champion from 1920 to 1923, won the national men's singles in 1928 and played on German Davis Cup teams from 1928 onward. In 1932 his spectacular victories over the English stars, Fred Perry and "Bunny" Austin, carried Germany to the Davis Cup Interzone Finals, and he was ranked as the sixth-best player in the world. Adolf Hitler's assumption of power coincided with Daniel Prenn's dismissal from the German Davis Cup team. Messrs. Perry and Austin were among those who decried this action.

Prenn may have been on the minds of the AAU delegates, but his case did not appear to concern the American Olympic

Committee. Two days after the AAU took its firm stand, the AOC adopted a more temperate resolution on the same subject, though it insisted on the principle of equal treatment for Jewish athletes. The architect of this compromise was Brigadier General Charles H. Sherrill, a delegate to the International Olympic Committee.

Representative Emanuel Celler, whose opposition to U.S. participation remained consistent throughout the Olympic debate, put it succinctly: "The Jew who is jeered on the streets simply because he is a Jew cannot be cheered in the arena because he is a champion." Representative Celler made his remarks on the floor of the House on September 12, 1934, and on September 27 Avery Brundage, president of the American Olympic Committee, announced that the United States had accepted the German invitation to participate in the Games.

After the threatening AAU resolution Mr. Brundage had gone to Germany to find out for himself about the status of the Jews. He had interviewed a wide range of Olympic officials, and Jewish sports and business leaders, to decide whether discrimination would be abolished in tryouts for the Olympic games. He had become convinced that it would. In a long and forceful speech to his colleagues on the committee, he announced that the German Jews were satisfied with their treatment from a sports point of view. Since the committee had agreed unanimously to consider the anti-Semitic situation in Germany only as it related to sports, the debate was not complicated by such extraneous considerations as concentration camps, economic boycott and terror in the streets.

While Mr. Brundage was convincing himself that equality of athletic opportunity existed in Germany, the list of places forbidden to Jews was growing. Now they included the gardens of Bad Dürkheim; the swimming pools and baths of Schweinfurt; the municipal baths of Karlsruhe, Freiburg, Gladbach and Dortmund; and the streetcars of Magdeburg. The roll call of towns closed to Jews increased each day, and through some lapse in public relations, included Garmisch-Partenkirchen, the scene of the 1936 Winter Olympics. This had apparently not aroused the wrath of Mr. Brundage and his colleagues on the American Olympic Committee, although such a sign would conceivably inhibit aspiring Jewish skaters and skiers.

In March 1935, one year before the start of the Olympics, the Jews, already barred from employment in government, the arts and the professions, were excluded from the manual crafts. On April 28 Minister of the Interior Wilhelm Frick gave advance notice of the Nuremberg Laws, which would be passed in September: he made a public announcement, reported by the world's press, that the time had come to deprive all German Jews of their citizenship. But the Jews, according to Mr. Brundage's information, would be given equal access to training facilities and an equal opportunity to compete for places on a team representing a country in which they were not even citizens.

Foreign correspondents reported from Germany that the anti-Semitic line would be softened in preparation for the Olympic games. But there was no evidence of this in the actions of Julius Streicher, the Nazi leader of Franconia and founder of *Der Stürmer*. On June 23, 1935, he spoke to an audience of two hundred thousand at the summer-solstice festival on Hesenberg Mountain. Streicher took advantage of the solstice to exhort the boys and girls of the Hitler Youth:

"Your proper gathering place is this mountain, where, two thousand years ago, your forefathers gathered before the country had been infected by a race which at that time executed the greatest anti-Semite of all time, Jesus Christ, for high treason. Now this race is an enemy to all peoples and threatens the life of the German people. In front of this blazing fire, dedicate yourself to hatred of a people who goad nations into war to profit by it, to hatred of those who dishonor our women, to hatred of those who torture animals to death."

Warning the children to beware of Christian clergymen

sympathetic to Jews, Streicher continued, "Don't believe in priests as long as they defend people whom Christ called 'sons of the devil.' Don't go to confession. If you have any faults, cast them into the holy flame burning here on this holy mountain, and I will absolve you."

Any hopes that the German government might moderate its policies in a bid for international respect were shattered in the evening of July 15, 1935, when two hundred Nazis attacked Jews on the Kurfürstendamm, in the heart of Berlin's West End. Shortly after eight o'clock the Nazis swarmed through the cafés assaulting men and women who looked Jewish while the police watched with studied disinterest. Shouting "The best Jew is a dead Jew," they raided theaters and restaurants, smashed windows and left a trail of bleeding victims on the streets.

A husky Nazi, engaged in beating up two women, noted a young man glaring at him, and pointing to the prostrate ladies, shouted, "What do you think of that?" The young man, an Annapolis midshipman named Ernest Wood, Jr., promptly knocked the German down. Wood was arrested and fined $20.

The tall blond leader of the Nazis singled out a short, swarthy man he assumed to be a Jew and was beating him unmercifully as the man tried vainly to identify himself. Finally the victim managed to pull out his wallet and prove that he was a Bavarian storm-troop leader.

This act of violence was regarded as the worst since the advent of Nazism. Foreign correspondents related it to the attacks on the Christian churches which were also taking place around that time. A propaganda campaign was seeking to link the remaining Christian anti-Nazis with the Jews.

The issue of *Der Stürmer* on sale the day of the riot was headlined: "THE CHURCH AND THE JEW."

As a result of the Kurfürstendamm violence, Jewish organizations in the United States appealed once again to the State Department to take some action, and this time there were results—of a sort. Representatives of four major Jewish organizations wanted to meet with Acting Secretary of State William Phillips (Hull was out of town) on July 26. In preparing Phillips for the meeting, Rudolf E. Schoenfeld of the Division of Western European Affairs warned him in a memo that the Jewish groups would desire action "even so far as a public statement or representations by this Gorvernment." Schoenfeld suggested five kinds of response by Phillips in descending order of preference. Hopefully he could get away with the earnest statement: "We are following developments most closely." If that didn't suffice he could move to the second option: "We have asked the Embassy to keep us fully informed." If this was not enough Phillips could placate his visitors with "We desire to be as helpful as possible." If that seemed unsatisfactory, the Acting Secretary could "hope they will trust us to take any action developments might warrant." The fifth alternative, to be used only if all else failed, was the most radical. Phillips could say he was "disposed to invite a German representative to call and inform him of U.S. public opinion."

Schoenfeld's fears proved groundless. When Phillips met with the Jewish group he did not have to commit himself to any course of action. The eight-man delegation handed the Acting Secretary a memorandum elaborating on the physical assaults upon Jews, the effects of the economic boycott against them, and the deprivation of their civic and political rights. It also pointed out that "this reign of terror is also beginning to affect the lives of numberless Catholics and Protestants and liberals of every description . . .

"It is inconceivable that the American Government should stand passively by and neglect to lift its voice against these assaults upon humanity, or to utter its condemnation of the violation of the fundamental principles of human rights. Our country has traditionally recognized its moral and legal right, as well as its duty, to speak in behalf of those persecuted for their religious beliefs and for minority groups or races deprived of their just rights."

The memorandum then called for action: ". . . we respectfully call upon the government of the United States to protest against the racial and religious persecutions that now prevail in Germany and to take every step consistent with international practice to inform the German Government of the outraged sentiments of the American people."

In response Mr. Phillips drafted a two-paragraph letter, the substantive portion of which said: "I fully understand your solicitude regarding the experience which these groups are reported to be suffering in Germany. The concepts of religious freedom and liberty of conscience for all constitute the most fundamental principles of our own civilization and political faith. This being so, the American people are always sympathetic to the maintenance of these concepts in the United States as well as in other nations."

He sent this draft to President Roosevelt with the following note: "We are called upon to protest against the general persecutions. Our reply is so important and so charged with dynamite, from a domestic as well as an international viewpoint, that I do not wish to send any reply without your careful consideration and cordial approval."

The President considered carefully, approved cordially, and Phillips sent his letter. That was it. That was the American action. The State Department did not send an official communication to the German government and stated that it had no plans to do so. At his next press conference the President declined to discuss the matter.

Some further insight into the political mood of the time is furnished by Senator William H. King of Utah. On July 27, the day after the Jewish delegation visited Acting Secretary Phillips, King introduced a resolution calling upon the Senate Foreign Relations Committee to conduct hearings and elicit evidence concerning the mistreatment of Jews and Catholics in

Germany. The senator explained to the press that he wanted to find out whether there might be grounds for the United States to sever diplomatic relations with the Reich in protest against its racial and religious policies.

A few days later Senator King met Acting Secretary Phillips at a dinner party. He took Phillips aside and explained that his resolution was meant only as an expression of the feeling of many people, not as a basis for action. As Phillips noted in a memo for the file the next day, King said "that he, naturally, did not expect to push his resolution, and that if I had an opportunity to tell the President that was his idea, he would be very glad to have me do so."

Even at this time—that is, about two weeks after the Kurfürstendamm riot—Avery Brundage of the American Olympic Committee reiterated that he knew of no racial or religious reasons why the United States should withdraw its athletes from the Berlin games. Mr. Brundage was replying to a forceful statement by Jeremiah T. Mahoney, a former New York State Supreme Court justice who had become national president of the AAU. Mr. Mahoney, whose group had voted almost unanimously for withdrawal some months earlier, repeated this stand in light of the new reports of violence.

Brundage insisted that Germany had not broken her pledge to give Jewish athletes an opportunity to qualify. As he put it; "Regardless of in what country the Olympic games are held, there will be some group, some religion or some race that can register a protest because of the action of the government of that country, past or present."

A few days after Brundage's remarks, a dispatch from Berlin informed the American public of the case of Greta Bergmann, the high-jumping champion of Württemberg. When she attempted to enter the national field-sports championships, an important meet for those wishing to qualify for the Olympic team, she discovered that only members of the German Light Athletic Association were allowed to compete. This association denied membership to Jews, even those who could leap higher than anyone else in Württemberg. Miss Bergmann was not allowed to enter the meet.

The Reich sports commissioner, Hans von Tschammer und Osten, did not consider this a technical violation of the Reich promise of equal opportunity, though he did not offer Miss Bergmann any alternative. In any case, as German officials were quick to add, Miss Bergmann was only the sixth-best lady high jumper in Germany, even if she was the best in Württemberg.

The Olympic debate in the United States was interrupted temporarily by the passage of the Nuremberg Laws on September 15, 1935. These should have dispelled any remaining notions that the impending festival of sports would act as a brake upon Nazi excesses.

The new laws, as had been predicted five months earlier, deprived the Jews of German citizenship. They were now *Staatsangehörige,* or "subjects of the state," setting them apart from the *Volk* citizens, who were *Reichsbürger*. The Nuremberg Laws prohibited marriage or extramarital relations between Jews and Aryans upon penalty of imprisonment. As a new measure of humiliation, Jews were not allowed to employ female domestic help under forty-five years of age. They were also forbidden to fly the German national flag. This was a particular blow to the forty thousand war veterans of the Association of Jewish Front Fighters, who, in spite of their persecution, continued to petition for the right to serve the Fatherland.

The laws also stipulated that the swastika would replace the imperial colors as the national flag.

In a speech before the Reichstag at Nuremberg (a Reichstag which that morning had voted itself out of existence as a deliberative body), Hitler sounded an even more ominous threat about the future of the Jews. He hoped that the new laws would bring tolerable relations between Germans and

Jews, but "if this hope should not be realized and if international Jewish agitation should continue, the situation will have to be reconsidered. If the attempt at legal regulation fails again, the problem will have to be transferred from law to the National Socialist party for a final solution."

The warnings from Nuremberg did not move the sportsmen of the American Olympic Committee. The opposition to participation in the Olympics expressed by such small publications as *Commonweal* (Catholic) and *The Christian Century* (Protestant) and by most Jewish organizations was ignored.

In spite of the disfranchisement of the Jews, Dr. Theodor Lewald, chairman of the German Olympic organization committee, reassured the world about their equal opportunity to train for the games. Actually, Dr. Lewald had caused considerable embarrassment to the Germans. Long after he was chosen for the job, a Jewish grandparent was discovered on his family tree, but by that time he was so well known internationally that the Nazis decided to keep him on. When an American reporter inquired about the denial of membership to Jews by German sports clubs, Dr. Lewald answered heatedly, "Other clubs have a right to choose their own members, don't they? Does the New York Athletic Club have Jewish members? I can tell you that it does not."

General Sherrill of the International Olympic Committee was becoming increasingly short-tempered with those who were against U.S. participation. He pointed out that Olympic rules governed the selection, not the training opportunities given athletes. The general did not go along with the argument that withholding training facilities violated the Olympic code.

Furthermore, General Sherrill sensed a grave danger "in this Olympic agitation." If U.S. athletes saw their ambition frustrated by the Jews, "We are almost certain to have a wave of anti-Semitism among those who never before gave it a thought and who may consider that about five million Jews in this country are using the athletes representing 120,000,000

Americans to work out something to help the German Jews."

General Sherrill expressed views on politics as well as sports. Taking cognizance of a general outcry against Fascism, he praised Mussolini as "a man I have long known and admired, a gallant father who sent his own two sons into the thick of the fighting . . . " The general added wistfully that he wished Mussolini had an opportunity to come to the United States and suppress Communism as he had done in Italy.

But Herr Lewald, Avery Brundage and General Sherrill could not stop Jeremiah T. Mahoney of the AAU from expressing feelings about American participation. To him, the movement to transfer the Olympic games from Germany was not a political issue, as Brundage had charged, but a question of "humanity and Christianity."

The American embassy in Berlin, apprised of the developing Olympic controversy in the United States, decided to see for itself whether or not Jewish athletes in Germany were being treated fairly. A staff member was assigned to investigate and he came away with quite a different impression than had Mr. Brundage. Ambassador Dodd reported the results of the investigation in a message dated October 11, 1935.

At first the Jewish athletes had refused to discuss their problems with the embassy man but eventually they told him everything. They had been barred from open competition, denied the use of sports fields, and their letters of protest to the Reich sports leader and Olympic committee had not even been answered. One club had a sprinter named Schattmann of world rank who had been dropped arbitrarily, and of course everyone knew about the high-jumping Greta Bergmann. To compound the problems of the Jewish athletes, the new statute of the Reich League for Physical Exercise had stated that its qualification for membership included *weltanschaulich* (ideological) fitness. The league had decreed that Jews were not capable of this quality, therefore could not be members. Nor could Jews wear the badges issued for passing various sports tests.

Without ideological fitness, badges, playing fields or social relationships with other German athletes, the thirty thousand members of Jewish sports clubs were much harder pressed than Mr. Brundage had been led to believe.

But the embassy reseacher had a pleasant interview with Dr. Lewald who, in order to prove the nondiscriminatory nature of Nazi sports, showed him a letter from Karl Ritter von Halt, leader of track sports. The letter stated that the Jews had failed to qualify for the games: "The sole reason for this was always the fact that no Jew was able to qualify by his ability for participation in the Olympic team. Heil Hitler."

Avery Brundage's serenity about the treatment of Jewish athletes was undermined somewhat by the announcement that the Maccabee League, one of Germany's leading Jewish sports clubs, had withdrawn from any participation in Olympic tryouts because of its members' deprivation of citizenship. That disposed of one of the fictions by which the American Olympic Committee justified its position.

Brundage was further contradicted by the statement of forty-one American college and university presidents in twenty-seven states, urging the United States to withdraw from the games. "It is our considered judgment," wrote the presidents, "based upon the record of events which have transpired in Germany for the past two and a half years, that the inequities and discrimination practiced against Jews, Catholics, Protestants, labor, Masons and all independents are perpetuated in the field of sports and in the Olympic games."

With the annual AAU convention scheduled for December 1935, Judge Jeremiah T. Mahoney announced that he would offer a new resolution opposing American participation.

Mr. Brundage was unmoved. His committee had primacy over the AAU and he responded unequivocally to the Mahoney threat. The Olympic committee would send a team to Berlin, with or without the co-operation of the AAU. "Our athletes," proclaimed Brundage, "must not be denied the chance to carry the Stars and Stripes to victory abroad just because of treason for political reasons in some quarters at home."

The climactic AAU meeting took place on December 8 in New York City. As a former president, Brundage attended the tense five-hour session.

Aaron T. Frank of Oregon, second vice-president of the AAU, described Hitler as a tyrant and added, "I pledge my intellectual honesty, free from religious and racial prejudice, that the logic of the situation is on the side of nonparticipation."

To this John T. McGovern, president of the Intercollegiate Amateur Athletic Association of America, replied, "You have the right to say you are opposed to things in Germany but you shoot your own boys in the back if you say they cannot have their birthright of competition in the international Olympic games."

Fred L. Steers of Chicago, third vice-president of the AAU, backed up McGovern: "There is no case yet against Germany in anything where the International Olympic Committee has authority. Germany hasn't yet selected her team any more than we have. What you are trying here is not a case of sporting discrimination, but a moral judgment on Germany as a whole, which we have no right to impose on our athletes."

Steers then revealed that a questionnaire had been sent to all the American athletes who had placed first, second and third in the national AAU games and the National Collegiate Athletic Association outdoor championships, as well as to other Americans holding Olympic records. Of the hundred and forty replies, only one opposed participation. It was from a Tulane University sprinter named Herman Neugass.

The president of the South Atlantic Association, though opposed to participation, acknowledged the AAU's secondary role in the Olympic decision. Then he said, "We can shout to heaven and not shut off participation but it's our duty just the same to shout."

The president of the Intercollegiate AAU, an undergraduate at the University of Pennsylvania, said he was speaking on behalf of the younger generation and that "we are all for participation in the Olympic games."

This brought a burst of applause, which soon subsided as the next speaker, C.W. Romine of the Indiana-Kentucky district, characterized the Hitler government as "diabolical, indecent and unsporting."

One of Jeremiah Mahoney's most ardent supporters, Louis di Benedetto of the Southern Association, said that participation by an American athlete would be a "betrayal of honor and sportsmanship by any Catholic, Protestant or Jew who loves his God."

Judge Aaron Steuer attempted to bridge the contending groups with a compromise proposal: "Brundage says conditions are all right in Germany. Mahoney says they are not. That is a question of fact that cannot be decided by resolutions, calling names, or listening to the viewpoint of every speaker."

Steuer then suggested that an investigating commission be sent to Germany to study conditions on the spot. He said he was sure that funds could be raised to cover the expenses of the commission, but Federal Judge Murray Hulbert, a former president of the AAU, opposed that notion.

Said Judge Hulbert, "If the sources to be tapped are the same sources to which the American Olympic Committee will apply to send a team to Berlin, I don't want the funds necessary for athletes to be used to send a committee to investigate Germany."

The Steuer proposal was rejected. When all the oratory had ended, the AAU voted to participate in the Olympics, defeating Jeremiah T. Mahoney by a mere 2 votes. Mahoney then resigned as president and was immediately succeeded by Brundage, who said that now the AAU could go about its business of getting America's youth to the Olympics.

There was one further bit of convention business. Gustavus T. Kirby, another former AAU president who had originally favored withdrawal from the Olympics and then shifted his position, proposed a resolution declaring that the certification of U.S. athletes for the Olympics must not be "construed to imply endorsement of the Nazi government." The resolution was passed.

The refusal of the United States to withdraw from one of the great propaganda festivals in Nazi history was one of an endless series of decisions which played into the hands of Adolf Hitler and, however inadvertently, enhanced German prestige. The Olympic torch of 1936 did not reveal to the world the dark corners of Germany, the material poverty of its dispossessed Jews or the spiritual poverty of its silent Christians. The brilliant Olympic victories of American Negroes were not even acknowledged by Hitler. He was too busy in this year after the Nuremberg Laws exulting in the triumph of German organization and the quiescent co-operation of a willing world.

After the Olympics the AAU acknowledged the moral judgment of Jeremiah T. Mahoney and once again elected him as president by an overwhelming margin over Avery Brundage's candidate. But it was a year too late and the anti-Semitic posters that had been removed for the Olympic games once again covered the walls of the Third Reich.

■ X ■

"I Cannot Remain Silent . . ."

ON JANUARY 1, 1936, AFTER TWO YEARS AND two months of frustration, James G. McDonald resigned as League of Nations High Commissioner for Refugees (Jewish and Other) Coming from Germany. His letter of resignation and its attached documentation filled twenty-seven printed pages. Excerpts of this material were featured by newspapers everywhere but in Germany.

In a restrained but devastating indictment of Nazi racial policies, McDonald summoned the nations of the world to meet the German challenge by direct political action. He called for a radical change in the League's approach to refugee problems, pointing out that as High Commissioner, detached from the direct authority of the League, he had been powerless to act. His duties had been restricted to caring for refugees from the Reich, but the flood of impoverished outcasts streaming across Germany's borders into neighboring countries had transformed the issue from an internal German question to an international problem. The forced exodus must be stopped. McDonald proposed to the Secretary-General of the League that the problem be solved at its source—the German government:

"The developments since 1933, and in particular those following the Nuremberg legislation, call for fresh collective action in regard to the problem created by the persecution in Germany. The moral authority of the League of Nations and of State Members of the League must be directed towards a determined appeal to the German Government in the name of humanity and of the principles of the public law of Europe."

McDonald closed his letter of resignation on a prophetic note:

"But convinced as I am that desperate suffering in the countries adjacent to Germany, and an even more terrible human calamity within the German frontiers, are inevitable unless present tendencies in the Reich are checked or reversed, I cannot remain silent . . . When domestic policies threaten the demoralization and exile of hundreds of thousands of human beings, considerations of diplomatic correctness must yield to those of common humanity. I should be recreant if I did not call attention to the actual situation, and plead that world opinion, acting through the League and its Member-States and other countries, move to avert the existing and impending tragedies."

McDonald's documented analysis of German legislative and administrative actions against the Jews comprised a complete catalogue of the debasement of German law, medicine, education, journalism, commerce and industry.

During his two years as High Commissioner, McDonald had carried on a tireless search for havens for the Jews. He warned everyone who would listen that the German persecution was not a temporary aberration. Months before his resignation he had met in Europe with Sigmund and Erich Warburg of the great German Jewish banking family. He described the meeting in a letter to Erich's uncle, Felix Warburg, the philanthropist who then headed the Joint Distribution Committee:

"Everything Erich and Sigmund had to say confirmed my own worst impressions and fears about the situation as it has been developing since the Nuremberg legislation. The question in everybody's mind is what can be done. On only one point is there complete agreement: the need for immediate action is overwhelming . . . On the assumption that the present tendency in the Reich will be carried through to its logical conclusion, the necessity for relief measures on a scale heretofore not undertaken, and except in very few quarters envisaged, seems to me absolutely clear."

McDonald then suggested to Felix Warburg that plans be made for the immigration of fifteen to twenty thousand young Jews each year: "The Jewish Communities, particularly in Great Britain and the United States, must now at last realize the truth, bitter and terrible though it is, which you and I and some of the rest of us have tried to drive home to them for more than two years—there can be no future for Jews in Germany."

Warburg sent McDonald's letter to Governor Herbert Lehman of New York, who forwarded it to President Roosevelt with a plea that the immigration quota of Jews from Germany be increased. Roosevelt turned the letter over to the State Department, where a reply was prepared informing Lehman that there was no Jewish quota and that a maximum of 25,957 Germans could be admitted annually to the United States without reference to their religious beliefs. The letter went on to reveal that 14,202 Germans of all faiths had entered the United States from 1932 to 1935, an average of 3,550 per year. There was no reference to McDonald's proposal for the immigration of fifteen to twenty thousand young people each year, no explanation of why the numbers admitted fell so far below the quota.

Just before he resigned, McDonald visited the British Foreign Office with a proposal to evacuate one hundred thousand young Jewish men and women from Germany during the next four or five years, the immigration to be financed completely by Jewish organizations. He explained that the Foreign Office would be expected to intercede with the German government to obtain its co-operation in the orderly evacuation.

The Foreign Office officials were outwardly impressed. They informed McDonald that his scheme "would be studied promptly and sympathetically," and wired the British embassy in Berlin for an opinion. The embassy advised the Foreign Office against any British intervention, and this decision was relayed to Washington.

In February 1936, a month after his resignation, McDonald called on Undersecretary of State Phillips. Unaware of the British refusal to intercede, he urged Anglo-American co-operation in appealing to the German government and reminded Phillips of Britain's sympathetic response. Phillips circulated McDonald's suggestion within the State Department and received a negative reaction. Rudolf Schoenfeld of the Division of Western European Affairs replied characteristically: "This would involve intercession in behalf of a non-American group for the purpose of obtaining for them preferential treatment as compared with other groups, among which are Americans having funds and property in Germany." John Farr Simmons concurred, stating that no special facilities were possible for the admission of such groups of refugees. In the end, there was neither British nor American intercession.

The League of Nations also failed to heed McDonald's plea that it strengthen its role in refugee matters. The League's power and prestige had been undermined by its indecisive response to the Italian invasion of Ethiopia, the withdrawal of Germany and the nonparticipation of the United States. It responded to McDonald's challenge with customary weakness.

On February 14, 1936, the League appointed Sir Neill Malcolm, a retired British brigadier general, to succeed McDonald as High Commissioner for Refugees. Far from broadening his scope, the League narrowed it, as Sir Neill soon announced: "I have no policy, but the policy of the League is to deal with the political and legal status of the refugees. It has nothing to do with the domestic policy of Germany. That's not the affair of the League. We deal with persons when they become refugees and not before."

As it became clear that the League of Nations offered no hope, the leaders of British Jewry took the initiative in developing plans to evacuate their German brethen. Sir Herbert Samuel, a former Cabinet minister; Lord Bearsted, whose father had been Lord Mayor of London; and Simon Marks, a founder of the Marks and Spencer stores, made a pilgrimage to the United States to enlist the support of the American Jewish organizations. The British emissaries, representing a Jewish population one-twelfth that of the United States, offered to raise one-third of a $12,000,000 fund to assist in relocating the refugees. The Americans agreed, but the unanswered question remained: Who would take the refugees?

The Jews of Palestine were perhaps the only people in the world anxious to accept refugees unrestrictedly. In 1917 Britain's Balfour Declaration had favored the establishment of a Jewish national home in Palestine, an action later approved by the League of Nations. In 1922 the League had appointed Britain to rule Palestine as a mandate.

The Arab population of Palestine was violently opposed to an influx of Jews, and in 1936, as the Jews sought to escape from Germany, Arab rioting and terrorism intensified. The British Foreign Office, ever responsive to Arab pressures, refused to sanction unrestricted immigration.

With refugees facing increased difficulty in migrating to Palestine, and large sums of money being collected in their behalf, it appeared that renewed pressure would be exerted to open the doors of the United States.

On May 15, 1936, Consul General Erhardt in Hamburg sent a seventeen-page message on this subject. He cautioned that American Jews might attempt to pressure the State Department to liberalize its procedures for issuing visas. Perhaps they would even try to place Jews in a new and special category—"political refugees."

"It is entirely possible," he wrote, "that the United States will find itself receiving nearly the full quota of 25,000 German Jews yearly, by 1937."

There was another interesting revelation in the dispatch from Hamburg. The immigration laws imposed no qualifications on the relationship between the prospective immigrant and the sponsor who signed his affidavit of support. Nevertheless, as the case histories from Rotterdam indicated, consuls had rejected many an immigrant on the ground that the sponsor relationship was not close enough even when it involved brother and sister.

Consul General Erhardt mentioned in his lengthy dispatch that these restrictions had been imposed by State Department administrative regulations. "It is of course realized that a strict adherence to the administrative ruling in regard to the requirement of affidavits from close blood relations was made as a rough and ready means, at a time of great unemployment and economic stress, to limit the number of foreign competitors for the available jobs in the United States." According to Erhardt, the Jews were relying on the relaxation of this ruling.

Shortly after the Erhardt dispatch, Sir Herbert Samuel complained to Felix Warburg about the harsh attitude of American consuls. Although Sir Herbert had been assured personally by Franklin D. Roosevelt that consuls would not enforce the rules too rigidly in Germany, he forwarded a variety of grievances compiled by German Jews who had experienced the full weight of American bureaucracy. According to Sir Herbert, the Stuttgart consulate was so deluged with visa applications that one thousand letters lay unopened. He added that the United States consulates in Frankfurt and Cologne were not empowered to issue visas, which further narrowed the bottleneck.

In Hamburg, Consul General Erhardt was accepting affidavits of support only from the parent, child, uncle or aunt of a prospective immigrant. According to Sir Herbert's informants, the Hamburg consulate objected to the affidavits from brothers- and sisters-in-law and rejected outright those from distant relatives.

Sir Herbert's letter of complaint was sent to the President and relayed to the State Department, which prepared a reply for Roosevelt's signature. The response assured Sir Herbert of the consuls' fairness and informed him that two clerks had been hired and two additional consular officers transferred to Stuttgart to handle the deluge of applications.

Roosevelt's reply stated blandly that "A promise of support made by a close relative will naturally be given more weight than one from a distant relative . . ."

The isolationist temper of the United States had been reinforced by the Neutrality Act of 1935, but Americans now began to express apprehensions about the heartlessness of their immigration policies. The official explanations were unconvincing and public protest mounted. The fears of many Americans were reinforced by a Nazi chorus proclaiming the eventual destruction of the Jews.

A notable example was provided by Julius Streicher, whose pornographic, anti-Semitic sheet, *Der Stürmer,* was one of Germany's most popular publications. During the 1936 Nazi party congress in Nuremberg, Streicher addressed a closed meeting of anti-Semitic journalists from Europe and the Americas. Some members of his audience repeated the text of his remarks to outsiders. The *New York Times* was one of the newspapers which printed the details.

Streicher stated bluntly that in the last analysis, extermination was the only real solution to the Jewish problem. It was, after all, a world rather than a German problem. If a final solution were to be reached, said the *Gauleiter* of Franconia, "one must go the bloody path." These measures would be justified, he declared, "because the Jews always attained their ends through wholesale murder and have been responsible for wars and massacres. To secure the safety of the whole world they must be exterminated."

When these and similar outbursts by high-ranking Nazis were quoted in responsible journals, there was a sharp increase in demands that the United States ease its immigration procedures. This could be accomplished by President Roosevelt's cancellation of Herbert Hoover's executive order on "public charges," and by new directives instructing consuls to accept refugees to the maximum extent permitted by the quota. The perfect setting for a presidential announcement was at hand. On October 28, 1936, Franklin D. Roosevelt was scheduled to speak at the commemoration of the fiftieth anniversary of the Statue of Liberty.

Professor John Dewey was among those who urged the President to take advantage of the occasion. The distinguished philosopher-educator wrote to Roosevelt a week before the ceremony:

"Fifty years ago, at the Statue, this country was spoken of as an asylum of the oppressed, a haven for political refugees who had been driven from their homelands. Today this tradition is in danger of being completely discarded. The gates have been closed to immigrants and, for the last five years, more people have been leaving the United States than have been entering it . . . We urge you to declare . . . that this country will live up to its promise of equal opportunity for the immigrants within its borders and that it will re-establish the proud principle it once maintained as an asylum for political and religious refugees."

The President did not respond to the suggestion. In his Statue of Liberty speech he did not refer to the refugee crisis or its solution. "For over three centuries," he said in that mellow, intimate voice, "a steady stream of men, women and children followed the beam of liberty which this light symbolizes. They brought to us strength and moral fiber developed in a civilization centuries old but fired anew by the dream of a better life in America . . . Within this present generation that stream from abroad has largely stopped."

Roosevelt did not elaborate on why that stream had become a trickle, how it had been dammed by impassable administrative walls buttressed by endless regulations. Behind those walls, hundreds of thousands of men, women and children struggled in vain for a glimpse of that "beam of liberty" described by the President.

But neither the President nor his cautious State Department could continue American policies so clearly at variance with the national tradition and the object of so much criticism by numerically small but highly regarded groups of citizens representing leadership in education, religion, and the arts and sciences.

Jarred by the extent of this criticism, the State Department assigned J. Klahr Huddle, a Foreign Service inspector, to review visa procedures. Centering his study on the Stuttgart consulate, Huddle concluded that the admission of German Jews to the United States did not pose a great risk at all. He reported to State about the unusual character of German Jewish immigration: ". . . Many of the immigrants come from the better-class families and . . . although they frequently have only distant relatives in the United States, these . . . have a sincere desire to assist their relatives in Germany, so that the likelihood of their becoming a public charge is very remote."

Mr. Huddle's unexpected conclusion impressed Eliot B. Coulter, assistant chief of the Visa Division. Coulter had been under some pressure from Assistant Secretary of State Wilbur Carr, who apparently had the uneasy feeling that some of the complaints about the American consuls were justified.

Coulter sensed a new liberalization. He reported back to Carr that State Department personnel were basing their decisions on the possibility that a distant relative of an alien might not live up to his moral and legal obligation to support him. Consular refusals, said Coulter, should be based on the *probability,* not the *possibility* that the applicant might become a public charge.

"We know," wrote Coulter, reflecting the sudden wave of concern for Hitler's victims, "that the Jewish people often have a high sense of responsibility towards their relatives . . . and that they feel keenly the difficult lot of their kin in Germany and the lack of a future in that country for the younger generation." In such cases, he suggested evidence of financial ability should be sufficient.

Coulter included some related examples of consular abuses. One concerned Dr.——, who had visited Coulter because visas had been refused two of his relatives.

Dr.——, with assets of more than $100,000, had helped his wife's cousin to come to the United States. Now he wished to bring over other relatives, a husband and wife who had escaped from Germany to Belgium. The American consulate in Antwerp had refused to issue visas to the couple because Dr. —— had not supported them in the past and because he had already assumed responsibility for one refugee.

Dr.——, whose only other dependent was his wife, felt that his resources were sufficient to guarantee that the additional newcomers would not become impoverished, a theory with which Coulter agreed. As Coulter put it to Carr: "There is a ring of sincerity in his anxiety over the prospective fate of these persons if they are forced to return to Germany . . . I believe that visas might properly be issued because it does not appear 'likely' that they will become public charges."

Coulter recounted similar case histories from Stuttgart and Berlin and stated flatly that visa applications of equal merit had been turned down in Paris, Warsaw, Rotterdam, Athens and other consulates.

Carr penciled the following notation in the margin of Coulter's memorandum: ". . . some [consuls] have the mistaken idea that the consul has a responsibility for keeping visas down to a minimum number instead of his real responsibility of making a fair evaluation of the evidence and basing the decision on that."

The internal debate which began in November 1936 culminated in the issuance of new visa instructions on January 12, 1937. The directive, addressed to consular and diplomatic officers, began:

"There have been an increasing number of complaints received by the Department and some recent public criticism that the visa work of the consuls is not being carried out in a fair and impartial manner, particularly, that the public charge provisions are not being properly administered and that the consuls are acting under the mistaken idea that they are responsible for keeping the issuance of visas to a minimum." (The next line in Coulter's first draft of the instructions read: "Examination of the complaints and review of consular visa correspondence show that there is a real basis for adverse criticism." This line was deleted from the final draft.)

The letter cited complaints that persons applying for visas had been received discourteously and had not been permitted to present documents or discuss their cases. Later they had been told that they required additional documents.

Most important, the new instructions emphasized *probability* rather than *possibility* as the criterion for determining the likelihood of an applicant becoming a public charge. Coulter went so far as to state that if a case was decided on the basis of *possibility*, "Such action affords ground for just criticism of the officers and the Department." A visa should not be denied an applicant simply because his support was guaranteed by a distant rather than a close relative.

In rebuttal, most of the consuls denied that there had been inequities in the past and assured the department that they would continue to display their usual fairness, courtesy, sympathy and understanding. But there was one unorthodox response.

From Rotterdam Consul Homer Brett wrote jubilantly: "If it is permissible for a consular officer to express an opinion regarding an instruction from the Department I would like to say I am very happy to have this assurance that the policy set forth . . . September 30, 1930, and in subsequent oral and written instructions in the same sense, has been abandoned and that America is once again to resume its historic and glorious position as a land of refuge for the downtrodden and oppressed . . . It is good now to have a plain instruction that the law is to be enforced as it is written and not according to forced interpretations."

The new instructions to consuls represented a belated admission by the State Department that the charges made by its critics were accurate. The liberalization helped to increase German and Austrian immigration from 6,642 in 1936 to 11,536 in 1937 and 17,868 in 1938. But the total still fell far short of the combined German and Austrian quotas of 27,370 per year.

Consul Brett's enthusiasm may have been refreshing, but it proved to be premature. The liberalization of the "public charge" provision was more than offset by the events of 1938, a year which illustrated the vivid contrast between American apathy and Nazi action.

■ XI ■

1938: Evian

"WE REALLY DIDN'T KNOW WHAT THE NAZIS were doing at the time" is a familiar refrain in contemporary American discussions of the murder of six million Jews and of the specific events which preceded their final journey to the gas chambers.

Man's memory is clouded by time. The events of 1938, which foreshadowed mass murder, were widely publicized. They made headlines day after day in the United States and Great Britain, were described on the radio and filled the pages of the mass magazines.

The German annexation of Austria in March 1938 triggered the most savage anti-Semitism since the rise of Hitler. Following the fall of the Schuschnigg government, the 200,000 Jews of Austria (180,000 of whom lived in Vienna) were subjected to torments which made the persecution in Germany seem moderate. The following are brief excerpts from the *New York Times* during the first days after the German takeover:

March 16

"Adolf Hitler has left behind him in Austria an anti-Semitism that is blossoming far more rapidly than ever it did in Germany. This afternoon the Jewish quarter of Leopoldstadt was invaded by triumphant crowds that called families from their houses and forced them to kneel and try to scrub from the pavements slogans such as 'Hail Schuschnigg' which were part of the former Chancellor's plebiscite campaign. This humiliation was carried out under the supervision of Storm Troopers wearing swastika armlets. The crowds were composed . . . of some of the worst elements of the population, assembled to jeer at the Jews, and shouting, 'Perish Jewry!' 'Out with the Jews!' "

March 18

"There have been many cases of men in Storm Troop and Elite Guard uniforms entering Jewish-owned shops and carrying off whatever goods they fancied as well as money, and going into private houses and demanding large sums of money, or in default of personal jewelry, other valuables. In other cases not only are automobiles removed but their owners are also asked to hand over money for gasoline."

March 20

"The death carts of the Anatomical Institution are busy daily collecting the bodies of those poisoned by their own hands or by those nearest and dearest to them. Death seems to them the kindest gift to those, well-favored or humble, for whom once smiling Austria has become a vast prison from which there is no outlet and within which all chance of a livelihood is dead . . . Is this Vienna . . . with its truckloads of palefaced citizens being hurried through the streets to vanish through the great gates of the central prison—for many of them the first stage of the journey to the concentration camp?"

March 23

"It is becoming clear that whereas in Germany the first Nazi victims were the Left political parties—Socialists and Communists—in Vienna it is the Jews who are to bear the brunt of the Nazis' revolutionary fire. In a fortnight the Jews have been brought under an infinitely severer regime that was reached in Germany after a year. That is why the daily list of suicides is so great, for the Jews are exposed to arrest, plunder, deprivation of their opportunity for a livelihood, and mob fury."

The world's press reported that suicides among Jews in Vienna had risen to two hundred daily and that Austria had closed the frontiers to her Jewish citizens. Italy, Switzerland and Czechoslovakia sealed their own borders and thus double-locked the gates of their neighbor. "The rape of Austria," as Churchill later characterized it, was only one storm signal. The Japanese, proclaimed allies of the Nazis, were driving deep into China while Italy and Germany were testing their weapons alongside the Fascist forces of Francisco Franco, in revolt against the legitimate government of Spain.

The Neutrality Law, first passed by the United States Congress in 1935 and subsequently renewed, played into the hands of the dictators. It punished the victims of aggression by denying them arms. Although Roosevelt opposed the law, he had lacked the courage to veto it. In spite of his record-breaking eleven-million-vote victory over Landon in 1936, the President had refused to exploit this mandate by educating the nation to dangers he recognized clearly. He had not even mentioned foreign policy in his inaugural address. In October 1937 he finally spoke out about the necessity of quarantining aggressors. Isolationists and pacifists reacted with violence to the President's speech, and this, combined with the silence of his own Democratic colleagues, forced him to retreat. He denied vigorously that he was contemplating more active international measures.

In March 1938, as the Austrian republic fell before external aggression and internal treason, Franklin D. Roosevelt was preoccupied with a domestic economic recession and the continuing problem of some ten million unemployed. Although he appeared powerless to influence international events, neither he nor his Administration could continue to ignore the Austrian disaster. It dominated the daily newspapers of every American family, as well as the classified dispatches that were circulated in the State Department and the White House. The United States would have to do something—something that would enable it to display humanitarian concern for the Austrian victims of Nazism.

On March 22, ten days after the first German troops had marched into Austria, the United States launched what appeared to be a bold plan of action. The President invited thirty-three governments to join in a co-operative effort to aid the emigration of political refugees from Germany and Austria. They included twenty Latin American republics, plus Great Britain, France, Italy, Belgium, Switzerland, Sweden, Norway, The Netherlands, Denmark, Canada, Australia, New Zealand and South Africa. The invitation specified that no country "would be expected or asked to receive a greater number of emigrants than is permitted by its existing legislation," but it emphasized that the freedom-loving nations must work together to solve the tragic problem.

The day the conference was announced, the President held an informal press conference at Warm Springs, Georgia. He reaffirmed the traditional role of the United States as a haven for the politically oppressed of all nations, but assured his listeners that the new proposal would not result in an increase or revision of U.S. immigration quotas. He added that it would be up to private groups rather than governments to finance any movement of refugees, and that Jews would not be the only beneficiaries of American generosity.

There was an instantaneous, massive reaction from church,

civic and women's groups, with generous offers of funds, assistance and encouragement. The Federal Council of Churches of Christ in America "hailed with appreciation" the U.S. proposal; the American Jewish Committee characterized it as "a splendid act" and the Hebrew Sheltering and Immigrant Aid Society called it "one of the great humanitarian acts of the twentieth century." Even the American Federation of Labor responded warmly, and its president, William Green, went so far as to say that "refugees have proved themselves through the years to be our finest citizens. It would be cruel, illogical and entirely out of keeping with our American principles if we were to close our doors to them now." Green had only one small reservation. The United States should admit no more than the number of immigrants provided by law, because of the competition for jobs.

The reaction to Roosevelt's proposal might have been less exuberant had the public known the motives behind it. An internal State Department memorandum prepared later in 1938 by an official of the Division of European Affairs (formerly known as the Division of Western European Affairs) described the origins of the Evian Conference with cold detachment.

The Nazi absorption of Austria had brought about increased public demand for State Department action in behalf of refugees. "Dorothy Thompson and certain Congressmen with metropolitan constituencies were the principal sources of this pressure," said the memorandum.

To counteract this outcry, Secretary Hull, Undersecretary Welles and two lesser colleagues had decided that it was preferable for the department to "get out in front and attempt to guide the pressure, primarily with a view toward forestalling attempts to have the immigration laws liberalized."

It was Summer Welles who had come up with the idea of an international conference and the President had approved. On this noble note the Evian Conference was born. It would be months in planning, would silence the critics of apathy, and if all worked well, would divert refugees from the United States to the other co-operating nations.

The Germans responded to the U.S. refugee plan with contempt. Chancellor Hitler, never losing an opportunity to deflate democratic pretense, said in a speech at Königsberg, "I can only hope and expect that the other world, which has such deep sympathy for these criminals, will at least be generous enough to convert this sympathy into practical aid. We, on our part, are ready to put all these criminals at the disposal of these countries, for all I care, even on luxury ships."

On April 13 President Roosevelt met at the White House with Protestant, Catholic and Jewish leaders to discuss the new international effort. The delegation included former High Commissioner James G. McDonald, who would become chairman of the President's Advisory Group on Political Refugees.

Two days before the meeting Undersecretary Welles had sent the President a note briefing him on matters to be taken up with the visitors. ". . . So far as this Government is concerned, there is no provision for Government aid to immigration and prospective immigrants . . . In no event would commitments be taken outside of the framework of our present immigration laws and practice . . . under the present quotas established by law it [the United States] has as liberal an immigration policy as any country today."

As the United States was waiting for replies to its invitations to the refugee conference, Nazi pressure on Austria intensified. By early April it was estimated that thirty-four thousand Viennese had been arrested. The wave of suicides was noted by Propaganda Minister Josef Goebbels in a speech before twenty-five thousand Austrian Nazis:

"There is talk of mass suicides of Jews in Vienna. It is not true. The number of suicides remains unchanged; the difference is that whereas Germans committed suicide before, it is now Jews. We cannot protect every Viennese Jew with a special policeman to prevent him from committing suicide."

The special policemen were busy throughout Austria. Consider the widely reported fate of the Jews of Burgenland, an Austrian province situated near the junction of the Austrian, Czech and Hungarian frontiers. As a young man, the Austrian citizen Adolf Hitler had lived in this lovely land of hills and vineyards. Several thousand Jewish families had lived in Burgenland for centuries but their presence now desecrated its sacred soil.

One Sunday morning in April 1938, residents of the Czech village of Theben heard feeble cries of help from the Danube River. A Czech patrol found fifty-one Jews huddled on the rough stones of the breakwater. Their property had been confiscated and they had been evicted from their villages. Austrian storm troopers had taken them to the breakwater and left them at night without food, money or warm clothing.

The group included an eighty-two-year-old rabbi and his sick wife, and many other women and children as well. The Czechs took them ashore, fed them, dressed the wounds of those who had been beaten by the storm troopers, and sheltered them for the night. Having demonstrated their hospitality, the Czechs then drove the Jews across the Hungarian border. But the Hungarians didn't want them either and eventually forced thirty-five of them back to Austria, where they were imprisoned in storm-troop barracks. The remainder hid at night in the Hungarian woods and were finally taken aboard an old French barge. They languished at a mooring for five months until the authorities ordered their departure. The barge and its human cargo drifted down the river and that was the last that was heard of it.

On April 26, Vienna's *Völkischer Beobachter* commented on President Roosevelt's impending refugee conference: "We cannot take seriously President Roosevelt's appeal to the nations of the world as long as the United States maintains racial quotas for immigrants."

The Nazis demonstrated malevolent efficiency in utilizing these immigration restrictions to rob the Jews materially and torture them emotionally. In Vienna they first imprisoned their victims. After a number of weeks of brutality and starvation they offered to release them. In return the Jews were required to pledge that they would relinquish their property and leave the country within four to six weeks.

Three thousand Jews a day waited in vain for visas at the American consulate in Vienna, while ten thousand applications lay unanswered at the Australian consulate. The Nazis now enjoyed what for them was the best of all possible worlds —they were able to acquire valuable property while retaining the impoverished former owners as hostages.

At the same time that Americans were reading about the assault on the Jews in Austria, Berlin newspaper correspondents quoted from a new German textbook, Julius Streicher's *First Reader*. In the opening chapter a mother tells her son what Jews are like:

"Just as one poisonous mushroom can kill a whole family," she explains, "so can one Jew ruin a whole city—even a whole nation."

In a section on religion, the Streicher textbook exhorts its young readers: "Remember that the Jews are children of the devil and murderers of mankind . . . . Whoever is a murderer deserves to be killed himself."

In this atmosphere Hermann Göring, Commissar for the Four Year Plan, began the final confiscation of Jewish property in Germany and Austria. He issued a decree ordering all Jews to report their possessions in excess of 5,000 marks ($2,000). As the status of the Jews continued to deteriorate, attempts by individual Americans to liberalize immigration to the United States were turned aside by the State Department. In one such effort six Jewish congressmen, including Emanuel

Celler of New York and Adolph Sabath of Illinois, met with George Messersmith, who had left Berlin to become Assistant Secretary of State. They asked what they could do to assist in the impending refugee conference and how they could help to ease the immigration procedures.

As Messersmith reported to Cordell Hull in a memo, he had told them he thought it undesirable to have any discussions in the immigration committees of the House and Senate "of bills tending toward liberalizing our present immigration laws." According to the Assistant Secretary, such debates might lead to more rather than fewer restrictions. Messersmith must have been quite persuasive. He informed Hull that the six congressmen had agreed unanimously to accept his advice. They would try to discourage new legislation as well as the discussion of more liberal bills already introduced.

On May 12 France approved of Evian-les-Bains as the site of the refugee conference. The luxurious resort on the French shore of Lake Geneva would provide excellent accommodations for representatives of the thirty-two nations which would attend. Only Italy and South Africa had declined, and the latter was sending an observer. The conference would not begin until July, so there was plenty of time for preparation. No doubt the weather would be lovely.

The United States announced that Myron C. Taylor, former chairman of the U.S. Steel Corporation, would be its principal representative at the conference. (By 1943 Taylor had become disenchanted with American immigration policy and threatened to disassociate himself from it, but in 1938 he was hopeful about progress.) With thirty-two nations compiling material for the conference and people of Myron C. Taylor's caliber dedicating themselves to the refugee problem, the precarious situation of the Jews was held in abeyance between May and July. Nothing was done to ease the rigidity of the immigration procedures, which proved particularly tragic for a thirty-six-year-old German Jewish woman named Luise Wolf.

Luise Wolf had arrived in New York on a six-week visitor's permit. During her stay she hoped to obtain an affidavit attesting to her means of support so she could assure the United States of America that she would not become one of its public charges. Then she would become a bona-fide immigrant.

In Munich she had worked as a saleswoman to support her sick mother and herself, but was discharged as a non-Aryan. At the Clara de Hirsch Home for Working Girls, where she lived in New York, she was regarded as a well-educated, quiet person, but somehow she had not been able to obtain her affidavit. She was scheduled to return to Germany on May 27. On May 25 Luise Wolf leaped to her death from a fifth-floor window of the Home. A return ticket to Germany and $15 were found in her purse.

Such tragedies seemed needless to many Americans, especially since U.S. immigration quotas were unfilled. On June 7, 1938, a delegation of the Jewish People's Committee for United Action Against Fascism and Anti-Semitism visited the White House and presented 120,000 signatures on petitions proposing that the unused quotas from any country be made available for the admission of refugees from other countries. Presidential secretary Marvin McIntyre met the group, accepted the petitions and then sent a note to Sumner Welles:

"Personally I do not see much necessity for any reply except that a more or less courteous but stereotyped answer signed by me may head off insistence in the future for a specific reply. What do you think."

Welles thought so too.

A few months later the Jewish People's Committee presented 245,325 additional signatures obtained from people of all faiths. These were filed with the first batch. Although there were many non-Jewish signatories to these and other petitions, and although leading Protestant and Catholic clergymen spoke out frequently against the Nazi actions, there was no national outburst of Christian indignation. Shortly before the Evian Conference, James McDonald renewed a familiar campaign as he accepted the Albert Einstein Medal for Humanitarian Services. Pointing out that Protestants and Catholics were also being persecuted, he said that it was time that non-Jews became aware of the problem.

"The only really discouraging element," he said, "is that the Christian world, in this country and in other countries, should to such a very small extent take in the meaning of this current attack upon the principles of civilized society. Until Protestants and Catholics as well as Jews come to see that the things they hold dear, even as the things Jews hold dear, are threatened—not until then will there be an adequate response to enable refugees from central Europe to be cared for."

Much more typical than McDonald's eloquence in behalf of the refugees was the action of the New York State encampment of the Veterans of Foreign Wars. With the imminent Evian Conference in mind the VFW passed a resolution disapproving the admission of any refugees to the United States and calling for the suspension of all immigration for ten years. That accomplished, the VFW noted first prize and a gold cup to the drum and bugle corps of its Syracuse post.

Even as the VFW and other "patriotic" groups were fighting the admission of refugees, the American and British press reported the large-scale movement of Austrian Jews to the Dachau concentration camp near Munich.

On June 19, two weeks before Evian, the London *Times*'s Vienna correspondent wrote: "Demoralization is pursued by constant arrest of the Jewish population. No specific charge is made, but men and women, young and old, are taken each day and each night from their houses or in the streets and carried off, the more fortunate to Austrian prisons, and the rest to Dachau and other concentration camps in Germany. These raids are not restricted to the rich; they include doctors, lawyers, merchants, employes, poor artisans and peasants. There can be no Jewish family in the country which has not one or more of its members under arrest. The state of hopelessness and panic which is engendered can be imagined . . . The authorities demand rapid and impossible emigration. The Jews would welcome evacuation, but for most it is impossible. Only a few still own any considerable property and they cannot take out even that tithe that hitherto Jews leaving Germany have been able to save. Thousands turn in despair to relatives and friends abroad, beseeching them to obtain permanent or temporary visas. Thousands stand outside the consulates of America, England and other countries, waiting through the night for admission so that they may register their names . . . Already in the public schools the segregation of Jewish children from 'Aryans' is complete. The youngest are not spared; infants of the kindergarten can no longer play in public parks and on the door of their school the legend is painted: 'Cursed be the Jew.'

Perhaps no one described the challenge of Evian more eloquently than Anne O'Hare McCormick, columnist of the *New York Times*. Two days before the conference opened, she wrote: "It is heartbreaking to think of the queues of desperate human beings around our consulates in Vienna and other cities waiting in suspense for what happens at Evian. But the question they underline is not simply humanitarian. It is not a question of how many unemployed this country can safely add to its own unemployed millions. It is a test of civilization . . . Can America live with itself if it lets Germany get away with this policy of extermination, allows the fanaticism of one man to triumph over reason, refuses to take up this gage of battle against barbarism?"

Unknown to Miss McCormick and to the reporters gathering to cover the conference, Myron Taylor had met earlier with Sir Michael Palairet, the deputy head of the British delegation. Taylor told him that American Jewish leaders were anxious that Dr. Chaim Weizmann, head of the Jewish Agency for Palestine, be given an opportunity to present the case for immigration to Palestine either during the conference or at a private session. Sir Michael replied that his government "would naturally prefer that this meeting should not take place." Taylor promised him that he would not even talk to Weizmann prior to the conference.

Palestine had received more Jewish refugees than any other country, but the British had excluded its most eloquent spokesman, Dr. Weizmann, even before the conference began. His Majesty's delegation, led by Lord Winterton, managed to evade this delicate subject for the duration of the conference.

Even before the conference opened it was clear that the United States and Britain, to whom the others looked for leadership, had utterly disparate viewpoints. The vigorous Myron Taylor advocated relief for millions of refugees through a new Intergovernmental Committee, detached from the League of Nations. The cautious and ineffectual Lord Winterton, speaking for the British Foreign Office, preferred an expansion of the League's High Commission for Refugees, the doddering relic from which James McDonald had resigned. The French, led by Senator Henry Bérenger, were prepared to observe the Anglo-American duel, serene in their knowledge that they had welcomed more refugees than most and wanted no more.

Clarence K. Streit of the *New York Times* observed this preliminary maneuvering and reported its relationship to hundreds of thousands of desperate refugees: "These poor people and these great principles seem so far away from the Hotel Royal tonight. To one who has attended other conferences on Lake Geneva, the most striking thing on the eve of this one is that the atmosphere is so much like the others . . . The object and the players have changed but the atmosphere remains that of a none too trustful poker game, particularly as between the three great democracies, the United States, the United Kingdom and France."

. . .

On July 6, 1938, after much introductory skirmishing, the highly publicized Evian Conference was called to order. The first major controversy tackled by the delegates had nothing to do with refugees. It concerned the selection of the conference president. This dispute went on for two days. Curiously, the United States fought for the selection of Senator Bérenger, the French for Myron Taylor. In the end the pro-Taylor forces triumphed.

When the delegates finally turned to substantive issues it became clear that it would take more than the dedication of a Myron Taylor to rescue the conference: one after another the nations made clear their unwillingness to accept refugees. Since the business meetings were closed to the press, they did not risk public exposure.

Australia, with vast, unpopulated areas, announced: "As we have no real racial problem, we are not desirous of importing one." New Zealand was unwilling to lift its restrictions. The British colonial empire, reported Sir John Shuckburgh, contained no territory suitable to the large-scale settlement of Jewish refugees. Canada wanted agricultural migrants and none others. The same was true of Colombia, Uruguay and Venezuela.

Peru was particularly opposed to the immigration of doctors and lawyers lest such an intellectual proletariat upset the unbridled power of its upper class. The Peruvian delegate pointedly remarked that the United States had given his country an example of "caution and wisdom" by its own immigration restrictions.

France, whose population already included two hundred thousand refugees and three million aliens, stressed that it had reached its saturation point.

Nicaragua, Honduras, Costa Rica and Panama issued a joint statement saying that they could accept no "traders or intellectuals." Argentina, with a population one-tenth that of the United States, reported that it had welcomed almost as many refugees as the United States and hence could not be counted on for large-scale immigration.

The Netherlands and Denmark reflected their traditional humanitarianism. Though Holland had already accepted twenty-five thousand Jewish refugees, it offered itself as a country of temporary sojourn. Denmark, so densely populated that its own citizens were forced to emigrate, had already taken in a disproportionately large number of German exiles. Within its narrow limits, it would continue to do so.

And the United States, the nation at whose initiative the conference had convened, what would it offer? The answer was soon in coming. The United States, with its tradition of asylum, its vast land mass and its unlimited resources, agreed, for the first time, to accept its full, legal quota of 27,370 immigrants annually from Germany and Austria. That was the major American concession made at Evian.

Although Myron Taylor lacked the power to vitalize American immigration policy, he soon demonstrated that he could overcome British lassitude. As His Majesty's representative continued to battle at Evian for the retention of the impotent League of Nations High Commission for Refugees, Taylor prepared a detailed exposition of the need for a new approach. He sent a draft to Secretary Hull, paragraph five of which stipulated:

"The new urgency created by the Austrian development demands a fresh approach to the German Government in an effort to arrange more favorable conditions of migration than now exist. The existing terms of reference of the League's High Commissioner do not permit an approach to the German Government. A fresh approach under the auspices of the Intergovernmental Conference meeting at Evian should be attempted in an effort to change the present intolerable situation in which increased numbers of refugees now find themselves."

Secretary Hull wired back, evincing that zealous caution

with which he approached all matters of life and death: "Paragraph five to be used guardedly and only orally since we do not wish to appear to assume responsibility for making an approach to the German Government."

Taylor's guarded, oral use of paragraph five helped to carry the day against the British. The participants in the Evian Conference established the Intergovernmental Committee on Refugees, with permanent headquarters in London. The new organization would be independent of, but would co-operate with, the League. Unfortunately, its leadership would consist of the same personalities who had dominated the Evian meeting. They would accomplish just as little.

The Evian Conference adjourned on July 15 and it was announced that the new Intergovernmental Committee would meet in London in August. Its first task was to commence negotiations with Germany for an orderly solution of the refugee problem. Judging by the reactions of that nation's newspapers to the Evian discussions, the task would not be easy.

The *Danziger Vorposten,* aware that no new gates had been opened to the Jews, commented: "We see that one likes to pity the Jews as long as one can use this pity for a wicked agitation against Germany, but that no state is prepared to fight the cultural disgrace of central Europe by accepting a few thousand Jews. Thus the conference serves to justify Germany's policy against Jewry." The *Nationalsozialistische Parteikorrespondenz* stated that Evian had revealed "the danger which world Jewry constitutes."

American and British press reactions were almost as bitter, though for different reason. Several publications pointed out that "Evian" spelled backwards is "naïve," and *Time* magazine observed wryly. "Evian is the home of a famous spring of still and unexciting table water. After a week of many warm words of idealism and few practical suggestions, the Intergovernmental Committee on Political Refugees took on some of the same characteristics."

Although some of the British press felt that Evian had been useful in establishing machinery which might ultimately help the refugees, the *Daily Herald* disagreed, "If this is coming to the help of the refugees, then what would the nations do if they meant to desert them?"

To most observers, the Evian Conference had accomplished too little, but to the medical professions of Great Britain and the United States it appeared to have accomplished too much. Their organizations conjured up hordes of incompetent, fee-splitting refugee doctors shattering the ethical basis of Anglo-Saxon medicine and, by the way, stealing patients from their hospitable hosts.

Before the Evian Conference adjourned, the British Medical Association had threatened a "stay-in strike," stating that "no member of the medical profession wishes to see the country inundated with emigrés." At that time the refugee doctors comprised less than one-third of one percent of England's physicians.

In Britain this attitude was not confined to the more capitalistically inclined practitioners. Socialist doctors, at their annual union conference, complained about the "dilution of our industry with non-union, non-Socialist labor." The Medical Practitioners Union, in a burst of Marxian idealism, objected not to the admission of refugees "but to their being allowed to practice."

For once the Socialist and free-enterprise practitioners agreed. Lord Beaverbrook's *Sunday Express* published a fearsome editorial, charging that "just now there is a big influx of foreign Jews into Britain. They are overrunning the country. They are trying to enter the medical profession in great numbers. They wish to practice as dentists. Worst of all, many of them are holding themselves out to the public as psychoanalysts. A psychoanalyst needs no medical training but arrogates to himself functions of a doctor. And he often obtains an ascendancy over a patient of which he makes base use if he is a bad man." There was an uncomfortable similarity between the *Express* editorial and *Der Stürmer*'s tales of German patients in the clutches of Jewish doctors.

The American Medical Association did not charge that unqualified Jewish psychoanalysts were gaining ascendancy over the minds of helpless gentile patients, but it registered alarm about immigration.

Dr. Olin D. West, the secretary and general manager of the AMA, wrote a letter to Secretary Hull regarding inquiries he had received from his physician members about the frightening influx of European practitioners. Fully a month before Orson Welles terrified radio listeners with his invasion from Mars, Dr. West asked about the rumor that "approximately 500 members of professions from central European countries recently embarked for the United States on one vessel and that at this very time approximately 175 physicians from one of the European countries that has recently adopted strict measures that will prohibit physicians of a certain race from further pursuit of their professional careers in that country are to sail within the next few days for the United States."

Cordell Hull, who knew better than anyone how impossible it would be for five hundred Jewish physicians to be headed toward the United States on one ship, with stethoscopes at the ready, asked Assistant Secretary Messersmith to reassure the good doctor. In his reply Messersmith eased Dr. West's fears of special consideration for refugee doctors: each and every physician would have to fulfill every single immigration requirement before sailing to the United States.

The attitude of organized medicine (as distinct from the attitude of individual American physicians) was perhaps best illustrated by the magazine *Medical Economics.* Its article "Refugees, Unlimited" purported to give a factual account of foreign doctors arriving in a steady stream, ready to debase American medicine. "Waiting to welcome them are the newspaper 'sob sisters,' whose livelihood has long consisted of drumming up pity for the 'downtrodden'; sympathetic immigration officials to give them preference in the quotas; amenable boards of regents to grant them licenses without examination . . ."

The article listed some of the characteristics of the refugee doctors: they charged fifty cents a visit, their diagnoses were hasty, their surgery radical. *Medical Economics* was pleased that the AMA's governing House of Delegates had recommended that only American citizens be permitted to practice medicine. This would deny the refugees an opportunity to earn a living for at least five years.

"No ready-made solution seems to fit the problem," concluded *Medical Economics*. "Meanwhile cheap competition streams down the gangplank."

There were, of course, many physicians who realized that American medicine would be enriched by the talents of some of the world's outstanding physicians, surgeons and researchers. One American who welcomed the newcomers was Dr. Lawrence S. Kubie, secretary of The American Psychoanalytic Association. Dr. Kubie headed a physicians' committee to assist the new arrivals. It was a frustrating experience, as he explained in a letter to President Roosevelt. He described the new, restrictive legislation by which various states sought to prevent the refugee doctors from practicing. Ironically, the most severe laws had been hurried through the legislatures of those states which needed doctors most. As Dr. Kubie informed the President, "now scarcely half a dozen states are left to us as havens for these unfortunate scientists . . . In this matter states have behaved as though they were countries with a protective tariff."

The plight of German and Austrian doctors became worse immediately after Evian. Although virtually all areas of medical practice were closed to them, they had been permitted to keep their licenses and to care for Jewish patients. On August 3 the Nazis decreed that the licenses of all Jewish physicians would expire on September 30. As a result, scores of Germany's leading physicians lined up for hours at the U.S. consulates, only to be told that the German quota was filled for the next two to three years.

The day after the Germans issued the doctors' decree, the Intergovernmental Committee on Refugees convened in London. Myron Taylor stated frankly and earnestly that it was necessary to find new homes for 660,000 persons still living in Germany and Austria. Of this total, 300,000 were Jews; 285,-000 were Christians of sufficient Jewish ancestry to fail the Nuremberg racial tests; and 75,000 were Roman Catholics. At the present rate of emigration, warned Taylor, this resettlement would take sixteen years. A way must be found to accomplish it in five years or less. Taylor emphasized the need for German co-operation in this effort.

This would be the primary task of George Rublee, a new personality in the refugee drama. Rublee, a lawyer of Huguenot descent, had been persuaded by Franklin Roosevelt to become the new director of the Intergovernmental Committee. A partner in the law firm of Covington, Burling and Rublee, he had long been a troubleshooter in international affairs. As legal adviser to the U.S. embassy in Mexico, he had aided Ambassador Dwight Morrow in a delicate matter involving church-state relations. He had also served with distinction as an adviser to the U.S. delegation at the London Naval Conference of 1930. Coupled with these victories were equally striking defeats as a crusader for the League of Nations and as an adherent of Teddy Roosevelt's Bull Moose movement.

The complexity of Rublee's personality was captured eloquently by one of his law associates, Dean Acheson. The former Secretary of State has written that Rublee's life was like the movement of a symphony, "a movement with alternating themes, one of contented languor touched with melancholy, the other a passionate, almost demoniacal seizure which carried him to heights of brilliant and tireless effort, ending in the tragedy of frustration and failure, followed again by the melancholy languor."

Though Rublee assumed direction of the Intergovernmental Committee's activities, Lord Winterton continued as its chairman, devoting himself officially to matters of protocol and unofficially to the protection of British Middle East policy.

As Rublee turned his considerable talents to his challenging assignment, the Jews were subjected to yet another form of harassment. As of January 1, 1939, Jewish males whose first names were not distinctly Jewish must add the middle name of Israel. Jewish women, whose names did not immediately identify them as such, must add that of Sarah. The Nazis were obliging enough to draw up a list of 185 male and 91 female names which they considered to be Jewish. Among them were such male designations as Abimelech, Ahasuer, Akiba, Esau, Itzig and Zedekia. The female names were equally exceptional, among them Brocha, Feigle, Millkele, Simche and Zorthel.

Under this law, newborn children must be given only these "approved" names, and adult name changes must be recorded in birth and marriage certificates. Failure to comply would be punishable by six months in prison.*

George Rublee, faced with accelerated manifestations of the German national psychosis, proceeded with his difficult task. He would try to persuade member governments to lower immi-

* According to an affidavit submitted during the Nuremberg Trials, it was Hans Globke, an official of the Interior Ministry, who had drawn up the decree ordering the name changes and who had prepared the list of "approved" Jewish names.

Globke's contribution to the harassment of the Jews did not handicap his postwar career. For many years he was one of Chancellor Konrad Adenauer's closest associates, first as *Ministerialdirektor* in the Chancellor's office and later as *Staatssekretär*, an even higher designation.

gration barriers while he laid the groundwork for an approach to the Germans. But even as he began, the Nazis struck a brutal blow at his hopes.

On October 28, 1938, the Germans deported thousands of Polish Jews, triggering a chain of events which would spark the most virulent Nazi reprisal of the prewar era.

■ XII ■

1938: The Night of Broken Glass

ON OCTOBER 28, 1938, EMBOLDENED BY THE world's passive response to their anti-Semitism, the Germans launched an assault against thousands of Polish Jews who had lived for many years in the Reich. It was a brutal action even by Nazi standards. They snatched children from the streets without notifying their parents, and jammed them, along with thousands of others, including the aged and infirm, into trucks and trains bound for the Polish border. The Jews were allowed to take only 10 marks ($4) and the clothes on their backs. About ten thousand were dumped across the border. In bitter cold they sought refuge in empty railroad cars, in the open no man's land between the German and Polish frontiers, or in abandoned, heatless barracks.

During the following days the attention of the world was drawn to the precarious state of the deportees, particularly to several thousand enduring the most extreme hardships at the Polish border station of Zbaszym. Among this mass of human misery was the Zindel Grynszpan family of Hanover. One of the sons, seventeen-year-old Herschel, had fled to Paris earlier.

His father wrote him a letter describing the family's suffering. The boy, who had been overwrought since he left Poland, bought a pistol and on November 7 went to the German embassy in Paris with the intention of assassinating Ambassador Johannes von Welczeck. He demanded to see the ambassador but a minor official, Ernst vom Rath, was delegated to deal with the visitor.

It is a tragic irony that even as Vom Rath walked toward his death he was being investigated by the Gestapo because of his opposition to anti-Semitism. The moment the shots were fired into his body, Vom Rath's heresy was forgotten and his martyrdom assured. As he lay unconscious in Paris the German press fomented a massive reprisal against the Jews. Grynszpan, in the custody of French police, broke down and cried, "Being a Jew is not a crime. I am not a dog. I have a right to live and the Jewish people have a right to exist on this earth. Wherever I have been I have been chased like an animal."

On the afternoon of November 9 Ernst vom Rath died of his wounds. At two o'clock the next morning a wave of arson, looting, murder and arrest began which stunned even a world by now immune to Nazi excesses. The "spontaneous" demonstration had been organized on teletyped orders from Reinhard Heydrich, who commanded the Security Service organization under Heinrich Himmler.

In the ensuing orgy some 195 synagogues were burned, more than 800 shops destroyed and 7,500 looted. The streets of Germany were littered by the shattered shop windows and the disaster became known as the "night of broken glass," or the *Kristallnacht*. Twenty thousand Jews were arrested and taken to concentration camps. Official German figures listed thirty-six killed, but newsmen and diplomatic observers counted many more deaths.

The *New York Times* headlined its report of November 11, 1938: "NAZIS SMASH, LOOT AND BURN JEWISH SHOPS AND

TEMPLES UNTIL GOEBBELS CALLS HALT," and its correspondent Otto D. Tolischus wrote:

"A wave of destruction, looting and incendiarism unparalleled in Germany since the Thirty Years' War, and in Europe generally since the Bolshevist revolution, swept over Great Germany today as National Socialist cohorts took vengeance on Jewish shops, offices and synagogues for the murder by a young Polish Jew of Ernst vom Rath, third secretary of the German embassy in Paris.

"Beginning systematically in the early morning hours in almost every town and city in the country, the wrecking, looting and burning continued all day. Huge but mostly silent crowds looked on and the police confined themselves to regulating traffic and making wholesale arrests of Jews 'for their own protection.' "

The Austrian Nazis, not to be outdone, joined the carnage. All twenty-one of Vienna's synagogues were set afire, and eighteen were completely destroyed. In some communities every male Jew was sent to a concentration camp.

Detailed descriptions of the Nazi barbarism were forwarded by diplomatic representatives in all parts of Germany to the British Foreign Office and the State Department. The American consul in Stuttgart sent a dispatch to Ambassador Hugh Wilson in Berlin: ". . . the Jews of southwest Germany have suffered vicissitudes during the last three days which would seem unreal to one living in an enlightened country during the twentieth century if one had not actually been a witness of their dreadful experiences . . . the horror of midnight arrests, of hurried departures in a half-dressed state from their homes in the company of police officers, of the wailing of wives and children suddenly left behind, of imprisonment in crowded cells and of the panic of fellow prisoners."

The Stuttgart consulate was described as "a mass of seething, panic-stricken humanity . . . For more than five days the office has been inundated with people. Each day a larger and larger crowd has besieged the Consulate, filling all the rooms and overflowing into the corridor of a building six stories high. Today there were several thousand."

The consul had seen men and boys sacking Jewish shops while the police looked on, smiling. Practically all the male Jews between eighteen and sixty-five had been arrested.

British Consul General Bell in Cologne reported to Sir George Ogilvie-Forbes, the counselor of the British embassy in Berlin: "Personally I have been more shocked by the cold-blooded and calculated manner in which action was taken than by anything else about the recent events. Yet I am inclined to think that the Führer knows his Germans."

Sir George wired his Foreign Secretary, Lord Halifax, that the murder of Vom Rath "has only accelerated the process of elimination of the Jews which has for long been planned . . . 500,000 people deliberately excluded from all trades and professions . . . Misery and despair are already there, and, when their resources are either denied to them or exhausted, their end will be starvation. The Jews of Germany are, indeed, not a national but a world problem, which, if neglected, contains the seeds of a terrible vengeance."

British consul general Gainer in Vienna noted that three times during the night, storm troops had arrested all the men in the long lines awaiting the opening of the British consulate at eight-thirty. In this same dispatch Gainer reported that the Nazis had attacked Jews who were lined up outside the U.S. consulate, beating them until the American consul general, "unable to bear the spectacle," insisted upon police intervention.

The British and American newspapers reported that twenty thousand Jews rounded up during the "night of broken glass" were being held in three concentration camps: Dachau near Munich, Oranienburg-Sachsenhausen north of Berlin and Buchenwald in the Weimar area.

These camps had all been mentioned earlier by the press. A Reuters dispatch of August 11, 1938, which had appeared in English newspapers, including the *Manchester Guardian,* made it clear that the German public was also quite aware of their existence: "Everybody in Weimar knows of the Buchenwald and will readily indicate in general terms where it is, but no one mentions the dread words 'concentration camp.' "

After a detailed description of the extreme hardships facing sixty thousand of the eighty thousand Jews of Berlin, the Reuters story continued: "But more poignant than loss of work or business is the news of friends who suddenly disappear and are engulfed into the great concentration camp of Buchenwald. From this dread spot in the heart of beautiful Thuringia, the relatives of those interned there have sometimes received a curt official intimation that the prisoner has died on a certain date, that he has been cremated, and the ashes may be collected. Sometimes these notices reach the relations very soon. The Buchenwald is not a healthy place."

Diplomatic reports were even more specific. A message to the British Foreign Office in 1938 confirmed the daily deaths at Buchenwald, adding that relatives of the victims were required to pay 3 marks ($1.20) for their ashes.

The same dispatch reported the mistreatment of three thousand prisoners, 96 percent of them Jewish. One man suffering from heart trouble was unable to walk rapidly enough to suit the guards and his fellow prisoners were ordered to drag him face downward, tearing his flesh until his features were unrecognizable. The prisoners were awakened at three-thirty in the morning and after hours of standing at attention, the sick were asked to step forward. The commandant, carrying a riding whip, conducted inspection of the ailing. Those whom he declared fit were whipped about the face. Organized floggings occurred during afternoon roll call.

A former Buchenwald prisoner prepared a statement for the British Foreign Office which began: "Only a few miles from

Goethe's Weimar, situated in the midst of a pleasant beech forest, ringed around with barbed-wire fences, guarded by SS detachments and machine guns, lies the new City of Sorrow, the concentration camp of Buchenwald."

Dachau after the *Kristallnacht* was described in a report by the British consul general in Munich. There were now fourteen thousand Jewish prisoners in the camp. Their heads were shaven and they wore coarse prison suits on which the yellow Star of David had been stamped. If and when they were released, they were required to sign statements that they had been well treated, but many had died, according to the consul.

In 1938 the concentration camps were not the centers of mass extermination they later became; nevertheless, death was a frequent visitor. The names of prominent victims, far from being secret, were published openly in the non-German press. Deaths at Dachau were announced frequently in British newspapers, as for example:

News Chronicle: Baron von Lessner, former president of the Catholic Schools Association, a foe of both the Nazis and the Social Democrats, dead at Dachau. He was in perfect health at the time of the arrest but died at the age of fifty, a few months after entering the camp.

London *Observer:* Richard Schmitz, former anti-Nazi mayor of Vienna, dead after three months of imprisonment.

London *Times:* Dr. Robert Hecht, former legal adviser to Austrian Chancellors Dollfuss and Schuschnigg, died at Dachau.

These and many other killings were reported in 1938 and the world knew that the shipment of twenty thousand Jews to concentration camps after the "night of broken glass" signaled more than conventional imprisonment.

The barbarities of the *Kristallnacht* were reviewed in minute detail in the House of Commons by Philip Noel-Baker, a Labour party member who later won the Nobel Peace Prize. Mr. Noel-Baker urged large-scale loans and large-scale hospitality for German refugees, describing them as "very able, resourceful, educated people—one of the best investments in the world . . .

"Dr. Goebbels," concluded Mr. Noel-Baker, "said the other day that he hoped the outside world would soon forget the German Jews. He hopes in vain. His campaign against them will go down in history with St. Bartholomew's Eve as a lasting memory of human shame. Let there go with it another memory, the memory of what the other nations did to wipe the shame away."

The American public responded to the *Kristallnacht* with similar outrage. The White House and the State Department were inundated with messages from religious and civic groups, and with resolutions for action adopted by public meetings in Cincinnati, Minneapolis, Kansas City, Salt Lake City, Boston, Memphis, New York, Spokane and Detroit. There were pleas from Lincoln, Nebraska; Manchester, New Hampshire; Amarillo, Texas; Canton, Ohio; Shreveport, Louisiana; and many others. They demanded protest, action and rescue.

There was one notable exception. Father Charles E. Coughlin, the Detroit priest whose anti-Semitic radio broadcasts had been hailed by the Nazi press, described the German violence as a "defense mechanism" against Jewish-sponsored Communism. His view was not shared by the U.S. press which, almost without exception, denounced the Nazis.

Buffalo *Courier-Express:* " . . . the Berlin government must be regarded as leading lynching mobs against Jews in Germany."

St. Paul *Dispatch:* "Reprisal against a whole people for the crime of an overwrought youth is a throwback to barbarity."

Syracuse *Post-Standard:* "Humanity stands aghast and ashamed at the indecency and brutality that is permitted in Germany."

Hartford *Courant:* "The people outside Germany who still value tolerance, understanding and humanity, can no more keep silent in the face of what has just taken place than they would in the face of any other barbarity."

But the United States government, the official voice of those people who "can no more keep silent," remained silent.

Propaganda Minister Goebbels, aware of the outcry across the sea, made a statement to representatives of the foreign press. He would not reply to charges of "gangsterism and medievalism," he said, because they were beneath his dignity, but once again he challenged the democracies: "If there is any country that believes it has not enough Jews, I shall gladly turn over to it all our Jews."

There were no takers.

The cruelty of the *Kristallnacht* did not end with the shattering of the last pane of glass. On November 12 the German government imposed a fine of 1,000,000,000 marks (approximately $400,000,000) on the Jews as "money atonement" for the death of Vom Rath. In addition, they ruled that the Jews would be responsible for the repair of the astronomical damage to shops and homes. They must pay all costs and the work must start immediately. Furthermore, they would not be permitted to collect insurance on their damaged buildings. A committee chaired by Reich Minister Hermann Göring issued a communiqué stating that the Jews were responsible "for all the damage to Jewish businesses and homes resulting from the people's resentment toward the agitation of international Jewry against National Socialist Germany during November 8, 9 and 10, 1938."

The billion-mark fine, which was to be paid in four installments beginning December 15, jolted the hopes of George Rublee, the American recently appointed as director of the Intergovernmental Committee on Refugees. Rublee was waiting in London for an invitation to begin discussions with German officials in Berlin. His mission could succeed only if the Germans co-operated in permitting the Jews to emigrate with some of their assets. But after the billion-mark fine, there would be no assets left.

On November 14 Rublee wired Secretary Hull, explaining that "The attack on the Jewish community in Germany on the one hand and the indifference of the participating governments to the fate of the victims on the other has brought the affairs of the Intergovernmental Committee to a critical state where, in our opinion, immediate action is required if the President's initiative is to lead to a positive result . . .

"With the exception of the United States, which has maintained its quota, and the British Isles, which are admitting immigrants at a current month's rate equal to the rate immigrants are being admitted to the United States, doors have been systematically closed everywhere to involuntary emigrants since the meeting at Evian."

Rublee's quest for havens had been frustrated by the disinterest of the Latin American republics, the French, English and Dutch colonies and representatives of the British dominions. Indeed, since Evian, new and more restrictive immigration regulations had been adopted by such conference participants as Argentina, Chile, Uruguay and Mexico. As for the possibility of a meeting with German officials, Rublee reported to Hull: "My chances of being received are receding."

On the same day that Rublee sent his dismal report, Assistant Secretary of State George Messersmith, whose long diplomatic service within Germany had been marked by eloquent and perceptive reporting, sent a strong memorandum to Hull:

"Of all the many acts of the present German Government against innocent and defenseless peoples, these last are the culmination. For a Government to order and to carry through such wholesale action against a part of its people, and to threaten the rest of the world with further action if it should even pass censure, is an irresponsible and mad act that our Government cannot pass unnoticed.

"We have throughout our history let it be known where we

stand on matters of principle and the decencies . . . Whenever such acts in the past have been committed, or permitted by Governments, in countries which the world has considered less civilized, we have spoken and acted. The proud record of this Government, and of our public conscience shows this (Russia, Turkey, Rumania). When a country which vaunts its civilization as superior commits in cold blood and with deliberation acts worse than those we have in the past dealt with vigorously, the time has come, I believe, when it is necessary for us to take action beyond mere condemnation.

"It is my belief that unless we take some action in the face of the events in Germany of the last few days, we shall be much behind our public opinion in this country."

Messersmith thought it prudent for Hull to ask President Roosevelt that Ambassador Wilson be recalled from Germany "for consultation." According to Messersmith, this might stem the orgy and give the Germans "food for thought."

He added that if Wilson was recalled, it could not affect the Intergovernmental Committee on Refugees adversely, "for it has been quite obvious that the German Government does not wish to receive Rublee except to use his visit as a pawn in the game of endeavoring to secure a basis for economic negotiations of a wide character which, in any event, we could not enter into."

Hull reacted to the suggestion with uncharacteristic speed. He consulted with the President immediately and that same day he sent Ambassador Wilson a telegram informing him that the situation within Germany was so shocking that the President "desires you to report to him in person."

The action was not technically a recall, which would have been regarded as a serious diplomatic action. But the implication was clear. Since it was the first time an American ambassador to a major power had been summoned home in such a manner since the First World War, it created a sensation.

More than two hundred correspondents, anticipating the

President's comments about Germany, attended his news conference on November 15. They found him in good humor, smoking a cigarette from his long holder, his expression jaunty, his mood confident. His demeanor changed as he picked up a prepared statement and read it to the reporters:

"The news of the past few days from Germany has deeply shocked public opinion in the United States. Such news from any part of the world would inevitably produce a similar profound reaction among American people in every part of the nation. I myself could scarcely believe that such things could occur in a twentieth century civilization. With a view to gaining a firsthand picture of the situation in Germany I have asked the Secretary of State to order our Ambassador in Berlin to return at once for report and consultation."

In response to inquiries about the crucial situation of the refugees, the President said that the Intergovernmental Committee was enlarging its scope because of the German situation.

Had the President considered where the refugees might go?

He had given a great deal of thought to it but was not yet ready to make any announcements.

Then a correspondent asked if Mr. Roosevelt would recommend to Congress that immigration laws be modified to permit the entry of more refugees to the Unied States. The President replied in the negative. No modifications were contemplated.

The symbolic withdrawal of Ambassador Wilson and the President's brief verbal chastisement of Germany comprised the total American response to the *Kristallnacht*. The United States continued its trade relations with the Third Reich, a fact which impelled thirty-six of the most prominent writers of the United States to send a telegram to the President:

"We feel we no longer have any right to remain silent, we feel that the American people and the American government have no right to remain silent. Thirty-five years ago a horrified America rose to its feet to protest against the Kishinev pogroms in Tsarist Russia. God help us if we have grown so indifferent to human suffering that we cannot rise now in protest against pogroms in Nazi Germany. We feel that it is deeply immoral for the American people to continue having economic relations with a country that avowedly uses mass murder to solve its economic problems."

Signers of the telegram included Eugene O'Neill, Robert Sherwood, John Steinbeck, Pearl Buck, John Gunther, Edna Ferber, Sidney Howard, Lillian Hellman, George S. Kaufman, Robinson Jeffers, Van Wyck Brooks, Marc Connelly, Clifford Odets, Thornton Wilder and Dorothy Thompson.

Pressure for more decisive American action came from within the State Department as well as from without. One of the strongest voices was that of the United States ambassador to Poland, Anthony Drexel Biddle, Jr. After the *Kristallnacht,* Biddle notified Secretary Hull that according to reliable informants in Germany, "Nazi officialdom considered world opinion bankrupt. They believed people abroad would undoubtedly throw up their hands in horror, but they would do nothing about it . . . I consider these recent Nazi excesses in addition to those recently perpetrated against the Catholic clergy in Vienna and subsequently the Protestant clergy . . . as nothing short of a challenge to modern civilization."

Biddle reminded Hull that a vast danger lay in the repercussions to unchecked Nazism in nearby states: 445,000 Jews in Hungary were already subject to anti-Semitic laws. Reports throughout 1938 had described increasing pressure on the 900,000 Jews of Rumania as its Fascist government mimicked Nazi measures. As for Poland, Ambassador Biddle had warned again and again that the economic condition of her 3,500,000 Jews had deteriorated severely and that anti-Semitic laws were on the horizon.

Biddle was an accurate prophet. Hungary and Rumania, as eventual allies of Germany, would demonstrate their expertise in exterminating Jews. In 1902 the United States had intervened in Rumania with good effect, but those days were past. The information mounting in State Department files would not be put to use; the license of Hungary, Rumania and Poland to maltreat the Jews would not be challenged; and the Biddle reports would survive as mementos of unheeded warnings.

The philosophical attitude of the State Department in this period immediately after the "night of broken glass" was expressed in a memorandum summarizing the refugee situation. Prepared for the Division of European Affairs, it was designed to point up the role of the Intergovernmental Committee on Refugees, then floundering in London.

"It is easy to dismiss the whole problem by saying, 'Nobody wants any more Jews.' That is unquestionably true, but the problem remains to be solved and this Government is committed to solving it. The failure of the Intergovernmental Committee would involve a serious loss of prestige for this Government."

The Foreign Service officer who authored this document concluded on a generous note: "Whatever anyone may think individually about Jews, the sufferings these people are going through cannot but move the humanitarian instincts of even the most hard-hearted."

The humanitarian instincts of the British Foreign Office were also aroused, but His Majesty's Palestine policies prevented their fulfillment. The Arab revolt against the English in Palestine posed a great threat to Whitehall. Masterminded by the pro-Nazi Grand Mufti, it jeopardized Britain's influence in the Middle East. It also threatened the last bastion of Jewish immigration. Perhaps the English were casting about for other sanctuaries for the Jews in order to maintain their humanitarian reputation, while at the same time reassuring the Arabs that Jewish immigration would be curtailed. In any event, on November 17, two days after Franklin Roosevelt's press conference, the British ambassador called upon Sumner Welles with a novel proposal.

Sir Ronald Lindsay announced that Britain would be willing to relinquish some of the sixty-five thousand places it had been allocated on the United States immigration quota "in order that the remainder . . . might be utilized for the purpose of permitting German refugees to enter the United States." The implications of the offer were staggering. England's quota was more than twice that of Germany's but only four thousand British immigrants had arrived in 1938. The unused portion offered vast relief possibilities.

The urbane Mr. Welles was unruffled by the suggestion. According to his own account of the conversation, he told Sir Ronald that immigration quotas were established under law and were not the property of the nations to whom they were granted.

He explained that there were insuperable obstacles from a legal standpoint, and in his own words, "I further thought that the Ambassador would understand that there were likewise objections from the standpoint of policy. I reminded the Ambassador that the President had officially stated once more only two days ago that there was no intention on the part of this Government to increase the quota already established for German nationals. I added that it was my very strong impression that the responsible leaders among American Jews would be the first to urge that no change in the present quota for German Jews be made."

In invoking "legal" obstacles to acceptance of the British offer, Welles had fallen back on a convenient subterfuge, one that had been used and would be used until late in the war to block rescue action. The ephemeral nature of "legal" obstacles was illustrated just two days after Sir Ronald Lindsay's offer. President Roosevelt announced that, contrary to legal procedure, twelve to fifteen thousand German refugees who had come to the United States on visitor's visas would not be forced to depart when they expired. The President had given instructions to extend their visas an additional six months and thenceforth to renew them for as long as might be necessary. He made it clear that the United States would not just stand by and let them return to concentration camps and other types of punishment. Technically the President's decision was illegal. The German government had announced that it would cancel the passports of all nationals who did not return to the Fatherland before December 30. The refugees would become resident aliens without valid passports. This was contrary to American law and Roosevelt was aware of it. At his next press conference he emphasized that he would not permit legal technicalities to block humanitarian action.

Chairman Martin Dies of the House Committee on Un-American Activities challenged the President's right to extend the visas, but there were no other serious objections and the refugees were permitted to renew their visas until such time as they completed arrangements to qualify for citizenship. A substantial number of them happened to be teachers and university professors who subsequently made significant contributions to American education and science. It was clear that legalities could be circumvented under emergency conditions.

In justice to Welles, the transfer of a portion of the British quota to the German might have posed more difficult problems than Roosevelt's extension of the visitor's visas. But there were, at the time, a variety of proposals which might have accomplished the same purpose. Most were suggested by Jewish groups, although Welles was correct in stating that some American Jews opposed changes in the quota. There was fear among a small but influential segment of Jewry that increased immigration might aggravate domestic anti-Semitism. Although this was a convenient excuse for Welles, it does not appear that American policy was affected any more by the behavior of timid than of forceful Jews.

One of the most frequent proposals by Jewish organizations

involved the mortgaging of future quotas. For example, it was suggested that eighty-two thousand refugees entitled to enter the United States from Germany during a three-year period might be admitted immediately in view of the emergency. Future German immigration would then be cancelled until the numbers were stabilized. In that manner the total admitted over the full period would not exceed the limit of the law.

Secretary of Labor Frances Perkins discussed this possibility with President Roosevelt on November 17, 1938. She emerged from their conference stating that "a cautious approach is necessary to be certain we are doing the right thing and that the American people will co-operate." She added that there had been no decision to attempt to revise the immigration law because the sentiment of the American people had not yet been crystallized; that is, there was no public outcry for a change. In view of the President's almost daily reiteration that the immigration law would not be revised, it is difficult to conjecture how this could have been expected.

Roosevelt, though unwilling to act decisively, was concerned about the immigration dilemma, as he revealed to Myron Taylor in a confidential letter of November 23, 1938:

"The Intergovernmental Committee on Political Refugees which your devoted and effective efforts created at Evian and launched at London has not yet produced the concrete results I had hoped. This has been due to forces and circumstances beyond the control of any of us but I feel that the time has come when a special effort must be made to make the Committee's work really effective. We must produce concrete and substantial results and we must produce them soon."

The President informed Taylor that he was sending him to London as his personal representative on refugee matters. "It is essential," wrote Roosevelt, "to create the proper spirit in the countries of potential settlement and to lead them to see this problem as one which is humanitarian in its urgency but from which they can draw ultimate practical benefit . . . I do not believe it either desirable or practicable to recommend any change in the quota provisions of our immigration laws. We are prepared, nevertheless, to make any other contribution which may be in our power to make."

Roosevelt and the British were in fact considering the possibility of large-scale resettlement of the Jews in thinly populated colonial areas of the world. The British had started studies (they would turn out to be long-range studies) of Northern Rhodesia, British Guiana and Kenya and were considering the acceptability of the former German colony of Tanganyika.

In October, Roosevelt had written to Isaiah Bowman, the distinguished geographer and president of Johns Hopkins Univeristy, inquiring about the feasibility of settling the Jews in the Venezuelan plateau north and south of the Orinoco River. Bowman sent a discouraging reply, calling the President's attention to the region's heat, rain and ticks. On November 2, 1938, the President wrote to Bowman again:

"Frankly what I am rather looking for is the possibility of uninhabited or sparsely inhabited good agricultural lands to which Jewish colonies might be sent . . . all this is merely for my own information because there are no specific plans on foot . . ."

In December, Bowman sent the President a twenty-six-page summary of world-wide settlement possibilities. He estimated that it would cost half a billion dollars to scatter the refugees throughout Africa, South America, Southeast Asia and Australia—that is, provided they were accepted by the host countries. Roosevelt thanked him.

Within Germany, which now included Austria, the pressure continued to mount on the seven hundred thousand remaining non-Aryans. They were forbidden to enter parks, museums, concert halls and certain streets; in some cities their telephone service was disconnected and their radios seized. In Munich,

Leipzig and Nuremberg they were not permitted to buy food. It was impossible for them to get medical attention in Munich because all the Jewish physicians had been arrested.

The lines around the U.S. consulates lengthened. The Stuttgart consulate, empowered to issue 850 visas per month, received 110,000 applications.

Nazi officials now announced their intention to establish ghettos in the slums of major cities. Those Jews living in more desirable sections would be evicted from their apartments. As rumors spread of the pending evictions, eager Aryans swamped the housing authorities with applications for a chance to replace their dispossessed neighbors. These Germans were no doubt among that vast number which was unaware of what was happening to the departed tenants. They were perhaps less well informed than the Americans and the English whose newspapers kept them abreast of each new Nazi measure. The Associated Press dispatch of November 27, which described the Aryan demand for Jewish apartments, noted the removal of signs from eighty Vienna streets named for distinguished Jews. According to the AP, one of the men whose memory was to be eradicated, Joseph von Sonnenfels, "was responsible for the abolition of torture as a method of police investigation . . ." The pogrom that followed the "night of broken glass" made it clear that a street sign honoring Von Sonnenfels was quite inappropriate in the Third Reich. It was clear too that an event like the *Kristallnacht* would have occurred eventually even if a Herschel Grynszpan had not murdered an Ernst vom Rath. According to both newspaper and diplomatic reports, vast new accommodations had been added to the concentration camps long before the fatal shots in Paris.

In retaliation for the summoning home of Ambassador Wilson, the German government sent for its own ambassador, Hans Dieckhoff. On November 22 he paid a farewell visit to Secretary Hull, who jotted down a description of their meeting: "The Ambassador of Germany came in on his own request. I felt no spirit of cordiality and naturally acted accordingly. The Ambassador sat down and said that he was being recalled and had come in to say goodbye. I said I hoped he would have a safe voyage. That ended the conversation."

On that high note of indignation the Secretary of State of the most powerful democratic nation on earth bade farewell to the representative of the most barbarous regime of modern history. Later Dieckhoff would prepare a list of prominent American Jews whose names could be used by German propagandists. He would make a point of mentioning that Mrs. Hull was Jewish.

Even as Dieckhoff departed from the United States the Nazi press described the ultimate intentions of the Hitler government. On November 23, 1938, Hitler's official newspaper, the *Völkischer Beobachter,* proclaimed in its leading editorial that the German people had embarked upon "the final and unalterably uncompromising solution" of the Jewish problem.

Das Schwarze Korps, the organ of the black-shirted Elite Guard and the Gestapo, was more explicit. In a lurid front-page article the newspaper pointed out that many Germans had argued that the Jewish question should have been solved "completely and with the most brutal methods in 1933. This view was right, but it had to remain theory because at that time we lacked the military power we possess today . . . Because it is necessary, because we no longer hear the world's screeching and because, after all, no power on earth can hinder us, we will now bring the Jewish question to its totalitarian solution."

The article outlined the future of the German Jew: elimination from the German economy; ghettoization with an identifying mark so that each individual might be recognized as a Jew; and utter isolation. Under these circumstances, reasoned *Das Schwarze Korps,* the Jews would become impoverished and then forced to turn to crime.

"But let nobody suppose," concluded the article, "that we shall look calmly on such developments. We do not intend to permit hundreds of thousands of pauperized Jews to become a breeding place for Bolshevism or catch basin for politico-criminal subhumans. Were we to tolerate that, the result would be a conspiracy of the underworld such as is possible and thinkable in America, perhaps, but not in Germany.

"At this stage of development we should therefore face the hard necessity of exterminating the Jewish underworld in the same way in which we in our orderly state are wont to exterminate criminals, i.e., with fire and sword. The result would be the actual and definite end of Jewry in Germany and its complete extermination."

The editorial and the article were reprinted in the United States and Europe. It was November 23, 1938, two years and eight months before Hitler would order the implementation of plans for the final solution of the Jewish problem.

■ XIII ■

The Attempt to Buy Lives

AS DIRECTOR OF THE INTERGOVERNMENTAL Committee on Refugees, George Rublee had been waiting in London since October 1938 for an invitation to begin discussions in Berlin. Ignored by the Germans, brushed off by Ambassador Joseph P. Kennedy in London and thwarted in his efforts to locate new homes for refugees, Rublee managed in December to wangle a conference with Dr. Hjalmar Schacht, president of the Reichsbank, who chose London as the meeting place. They conferred under the most disadvantageous circumstances for Rublee. There was no bargaining; Schacht simply presented a plan for acceptance or rejection. But for all his apparent rigidity, Germany's "financial wizard" viewed these talks as a unique opportunity—with Rublee he could play the humanitarian while filling Germany's coffers. Schacht presented his "package deal" for the liberation of the Jews: payment of 3,000,000,000 marks ($1,200,000,000) coupled with a complex scheme to force the émigrés to bolster German exports as they reconstructed their lives in other countries; in return the Nazis would release fifty thousand Jewish "workers" a year for three years.

It was clear that the Germans would contribute nothing to the resettlement of their outcasts, the departing Jews would be stripped of everything, and some four hundred thousand members of their families would be left behind as vulnerable targets for future blackmail. "The plan," Sumner Welles cabled Rublee, "is generally considered as asking the world to pay a ransom for the release of hostages in Germany and to barter human misery for increased exports."

Jewish organizations in the United States joined Welles in condemning the Nazi offer. Leaders of the World Jewish Congress adopted a resolution stating that Jews would refuse any solution of the refugee problem which rewarded Germany for her policy of robbery and expulsion.

Up against a wall of universal disapproval, Schacht invited Rublee a few weeks later to resume talks in Berlin. Now the American had an improved bargaining position, a fact which became apparent immediately. Schacht suggested a compromise arrangement, this time omitting any link to German exports. Before Rublee could exploit this new opportunity, he was notified by telephone that "the Führer has deprived Dr. Schacht of his office, wherefore he is unable to continue the negotiations."

The "wizard's" demotion was caused more by his disagreement with changes in Germany's financial policies than by his apparent accommodation to Rublee. This became evident when the Nazis indicated that they wished to continue the talks. At the end of January 1939, Hermann Göring delegated an adviser in the Ministry for Economic Affairs, Helmuth Wohlthat, to continue the negotiations for Jewish emigration.

In spite of Rublee's dedication and legal skill, one essential element of reality was lacking in his proposals. The Nazis across the table knew there was no nation or territory prepared to admit Jews in significant numbers. The one Jewish newspaper still published in Germany (under the direction of the Propaganda Ministry, of course) observed during the Rublee-

Wohlthat talks that "the United States, which initiated the Evian Conference, should be reminded of its moral duty to set other immigration countries a good example with a generous gesture. If the United States could decide to accept 100,000 Jews from Germany conditionally, they could remain in the thinly settled regions in the West of that country and would make a very valuable contribution to the solution of the emigration problem." Alaska was mentioned specifically as an example of an underpopulated area which might absorb vast numbers of immigrants. (No doubt Propaganda Minister Goebbels sought to embarrass the United States with these suggestions.)

In February 1939 Wohlthat unexpectedly announced that Germany was ready to authorize an orderly emigration of its Jews. The exodus would begin with 150,000 wage earners, from fifteen to forty-five years of age, who would be permitted to emigrate during the next three to five years. During that period there would be no new pressures or penalties against the remaining Jews. Later the 150,000 wage earners would be joined by their wives, children and dependents. The Third Reich would even retrain emigrants for work in their new homes, and Wohlthat went so far as to promise that Jews in concentration camps would be released once the program got under way.

The financial arrangements for the mass movement were not stated precisely, but in broad outline they appeared to represent an improvement over the earlier German attempts at extortion. The immigrants' travel expenses, as distinct from other costs of resettlement, would be financed by a trust fund amounting to at least one-fourth of the remaining Jewish wealth in Germany. According to Wohlthat, this fund would be organized by Hitler's government and administered by three trustees—two Germans and one foreigner. Wohlthat further pledged that Germany would rescind its 25 percent "flight tax." This levy against all Jews fleeing the Third Reich had contributed substantially to their status as destitute refugees.

No one seemed to know why the Germans had become so generous so suddenly. There was conjecture in the U.S. press that Göring had become alarmed by the excesses of his brown-shirted followers. Their vandalism and looting, directed originally against the Jews on the *Kristallnacht,* was now beginning to spread to non-Jewish targets. Some observers believed that the Nazi government might be losing control of its more fanatic elements and that the orderly departure of the Jews would remove the excuse for internal violence. Others attributed the new German moderation to the sharp decline in exports which had followed the November rioting. The condemnation of Germany by world-wide public opinion had affected businessmen if not their governments.

Whatever the reasons, Rublee was elated by the new German proposal. His optimism was heightened by simultaneous news of progress in the effort to locate homes for the refugees. The Philippine Commonwealth declared that it was considering the acceptance of one thousand annually and would examine the possibility of mass settlement in Mindanao; Generalissimo Trujillo's Dominican Republic would admit as many as a hundred thousand if adequate financing were assured; and The Netherlands had dispatched a commission to investigate potential havens in its colonies.

Rublee was warned by members of the Intergovernmental Committee that the Nazi offer should not be taken at face value. The financial details were still cloudy and there was an unexplained German refusal to include non-Jewish political refugees, including seventy-five thousand Catholics who wished to emigrate. Rublee was reminded that German assurances of good treatment of the Jews might be invalidated by one bullet hitting a Nazi anywhere in the world or by a fabricated incident that would again expose the Jews to the full fury of their captors.

The American negotiator, now eager to complete his mission and return to his law practice, visited Göring and was assured that Wohlthat's proposal had been made with the Generalfeldmarschall's full knowledge and consent. According to Göring, Hitler himself had approved the arrangements.

To the doubters Rublee retorted that the Intergovernmental Committee must accept German assurances of good faith. After all, the whole purpose of the Evian Conference had been to prepare for an agreement with the Hitler government. The London *Times* was among those sharing Rublee's viewpoint. Said the *Times* in an editorial: "It is certainly well worth while of the governments represented on the Evian committee to take these proposals at their face value and to construct their own plans for dealing with refugees accordingly."

In a hopeful telegram to Hull, Rublee called the German plan "a substantial departure from their previous policies" and he added that "they will put their program into effect when they are satisfied that the countries of immigration are disposed to receive currently Jews from Germany in conformity with the program."

Hull's political antennae must have quivered at this reference to countries of immigration, for he replied: "Insofar as our immigration laws are concerned, it is unthinkable that we could admit the right of another government to say whom we should or should not admit." Nevertheless, the Secretary of State congratulated Rublee on his achievement and made it clear that the success was unexpected. For one thing, the informal talks between Rublee and Wohlthat had taken place in a diplomatic no man's land, and each party was expected to proceed separately once general agreement had been reached. Technically Germany refused to accept the Intergovernmental Committee's intercession on behalf of German citizens, but this wary attitude was not unique to the Germans. Hull himself had stressed that German action in liberating the Jews should be taken unilaterally and not in concert with the Intergovernmental Committee. All this put Rublee in a somewhat ambiguous position, but he remained enthusiastic about the new German offer and the ensuing events.

Since the internal German trust fund would cover only part of the traveling expenses of the refugees, it would be necessary to raise a vast sum outside of Germany for the actual resettlement of the Jews, including the purchase of land and construction of housing. Members of the Intergovernmental Committee agreed that they should play no role in this endeavor. Instead, at the initiative of British Jews, the first steps were taken to create an international corporation which hopefully would lend as much as $300,000,000 to the destitute émigrés. This corporation would be entirely separate from the internal trust fund which would be organized by the German government.

With arrangements for the internal trust fund and international corporation under way, Rublee, convinced that he had achieved a provisional agreement with the Germans, resigned as director of the Intergovernmental Committee. The work of refining and implementing the plan was left to his successor, Sir Herbert Emerson. Rublee's resignation was effective February 13, 1939.

Ten days later the Germans gave the first indication that they had no intention of carrying out the agreement. Hermann Göring announced a new decree ordering "all German or stateless Jews" to surrender within two weeks all jewelry and objects of gold, silver and platinum, including silver knives, forks and spoons. This violated Wohlthat's assurances that there would be no further harassment of the Jews.

Two days later an even harsher announcement battered the foundations of the Rublee-Wohlthat plan. The Jewish community was ordered by police to provide the names of one hundred persons each day; those named would be required to leave Germany within two weeks. This set in motion the very panic which Rublee had sought to avert. There was as yet no place for the Jews to go and the police threatened severe punishment to those who remained beyond the two weeks. Simultaneously a new wave of economic disaster rolled across the Jewish community. Jews leaving Germany were required to pay an additional tax of up to 10 percent of the gross value of their possessions. The Nazis claimed that this would be put into a special fund to care for older Jews remaining in Germany. This payment would supplement the 20 percent fine still being levied on the Jews because of the death of Vom Rath and the 25 percent flight tax, which, in spite of Wohlthat's pledge, had not been rescinded. As if the above measures were not sufficient, Nazi ingenuity had devised an additional penalty; the departing Jews would now also pay an amount equal to the value of any new goods they wished to take out of the country.

The procedure for this legalized robbery would be as follows: as soon as the police received their daily quota of one hundred names, those chosen would pay the various fines listed above. They would then receive passports stamped with a large *J* to simplify immediate classification and would be ordered to obtain a visa from some country within fourteen days. The concentration camps and other German refinements awaited those unable to emigrate.

Sir Herbert Emerson, the new director of the Intergovernmental Committee, and his colleagues agreed that the new German regulations made their task virtually impossible. Nevertheless, there were fitful efforts to resume the negotiations, and Sir Herbert's vice-director, the American Foreign Service officer Robert T. Pell, continued to meet with Wohlthat.

In March 1939 Wohlthat inquired about the availability of areas for Jewish settlement. Pell put the question to the State Department, which replied that hoped-for sanctuaries had not yet materialized. Information about the Dominican Republic and British Guiana would not be available until mid-April, and the mission to Mindanao was still in the organizational stage. There seemed to be less than a sense of urgency about completing the various surveys of potential asylum. Meanwhile no action had been taken on the two key elements in the Rublee-Wohlthat plan; the Germans had done nothing to create their internal trust fund, and the British and American Jews, attempting to establish a private, international corporation, were floundering in disagreement.

Myron Taylor reported that there were three stumbling blocks to the establishment of the corporation. The British and American financiers feared that their activity might revive ancient accusations about "international Jewry"; they were concerned that an agreement with the German government might appear to condone Nazi racial policy and confiscation of property; and they were worried about the possibility that the corporation might strengthen the Germans economically.

In May the Gestapo permitted representatives of the German Jews to visit London to plead with the Intergovernmental Committee for immediate action. Pell attended the meeting. He reported to the State Department that the Jews had been told by the Gestapo that the international corporation must be established and refugee settlements located or "the German authorities would return to the shock tactics which were so successful in ridding Germany of Jews in the past."

Lord Winterton, in his lofty role as chairman of the Intergovernmental Committee, told the desperate Jews that the German police would not dictate to his committee "what it was and was not to do . . . There was a limit to the absorption of immigrants, whatever their race or religion, beyond which it was dangerous to go and it should be understood by the German authorities that the outside governments would not exceed this limit."

The Jewish delegation from Berlin explained that the Gestapo had enjoined them to return with a plan, and they begged for some piece of paper with which to placate the Nazis. According to Pell, "Emerson was adamant in his refusal to give them either a plan or a program.

"The group from Berlin was obviously very distressed," he continued. Next, they implored Emerson to send a letter to Lord Reading, a leading British Jew, assuring him that the committee would strive to bring a number of Jews from Germany. The delegation from Berlin would take a copy of this letter to the Gestapo as evidence of the committee's continuing activity. Emerson declined to write the letter.

The German visitors, by now frantic, asked Emerson simply to send Lord Reading a routine letter stating that the committee was proceeding with its assigned work and hoped to carry out its task successfully. "Emerson refused even to consider this minimum plea," wrote Pell.

The Jews returned to Berlin empty-handed.

In June 1939 the British, responding to relentless public pressures, suggested the possibility of raising $100,000,000 for refugee resettlement over a five-year period with governments matching the amounts raised by private subscription. The British acknowledged that this departed from the Evian agreement that all such financing must come from private sources, but they argued that the entire refugee effort would collapse without the infusion of government funds.

The Americans promptly discouraged the British suggestion. Hull reminded the Foreign Office that the matching of funds ran counter to congressional practice. In a cable to the State Department, Pell and Theodore Achilles, the third secretary of the American embassy in London, revealed another objection: if the new plan were adopted it would place the British "in a strong moral position" which they would exploit in the press. This was an upsetting thought to Pell and Achilles, who explained that "we who have contributed more than any other government or people to the solution of the refugee problem should get full credit before the public."

In another communication to the State Department on the same subject, Pell wrote: "To ask the general public and its representatives in Congress, most of whom have no direct interest in the problem other than a remote humanitarian one, to approve expenditures for this purpose would be Utopian."

During the controversy Sir Herbert Emerson, searching for the cause of the Intergovernmental Committee's failure to help the refugees, finally came up with the villain. "The trouble in this whole refugee affair," he told Pell, "was the trouble of the Jews and most eastern people. There was always some other scheme in the background for which they were prepared to sacrifice schemes which were already in hand."

The only tangible result of the endless studies of refugee havens was the founding of a small colony in the Dominican Republic. Herculean efforts by an American attorney, James N. Rosenberg, resulted in the placement of several hundred refugees, a far cry from the hundred thousand which the Dominican government had promised to welcome. In spite of its consistent record of failure, the Intergovernmental Committee remained the single international instrument for refugees, and Franklin Roosevelt refused to scrap it or replace it.

In a postscript to the dismal negotiations of 1939 Robert Pell, who was now the assistant chief of the State Department's Division of European Affairs, became aware that the President favored another meeting of the Intergovernmental Committee. As the committee's former vice-director he tried to dissuade FDR by a forceful memorandum:

"Assuming that this Government is genuinely concerned with ways and means of contributing to the alleviation of the political refugee situation, it must be said with all frankness that the practical approach is not through a meeting of a number of Ambassadors and Ministers under the aegis of Lord Winterton at Paris or some other point. These gentlemen, as in the past, will make pretty speeches, or in most cases will not speak at all. Mr. Taylor will offer a large banquet. A few of the representatives will make reports to their Governments, but most frankly admit that they do not even do that. The hopes of the unfortunate refugees will be raised by the announcement that a meeting is to be held and, as on previous occasions when the Committee has assembled, will be dashed to even lower depths after the session."

In a reply addressed to Secretary Hull, Roosevelt disagreed with Pell. The President asserted that the long-range purpose of the Intergovernmental Committee was important: "Even if this proposed meeting only 'makes pretty speeches,' it is worthwhile keeping this Committee very definitely alive."

In a technical sense, the committee remained alive.

■ XIV ■

"Suffer Little Children . . ."

EARLY IN 1939, AS GEORGE RUBLEE WAS negotiating for the release of German Jews, a campaign was launched in the United States to create a temporary haven for twenty thousand German children. The lead had already been taken by several countries: The Netherlands had reacted to the *Kristallnacht* by welcoming seventeen hundred German Jewish children, and overcrowded Belgium admitted several hundred more. But the most dramatic response was that of Great Britain, which opened its crowded island to more than nine thousand refugee children. The American journalist Quentin Reynolds reported the arrival at Dovercourt camp of these outcasts of a land whose laws had barred them from parks and playgrounds.

"When they heard the incredible news that no '*verboten*' signs existed at Dovercourt, they gave happy cries and rushed out onto the grass and rolled in it like kittens rolling in catnip. They tore tufts of it and pressed it against their cheeks. This was the first freedom any of them had ever known."

On January 9 a delegation of Roman Catholic and Protestant clergymen presented a petition to the White House calling upon the United States to open its doors to German children: "Working within and under the laws of Congress, through special enactment if necessary, the nation can offer a sanctuary to a part of these children by united expression of its will to help."

Senator Robert F. Wagner of New York, attempting to implement the clergymen's proposal, introduced a resolution in the Senate, and Representative Edith Nourse Rogers of Massachusetts offered an identical measure in the House of Representatives. Known as the Wagner-Rogers Bill, or Child Refugee Bill, it proposed that a maximum of ten thousand children under the age of fourteen be admitted in 1939 and a similar number in 1940. Their entry would be considered apart from and in addition to the regular German quota. They would be adopted temporarily by American families, with costs and responsibilities assumed by reputable individuals and organizations. The children would not be permitted to work, thus avoiding labor union charges of unfair competition, and they would be reunited with their parents as soon as safe living conditions were re-established.

The migration of the children would be supervised by the American Friends Service Committee. Appropriately it was the Quakers who had once saved the lives of German children. After the First World War the Friends had fed more than a million starving German children.

With their characteristic blend of idealism and pragmatism, the Quakers worked out the complex details of moving the twenty thousand children to the United States. In collaboration with child-care specialists, physicians, psychologists and refugee organizations of all faiths, they developed procedures for the selection, transportation, reception and distribution of the children. Clarence Pickett, executive secretary of the Quakers, was named to direct a large nonsectarian committee, assisted by Cardinal Mundelein of Chicago and Canon Anson Phelps Stokes of Washington Cathedral. Other committee members included Herbert Hoover; Alf Landon; William Allen

White; Owen D. Young, president of the General Electric Company; and some of the nation's leading educators, clergymen and businessmen. Hopefully their influence would persuade Congress and the American people to accept the youngsters as a group apart from the regular German quota.

Within a day after the plan was announced, four thousand families of all faiths had offered to adopt the children. Newspapers throughout the nation reported hundreds of telephone and mail inquiries from interested citizens.

Mrs. Roosevelt supported the Wagner-Rogers Bill, as indeed she backed every attempt to aid refugees. The President had not committed himself but the official White House attitude soon became known. Eddie Cantor was one of the first to find out.

Cantor, the popular comedian and singer, admired Roosevelt unreservedly. A warm, sentimental man, he had created the March of Dimes for the President's favorite cause, the National Foundation for Infantile Paralysis. Now the pop-eyed star of radio and films responded with characteristic enthusiasm to the proposal to admit refugee children. On January 12, 1939, he addressed an emotional letter to presidential secretary Marvin McIntyre. Cantor wrote that there were many more than ten thousand families in the United States willing to adopt the children, that far from hurting the nation economically, the arrival of the ten thousand would mean increased purchases of food and clothing.

"My dear Marvin," wrote Cantor, "for generations to come, if these boys and girls were permitted entry into this country, they would look upon our leader as a saint—they would bless the name of Franklin D. Roosevelt . . . If it met with the approval of the President, and Congress, I would furnish you with the names and references of the families willing to adopt these unfortunate children."

McIntyre sent Cantor's letter to Sumner Welles with a covering note: "The attached is self-explanatory and the President thought I might send it to you for your reaction. Confidentially, Eddie has been a very ardent worker for the Foundation, etc. I am wondering whether you could send him a discreet little note of appreciation or whether it would be safe for me to do it."

Welles thought it would be quite safe for McIntyre to reply, so the presidential secretary wrote to Mr. Cantor: "There is a general feeling, I believe, even among those who are most sympathetic towards the situation in which so many thousands of persons find themselves abroad, that it would be inadvisable to raise the question of increasing quotas or radical changes in our immigration laws during the present Congress. There is a very real feeling that if this question is too prominently raised in the Congress during the present session we might get more restrictive rather than more liberal immigration laws and practices."

Roosevelt feared the antagonism of Congress, for at that very moment he was seeking half a billion dollars from an isolationist Congress to expand the Air Corps and to construct naval bases. The President's priority clearly went to defense.

Many years later Eleanor Roosevelt would explain her husband's seeming indifference to crusades in which she participated actively. "While I often felt strongly on various subjects," she wrote in *This I Remember,* "Franklin frequently refrained from supporting causes in which he believed, because of political realities."

According to Mrs. Roosevelt, this accounted for the President's failure to give priority to such domestic matters as anti-lynching and anti-poll tax legislation. "When I would protest, he would simply say: 'First things come first, and I can't alienate certain votes I need for measures that are more important at the moment by pushing any measure that would entail a fight.' "

Mrs. Roosevelt, however, persisted in her efforts to awaken her husband's interest in the Wagner-Rogers legislation. While he was vacationing aboard the U.S.S. *Houston* she sent him a telegram: "Are you willing I should talk to Sumner and say we approve passage of Child Refugee Bill. Hope you are having grand time. Much love. Eleanor."

Mrs. Roosevelt's gentle persuasion did not work. Perhaps the President was inhibited by the sixty anti-alien bills before the Seventy-sixth Congress. Paradoxically, though he seemed indifferent to the fate of the children, he was warning Myron Taylor of impending new disasters facing the Jews.

On January 14, 1939, he cabled Taylor: "The fact must be faced that there exists in Central and Eastern Europe a racial and religious group of some seven million persons for whom the economic and social future is exceedingly dark. While the Intergovernmental Committee has wisely treated the German refugee problem as being one of involuntary emigration regardless of race, creed or political belief, it must be frankly recognized that the larger Eastern European problem is basically a Jewish problem. Acute as the German problem is, it is, I fear, only a precursor of what may be expected if the larger problem is not met before it reaches an acute stage and indications are rapidly increasing that such a stage may be reached in the near future."

Roosevelt doubted that Palestine could absorb a sufficient number of refugees and suggested that the Jews' best hope for resettlement lay in Africa, specifically in the Portuguese colony of Angola. He instructed Taylor to discuss with Prime Minister Neville Chamberlain the possibility of a British approach to the Portuguese dictator Salazar.

The British responded enthusiastically at first but eventually rejected the proposal. The Foreign Office explained that Portugal was sensitive about its colonies and might become offended by the suggestion.

As if to confirm Roosevelt's fears of more widespread anti-Semitism, Adolf Hitler made a speech on January 30 commemorating the day he had seized power six years before. He was quite candid: "Today I wish to be a prophet once more. Should international Jewry, inside and outside Europe, succeed once more in plunging the nations into war, the result will not be the Bolshevization of the earth and through it the victory of Jewry, but the annihilation of the Jewish race in Europe."

On March 15 Hitler, encouraged by the abject Franco-British surrender at Munich, dismembered Czechoslovakia. In the process he added more than three hundred thousand Jews to those already under his domination. Bohemia and Moravia became a Nazi protectorate and the Germans clamped an iron grip on Prague, which was crowded with Jewish refugees.

Slovakia was sliced from the former republic, and with the blessing of the Nazis, became an independent state under the leadership of the anti-Semitic priest Monsignor Josef Tiso. Carpatho-Ukraine, another portion of shattered Czechoslovakia, fell to Hungarian invaders. They too had received Nazi permission to plunder the corpse of the republic. In the three sections of the erstwhile democracy the new rulers were in agreement on how to treat the Jews.

Thus, by April 1939, when the first of two congressional hearings began on the proposal to admit twenty thousand children, all illusions about Nazi moderation had ended.

At the opening of the first hearings, held jointly by subcommittees of the House and Senate committees on immigration, a letter from Secretary Hull was read. As might have been anticipated, he wished to remind the legislators that the Wagner-Rogers resolution opened the door to a departure from the quota system. Moreover, granting twenty thousand German visas in addition "to an estimated 30,000 immigration visas now being issued annually in that country will inevitably necessitate increased clerical personnel, unfamiliar with the law and regulations, as well as additional office accommodations."

Senator Wagner made a fervent appeal for the passage of

his resolution. He reminded the committee members that the nation's leading Catholic and Protestant clergymen had signed a petition supporting it and he made a point that would be reiterated over and over during the following months: almost half the youngsters to be admitted would *not* be Jewish. He produced editorials from fifty-eight newspapers in favor of the bill, and he described the generosity of Great Britain, France, Belgium and The Netherlands in offering sanctuary to boys and girls from Germany.

Senator Wagner recalled Alexander Woollcott's story of the Jewish boy in Prague who entered a travel agency and said he wanted to buy a ticket.

"Where to?" asked the clerk.

"Well, what kind of tickets have you got?" inquired the boy. The clerk yawned and pushed forward a globe of the world.

The boy examined every inch of the globe, then said, "Haven't you got anything better?"

Wagner described the care with which the Quakers had organized every detail of the migration, the impeccable leadership of the Non-Sectarian Committee, and the spontaneous response of Americans from all walks of life. He stated that the admission of twenty thousand children could be of little economic consequence to a nation of 130,000,000.

He closed with the Biblical injunction: "Suffer little children to come unto me and forbid them not; for of such is the Kingdom of Heaven."

Former President Hoover and former presidential candidate Landon informed the committee of their support of the bill, as did representatives of the American Federation of Labor and Congress of Industrial Organizations.

Clarence Pickett, the Quaker who had agreed to lead the children's odyssey, asserted at the hearing that an issue more profound than that of helping German children faced the members of Congress. "That issue," he said, "is whether the American people have lost their ability to respond to such tragic situations as this one. If it turns out that we have lost that ability, it will mean that much of the soul has gone out of America."

Then came the opposition.

Francis H. Kinnicutt, president of the Allied Patriotic Societies, represented thirty organizations opposed to the legislation. These included the New York County organization of the American Legion, American Women Against Communism, Dames of the Loyal Legion, Veterans of Foreign Wars, United Daughters of the Confederacy, Daughters of the Defenders of the Republic, Society of Mayflower Descendants, Sons of the American Revolution, Daughters of the American Revolution, Lord's Day Alliance of the United States, and similarly titled groups.

Kinnicutt minced no words. He told the committee members that "we must recognize that this is just part of a drive to break down the whole quota system—to go back to the condition when we were flooded with foreigners who tried to run the country on different lines from those laid down by the old stock . . . Strictly speaking, it is not a refugee bill at all, for by the nature of the case most of those to be admitted would be of the Jewish race. And in the last two years we already have admitted eighty thousand Jewish refugees . . .

"The bill, if passed," said the spokesman for the patriots, "will be a precedent . . . in response to the pressure of foreign nationalistic or racial groups, rather than in accordance with the needs and desires of the American people."

The American Legion had earlier announced its support for Senator Robert R. Reynolds' bill abolishing all immigration to the United States for the next ten years. A North Carolinian of virulent racial views, Reynolds had become the principal spokesman for the restrictionists, surpassing even Martin Dies.

Colonel John Thomas Taylor, the American Legion's lobbyist, reaffirmed his organization's support of the Reynolds' bill and its opposition to the Wagner-Rogers proposal. "If this bill passes," warned the colonel, "there is no reason why we should not also bring in twenty thousand Chinese children. Certainly they are being persecuted too."

Representative Kramer of California reminded Colonel Taylor that the Oriental Exclusion Act would prevent the entry of the Chinese. To this the colonel replied contemptuously, "Why, you don't mean to say you'd let that law stand in the way of such great humanitarian ideals?"

The parade of hostile witnesses continued with Mrs. Agnes Waters of Washington, who claimed to represent the widows of World War I veterans.

"I am the daughter of generations of patriots," she proclaimed. "This nation will be helpless to guarantee to our children their rights, under the Constitution, to life, liberty, and the pursuit of happiness if this country is to become the dumping ground for the persecuted minorities of Europe. The refugees have a heritage of hate. They could never become loyal Americans." She characterized the prospective immigrants under fourteen years of age as "thousands of motherless, embittered, persecuted children of undesirable foreigners." She called them "potential leaders of a revolt against our American form of government . . .

"Why should we give preference to these potential Communists?" she asked. "Already we have too many of their kind in our country now trying to overthrow our government."

Mrs. Charles Fuller Winters, representing a Michigan group called Young Americans, Inc., testified in a somewhat similar vein: "I say if we are going to keep this country as it is and not lose our liberty in the future, we have got to keep not only these children out of it, but the whole damned Europe."

Margaret Hopkins Worrell, national legislative chairman of the Ladies of the Grand Army of the Republic, said her group agreed with Mrs. Winters "that the women of America should arise and defend their own children."

The Child Refugee Bill was next attacked by John B.

Trevor, representing the 115 patriotic societies of the American Coalition. Trevor, it will be remembered, had dedicated much of his public career to the cause of deporting the alien insane, but he was equally upset by the arrival of the alien sane. He too advocated a ten-year suspension of all immigration.

Trevor cited the outcome of a public-opinion poll which had been published in the April issue of *Fortune* magazine. Respondents had been asked, "If you were a member of Congress would you vote 'yes' or 'no' on a bill to open the doors of the United States to a larger number of European refugees than now admitted under our immigration quotas?" The results had been overwhelming: 83 percent had said "no," 8.3 percent had replied "Don't know" and a mere 8.7 percent had answered "yes."

Fortune reported that only 6.3 percent of the Protestants and 8.3 percent of the Catholics favored an increase in the quotas. In sharp contrast, 69.8 percent of the Jews called for larger quotas. "Here is an American tradition put to the popular test," concluded the editors of *Fortune*, "and here it is repudiated by a majority of nearly ten to one . . . The answer is the more decisive because it was made at a time when public sympathy for victims of European events was presumably at its highest."

In calling the attention of senators and congressmen to the *Fortune* findings, John B. Trevor illustrated effectively the gulf in American public opinion separating sympathy and action. Some months earlier a Gallup poll had revealed that 94 percent of the American people disapproved of the German treatment of the Jews, while 97 percent disapproved of the treatment of Catholics. Now the *Fortune* poll made it clear that mere disapproval of Nazi policies did not imply a willingness to take action against them. Franklin Roosevelt had put his political finger to the wind and had gauged its direction accurately. The thousands of Americans who had signified their interest in adopting youngsters were not representative of a universal American feeling. In the absence of presidential leadership, the Ladies of the Grand Army of the Republic appeared to reflect the American mood more accurately than the religious, civic or liberal groups.

In the face of the fierce opposition to the refugee children, the gentle testimony of witnesses such as Bishop Bernard Sheil, representing Cardinal Mundelein of Chicago, was barely audible.

"In providing them a sanctuary where they can grow up in the ways of peace and walk in the paths of righteousness," the bishop said of the children, "we will help not only them but ourselves. If we suffer little children to come unto us, we will demonstrate to the world our own devotion to the sanctity of human life."

The Unitarians spoke out in favor of the bill and Rabbi Stephen S. Wise appeared in its behalf. So did the YMCA and the YWCA and the Federal Council of the Churches of Christ, whose twenty-four Protestant denominations included twenty-two million church members.

The first hearings on the bill adjourned on April 24. The second, to be held before the House Committee on Immigration, would begin a month later. In the interim, supporters of the bill, alarmed by the passionate outpourings against it, sought to calm their antagonists.

Dr. Henry Smith Leiper, secretary of the Federal Council of Churches, focused public attention on the fact that refugees, far from becoming an economic burden to the United States, were stimulating the development of new industries and providing employment to American workers. Whole industries which had never existed in the United States had been transplanted from Europe by the refugees—Czechoslovakian glass, German dental tools, synthetic resins, Austrian handmade jewelry, needlepoint and tooled leather.

In a series of speeches Dr. Leiper supported his argument

with examples of businesses founded by refugees: a real estate development which had hired two hundred workers; a mill in Lawrence, Massachusetts, producing hosiery formerly imported from Germany; a dress firm employing seventy-five New Yorkers; and a Chicago shoe factory which had provided jobs for 147 previously unemployed craftsmen.

As might be expected, the Quakers were also active in support of the bill. Seeking to dispel the widely held myth that the nation was swarming with refugees, they published a booklet entitled *Refugee Facts.* According to official statistics, a total of 241,962 immigrants from all parts of the world had entered the United States in the six years from July 1, 1932, to July 1, 1938. During the same period 246,000 persons had left the country permanently, a *decrease* of almost 5,000 in the total population. Readers were reminded that the United States had admitted only 26 percent of its German quota during those six years.

Clarence Pickett spoke tirelessly in support of the Child Refugee resolution. He reported the findings of a British study which revealed that eleven thousand refugees had created fifteen thousand new jobs in England, and he kept hammering away at the fact that 31 percent of the German refugees admitted to the United States were Christian.

But on May 4 the national executive committee of the American Legion approved the recommendation of its National Americanism Commission to oppose the Wagner-Rogers measure because "it was traditional American policy that home life should be preserved and that the American Legion therefore strongly oppose the breaking up of families, which would be done by the proposed legislation." Apparently the spokesmen for the veterans regarded it as preferable for a family to remain together in a concentration camp than to send its youngsters to freedom in the United States.

The Americanism Commission was not opposed to all pending legislation in the field of immigration. It backed three of

Martin Dies's bills ostensibly aimed at alien radicals and it applauded other measures calling for swifter deportation procedures.

In New York City the new favorite of the "patriotic" lobby, Senator Robert R. Reynolds of North Carolina, addressed the American Defense Society. Calling for a repudiation of the Wagner-Rogers proposal, he warned that in the event of war, America would be swarming with spies. "The danger is from within," he declared, assailing "certain minorities." He charged that Americans were "asleep at the switch" and unaware of the activities of these minorities.

One of the most enthusiastic members of his audience was Fritz Kuhn, the Führer of the German American Bund. Asked about the senator's talk, Kuhn said, "I liked it very well. I would underline everything."

On May 17, 1939, a week before the House Committee on Immigration resumed the hearings on the proposed Wagner-Rogers legislation, the British published their White Paper on Palestine. It dealt a new and devastating blow to the Jews, limiting their immigration to seventy-five thousand during the next five years. The White Paper shut off escape from Europe at the very moment it was needed most. Total Jewish population would be held to one-third that of the Arabs, and the sale of land to Jews would be heavily restricted. In response to Arab violence the British announced that no further Jewish immigration would be permitted after the termination of the five-year period "unless the Arabs of Palestine are prepared to acquiesce in it."

"It is in the darkest hour of Jewish history," proclaimed the Jewish Agency for Palestine, "that the British Government proposes to deprive the Jews of their last hope and to close their road back to their homeland. It is a cruel blow, doubly cruel because it comes from the Government of a great nation which has extended a helping hand to the Jews and whose position in the world rests upon foundations of moral authority and international good faith. This blow will not subdue the Jewish people. The historic bond between the people and the land of Israel will not be broken."

It was a brave statement but the narrow gates of refuge were almost shut.

From the moment the House Immigration Committee, chaired by Representative Samuel Dickstein of New York, began the second round of hearings, it was clear that the proposal to admit twenty thousand children was in serious jeopardy.

Representative A. Leonard Allen of Louisiana set the mood as he questioned an American Federation of Labor lawyer who had supported the bill. He asked the A.F.L. man whether he would also agree to admit Polish, Russian and French children. The attorney replied that that was not the issue before the committee.

"In other words," snapped Allen, "you are a restrictionist until certain powers in the country begin to clamor for a certain bill and then you are ready to flop, is that right? . . . The Federation can do as it wishes to do, but I am going to stand for America. Put that down in the record."

Joe E. Brown, the wide-mouthed movie comedian, testified simply and eloquently about the need for the legislation. When he was challenged by the congressmen to state whether or not he personally would adopt a child, Brown quietly replied that he and his wife had already adopted two baby girls and that a young Serbian boy had been living with them for seven years.

This did not pacify Congressman Allen. "Would the gentleman advocate bringing the hordes of Europeans here," he asked, "when the record shows we have thousands and thousands of poor people in this country who are in want?" Brown assured the gentleman from Louisiana that his intention was not to harm Americans.

Frank P. Graham, president of the University of North Carolina, testified that the Wagner-Rogers proposal was consistent with the American tradition of providing a haven for religious and political refugees.

"That is the form of our government," agreed Chairman Dickstein, "but as a matter of fact, we have never done the things we preach. So far, during my time here, I do not think we have done that. We talked about it."

A rural Carolinian named Hugh McRae thought that the South could benefit from an infusion of new blood and said that he welcomed the prospect of refugees. This upset the Southern congressmen, who did not seem to share McRae's view.

A number of witnesses who had recently returned from Germany offered firsthand testimony of Nazi barbarism. Clarence Pickett described the fate of children banned from schools and parks and spat upon in the streets while their fathers languished in concentration camps. He repeated the sentiments of a Catholic priest who had said that the saddest thing of all was to see Aryans in church moving away from non-Aryans who had considered themselves Catholic for generations.

Pickett pleaded with the committee: "Unlike such catastrophes as fire or earthquake or tidal wave, which have commanded the help of America to unfortunates abroad so often in the past, this catastrophe threatens not only death but a living death, to thousands and thousands of children."

Quentin Reynolds testified on the basis of his two extended stays in Germany. In an exchange with Chairman Dickstein he made it clear that he believed the worst was yet to come.

DICKSTEIN: Do you contemplate . . . that there will be another pogrom?

REYNOLDS: I not only contemplate it, but I am confident the complete pogrom is not very far away.

DICKSTEIN: In other words, there will be a new slaughter?

REYNOLDS: Yes, there is no doubt about that.
DICKSTEIN: Annihilation?
REYNOLDS: Yes, a complete pogrom.

When Congressman Allen asked where the thousands of German children would find homes, Dickstein turned to Reynolds and said, "Between you and me we can dispose of the ten thousand."

"Yes, in an hour," replied Reynolds.

As the hearings continued, the restrictionists concentrated their fire on the bill's alleged threat to the quota system. They were quite willing to admit the youngsters *within* the German quota and they pointed out that past German immigration had fallen more than ten thousand below the quota limits.

Chairman Dickstein agreed that this had been true in the past, but pointed out that the present German quota was swamped with applicants and filled for years ahead. The opponents of the legislation then suggested that the children be given preference over the adults who had already filed for immigration.

Colonel John Thomas Taylor, making his return appearance on behalf of the American Legion, echoed this theme. "If the real purpose is to help these children," he argued, "the matter can be handled by giving them preference within the regular immigration quotas this year and next."

John B. Trevor returned to champion the quota system and submitted a list of his 115 organizations. In addition to groups already named, the American Coalition of Patriotic Societies represented the united passions of the Colonial Order of the Acorn, the American Christian Crusade, American Vigilant Intelligence Federation, Order of Colonial Lords of Manors in America and the Tax Evils Committee of Council Bluffs, Iowa.

A novel argument against the legislation was presented by F. W. Buck, representing the Defenders of the Constitution, a group which had somehow escaped the jurisdiction of John B. Trevor. Mr. Buck said he was worried about anti-Semitic reactions in the United States to the arrival of the twenty thousand children.

Chairman Dickstein reminded Mr. Buck that Protestant and Catholic children would also be entering the country if the bill passed.

"We feel the bill will tend to create more opposition to the Jews," Mr. Buck insisted, "and we don't want to do that, because they're nice people."

The hearings before the House Committee on Immigration ended on June 1. The next day President Roosevelt received a memo from "Pa" Watson, one of his aides. Watson reported that Representative Caroline O'Day of New York had asked for an expression of Mr. Roosevelt's views on the Wagner-Rogers Bill. The President picked up a pencil and scrawled on the memo: "File No Action FDR."

On July 1 the Child Refuge Bill was finally reported out with one modification: the twenty thousand youngsters' visas over the next two years would be issued against the German quota, not in excess of the quota.

Senator Wagner, the German-born Catholic who had pioneered in labor legislation and who had experienced the benefits of immigration, was appalled by the amendment. He realized that the twenty thousand children might become twenty thousand death warrants for the adults they would displace.

"The proposed change," he said, "would in effect convert the measure from a humane proposal to help children who are in acute distress to a proposal with needlessly cruel consequences for adults in Germany who are in need of succor and are fortunate to obtain visas under the present drastic quota restrictions."

Wagner took the only course now open to him. He withdrew his legislation. The plan was dead. The ladies of the Grand

Army of the Republic and the philosophers of the American Legion had triumphed. They had won their war against the children. The aliens had tried to breach the walls of the mighty Republic but the patriots had withstood their assault.

■ XV ■

The Voyage of the St. Louis

EVEN AS THE CONGRESS AND THE PEOPLE OF the United States were debating the merits of admitting the refugee children, a drama of human survival was being enacted on the high seas. It was a voyage which would hold up a mirror to mankind.

On May 13, 1939, the Hamburg-American Line's luxurious *St. Louis* sailed from Germany with 936 passengers. They were bound for Havana, Cuba—930 of them Jewish refugees, among the last to escape from the Nazis' narrowing vise. Inscribed on each passport was a red *J* and in each mind the memory of six years of ever-increasing terror.

Each refugee had managed to scrape together $262 for passage, plus $81 as a guarantee for return fare in the event Cuba would not accept them. But this was a mere formality, since they all held official landing certificates signed by Colonel Manuel Benites, Cuba's director general of immigration.

For 734 of the refugees, Cuba would be but a temporary sanctuary, a way station en route to their future home—the United States. They had fulfilled U.S. immigration requirements, completed labyrinthine forms and now held quota numbers which would permit them to enter the United States from three months to three years after their arrival in Cuba.

Since the refugees could not get into the United States immediately, the Cuban landing certificates were literal lifesavers. The Hamburg-American Line had bought them from representatives of Colonel Benites and had resold them at an average of $150 apiece. As the Jews had long since been removed from the economic life of Germany, and as all their possessions were gone, fined or sequestered, the effort of raising these sums had been prodigious. Few were left with more than the $4 in cash they were allowed to take abroad.

But the memory of the *Kristallnacht* in November 1938 was still fresh in their minds, and the afterimage of burning synagogues and brown-shirted mobs still clear. That moment of horror passed, but afterward they had no longer been allowed to walk in the parks and even their passage through the streets was restricted to prescribed routes of drabness. Suddenly they had been plucked from the shabby streets of their ghettos, and through the alchemy of a Benites landing certificate, ushered into the carpeted public rooms of a luxury liner. Defined as subhuman by their oppressors, they were now serenaded by a German string quartet, performers and audience responding as though the first six years of the Third Reich had been left on the receding shore.

There was Dr. Max Loewe, a lawyer from Breslau who at the age of fourteen had fought for his Fatherland in the World War and had been decorated for heroism. He was traveling with his mother, his wife Elise, and their children Ruth, age seventeen, and Fritz, twelve. Dr. Loewe limped when he walked, for the soles of his feet had been beaten in a concentration camp. His whole family looked forward to their new life except for the elderly grandmother, who cried continuously.

There were the Guttmanns, who had married in Berlin and were honeymooning aboard the *St. Louis*. Eva Broeder, a twenty-one-year-old art student, observed them with special attention, because her fiancé would be waiting on the dock in Havana. So would the wife and small children of Bruno Glade, a concert pianist from Berlin.

The poster artist Moritz Schoenberger could now plan contentedly for his new life. His wife and eighteen-year-old daughter were already in the United States, preparing to meet him in Cuba. Moritz Weiler, an elderly university professor, was less optimistic. It would be difficult to begin life again and there would be no loved ones waiting in Havana, but at least he would find a haven after the years of terror. For sixty-seven-year-old Rabbi Gelder the voyage had only one objective—final reunion with his two sons who had preceded him into exile.

One of the busiest passengers was Frau Feilchenfeld of Breslau; she was traveling with her four children, ranging from one to eleven, traveling toward reunion with her husband in New York.

As they sailed from Hamburg on that happy day, none was aware that eight days earlier President Federico Laredo Bru of Cuba had signed decree number 93 invalidating their landing certificates. From now on refugees would be required to carry visas approved by the Cuban State, Labor and Treasury departments. The thousands upon thousands of blank landing certificates sold to the Hamburg-American Line for resale to desperate refugees were worthless.

The new Cuban regulation had been brought to the attention of the company before the ship sailed, but somehow the passengers had never been notified—nor had Captain Gustav Schroeder, the extraordinary commander of the *St. Louis*.

Before the first hint of trouble, the voyage of the *St. Louis* was a dreamlike odyssey, a moment out of time, an excursion from reality. The travelers were not treated as refugees but as passengers with all the attentions and courtesies to which fare-paying guests are entitled. The usual deck games, *dansants* and polite conversation occupied the day. The voyagers reclined in deck chairs, sipped their coffee and enjoyed excellent meals in the elegant dining rooms. One would never know from the attitude of the stewards that they were serving members of a despised race. It was perhaps too soon for the passengers to realize that they were being guided on this unusual voyage by an unusual German. Captain Schroeder was making amends on this one journey for the entire German nation.

But before the ship reached Havana, telegrams from Cuban officials indicated that there was doubt, serious doubt, about the validity of the passengers' documents. These first warning notes shattered the illusion of a graceful pleasure cruise and a wave of panic swept the ship. The fears which had been dissipated by days of civilized treatment returned with their old clutching intensity. Professor Weiler fell ill and declined rapidly. Even the ship's comedian, Max Schlesinger of Vienna, had difficulty in forcing smiles from his fellow passengers.

The questions were endless. What about loved ones waiting at the pier? Would passengers be permitted ashore while their papers were being studied? Could children come aboard? What about baggage and furniture shipped ahead? And how was it possible that the signature of Manuel Benites, director general of immigration, authorizing the undersigned to land in Cuba, could be open to question?

The 734 passengers who held American immigration quota numbers considered that they had an extra margin of safety. If their worst fears were justified and the ship was forced to return to Germany, surely the United States would waive the formalities of delay to save their lives.

Captain Schroeder sought to relieve the wild apprehensions gripping his passengers. He assured them that he would make every effort to influence the Cuban authorities to honor the landing certificates. But it was 1939 and the refugees knew the scent of danger. Nothing was unimaginable. They had seen too many impossible cruelties to doubt the probability of yet another. In the midst of their anguish Professor Weiler died.

Later Captain Schroeder described his passing. "It broke his heart to feel that in his old age, he had to leave the land where, all his life long, he had worked on the best of terms with his colleagues . . . one felt that his will to live had gone." Moritz Weiler was buried at sea. Captain Schroeder feared that the presence of his body aboard the *St. Louis* would give the Cuban government an excuse to turn away the ship.

On May 27 the *St. Louis* docked at Havana. No one was allowed ashore. Guards patrolled the pier, preventing friends and relatives of the passengers from boarding the ship. Those who had come to greet the refugees hired boats and circled the ship, shouting messages of encouragement. They included Eva Broeder's fiancé, Moritz Schoenberger's wife and daughter, and Bruno Glade's family.

One man paddled a canoe close to the *St. Louis* while his wife held their two babies at the porthole. The scene was repeated day after day. At night searchlights attached to the sides of the vessel probed the surrounding waters to reveal any passengers trying to swim to freedom.

Twenty-eight passengers were allowed to leave the ship. Twenty-two were refugees who, skeptical of the landing certificates, had hired lawyers in Europe to obtain more complete documentation. For payment of legal fees plus $500 they had received visas authorized by the Cuban State, Treasury and Labor departments. The other six passengers permitted to leave the *St. Louis* permanently consisted of a Cuban couple and four visiting Spaniards. Nine hundred and eight passengers remained aboard.

The Cuban government position was that the landing certificates had been sold illegally, and Cuba must insist upon strict adherence to its laws. Furthermore, Cuba had admitted a greater number of refugees proportionately than the richer nations. The government neglected to mention that the arrival of the *St. Louis* had coincided with a wave of anti-Semitism in the Cuban press, radio and Congress, together with fierce rivalry among pro and antigovernment forces for the millions of dollars which might be extracted from desperate refugees.

The passengers' distress became a front-page newspaper story in the United States. The fact that a German vessel had carried a large number of refugees toward safety only to be rebuffed at the very gates of salvation added a bizarre note. The press conjectured whether they would return to face slow death in a ghetto or a concentration camp. American readers followed the story with fascination.

On May 28 the Joint Distribution Committee sent two representatives to Havana. One was Cecilia Razovsky, the social worker who earlier had organized German Jewish Children's Aid. She would concentrate on arrangements for the housing, schooling and well-being of the *St. Louis* passengers if they were permitted to enter Cuba. The JDC's second emissary was Lawrence Berenson, a prominent New York lawyer who had headed the Cuban Chamber of Commerce in the United States. He was assigned to negotiate with the Cuban government for the landing of passengers. Among other assets, Berenson had been a personal friend of Fulgencio Batista, Chief of Staff of the Cuban Army. The JDC had authorized the lawyer to post a bond up to $125,000 guaranteeing that none of the passengers would become economically dependent upon the Cuban government. The JDC was prepared to offer further assurances that the refugees would not seek employment in Cuba while they awaited reimmigration.

President Bru agreed to meet Berenson on June 1, but on May 31 Captain Schroeder was notified that the *St. Louis* must depart the following day. The captain, who had been trying to contact the President himself to urge that the refugees be permitted ashore, notified Cuban authorities that he feared a wave of suicides if the ship were forced to leave.

That very day, as if to justify his captain's prediction, Max Loewe, the lawyer from Breslau, World War hero and former concentration camp inmate, slashed his wrists and leaped overboard. He was pulled from the water and rushed in grave condition to a hospital ashore. He was thus the first of the unauthorized refugees to touch Cuban soil. His wife and children were not permitted to leave the ship.

On June 1, prior to his meeting with Berenson, President Bru signed a decree ordering the ship to leave Havana but postponing its departure until the next day. The decree provided that in the event of noncompliance, the Cuban navy would "conduct" the vessel outside of Cuban waters.

Despite the announced departure, the President kept his appointment with Berenson. The Cuban Chief Executive was cordial and stated his sympathy for the refugees. He indicated hostility only toward the Hamburg-American Line, which he felt was attempting to lessen the dignity of his government by pressuring for admittance of its passengers.

Berenson outlined the JDC plan in general terms. In discussing the bond, he pointed out that it would be reduced proportionately as the refugees were admitted to the United States. It was clear in this opening conversation that the JDC had not set aside any sums for the private pockets of Cuban officials.

The President was courteous but adamant. "I have already stated that the ship must go out," he said. "I won't permit it to remain in the harbor. I will talk with you after that is done."

Bru then indicated that the *St. Louis* need sail only to the twelve-mile limit. and he implied that thus Cuba would save face while he and Berenson negotiated specific terms for the eventual landing of the passengers.

Berenson, in constant telephone contact with the Joint Distribution Committee in New York, communicated his guarded optimism about ultimate success. But there was a new and serious worry. JDC suggestions in Washington that the government offer temporary haven to those refugees who possessed U.S. immigration numbers had been rebuffed unqualifiedly. There would be no compromise with the immigration laws. More than that, the State Department notified the JDC that it knew of no South American country which would permit the refugees temporary entry. It was up to Berenson.

On Friday, June 2, at 11 A.M., the *St. Louis* sailed for Hamburg with its 907 passengers. Hardened newspapermen in accompanying launches wept openly as hundreds of refugees lined the rails imploring Cuba for mercy and straining for a final sight of loved ones on the dock. The refugees had been reassured by Captain Schroeder that he would delay as much as possible at sea while negotiations continued ashore, but nevertheless, the destination *was* Germany. Although the Cuban government had admitted that its officials had not been entitled to accept payments for the landing certificates, it neglected to return $150 to each of the destitute passengers.

Rabbi Gelder, whose two sons were on the pier, was heard to murmur, "I wish that I could have shaken their hands."

Eva Broeder saw her fiancé and exchanged hurried messages but they were never close enough for a private word.

A pantomime was enacted by twenty-three-year-old Gerda Weiss and her fiancé who had brought the marriage license and ring to the pier. The pantomime ended with waves of goodbye, perhaps forever.

Max Loewe remained at Calixto García Hospital in serious condition after his suicide attempt. His wife, mother and two children were still not allowed ashore.

Captain Schroeder, who had written to President Bru that he would not be responsible for the fate of the refugees if they returned to Germany, had posted an encouraging message on the bulletin board: "The shipping company is going to remain in touch with various organizations and official bodies which will endeavor to effect a landing outside Germany. We shall try to stay somewhere in the vicinity of South American countries."

Cecilia Razovsky, whose plans for housing the refugees in Cuba now seemed academic, switched her attention to the morale of the passengers. Each day she sent a series of telegrams to the ship describing efforts that were being made to find sanctuary. To forestall suicide attempts aboard the *St. Louis,* word was spread that the U.S. government had authorized the refugees' landing in New York if efforts for their entry into Cuba failed. But, as the *New York Times* observed: "Kept from them was the news from Washington that government officials there said no arrangements had been made for them to land in New York or any other United States port."

As the *St. Louis* steamed very slowly under the concerned command of Captain Schroeder, Lawrence Berenson found himself in an utterly confusing tug of war with shifting Cuban factions. A Havana lawyer who was assisting him said that he had seen a letter in President Bru's handwriting empowering two of his henchmen to collect $500,000 in cash from Berenson in exchange for sanctuary for the *St. Louis* passengers.

Soon after this report two men identified themselves on the telephone as representatives of the President and requested an appointment. Berenson refused to meet them, whereupon they threatened to shoot him. Later, as Berenson walked in the park, two men darted from the bushes and demanded the $500,000 they said they knew he was carrying. Berenson emptied his pockets to prove that he was not strolling in the park with half a million dollars, so the men left without harming him.

Berenson's next meeting with the President was scheduled for Sunday, June 4. His old friend Batista, who had refused to see him (he was sulking at army headquarters in Camp Colombia while his rival Bru was ensconced in the presidential palace), sent word through an emissary that Berenson should not yield to Bru's exorbitant demands. The situation was further complicated when a former associate of Benites, who had been removed as director general of immigration, burst into Berenson's room late at night.

"I know that you have one million dollars right there in your pocket," he said. Speaking on Benites' behalf, he offered to arrange for the reception of the *St. Louis* passengers on Cuba's Isle of Pines. It would cost Berenson a mere $450,000. This would include a $50,000 fee and a $150,000 contribution to Batista's next election campaign.

Berenson reported the Benites proposal to Batista via an intermediary of the Chief of Staff. "Absolutely nothing doing on shakedowns," replied Batista. "We will do this job without any such talk."

The emissary then told Berenson that the JDC bond would be sufficient and that both Bru and Batista would co-operate to settle the problem. He assured the lawyer that all arrangements would be completed in time for his meeting with President Bru.

On Sunday, the hopeful Berenson arrived at the President's country estate, only to realize immediately that no arrangements had been made.

"We have to have a cash deposit," said the President, tight-lipped. He then announced his terms: $500 for each man, woman and child *plus* full maintenance guarantees—almost $1,000,000. Berenson said it would take time to raise such an amount; Bru told him that the ship could be recalled if the money was available within forty-eight hours.

The Havana lawyer who had been assisting Berenson was present at the meeting. Surprised that Berenson had not accepted the Cuban President's proposal, he became angry. "Berenson," he snapped, "you know those rich Jewish fellows from Sears, Roebuck and Kuhn, Loeb can underwrite a million dollars in ten minutes. My friend was telling me how they all sit around and one says, 'I'll give you fifty thousand dollars and the next fellow says, 'I'll give you sixty thousand dollars.' "

While Berenson and the President discussed the cash requirements for rescue, the *St. Louis* hovered off the city of Miami. Captain Schroeder was delaying his return to Hamburg as long as possible, offering his 734 passengers with United States immigration papers a glimpse of their future homeland. The United States Coast Guard cutter *244* shadowed the *St. Louis,* with orders to prevent any refugees from jumping overboard and swimming ashore.

Newspaper descriptions of the scene prompted Bishop James Cannon, Jr., of Richmond, Virginia, to write a letter to the *Richmond Times-Dispatch:*

". . . the press reported that the ship came close enough to Miami for the refugees to see the lights of the city. The press also reported that the U.S. Coast Guard, under instructions from Washington, followed the ship . . . to prevent any people landing on our shores. And during the days when this horrible tragedy was being enacted right at our doors, our government in Washington made no effort to relieve the desperate situation of these people, but on the contrary gave orders that they be kept out of the country. Why did not the President, Secretary of State, Secretary of the Treasury, Secretary of Labor and other officials confer together and arrange for the landing of these refugees who had been caught in this maelstrom of distress and agony through no fault of their own? . . . The failure to take any steps whatever to assist these distressed, persecuted Jews in their hour of extremity was one of the most disgraceful things which has happened in American history and leaves a stain and brand of shame upon the record of our nation."

While the *St. Louis* inched along the Florida coast, Lawrence Berenson received authorization from the JDC to make a new offer to the Cuban government increasing the bond to

$500 in cash for each passenger. Berenson checked with the American ambassador, J. Butler Wright, who urged him to keep the offer as low as possible; the State Department had told the ambassador that the Cubans were bluffing in their demands.

On June 5 President Bru called a press conference and announced Cuba's willingness to receive the *St. Louis* refugees in a camp on the Isle of Pines. The President added that it was absolutely necessary that the refugees' food, lodging, reembarkation and other needs be guaranteed. If these guarantees were not forthcoming by noon of June 6, the offer would expire.

Then President Bru told the press about his personal anguish: "The post that I occupy has painful duties, which oblige me to disregard the impulses of my heart and follow the stern dictates of duty."

Berenson had already prepared an itemized statement of the JDC's new proposal, involving an initial deposit of $443,000. By arrangement, the President's representative, a major in the secret police, would bring this statement to a meeting with Bru and Batista at ten o'clock in the evening.

Two hours before the presidential meeting, the major went to Berenson's house and picked up the document. He glanced at it quickly, assured Berenson that it would be accepted and promised that he would telephone immediately after the meeting. In any case, the major would meet Berenson at ten o'clock the following morning to iron out any remaining details.

There was no telephone call. The next day the frantic Berenson was unable to reach any of the Cuban officials. He went to the police station at ten o'clock, but the major had left word that he was detained at the presidential palace. The President, no doubt following the stern dictates of duty, had left word that he was not to be disturbed. During the morning there was one approach to Berenson by an intermediary of the major who inquired whether the JDC was prepared to give the major a gift "after this thing is over." Berenson said he would consider a small gift.

At noon the Cuban government announced that its deadline for the guarantee of the refugees' maintenance had passed and that its offer of sanctuary on the Isle of Pines had been withdrawn. The Havana lawyer whom Berenson had dealt with explained why the offer had been canceled. "They were aware of all that cash," he said, "and they finally realized that nothing was to be handed out."

Berenson asked the Cuban how much the government officials had expected as their personal payoff.

"At least three hundred and fifty thousand dollars, in addition to the deposits," replied the lawyer.

The JDC made one final effort to persuade the Cuban government, and deposited $500,000 in a Havana bank, but President Bru replied that the case was closed.

At eleven-forty on Tuesday evening, June 6, 1939, the *St. Louis* finally ended her idle cruising and set her course for Europe. Captain Schroeder would proceed directly—but slowly. A committee of passengers addressed a telegram to Franklin D. Roosevelt asking help for 907 passengers, "of which more than 400 are women and children." There was no reply.

On June 9, as the refugees sailed toward a fate that was no longer in doubt, the *New York Times* editorialized: "It is hard to imagine the bitterness of exile when it takes place over a faraway frontier. Helpless families driven from their homes to a barren island in the Danube, thrust over the Polish frontier, escaping in terror of their lives to Switzerland or France, are hard for us in a free country to visualize. But these exiles floated by our own shores. Some of them are on the American quota list and can later be admitted here. What is to happen to them in the interval has remained uncertain from hour to hour. We can only hope that some hearts will soften somewhere and some refuge be found. The cruise of the *St. Louis* cries to high heaven of man's inhumanity to man."

Nowhere in the *Times*'s editorial nor in the archives of the United States government is there a suggestion that the refugees be sheltered temporarily within the capacious boundaries of the United States. Nowhere was their grave danger related to the American experience. Except for the Jewish community there was no upsurge of feeling among the American people, all sons, daughters or descendants of immigrants, to come to the aid of these men, women and children floating across the Atlantic toward certain doom, guilty of no crime, accused of no offense, victims only of the accident of birth.

In all the United States only one organization rose to the challenge of the *St. Louis*—the Joint Distribution Committee. On June 9, with Captain Schroeder heading slowly—but directly—for Hamburg, the passengers sent the JDC a cry for help: "We ask in great despair your assistance for disembarkation at Southampton or asylum in benevolent noble France."

Morris Troper, the JDC's European chairman with headquarters in Paris, was put in charge of the rescue operation. Troper was barraged with telegrams from New York recounting the JDC's failure to find havens: "INTERVENTION COLOMBIA WITHOUT PROSPECTS STOP IMMIGRATION CLOSED"; "CHILE: NOTHING DOING ST. LOUIS ACCOUNT POLITICAL SITUATION"; "PARAGUAY YET UNDECIDED"; "ARGENTINE UNDERTAKING STEPS DOUBTFUL RESULTS." From the New York office he received an ominous cable: "REGARD THESE PASSENGERS AS DOOMED ONCE THEY REACH GERMAN SOIL . . . WE WOULD WANT TO BE ASSURED NO SINGLE POSSIBILITY OF ESCAPE SHOULD FAIL TO BE GIVEN UTMOST CONSIDERATION . . . TIME IS OF ESSENCE BOAT HAS COMPLETED MORE THAN HALF OF TRIP."

Another message on June 10 reaffirmed the continuing inability of the JDC to budge the United States government: "ANY IMMIGRATION THIS SIDE OF WATER . . . IS OUT OF

QUESTION. THIS WE HAVE NOT COMMUNICATED TO PASSENGERS BUT WISH YOU TO KNOW."

On the *St. Louis* itself the passengers formed a committee of the most stable personalities to prevent suicide by constant patrolling of the decks.

The children played a game which Captain Schroeder later described. Two small boys with stern expressions guarded a barrier constructed of chairs. Other youngsters lined up asking permission to pass through.

"Are you a Jew?" asked one of the guards.

"Yes," replied the child at the barrier.

"Jews not admitted!" snapped the guard.

"Oh, please let me in. I'm only a very little Jew."

In Paris, Morris Troper began a round-the-clock effort to find havens for his 907 charges. He concentrated on European relief agencies which the JDC helped to support, and once again guaranteed the maintenance costs of the passengers. First he telephoned Max Gottschalk, president of the Refugee Committee of Brussels. The next morning Gottschalk spoke to Belgian Minister of Justice Janson, asking him to admit 200 passengers, 150 with U.S. quota numbers. Janson said he would have to consult the Prime Minister. At twelve-thirty that same day the Chef du Cabinet phoned Gottschalk and told him that the Prime Minister had approved. Later Belgium agreed to accept an additional 50 passengers, all with American immigration papers.

Next Troper contracted Gertrude Van Tijn of the Amsterdam Refugee Committee. She wired Minister of Justice Goseling while some of her non-Jewish acquaintances approached Queen Wilhelmina. On June 12 Minister Goseling announced that Holland would welcome 194 of the passengers.

With sanctuary found in two countries and appeals underway in England, Portugal and Luxembourg, Troper wired Captain Schroeder, who was still making minimum speed toward Hamburg: "WISH INFORM YOU MAKING EVERY EFFORT

LAND YOUR PASSENGERS WITH SEVERAL POSSIBLE PROSPECTS ENROUTE WHICH WE HOPE WILL BECOME DEFINITE NEXT THIRTY-SIX HOURS."

Aboard the *St. Louis* the antisuicide patrol and the encouraging attitude of Captain Schroeder and his crew were calming the more volatile voyagers. Max Schlesinger, the irrepressible comic from Vienna, raced around the decks urging passengers to "get bronzed in the sun. We're on a cruise. Let's enjoy it." But passengers agreed that the most inspiring example was set by Frau Feilchenfeld, formerly of Breslau. Headed back toward Germany with her four small children, separated no doubt forever from her husband in New York, she maintained a bearing and dignity which bolstered the courage of those on the edge of panic.

Troper now met with Mme. Louise Weiss, secretary general of the Central Refugee Committee in Paris. At three-forty on June 12 Mme. Weiss telephoned him to say that she had just seen Foreign Minister Georges Bonnet, who said he would authorize the admittance of several hundred passengers if it was approved by Minister of the Interior Sarraut. At six o'clock Troper, Mme Weiss and others met with the minister. They informed him that Paul Baerwald, chairman of the Joint Distribution Committee, had reported from London that the British would probably admit 250 passengers. Minister Sarraut promptly agreed to accept a similar number.

On Tuesday, June 13, Troper wired the passengers' committee on the *St. Louis*: "FINAL ARRANGEMENTS FOR DISEMBARKATION ALL PASSENGERS COMPLETED HAPPY INFORM YOU GOVERNMENTS OF BELGIUM, HOLLAND, FRANCE, AND ENGLAND COOPERATED MAGNIFICENTLY WITH AMERICAN JOINT DISTRIBUTION COMMITTEE."

The reply was swift. "THE 907 PASSENGERS OF ST. LOUIS DANGLING FOR LAST THIRTEEN DAYS BETWEEN HOPE AND DESPAIR RECEIVED TODAY YOUR LIBERATING MESSAGE . . . OUR GRATITUDE IS AS IMMENSE AS THE OCEAN ON WHICH WE

ARE NOW FLOATING SINCE MAY 13 FIRST FULL OF HOPE FOR A GOOD FUTURE AND AFTERWARDS IN THE DEEPEST DESPAIR . . . ACCEPT THE DEEPEST AND ETERNAL THANKS OF MEN WOMEN AND CHILDREN UNITED BY THE SAME FATE ON BOARD THE ST. LOUIS."

The ship altered course to land its passengers at Antwerp, Belgium, where transportation would be provided to their respective countries of asylum. In Britain, France, Holland and Belgium, citizens' committees joined government officials in planning the reception and housing of the refugees.

Morris Troper attended one such meeting in Paris, presided over by M. Bussières, chief of the French national police. M. Bussières expressed his regrets that the United States, the country to which most of the refugees were bound eventually, had not been able to welcome them to an American port but instead sent them all the way to Europe. But everyone was too happy over the zero-hour rescue to consider the other implications of the month-long odyssey.

At four o'clock in the morning of June 17 Morris Troper, who had worked without rest from the moment Cuba rejected the *St. Louis*, boarded the ship in the waters off Flushing, two hours from Antwerp. Later he wrote; "No words can describe the feelings of everyone on the tug when sighting the *St. Louis* with its human cargo, all standing as one man along the rails on the portside of the steamer."

One hundred children greeted the representative of the Joint Distribution Committee. Leisel Joseph, aged eleven, was the official spokesman. "Dear Mr. Troper," she said, "we the children of the *St. Louis* wish to express to you and through you to the American Joint Distribution Committee our deep thanks from the bottom of our hearts for having saved us from a great misery. We pray that God's blessing be upon you. We regret exceedingly that flowers do not grow on the ship, otherwise we would have presented to you the largest and most beautiful bouquet."

In the final disposition of the passengers, 214 went to Belgium, 287 to England, 181 to Holland and 224 to France. The 907th passenger turned out to be Mr. I. Winkler, a traveling salesman from Hungary who had got aboard the *St. Louis* inadvertently—an error, as he had found out, of considerable magnitude. As soon as the ship docked he hurried off as rapidly as possible.

Max Loewe, the lawyer left in the Havana hospital, recovered eventually and rejoined his family in France.

Sir Osbert Peake, Undersecretary in the British Home Office, announced that Britain's action in the *St. Louis* episode was not to be regarded as a precedent, and the London *Daily Express* echoed his words: "This example must not set a precedent. There is no room for any more refugees in this country . . . they become a burden and a grievance."

The story had a temporarily happy ending but the happiness was not to last for long. On September 1, 1939, World War II began with the German invasion of Poland. The only *St. Louis* refugees protected from the Nazi terror were those who had found sanctuary in Britain. Many—it is impossible to know how many—died in the German gas chambers following the Nazi invasions of Belgium, Holland and France. It may be that a few were able to utilize their American immigration numbers and sail past the Statue of Liberty to that final haven denied them earlier.

Captain Schroeder, unbeknownst to his Hamburg-American Line superiors, had considered beaching the *St. Louis* on the coast of England if the JDC efforts failed. He returned to Germany and was unmolested. After the war he was decorated by the West German government for his conduct.

The United States' rejection of the *St. Louis* passengers was not lost on Hitler or his propagandists. It was only one of many indications that his treatment of the Jews would not expose him to the wrath of the United States. The August 1939 issue of *Der Weltkampf* commented upon democratic pretense and reality:

"We are saying openly that we do not want the Jews while the democracies keep on claiming that they are willing to receive them—and then leave the guests out in the cold! Aren't we savages better men after all?"

▪ XVI ▪

Prelude to the "Final Solution"

FOLLOWING THE GERMAN INVASION OF Poland the reports of Nazi barbarities multiplied. They came from a variety of sources, including diplomatic channels, eyewitness accounts, the neutral press of Europe, and American correspondents of high reputation.

On January 23, 1940, a new Assistant Secretary of State, Breckinridge Long, took command of virtually all aspects of the refugee problem. Breck Long, the horse breeder and gracious host of Montpelier Hall, the loyal Democrat who had contributed so generously of his wife's funds to the party, found himself swamped by detailed reports of German brutality. The man who had praised the black-shirted Italian Fascisti now spent long hours studying the activities of their German partners. He read the diplomatic dispatches describing the murder of an estimated 250,000 Jews in Poland and he was shown accounts of refugees adrift among the ice floes on the Danube.

If occasionally the arduous nature of his duties caused him to overlook a dispatch, his daily newspaper filled the gap. For example, there was the January 30, 1940, Associated Press report from Berlin revealing that 465 urns containing the ashes of Jews had been shipped from Buchenwald to Berlin during the past three weeks. In February the press communicated the ominous news of the first removal of German Jews to Poland. Prior deportations had involved only "foreign" Jews, although a substantial number from the expanded Reich had already been shipped to Poland.

The American embassy in Berlin also reported this new development. Its dispatch of February 16 informed the State Department that the entire Jewish population of Stettin, numbering about twelve hundred, had been ordered out of their homes on seven hours' notice and then sent to Poland, allegedly for forced labor.

The embassy also knew of an order for the removal within a week of all Jews in the town of Schneidemühl "who are presumably also to be sent to eastern Poland . . . " The dispatch added that German authorities in Poland were making preparations to receive sixty thousand Jews from the Berlin and Vienna areas.

The initial report of the Stettin deportation was soon supplemented by detailed descriptions of the "resettlement" from newspaper correspondents in Berlin. The deportees included the inmates of two homes for the aged. The oldest was eighty-six and those who could not walk were carried to the railroad station on stretchers. It was difficult to conjecture how their physical labors in Poland could help the Reich. According to the published stories, the Stettin police provided printed forms by which the Jews signed away all their possessions except for marriage rings, watches, and the contents of one suitcase. Formally evicted from their homes and apartments, which were sealed by the Nazis, they boarded unheated freight cars at four o'clock in the morning. (Later it would be revealed that two hundred of the twelve hundred deportees had died within two months.)

The report of the Stettin deportation outraged at least one

high State department official, Assistant Secretary of State Adolf A. Berle, Jr. On February 17 Berle sent a memorandum to Breckinridge Long: "If the reports which reach us as to the fate of these unfortunates are only twenty percent true, it raises, in my judgment, a problem that ought to enlist our humanitarian interest . . . My personal view is that we cannot be party to any ultimate arrangement which sanctions that kind of cruelty on an organized scale."

On February 23, having received no reply, Berle addressed a similar communication to Secretary Hull: "I am of opinion that . . . we should register a protest. We did so during the far less significant, though more dramatic riots of a year ago November; and I see no reason why we should not make our feelings known regarding a policy of seemingly calculated cruelty which is beginning to be apparent now."

That same day Breckinridge Long replied to Berle's suggestion. He expressed sympathy "with the poor people involved" but "on the other hand, it is hardly necessary for us to make public expression of our feelings. Everyone in this country already knows and the civilized governments of the world are already cognizant of our feelings in the matter. Furthermore this is a question entirely within the power of Germany . . . We have known since the publication of *Mein Kampf,* and since the access of Hitler to power, that these poor people would be subjected to all kinds of improper treatment . . . We have given ample evidence of our sympathy by admitting to the United States a great many of these poor people but I doubt seriously if we should take an action which might tend to work the United States any closer to the state of war which exists in Europe and I feel that an action of this kind might be a step in that direction."

The Division of European Affairs supported Long's position, as did Secretary Hull, and Berle's proposal was turned down. Berle was (and still is) convinced that a powerful protest by a still-neutral United States might have been effective.

He reasoned that Germany was anxious to delay American belligerence and he believed that a loud and clear statement against Nazi inhumanity might have slowed the destructive machinery. At the very least it would have signaled the rest of the world that the conscience of the United States was not dead and that the eye of the American eagle was fixed on those committing crimes against humanity.

But America was silent and the deportations were accelerated. So was the war. In April 1940 Germany invaded Denmark and Norway; that same month the Nazis established the first enclosed ghetto, at Lódz, Poland. The 250,000 Jews in it were forbidden even on their own streets from 7 P.M. to 7 A.M.

The Nazis did not restrict their barbarity to the Jews. In May 1940 August Cardinal Hlond, the Polish Primate, informed Pope Pius XII that thirty-eight priests had been executed, hundreds imprisoned and churches desecrated. "The Pope is understood to have been so shocked," reported the *New York Times* correspondent from Rome, "that he is contemplating making a speech soon referring to Poland."

Before the Pope could express his outrage, Germany invaded France and a new cycle of refugee horror began. Between April and June 1940, France, Holland, Belgium, Norway, Denmark and Luxembourg fell to Nazi legions, and half a million more Jews became vulnerable to Germany's "final solution."

Now Britain stood alone. With Nazi air attack imminent, the American public demanded that English children be sheltered in the United States. Once again Franklin Roosevelt delayed, but this time his hand was forced. Raymond Clapper, who wrote a syndicated column, was one of many whose stinging criticism shook the White House. On July 6 Clapper described English preparations for the Nazi assault:

"Men and women are saying their final goodbys to each other. They are making ready to fight until death lays them down. But they want to spare their children. That is all they ask." Clapper urged that the United States and Canada shelter at least seventy thousand children, and he asked: "Then why has not the Administration asked Congress to change the law? I would be amazed if a single member objected. Then why doesn't President Roosevelt, the great humanitarian, do something? Ask Congress, Mr. Roosevelt."

Another journalist, Joseph Alsop, complained to the President that the U.S. Committee for the Care of European Children (of which Mrs. Roosevelt was honorary chairman) was receiving a thousand applications a day for English children but the effort was being smothered by State Department red tape. "I may add," wrote Alsop in a memorandum to the President, "that [Solicitor General] Francis Biddle privately indicated to me that the Justice Department saw no reason on earth why many of these changes in ruling and practice should not be made as they will save the lives of thousands."

On July 14, 1940, the State and Justice departments announced simplified procedures: the English children would be admitted on visitor's visas. Various charitable organizations would provide affidavits ensuring that the youngsters would not become public charges and that they would return to their parents when the danger had ended. This was remarkably similar to the planned rescue of twenty thousand German children, but contrary to the fate of that scheme, there was little objection to the English children. Ten thousand visas were quickly issued.

The opening of American doors to the English children was accomplished by the dedication and energy of private organizations rather than by the United States government. This was equally true of efforts to save European intellectual leaders whose anti-Nazi record and academic attainment doomed them to imprisonment or death. The United States immigration law permitted professors to enter the country on a non-quota basis if they had taught during the two previous years and had been guaranteed American teaching positions. Between 1933 and 1945 the Rockefeller Foundation contributed approximately $1,500,000 for the partial support of more than three hundred scholars for whom posts had been found at American universities. The foundation also assisted the Emergency Committee in Aid of Displaced Foreign Scholars, which eventually found positions for 459 of the 613 displaced professors on its rolls. One of the young men who distinguished himself in his work for the Emergency Committee was Edward R. Murrow.

One hundred and sixty-seven of Europe's most distinguished scholars staffed the University in Exile, founded by the New School for Social Research in New York City. Under the leadership of Alvin Johnson, the New School demonstrated the practicability of improving American education while at the same time snatching potential victims from the Nazis.

The academic rescue groups brought over refugees who enriched American life and contributed significantly to its defense during and after the war. Their ranks included no less than ten Nobel Prize-winners in physics: Albert Einstein, Niels Bohr, James Franck, Gustav Hertz, Jean Perrin, Enrico Fermi, Otto Stern, Felix Bloch, Emilio Segrè and Eugene Wigner. Together with such colleagues as Leo Szilard, Edward Teller, Bruno Rossi and Hans Bethe, they helped to usher in a new era of "American" science.

Most of these men arrived openly in one of the academic assistance programs. Others were liberated by the clandestine methods of the International Rescue Committee, which had been established in 1940 after the fall of France. Led by such figures as Elmer Davis, Robert M. Hutchins, Dr. George Shuster and Dorothy Thompson, it was supported by contributions from the Rosenwald, Warburg and Marshall Field families.

The committee's most daring operative was Varian Fry, a young journalist who established headquarters at Marseille in the unoccupied zone of France. In the thirteen months before his expulsion by the Vichy government, Fry and his friends spirited some fifteen hundred scholars, scientists, artists, religious and labor leaders to safety. These included the painters Marc Chagall and Max Ernst, novelists Franz Werfel and Lion Feuchtwanger (the latter was smuggled in women's clothes from a French internment camp), playwright Ferenc Molnár, harpsichordist Wanda Landowska and sculptor Jacques Lipchitz. Fry and his group established escape routes to Spain, thence to Lisbon and the United States. They forged papers, conquered the Vichy, Spanish and Portuguese bureaucracy and proved the feasibility of rescue. They maintained sympathetic liaison with Sumner Welles and Adolf Berle of the State Department and with Mrs. Roosevelt, but they operated on their own.

The only rescue program sponsored by the United States government during this period ran into immediate trouble. The President's Advisory Committee on Political Refugees was chaired by the redoubtable James G. McDonald, the former High Commissioner for Refugees. Beginning in July 1940, the committee selected, screened and transmitted the names of a limited number of distinguished Europeans to the State Department. According to the system, the department was supposed to notify consuls that visas might be issued to the persons recommended if they could be located and if the consuls had no objections.

On October 8, 1940, McDonald handed President Roosevelt a stiff memorandum: 567 names had been forwarded to the State Department in August and September but less than forty visas had been issued. Furthermore, wrote McDonald, "the Department of State now suggests that the arrangements be canceled because sufficient time has elapsed to provide for important key persons and because doubt exists that the activities of the persons recommended would be in accord with sound policies of national defense."

McDonald vigorously denied the charge. After all, the committee had been appointed by the President and included key representatives of the major faiths (Archbishop Joseph F. Rummel, Rabbi Stephen S. Wise and the Reverend Samuel McCrea Cavert of the Federal Council of the Churches of Christ), together with such prominent laymen as Hamilton Fish Armstrong, editor of *Foreign Affairs*. It seemed unlikely that they would approve persons of dubious character.

The President was also informed that some of the refugees selected by McDonald's committee had reached Lisbon, one of the last exit points in Europe, "but are still refused visas. To close this last avenue of escape," concluded McDonald, "is to condemn many scientists, scholars, writers, labor leaders and other refugees to further sacrifices for their belief in democracy and to bring to an end our tradition of hospitality to the politically oppressed. The original arrangements were wisely and soundly planned. Their purpose is still to be achieved."

McDonald's protest (one of a long line of McDonald protests) succeeded in part. The State Department was forced to carry out the President's mandate somewhat more expeditiously. But in his summary of visa activities, issued soon after the McDonald complaint, Breckinridge Long returned to his favorite theme: "In view of reports indicating that Nazi and other totalitarian agents are endeavoring to enter the United States in the guise of refugees, it has been considered essential in the national interest to scrutinize all applications carefully."

Fewer than half of the three thousand visas recommended by the McDonald committee were issued.

During 1940, America's robes of neutrality became increasingly ill-fitting. Massive expenditures for rearmament, the start of a two-ocean navy, and the passage of the Selective Service Act moved the nation closer to hostilities. Still, the President remained unwilling to challenge Congress with his own massive powers. In September he surmounted this caution. He announced the trade of fifty overage U.S. destroyers for British military bases in the Americas. This time Franklin Roosevelt acted without congressional sanction and with a good deal of trepidation. As James MacGregor Burns has described it:

"The President had performed many acts of compromise—perhaps of cowardice—in the White House, especially during his second term. But on September 3, 1940, he did much toward balancing the score. After years of foxlike retreats and evasions, he took the lion's role." Vital as the "lion's role" was to the rearmament of the United States, it did not extend to the civilian victims of the Nazis. To come physically to their defense in 1940 would of course have been impossible, but the failure to come to their moral defense was something else again.

Today that inactivity is often ascribed to ignorance; it is said that Nazi security prevented the outside world from knowing about the horrors within occupied Europe. As we have seen, the Nazi outrages in Poland, previews of more terrible deeds to come, were not concealed, nor was knowledge restricted to the inner chambers of the diplomatic establishment. In October 1940, for example, the Germans invited Alvin Steinkopf, an Associated Press correspondent in Berlin, on a one-week guided tour of the General Government of Poland, which had not been incorporated in the Reich but was German-ruled. Within this 42,500-square-mile area were the cities of Warsaw, Cracow, Radom and Lublin, and a population of thirteen million Poles, including two million Jews.

The Germans took Steinkopf through the Warsaw ghetto. In his AP story of October 12, which the Germans did not bother to censor, the reporter described the new, eight-foot concrete wall, behind which half a million Jews were crammed in an area that formerly had housed one-third that number. "The restraining walls are of comparatively little hindrance in normal times," Steinkopf continued. "But at a moment's notice the authorities, by posting eighteen policemen at the points of entry, can close off the entire district."

Steinkopf was accompanied in Warsaw by Dr. Wallbaum, an eminent Berlin physician serving as Minister of Health of the General Government. Dr. Wallbaum explained that the eight-foot barrier was "a wall against typhus," and Steinkopf was reminded by the German authorities that thirty thousand Jews had been quarantined several months earlier because they carried typhus-spreading vermin. Fortunately, their compassionate German protectors had fumigated the lice-infested dwellings with gas obtained from Germany, thus averting the outbreak of an epidemic.

Steinkopf could not know that in little more than a month the ghetto would be sealed, and that within less than two years, more than three hundred thousand of its inhabitants would be shipped to their death. Dr. Wallbaum's colleagues would once again use gas—this time at Treblinka, this time against men, women and children instead of lice.

There was something contagious in 1940-41 about the well-publicized Nazi freedom to plunder and torment Jews without arousing the world's wrath. It encouraged the "brown shirts" of other countries to revel in looting and sadism with impunity. Among them were the Rumanians, with their historic susceptibility to anti-Semitism.

Under the leadership of Marshal Ion Antonescu and the Iron Guard they rivaled the Nazis in destructive frenzy. Unlike Rumanian leaders of the early 1900's, Marshal Antonescu did not face the withering scorn and diplomatic condemnation of the United States. This was not the fault of the American minister to Rumania, Franklin Mott Gunther. In January 1941 he reported a massacre of more than seven hundred Bucharest Jews by Iron Guards. He included such details as the skinning of sixty Jewish corpses which were found hanging on hooks in a slaughterhouse. Gunther described the perpetrators as "ignorant primitive young savages whose dull vengeful minds responded to the German-controlled and inspired Rumanian press . . . It makes one sick at heart to be accredited to a country where such things can happen even though the real faults of inspiration and encouragement lie elsewhere."

Later in 1941, after Rumania had entered the war as an ally of the Germans, Gunther reported another massacre of Rumanian Jews, at Jassy. In a somewhat plaintive dispatch he pointed out that his personal efforts were weakened by the absence of firm instructions from the United States government: "On general principles I have lost no opportunity to indicate my own attitude of strong disapproval . . . I shall continue to hold this view up to light but, in the absence of specific instructions, I shall not seek further to trouble an already uncertain atmosphere by direct or specific representations."

Had the United States adopted a firm policy toward Rumanian persecution, it is possible that the deportation of 185,000 Jews to Transnistria might never have occurred. At the least, it is reasonable to assume that dictator Antonescu, whose desire to save his own skin became evident later in the war, would have demanded more moderation on the part of his subordinates.

As it was, Antonescu displayed unbridled brutality. Minister Gunther reported to Cordell Hull that the Rumanian leader had told a Spanish diplomat, "This is wartime and a good time to settle the Jewish problem once and for all." Gunther described the expulsion to Transnistria as "accompanied by innumerable kinds of frightfulness, including robbery, starvation, killings . . . This modern Captivity would seem deliberately calculated to serve a program of virtual extermination." He could not have been more prophetic.

In 1941 the Turkish minister in Bucharest suggested a plan for the relief of the Rumanian Jews. He proposed that Britain and France join Turkey in transporting three hundred thousand Jews across Turkey to Syria, and thence to Palestine for temporary sanctuary. The Turkish diplomat also requested the support of the United States and his plan was submitted to Cavendish Cannon of the State Department's Division of European Affairs. Without undue delay Cannon outlined the reasons for rejecting the Turkish suggestion. To begin with, he doubted whether there was sufficient shipping to handle the migration. Next, he argued that the mass movement to Palestine would upset the Arabs. Finally he provided his most convincing argument—the flight of the Jews from Rumania would lead to new pressures for asylum in the Western hemisphere. What's more, added Cannon, if we helped the Jews to emigrate it would demonstrate that Rumania's brutal policies worked. As it happened, the Turks did not press their initiative, so the United States could not be held responsible for the plan's failure. But the United States now erected another roadblock in the path of refugees.

In June 1941, new regulations were issued by the State Department making it virtually impossible for refugees with close relatives in occupied Europe to enter the United States. It was a major triumph for those who like Breckinridge Long saw subversion entering the land of liberty, cloaked in the shabby garments of a refugee.

The ruling applied to prospective immigrants from Norway, Holland, Belgium, occupied France, Czechoslovakia, Poland and the Balkans, as well as Germany and Austria. Its cumbersome wording did not conceal its deadly meaning:

". . . the fact that a relative of the first degree of consanguinity [father, mother, brother, sister, wife, children], with whom the applicant had maintained close family ties, remains abroad in any country or territory under the control of a country whose form of government is opposed to the form of government of the United States may be considered with other evidence that the ties between such relative and the applicant would make the entry of the applicant prejudicial to the public safety or inimical to the interests of the United States."

The order immediately affected some three thousand refugees awaiting transportation from Lisbon to the United States. Other thousands in Germany and German-dominated areas who had begun arrangements for later departure from Lisbon were halted abruptly. But an even more severe State Department ruling was yet to come.

On June 22 the Germans turned on their temporary ally and launched their invasion of the Soviet Union. A few days after the Nazi attack the State Department's Visa Division once again strengthened its capacity to reject the Jews. Each alien would now require two American sponsors, one to provide financial guarantees, the other to vouch for his moral integrity. In addition to the severe scrutiny of applicants leaving relatives behind, the would-be immigrant was now forced to hurdle three additions to the bureaucratic structure—the Primary Committee, Interdepartmental Visa Review Committee and Board of Appeals.

The new procedures also stipulated that elaborate forms had to be submitted directly to Washington for screening. The refugee, in flight for his life or living surreptitiously in an occupied country, first filled out both sides of four legal-size sheets known as Form BC. He sent six copies of BC to the Visa Division, which distributed them to representatives of the Immigration and Naturalization Service, Federal Bureau of Investigation, military intelligence, naval intelligence and State Department. Three to six weeks later these agencies, having checked their files, would report back on the applicant's suitability. If he qualified for what was now described as a "friendly" alien—that is, if he was *not* fleeing from Germany, Austria, Rumania, Hungary or Bulgaria—the Primary Committee could give an advisory approval. Following the approval, a quota number would be cabled to the consul nearest the applicant. Now the consul would swing into action: if he approved of the refugee he could issue the visa; if he objected, the case would be returned to Washington. If the refugee received a visa but could not obtain transportation during the quota year, the approval would become invalid and the procedure would start all over again.

If the Primary Committee rejected the application of a "friendly" alien, the case moved to the Interdepartmental Visa Review Committee. This committee tended to intimidate the refugee's sponsors. Some were challenged about their income or interrogated about their political beliefs. The representatives of military and naval intelligence appeared in uniform and it was not surprising that some sponsors, attempting to perform a humanitarian service, wondered why they had let themselves in for this treatment.

The refugee's problem was complicated by the difficulty he had in communicating with his sponsors in the United States. Witnesses and sponsors appearing in his behalf were often hard pressed to answer intimate questions about him, and their fear of committing perjury inadvertently further inhibited their testimony.

French, Belgian, Dutch and Czech refugees were among those who were regarded as "friendly" aliens. Theirs was a simpler task than the ordeal facing applicants classified as "enemy" aliens. Their cases passed upward through each committee and no advisory approval was permitted. If an "enemy" alien passed the scrutiny of both the Primary and Interdepartmental committees, his case would still be required to come before the Board of Appeals. That a case must come to Appeals after being presented successfully at lower levels was a unique State Department innovation.*

The handling of applications fell four and five months be-

* The severity of this procedure was moderated somewhat through the effective opposition by one member of the Board of Appeals, Frederick B. Keppel, at one time dean of Columbia College and later president of the Carnegie Corporation. Keppel's forthright denunciation of the screening procedures was responsible for the admission of many refugees who would otherwise have been rejected.

hind in this bureaucratic maze. Some foundered on the requirement that the refugee demonstrate that his acceptance would be of positive benefit to the United States, a subjective matter which defied verification.

Those rejected were permitted to reapply in six months, but were not informed of the reasons for the negative decision. The State Department told critics of this provision that if the refugees found out why they had been turned down, they might change the information on their next application. The severe new procedures slashed an already crippled immigration program to a few thousand a year.

James McDonald made his usual vigorous effort to eliminate discrimination against those refugees leaving close relatives in Europe and he urged simplification of the screening process. Of the former he wrote: "Our experience with refugees has convinced us that it is unnecessary, illogical, ill adapted to the purposes claimed for it, and cruelly burdensome on the refugees affected by it."

The new immigration requirements had also come to the attention of Albert Einstein. In July he wrote to Mrs. Roosevelt:

"I have noted with great satisfaction that you always stand for the right and humaneness even when it is hard. Therefore in my deep concern I know of no one else to whom to turn for help. A policy is now being pursued in the State Department which makes it all but impossible to give refuge in America to many worthy persons who are the victims of Fascist cruelty in Europe. Of course, this is not openly avowed by those responsible for it. The method which is being used, however, is to make immigration impossible by erecting a wall of bureaucratic measures alleged to be necessary to protect America against subversive, dangerous elements. I would suggest that you talk about this question to some well-informed and right-minded person such as Mr. Hamilton Fish Armstrong. If then you become convinced that a truly grave injustice is under way, I know that you will find it possible to bring the matter to the attention of your heavily burdened husband in order that it may be remedied."

Mrs. Roosevelt informed Professor Einstein that she would bring his letter to the President's attention "at once," but there is no indication in the presidential records that Mr. Roosevelt investigated the complaint.

The toughening of State Department visa policies coincided with a fateful decision by the Nazi leadership. On July 31, 1941, Hermann Göring sent a historic directive to Reinhard Heydrich, who headed the *Reichssicherheitshauptamt* (National Central Security Office) under Himmler:

"I herewith commission you to carry out all preparations with regard to . . . a total solution of the Jewish question in those territories of Europe which are under German influence . . . I furthermore charge you to submit to me as soon as possible a draft showing the . . . measures already taken for the execution of the intended final solution of the Jewish question."

Those measures included the establishment of four mobile killing units known as *Einsatzgruppen*. They followed on the heels of the German armies invading the Soviet Union, with a mandate "to carry out executive measures against the civilian population." Within five months, according to their own records, these groups had shot five hundred thousand Jews. Ultimately, about one and a half million Jews would fall before the bullets of the *Einsatzgruppen*. In spite of their conventional methods of murder they competed in efficiency with the more scientific techniques of the concentration camps.

The killings were on too massive a scale to be concealed even by the most rigorous security measures, and news of the massacres in Russia soon reached the outside world. Rumanian and Hungarian troops, as allies of the Germans, witnessed some of the shootings and reported the events in letters home. Unlike the Rumanians, many of the Hungarians were upset by the machine-gunning of men, women and children, and the eyewitness accounts of Hungarian officers were reported in the American press.

In September 1941 the Germans decreed that all Jews over the age of six must wear a yellow Star of David with the black superscripture *"Jude."* Each insignia cost 10 pfennigs. Newspaper reports coming out of Germany listed the thirty-five provisions of the new decree, including the warning that a Jew attempting to hide his Star under a briefcase or shopping bag would be subject to imprisonment in a concentration camp. The American public read about such strange sights as the two non-Aryan Catholic priests of Cologne who wore the Star of David on their cassocks.

In addition, there were eyewitness accounts by the small groups of refugees still managing to reach the United States. Particularly vivid descriptions were provided by fifty-six children who arrived in New York on September 24, 1941, on the Portuguese liner *Serpa Pinta.* As the result of massive efforts by relief agencies in France, they had been evacuated from Gurs, a muddy, windswept, disease-ridden internment camp in the unoccupied zone. When reporters asked about their parents, who had not been able to leave Gurs, the children broke down. They told of mothers and fathers who had died of starvation while trying to keep their youngsters alive, of others wasting away in utter despair.

Several of the children were ill and were moved to Ellis Island for treatment. A small brown-eyed girl remarked about this to a reporter: "It's horrible that the children are sick, but it's not as bad as throwing bread to Mommy."

Another child recalled the last sight of her father at Gurs. "Daddy looked frightful and old," she said. "He looked as thin as a snake."

. . .

In the months before Pearl Harbor, the Germans intensified their attack upon the Jews, and the State Department was informed of each step. Although reciprocal action had forced the closing of U.S. and German consulates in July, the embassy in Berlin remained open. Dispatches in October and November described deportations of Jews to Poland. Thousands of old people had been assembled in the ruins of Berlin synagogues; some had been forced to remain standing for as long as forty-eight hours in the synagogue at Levetzowstrasse. Two thousand had departed from Frankfurt on the Main, and an equal number were ready to leave Cologne. "These groups," said the embassy message, "consist almost entirely of elderly Jews but it is anticipated that under present plans all Jews in Germany will be deported within a few months."

Another dispatch from the embassy reported that "Jews in various German cities are at present being stripped of their belongings and herded into railway cars for shipment to Poland and an unknown fate."

On November 16 the embassy cabled that "many thousands of elderly Jews are being deported to the East, and stories are filtering back to Berlin to the effect that those already evacuated are being in effect exterminated by disease, cold, and starvation, and in some cases their outright massacre by their captors." The embassy added that a prominently displayed article by Josef Goebbels in *Das Reich* affirmed that Hitler's prophecy of January 30, 1939, regarding "the annihilation of the Jewish race in Europe" would be fulfilled. Vital statistics compiled by the Germans themselves supported the Propaganda Minister's boast. According to a Berlin report reprinted in London and New York, the death rate in the Warsaw ghetto was forty times higher than in the rest of the city. Starvation seemed almost as effective a weapon as bullets.

"Complete elimination of Jews from European life now appears to be fixed German policy," the *New York Times* had commented on October 28. It repeated the news that carloads of German Jews were heading eastward and noted that deportees were required to pay 90 marks for their transportation.

The Germans tried to keep these departures secret, but on October 29 a *Times* correspondent viewed the embarkation of perhaps a thousand Jews from a suburban Berlin freight yard. The reporter was not permitted near the train but watched the loading from outside the yard. He asked a man emerging from the station whether the train consisted of passenger or freight cars.

"Freight cars," replied the man, "but they are full of people."

After the United States entered the war on December 7, 1941, the American newspaper men and diplomats in Germany went home or were transferred to other posts, but the flow of information continued. It did *not* include a report of the conference held on January 20, 1942, in the Berlin suburb of Wannsee. With Heydrich presiding, this meeting was attended by five members of the Gestapo, and nine representatives of the ministries concerned with the "final solution." Adolf Eichmann was one of the Gestapo men in attendance. The meeting lasted an hour or so and included luncheon and drinks. Thirty copies of the transcript were prepared; they were later found among captured German documents.

Heydrich outlined his plan for implementing the Göring directive. "The Jews should now in the course of the final solution be brought to the East . . . for use as labor," he said. They would be used in road building, "in which task undoubtedly a large part will fall away through natural decline. The remnant that is able finally to survive all this, since this is unquestionably the part with the strongest resistance, must be given treatment accordingly, because these people, representing a natural selection, are to be regarded as the germ-cell of a new Jewish development, should they be allowed to go free."

The participants in the Wannsee conference knew that the Jews were to be liquidated but the precise nature of the "treatment" to be given the survivors of road building would not become clear for several months. It was not until the spring of 1942 that gas chambers were built in the Polish camps. Gerhart Riegner's message of August 1942, disclosing the use of Zyklon B gas, was the first detailed information about the "treatment," but it represented the continuation rather than the inauguration of Nazi mass murder.

Between the Wannsee conference, then unknown to the United States, and the Riegner message, which the State Department tried to suppress, a stream of events dramatized the paralysis of the Allies in the face of the Nazi massacre of the Jews. The combination of German extermination and American-British inhospitality to refugees drove many Jews to suicide. Others sailed on unseaworthy ships toward forbidden harbors.

The most tragic of these episodes involved the *Struma,* a 180-ton Rumanian vessel which normally carried a hundred passengers on coastal runs. On December 16, 1941, the *Struma* had picked up 769 refugees from the Rumanian port of Constanza, and though none of its passengers possessed British permits, began the slow voyage to Haifa, Palestine. Critically overloaded and endangered by a leaking hull and defective engines, it broke down off Istanbul. Turkish authorities would not permit the passengers to land unless they obtained British certificates for Palestine. The British refused.

The *Struma* remained at anchor for ten weeks. Finally, on February 24, in spite of protests by the captain that his ship was not seaworthy, the Turks towed the *Struma* to sea. Before the vessel faded from view the people ashore read the large banner made by the passengers. It said: "SAVE US!"

Six miles from shore the *Struma* sank. It is still not known whether it capsized, struck a mine or was hit by a torpedo.

Seventy children, 269 women and 428 men drowned. Two passengers swam to safety. Immediately after the *Struma*'s departure, local British officials received authorization from their superiors to issue Palestine certificates to the seventy children.

The world was shocked, but the British government remained unmoved. Harold Macmillan, Undersecretary for the Colonies, said in the House of Commons, "It is not in our power to give guarantees nor to take measures of a nature that may compromise the present policy regarding illegal immigration." Lord Cranborne, Secretary of State for the Colonies, taking note of the emotional reaction of some Englishmen to the tragedy, counseled, "Under the present unhappy situation in the world it is to a certain extent inevitable that we should be hardened to horrors."

For a short period there was anger in the United States over this latest demonstration of British Palestine policy but few Americans saw any similarity between the plight of the Rumanian refugees on the *Struma* and the difficulty of obtaining visas from the State Department.

On July 17, 1942, the Berlin radio announced the arrest of twenty thousand Jews in Paris for deportation to eastern Europe, and five days later the Nazis began their "resettlement" of the Warsaw ghetto, designed to wipe out the remaining 380,000 inhabitants.

These reports were confirmed by a variety of sources and widely publicized. In a letter read to a rally of twenty thousand at Madison Square Garden in New York City, President Roosevelt wrote: "The Nazis will not succeed in exterminating their victims any more than they will succeed in enslaving mankind. The American people not only sympathize with all victims of Nazi crimes but will hold the perpetrators of these crimes to strict accountability in a day of reckoning which will surely come."

All these events took place *before* Gerhart Riegner delivered the terrible news about Hitler's extermination order to the United States consulate in Geneva. In the long nightmare which had begun in 1933 with the progressive dehumanization of six hundred thousand Germans, this "final solution" was the logical rather than the unpredictable culmination of Nazi power. Yet Riegner's information was greeted with incredulity by men who had read an endless series of messages detailing the Nazis' inexorable degradation of the Jews. Programs of rescue suggested to the United States government had been obstructed, thwarted and delayed long after recognition by the highest authorities that the Germans were indeed carrying out a planned massacre of the Jews of Europe. Finally, after the direct presentation of evidence by the Treasury Department, Franklin Roosevelt had been shocked into action. In early 1944 he announced the formation of the War Refugee Board for "the rescue, transportation, maintenance and relief of the victims of enemy oppression and . . . the establishment of havens of temporary refuge for such victims."

The board went into action with a small staff, a small budget and the automatic animosity of the State Department. Its acting director was a relatively unknown thirty-four-year-old lawyer named John Pehle. Few thought the board could accomplish much. Pehle was one of the few.

Part III

THE RESCUERS

XVII
The War Refugee Board

FRANKLIN D. ROOSEVELT ANNOUNCED THE formation of the War Refugee Board on January 22, 1944. Three days later a cable drafted by John Pehle was sent over the signature of Cordell Hull to all United States embassies, consulates and other diplomatic missions. It ordered that "action be taken to forestall the plot of the Nazis to exterminate the Jews and other persecuted minorities in Europe."

The practice of suppressing unpleasant information had ended. The message specified that "communication facilities should be made freely available to . . . private agencies for all appropriate messages for carrying out the policy of this Government."

Pehle recruited a small staff of decisive men. Josiah DuBois, who had drafted the powerful report in preparation for Morgenthau's showdown with the President, was appointed the board's general counsel. James Mann of Glasgow, Kentucky, who had worked effectively with Pehle in the Treasury Department, accepted one of the board's most delicate assignments—liaison with the State Department. It was his responsibility to expedite the clearance and transmission of board cables moving over State Department communication facilities. In view of the continuing hostility of some Foreign Service officers, this proved to be a formidable chore.

The objective of the board's Washington staff, which never exceeded thirty, was to develop positive, new American programs to aid the victims of Nazism while pressing the Allies and neutrals to take forceful diplomatic action in their behalf. Crucial to the success of the board would be the performance of its field representatives assigned to U.S. embassies in the neutral nations of Europe: Turkey, Portugal, Switzerland, Spain and Sweden. Pehle envisioned them increasing the flow of refugees to the neutrals, who would then funnel them to safety in North Africa, Palestine, and North and South America. The departure of refugees from the neutrals during this lifesaving cycle would also make room for new arrivals from Nazi-occupied territories.

If the wearers of the State Department's old-school tie resented the board's invasion of their domain, they must have been appalled by the appointment of its first field representative, Ira A. Hirschmann. Hirschmann, assigned to the U.S. embassy in Ankara, Turkey, had received his diplomatic training as a department-store executive in New York City. His career took a spectacular turn at Lord & Taylor, whose sprightly public image was in large part the result of his imaginative advertising, promotion and merchandising. From Lord & Taylor he moved onward and upward at Saks Fifth Avenue and Bloomingdale.

But Hirschmann's horizons, as Pehle well knew, went beyond retailing. Appointed by Fiorello La Guardia as a member of the Board of Higher Education of New York City, he had championed academic freedom in the face of bitter political opposition. A gifted pianist and musicologist, he founded the New Friends of Music, which enriched the life of the city and had established new patterns of concert going. With all this, he had found time to serve as chairman of the board of the New School's University in Exile.

This involvement with refugee scholars inspired him to visit the Evian Conference of 1938. He was a private observer, but he carried a diplomatic passport by virtue of his acquaintance with the President. Disgusted by the hypocrisy of Evian he traveled directly from the conference to Vienna to get a first-hand look at the Nazis and to assist in the emigration of his wife's family.

In spite of his knowledge of the refugee problem he was startled to see long lines of Jews at the U.S. consulate. Realizing that most would not be admitted to the United States because they lacked financial sponsors, he rented a hotel suite and passed the word that he was prepared to act as their guarantor. His diplomatic passport and friendship with the American minister to Austria overcame the "public charge" problem, and in one day he accepted financial responsibility for more than two hundred prospective immigrants he had never seen before. None of them betrayed his trust.

When Hirschmann returned to America, he made up his mind to concentrate his energies on rescue work. He took a leave of absence from Bloomingdale's, and before the War Refugee Board was formally organized, he had volunteered to serve it in Turkey.

The strategic significance of neutral Turkey lay in its accessibility to refugees from Nazi-controlled Hungary, Rumania and Bulgaria. Once in Turkey, they could, theoretically, be moved by rail or sea to Palestine. But a bureaucratic minefield lay between the refugees and their objectives.

Hungarian Jews were denied permission by Rumanian authorities to travel through that country en route to Turkey. In their turn, the Bulgarians forbade transit papers to escaping Rumanian Jews who also sought to reach Istanbul. As if these were not sufficient barriers, the Turkish regulations allowed the entry of only nine families a week en route to Palestine from the three Nazi satellites.

The Jews who had run this formidable gauntlet would find themselves in Istanbul facing further hazard and delay. Immigrants to Palestine required certificates issued by Britsh authorities and it took nine weeks to get them, assuming that nothing derogatory was discovered about the applicant. Even then the immigrant could not depart for his promised land. Turkish bureaucracy imposed an additional six- to eight-week delay for exit visas.

Within days after the formation of the War Refugee Board, Ira Hirschmann reported to the U.S. embassy in Ankara. With strong support from the American ambassador, Laurence Steinhardt, he soon broke the bottleneck. First, Hirschmann persuaded Kemel Aziz Payman, the Turkish official who had delayed the visas, to streamline his languid procedures, and he impressed British officials with his mandate from the President of the United States. As a consequence, the fifteen- to seventeen-week lag in the issuance of British and Turkish documents was slashed to a maximum of three weeks. Hirschmann also found good use for the funds contributed by the Joint Distribution Committee. Working closely with representatives of the Jewish Agency for Palestine, who were operating covertly in Istanbul, Hirschmann fed these funds to the Black Sea captains, whose antiquated ships began ferrying Jews from Constanza in Rumania to Istanbul. The money was also used to obtain transit visas for travel through the Nazi satellites. Between April and August 1944, four thousand Jews were evacuated from the Balkans. From Turkey the refugees were transported by train to Syria, thence to Palestine.

Hirschmann and Ambassador Steinhardt arranged for their transportation and also assisted in obtaining the British permits for Palestine. Ironically, these had become available because only forty-three thousand of the seventy-five thousand Jews permitted to enter Palestine under the terms of the British

White Paper of 1939 had managed to evade the Nazis. The British had therefore extended the deadline for immigration.

Hirschmann also brought order to the chaos created by the presence of representatives of competing Jewish organizations in Istanbul. He co-ordinated their efforts with Christian rescue groups and unified the approach to temperamental and often venal Turkish officials.

In Washington the War Refugee Board was now bringing continuous pressure against the Axis satellites, reminding them that their mistreatment of the Jews would be remembered after the war. John Pehle and his colleagues fired off hard-hitting messages to the Axis powers via the neutrals, threatening retribution. This irritated the formalists at the State Department, who warned that these undiplomatic messages were placing the neutrals in an uncomfortable position. Nevertheless, they were delivered with good effect. In particular they struck terror in the Rumanian officials who had banished the Jews to Transnistria.

Ira Hirschmann in Ankara exploited this Rumanian fear. He had learned that Alexandre Cretzianu, the Rumanian minister to Turkey, did not share the Antonescu regime's anti-Semitic views, and he had armed himself with a letter from a former Rumanian ambassador to the United States. The letter urged Cretzianu to co-operate with Hirschmann and stressed the American determination to punish war criminals.

Through Gilbert Simond, a delegate of the International Red Cross, he arranged a meeting with Cretzianu at Simond's home. Prior to the establishment of the War Refugee Board, such a confrontation would have violated the law prohibiting dealings with enemy nationals. This regulation had been waived for representatives of the board, and Hirschmann's ability to "deal with the enemy" markedly enhanced his effectiveness.

At the start of their talk Hirschmann pointed out that a terrible fate awaited those of Cretzianu's countrymen who were adjudged war criminals. Then he demanded that the minister request his government to empty the Transnistrian concentration camps and return the Jews to their homes. By this date only 48,000 had survived of the 185,000 who had been deported and this helpless remnant lay in the path of the retreating German army. A massacre was inevitable and Hirschmann also informed the minister that the United States would hold the Rumanian government responsible. It did not take long to convince Cretzianu that he would share the fate of the other Rumanian officials, so he immediately agreed to recommend that the camps be evacuated and the Jews protected. In return Hirschmann promised to obtain four U.S. visas for the Cretzianu family.

This episode was not the Rumanian government's first exposure to a new and more vigorous American attitude. A few weeks earlier, at John Pehle's initiative, Stettinius had sent a cable to Ambassador Steinhardt asking him to pass the word to the Rumanians that the United States regarded their anti-Semitism as "criminal participation in Hitler's extermination campaign for which Rumania will be held accountable."

Hirschmann had met with Cretzianu on March 13. On March 17 the American embassy in Ankara was notified that the Rumanians had begun the transfer of Jews from the Transnistrian camps, and on March 20 Gilbert Simond relayed a message from the Red Cross in Bucharest that the safe return of the forty-eight thousand Jews had been completed.

Hirschmann also persuaded the Rumanians to issue transit visas, which enabled several thousand otherwise doomed Hungarian Jews to board rescue ships in Rumania for eventual sanctuary in Palestine. Thus the activities of one man, representing the United States government in Turkey, backed by concerned men in Washington and supported by a sympathetic ambassador, saved more than fifty thousand lives.

The tireless Hirschmann (who had long overstayed his leave of absence from Bloomingdale's) used similar techniques to pressure the Bulgarian government into revoking its anti-Semitic laws, which had been patterned after the Nuremberg legislation. Some twelve thousand "foreign" Jews had been deported from Thrace and Macedonia in 1943, and the forty-five thousand who remained within Bulgaria were living under a constant threat when Hirschmann made his first contact with the "enemy." Now his adversary was Nicholas Balabanoff, the Bulgarian minister to Turkey. Like Cretzianu, Balabanoff promised that he would urge his government to moderate its policies.

Hirschmann renewed his efforts in July, and after another meeting Balabanoff wrote to their mutual friend, Gilbert Simond: ". . . I consider that the policy of the new Bulgarian Government with regard to the Jews will be of a sentiment of justice and humanity. I do not exclude from my opinion . . . the possibility of reaching soon a completely normal state in the situation of the Jews at home."

This was still not sufficient for Hirschmann, who sent a sharp note to the Bulgarian: "We will not be satisfied until the two scandalous anti-Jewish laws are completely revoked and we expect the Bulgarian Government to take steps to this end with the least possible delay."

While Hirschmann threatened Balabanoff in Ankara, Pehle in Washington synchronized the overall offensive against the Bulgarians. Simultaneously, War Refugee Board representatives in other neutral capitals repeated the same theme to the local Bulgarian diplomats.

Early in August, Hirschmann and Balabanoff met again, and the American reported: "Monsieur Balabanoff arrived thirty minutes late and immediately appropriated a half-dozen of my Old Gold cigarettes for his wife." Hirschmann pressed the Bulgarian for a written statement affirming his government's intentions.

The following day, somewhat to Hirschmann's surprise, the letter arrived. Once again it was sympathetic and asserted that "arbitrary methods" would not be used against the Jews. Once again, however, it failed to guarantee a revocation of the discriminatory laws. Hirschmann now put in writing the advantages to the Bulgarian governnment if it abrogated the legislation. Taking a cue from his last conversation with Minister Balabanoff, he wrote: "Why send refugees in lost groups to strange lands if, as the Minister of their country asserts, they will gradually find themselves back in the position of respect and responsibility where they were before the war?" The letter was passed to the Sofia government by the daughter of a Bulgarian major general. It was one of several persuasive appeals. On August 30 the Bulgarian Cabinet announced that the laws would be revoked. This constituted the first cancellation of anti-Jewish legislation by any Axis country. It was particularly noteworthy because the United States and Bulgaria were still technically at war and the action represented direct defiance of Germany by one of its satellites.

There is a postscript to the Bulgarian story. In 1943, well before the establishment of the War Refugee Board, the Germans had repeated their order that the twenty-five thousand Jews in Sofia be deported to Poland—to certain death. Word of this impending disaster was flashed to Chaim Barlas, the representative in Istanbul of the Jewish Agency for Palestine. Barlas rushed to the residence of the one man who he thought could help him—Monsignor Angelo Roncalli, the Vatican's Apostolic Delegate to Turkey. The future Pope John XXIII had always listened sympathetically to Barlas and had always acted vigorously to help the Jews. Later Barlas described their first meeting:

". . . I realized that I stood before a man of lofty spiritual stature, who was truly interested in the sufferings that had befallen our people and who was prepared heart and soul to assist in whatever way he could. Whenever during my interviews he would hear of the news from Poland, Hungary and Slovakia, he would clasp his hands in prayer, tears flowing from his eyes."

When Barlas told Monsignor Roncalli of the impatient German demand for the destruction of the Jews in Sofia, the priest reacted with horror and indignation. He had served as Apostolic Delegate to Bulgaria and had developed a warm friendship with King Boris and the Queen. Now he assured Barlas that he would take immediate action, and began writing a message while Barlas was still in his presence. Later Roncalli wrote to Barlas, confirming that his message had been delivered to the King.

Barlas, who now lives in Israel, does not know the details of Roncalli's intervention but new information has been provided by Luigi Bresciani, a confidential servant to Roncalli in both Bulgaria and Turkey. Bresciani, today a sculptor in Bergamo, Italy, recalls the Monsignor's agitation after the Barlas visit:

"When Monsignor Roncalli found out about this, he wrote immediately a personal letter to King Boris. I had never before seen Monsignor Roncalli so disturbed. Before I carried this missive to a certain person able to put it personally into the hands of King Boris, Monsignor Roncalli read it to me. Even though calm and gentle as a Saint Francis de Sales come to life, he did not spare himself from saying openly that King Boris should on no account agree to that dishonorable action . . . threatening him among other things with the punishment of God."

Monsignor Roncalli's intervention came soon after the Jews of Sofia had been dispersed in the Bulgarian countryside, where they remained unharmed. King Boris died under mysterious circumstances in August 1943 and the safety of the Jews was once again in jeopardy. However, revocation of the anti-Semitic legislation one year later assuaged these fears.

One cannot measure the effects of the future Pope's intervention on the cancellation of the deportation order, just as it is impossible to ascribe the revocation of Bulgaria's anti-Semitic laws solely to the intervention of Ira Hirschmann. It is true that the Bulgarian people were never enthusiastic about anti-Semitism and that some politicians as well as ordinary citizens opposed the Nazi actions; nevertheless, Bulgaria had acceded to the deportation of twelve thousand Jews from Thrace and Macedonia. No doubt the appeals by the Vatican's highest ranking representative in the Middle East and by the emissary of the President of the United States played major roles in the rescue of at least twenty-five thousand Bulgarian Jews.

Pius XII remained silent but Angelo Roncalli, the stocky son of peasants who would one day inherit the throne of St. Peter, fought for the lives of the Jews, for they, as all men, were precious to him.

■ XVIII ■

Obstruction and Rescue

IN SPITE OF THE EARLY ACHIEVEMENTS OF the War Refugee Board, John Pehle was troubled—there was continuing obstruction of board programs within the lower echelons in the State Department.

On March 2, 1944, for example, the board drafted a telegram for Ambassador Winant in England. The ambassador was asked to remind the British of their offer at the Bermuda Conference to establish a camp for refugees at Cyrenaica, on the coast of North Africa. A year had elapsed without any British action, while the need for the camp had grown.

Jim Mann, Pehle's liaison with the State Department, made daily attempts to expedite the Cyrenaica cable as it drifted aimlessly from desk to desk. On March 24 he reported to Pehle:

"The news on the whole from the State Department front for the day cannot be considered too good . . . The Cyrenaica cable has not yet gone out and as a matter of fact cannot be located at the present time. This morning I had Mr. Warren [George L. Warren, a State Department specialist in refugee matters] call each person to whom the cable had been routed and it appears that it has not yet reached the African desk. However, it left the British desk day before yesterday . . . there is no excuse whatsoever for the delay."

Eventually the cable was sent, but by the time the British agreed to build the camp, other arrangements had been made for housing the refugees.

The War Refugee Board's demand for immediate action to rescue the remaining Jews struck deep-rooted prejudices within the State Department. A friend of Josiah DuBois' at State told him that he had overheard a Foreign Service officer complaining, "That Jew Morgenthau and his Jewish assistants like DuBois are trying to take over this place . . ."

"I tried to tell him you weren't Jewish, Joe," the State Department man said with a laugh, "but he wouldn't listen."

On one occasion Mrs. Ruth Shipley, who headed the Passport Division, called John Pehle and asked in all seriousness if the board employed any Americans. The bewildered Pehle replied that his staff was entirely American and asked the reason for the question.

"Well, I've never read cables like those your people send," she said. "They just aren't worded like *our* cables."

Mrs. Shipley was right. In place of the weak, apologetic appeals sent sporadically by Breckinridge Long and his associates, the new directives were urgent and uncompromising. Furthermore, they were not limited to the belligerent nations. The board challenged all the moral forces which had remained silent in the face of Nazi murder. Among them was the International Committee of the Red Cross.

The official history of the War Refugee Board, which until recently was classified "secret," notes that "The Board also appealed to the International Committee of the Red Cross time and time again to take direct and aggressive action to obtain humanitarian treatment for the helpless minorities being persecuted so viciously by the Germans. For many months, however, request after request from the Board met with the answer that the Germans would not permit the proposed action."

Officials of the Red Cross pointed out that they had no legal power to force the Germans to improve the treatment of the Jews. By international convention the Red Cross was concerned solely with the treatment of prisoners of war and interned civilians. Internees were defined as citizens of a belligerent nation trapped within an enemy's borders after the outbreak of war. They were guaranteed treatment comparable to that of prisoners of war. But the Germans had branded the Jews as *Schutzhäftlinge,* persons in protective custody. According to the Nazis they were stateless, and were treated as common criminals.

The Red Cross had directed a number of weak inquiries to the Germans about their treatment of the Jews but had never pressed the issue. They feared that excessive indignation would cause the Germans to cancel their arrangements for the civilized care of war prisoners and conventional internees. The spokesmen of the International Red Cross turned away complaints about their apparent neglect of the Jews with the somewhat familiar argument that they could not interfere in the internal affairs of a belligerent nation. After all, the Red Cross served all mankind impartially.

John Pehle and the War Refugee Board did not accept this explanation. On March 23, 1944, the board prepared a message to the Red Cross proposing that it urge Germany and its satellites to place Jews and other concentration camp inmates on a status equal to other prisoners'. If this was rejected the Red Cross should demand the right to ship and distribute food packages to inmates of the German camps.

Once again the State Department obstructed the board's message. For one thing, according to the regulations for the U.S.-British blockade of Europe, food parcels could not be sent to concentration camp prisoners because the Germans refused to follow the same procedure as at prisoner-of-war camps, where Red Cross inspectors were permitted to check the distribution of relief parcels. The blockade authorities reasoned that the Nazi guards might steal the food packages, which would aid the German war effort. The War Refugee Board, by urging a Red Cross presence in the concentration camps, hoped to abide by blockade rules while providing relief to the starving Jews.

The board's March 23 cable to the Red Cross was held up by the State Department until April 29, at which time Pehle forced its transmission. On May 17 Red Cross president Max Huber replied: the steps which the War Refugee Board wished the Red Cross to take "would go far beyond the limits of their traditional capacity, and the governments to whom such request might be addressed would not fail to view this proposal from that particular angle." What's more, Huber and his colleagues "might lay themselves open to objection that they were . . . trespassing upon internal concerns of a state should they attempt to act on behalf of certain categories of persons whom that state considered to be subject exclusively to its domestic legislation."

The International Red Cross replied with similar equivocation to the board's appeal that its staff in Budapest be enlarged. It was clear that the Germans were going to deport the eight hundred thousand Jews of Hungary, but there was only one Red Cross delegate in the capital. The board had requested that neutral nations, the Vatican and the Red Cross increase the number of their observers, in the hope that their presence would inhibit the Nazis.

In reply to the board's request, President Huber wrote that "under the present circumstances such mission might be considered as unrelated to the Committee's traditional and conventional competence." The mission of the Red Cross was to help war victims "without intruding into the domestic policy of any of those states."

The board snapped back: "It is difficult to believe that measures designed to check such slaughter directly or indirectly can be considered . . . as 'intruding into domestic policy' . . . If the measure is unprecedented, so is the emergency."

It was only after the Germans had deported more than four hundred thousand Hungarian Jews to Auschwitz that the Red Cross increased its delegation in Budapest. As a result, it played a major role in the subsequent rescue of the remaining Jews.

In fairness to the Red Cross it should be pointed out that in 1934 its International Committee initiated a proposal guaranteeing relief supplies for detained civilians of *all* categories during wartime. The draft was scheduled to be ratified at a diplomatic conference in 1940, but the start of hostilities prevented the meeting. Nevertheless, the Red Cross suggested to the belligerents that they voluntarily follow the proposed ruling for the treatment of civilians. Ironically, Germany was the only nation at war which did not reject the Red Cross appeal outright. The Reich agreed to abide by the change if adopted by the other combatants. It was not. Thus the Red Cross was denied the legal power to ensure equal treatment of vast numbers of detained and deported civilians.

In spite of the inflexible blockade regulations, an ingenious Austrian official of the International Red Cross had led a campaign which undoubtedly saved the lives of thousands and illustrated the feasibility of penetrating the concentration camps.

Prince Johannes Schwarzenberg, an anti-Nazi aristocrat, had fled from Vienna in 1938 to take up the hereditary Swiss citizenship enjoyed by his family for generations as a reward for military services once rendered. He joined the Red Cross administration in Geneva and eventually exploited an opportunity to provide food for Jews in the camps. In March 1943 the German Foreign Office agreed to let the Red Cross supply parcels to those deportees whose names and addresses were known to the international organization. This seemed a safe enough offer from the German point of view, since they had provided no lists of prisoners and Red Cross delegates were not permitted to enter the camps.

However, Schwarzenberg knew the names of thirteen prominent prisoners in the Oranienburg camp. To them he shipped food packages—with return receipts attached. When they came back to the Red Cross they caused a sensation. In addition to the signature of the addressee, each receipt bore the names of five to ten other prisoners with whom the food had been shared.

From this modest beginning, Schwarzenberg built a file of fifty-six thousand names from various camps. The original list from Oranienburg was supplemented by private organizations, individuals with special information, and secret dossiers compiled by intelligence agencies. Schwarzenberg was able to authenticate many of the signatures by contacting relatives and friends of the prisoners, and he convinced British blockade officials that the packages were not being diverted to the Nazis.

Schwarzenberg's fifty-six thousand names represented a small fraction of the deportees but they illustrated a determination and ingenuity which did not characterize the usual Red Cross approach to the problem. The International Committee did not become aggressive until Nazi defeat seemed inevitable. Only at this last point in the war did the Germans give Red Cross personnel access to the concentration camps. Then, utilizing funds provided by the Joint Distribution Committee and transmitted via the War Refugee Board, the Red Cross organized a massive distribution of food parcels which undoubtedly saved several thousand prisoners from starvation.

Although the principal Red Cross administrators failed in their modest efforts on behalf of the Jews, individual representatives in occupied Europe displayed striking heroism and resourcefulness. Red Cross delegate Georges Dunand risked his life carrying funds to Jews hiding in Slovakia. Toward the end of the war, delegate Hoeflinger prevented the German commandant of the Mauthausen concentration camp from blowing up the underground aircraft factories, which would have entombed forty thousand Jewish slave laborers. In Budapest the enlarged Red Cross staff provided protection for some thirty thousand Jews. Ankara delegate Gilbert Simond acted as intermediary for Ira Hirschmann's negotiations with Rumanian and Bulgarian representatives. But these efforts were small in relation to the principal activity of the Red Cross—the support and protection of three million Allied and Axis prisoners of war. The later expansion of Red Cross assistance to the "stateless" can be traced to the sharp criticism of the War Refugee Board.

On June 16, 1944, John Pehle notified Secretary of the Treasury Morgenthau that the board had finally triumphed in one of its most difficult battles:

"I am sure that you will be glad to know that the blockade has at last been broken as to the feeding of civilians in internment camps in enemy Europe. Following recent discussions we had with Dingle M. Foot, Parliamentary Under-Secretary of the British Ministry of Economic Warfare, an agreement has been reached with the British to permit the shipment of 100,000 food parcels a month for three months for distribution by the International Red Cross . . . The British proposed that the program be limited to detained persons in what was formerly unoccupied France. Since such a limitation is obviously unreasonable, we insisted that the proposed measure not be so limited and that it apply to any internment camps in Europe selected by the International Red Cross."

In its own official history the International Red Cross refers discreetly to its conflicts with the blockade and defends its position:

"Fortunately, through the energetic intervention of the War Refugee Board in Washington, set up in January, 1944, by

President Roosevelt, the Allied authorities yielded to the insistent requests of the International Committee of the Red Cross. The American supplies granted . . . for transmission to the concentration camps, which did not arrive in any considerable quantity until the end of 1944, provided relief for thousands of civilian detainees during the closing months of the war."

The speedy licensing procedures of the War Refugee Board expedited the transmission of funds to Switzerland to pay for Red Cross relief supplies and other rescue operations. $15,000,000 of the $20,000,000 funneled through the board represented contributions from the Joint Distribution Committee. Of this, more than $1,000,000 was given to the International Red Cross for the benefit of Christian as well as Jewish prisoners in concentration camps. This money had been raised by donations to the United Jewish Appeal. Without it, even limited rescue would have been impossible.

With this infusion of funds, Switzerland became the focal point for a wide variety of life-saving operations. In March 1944 the War Refugee Board chose Roswell McClelland, a thirty-year-old Quaker, as its representative in Switzerland. McClelland and his wife had worked for the American Friends Service Committee in France. They understood the plight of the Jews and were familiar with the ways of the Gestapo. The board's new representative was soon deeply involved in activities that saved thousands of lives.

Having lived in unoccupied France in 1941, McClelland was aware of the courage of its Catholic clergy. Now all France was controlled by the Nazis and McClelland knew of the desperate need for money to protect Jews and other anti-Nazis in hiding. The well-organized Social Service Section of the French resistance movement had collaborated with underground Jewish organizations, and with Catholic and Protestant clergy as well, to shelter thousands of threatened children. Mc-

Clelland relayed money from the Joint Distribution Committee to resistance emissaries in Geneva. This helped to sustain a clandestine printing plant in southeast France which turned out massive quantities of false documents. In March 1944 alone, its presses produced 1,895 identity cards, 1,300 work permits, 1,250 birth certificates, 428 military demobilization cards and 920 baptismal certificates. In that same period, names and dates on 1,500 genuine documents were removed chemically and revised to protect the holder from Nazi arrest.

McClelland also shipped large quantities of medicine and sanitary supplies into France; none was intercepted by the Nazis. Some of McClelland's money went to Father Godard, director of relief activities for Cardinal Gerlier of Lyon. Among his many feats *Père* Godard organized the release of two hundred wounded maquis prisoners. In a curious Teutonic version of justice, the Germans were restoring them to good health prior to their execution. This unique Nazi medical care was circumvented by the judicious use of *Père* Godard's funds and the maquis lived to enjoy the liberation of their country.

For those Jews who could not stay hidden in France, McClelland helped to organize escape routes across the Pyrenees into Spain. The hazardous fifteen-hour trek through the mountains was conducted by Spanish Republican and French guides who led at least one thousand hunted men, women and children to safety.

From Geneva the young Quaker dispatched funds to underground fighters in Slovakia who liberated fifteen hundred Jews from the concentration camps of Sered and Novaky. He financed prison breaks in Italy, freeing partisan leaders who had been condemned to death or deportation. McClelland also made contact in Switzerland with German political refugees banded together in the Freies Deutschland organization. Once a month these émigrés smuggled suitcases filled with inexpensive but unobtainable pocketknives, soap, razor blades, cigarettes and Swiss watches across the German border. The contents were used to bribe guards to look the other way as political refugees were spirited to safety in Switzerland.

Like Ira Hirschmann in Turkey, McClelland worked with well-organized, reliable underground groups from occupied Europe who lacked only money and supplies to aid the escape of Jews and other potential victims of the Nazis. The representatives of the War Refugee Board were not cloak-and-dagger operatives, but their authority from the President and their clear-cut commitment to values long blurred by political maneuvering and diplomatic duplicity invigorated the Europeans and strengthened their determination to continue the fight.

The record of the War Refugee Board was not unmarred, however; the years of official apathy could not be overcome in an instant of dramatic reform. There were many setbacks, the most serious occurring in Spain. There the United States ambassador, Carlton J. H. Hayes, firmly refused to permit the assignment of a board representative to his embassy. Morover, he deflected every board suggestion that he influence the Franco government to adopt more liberal refugee policies.

Hayes's defiance had begun the moment the board was established. To the cable announcing its formation and requesting that neutral governments increase their efforts to shelter refugees, Hayes replied that it was not "an opportune time." That was in January 1944.

The following month the board again cabled Hayes, with pleas that he get Spanish authorities to relax their border controls and make a public statement of their willingness to receive endangered persons. Hayes, taking a leaf from Breckinridge Long, countered with the argument that German agents might slip through if border controls were eased, and he refused to approach the Spanish government about a public statement.

Hayes maintained that the Spanish authorities were not handing refugees back to the Germans, but the War Refugee Board gathered contradictory evidence. On June 9, 1944, for example, twenty-three refugees from France, including women and children, arrived at the Spanish frontier town of Sallent. Border guards detained the Jews, then gave them false directions toward a supposedly safe area. They were well on their way toward German-held territory when they met a second group of refugees who warned them, and they returned to Sallent. This time the Spanish police forced twelve of the men into a truck and drove them back to Nazi-controlled France. En route the truck picked up twenty-six other refugees; the Germans shipped all thirty-eight prisoners to a concentration camp.

The same thing happened two days later at Bielsa. This time indignant townspeople, moved by the attempted suicide of a Dutch refugee, prevented the police from returning the Jews to the Germans.

In one memorandum protesting Hayes's inaction, Pehle wrote: "Not only has Ambassador Hayes refused to ask the Spanish Government to cooperate in implementing the President's policy with respect to refugees; he has even refused to explain the President's policy on the subject to that Government although requested to do so by the Board and the State Department."

Another member of the board staff, outlining the grievances against Hayes, wrote: "Upon the basis of the record to date, Hayes is apparently unwilling to permit a full exploration of the possibilities of expanding refugee traffic through Spain . . . and his apparent unwillingness to have private refugee organizations operate actively in Spain also seems to indicate either lack of understanding or lack of sympathy . . . it is difficult to avoid the inference that Hayes' main interest is to keep refugee operations as small and tightly controlled as possible rather than to exploit the full possibilities of Spain as a transit point for saving the lives of refugees now in enemy territory."

Hayes's obstructionism in Spain complicated the problems of the board's representative in Lisbon. Dr. Robert C. Dexter, formerly the European representative of the Unitarian Service Committee, had persuaded the Portuguese government to admit large numbers of children escaping from France via Spain, even though they lacked the proper papers. Without Hayes's full co-operation, fewer children would be accepted in Spain for transfer to Portugal.

According to the War Refugee Board's History: "In one memorandum on the matter, Dexter stated that solution of the conflict, if not the success of the Board's entire program for the Iberian Peninsula, was bound up with adequate representation in Spain. Representative Dexter went on to indicate that many of the difficulties that existed in Portugal could probably be overcome if the Board had a representative in Spain with the full backing of the Embassy there."

Pehle complained to both the President and Secretary Hull about the reluctant ambassador, but they refused to take any action. The board ignored the ambassador and went ahead with its rescue program. Perhaps the high point of Hayes's resistance was reached in May 1944, when he learned that rescue efforts were continuing through Spain without his concurrence. He demanded an explanation.

This prompted Congressman Emanuel Celler to urge his recall. "Because of the cruel recalcitrance of Mr. Hayes," said the congressman, "money for the relief and escape of refugees was sent to Portugal and several hundred were saved. Mr. Hayes resented this; his pride had been injured because his inaction had been circumvented. Mr. Hayes complained. It is noteworthy that had Mr. Hayes been willing to cooperate, thousands could have been saved through Spain instead of hundreds through Portugal . . . Will Ambassador Hayes be permitted to make policy in contradiction to the stated policy of our President? The time has come to put the screws upon the Francophile. Hayes should be recalled."

Hayes was not recalled. Later in 1944 he agreed to accept a board representative, but by that time France was in Allied hands and rescue through Spain was no longer necessary.

Ambassador Hayes's hostility was something the War Refugee Board could cope with—rescue could be detoured around him—but the frequent opposition of the British government could not be circumvented so easily. The possibility of mass rescue threatened England's Palestine policies; the vision of Jews streaming to Palestine seemed to upset Whitehall more than the vision of Jews walking to their death in the gas chambers. Although the British public and clergymen of all faiths expressed themselves earnestly on behalf of the Jews, the government sought to minimize the public outcry, through joint statements with its allies.

As a matter of fact, one might suppose from some of these major policy statements that the Jews had not even been included among Hitler's victims. The Moscow Declaration of 1943, signed by Roosevelt, Churchill and Stalin, did not mention them, although it specified that "Germans who take part in the wholesale shooting of Italian officers or in the execution of French, Dutch, Belgian or Norwegian hostages or of Cretan peasants, or who have shared in slaughters inflicted on the people of Poland or in the territories of the Soviet Union which are now being swept clear of the enemy, will know that they will be brought back to the scene of their crimes and judged on the spot by the peoples whom they have outraged."

The Big Three's omission of the Jews infuriated the World Jewish Congress, whose English section pressed the Foreign Office for a new and more specific statement. The issue came to a head after the formation of the War Refugee Board. In the belief that the Nazis' avowed drive to exterminate the Jews should be condemned and war criminals threatened with drastic punishment, the board drafted a forceful declaration which it hoped would be issued by President Roosevelt. The British government opposed the statement on the ground that similar declarations had been ineffective and had proved "embarrassing" to the Allies.

John Pehle reacted immediately to the British argument. On February 11 he wrote to Undersecretary Stettinius, stressing that the leaders of the enemy nations must be convinced that the Allies were dedicated to the rescue of the Jews. Pehle argued that a change in enemy attitudes, brought about by a new realization of Anglo-American determination to rescue the Jews, could result in the saving of many more lives than complicated rescue programs.

As for the British fear of "embarrassment," Pehle was quite blunt. There would be no embarrassment if England was sincere in her desire to prevent murder.

"On the other hand," wrote Pehle, "if the position of such government is that expressed by certain British officials to our Embassy in London in December—in simple terms that they were apparently willing to accept the probable death of thousands of Jews in enemy territory because of 'the difficulties of disposing of any considerable number of Jews should they be rescued'—and if this attitude is known to the Germans by virtue of the actions if not the words of such government, then the contention that a declaration might embarrass such government has some significance."

Pehle agreed with the World Jewish Congress' objections to the Moscow Declaration. "Any statement on our part," he wrote to Stettinius, "which omits any specific reference to the Jews loses much of its effectiveness in Germany and among her satellites by reason of the omission."

On March 24, 1944, President Roosevelt issued the strong

statement drafted by the War Refugee Board. That same day he promoted John Pehle from acting executive director to executive director of the board.

The March 24 presidential statement on Nazi criminality was not a polite pronouncement couched in diplomatic terms and released into the empty air to be forgotten. It was a direct warning to Germany and its satellites, and it was relayed by every conceivable means, including foreign-language broadcasts by the Office of War Information, publication in underground newspapers, and in leaflets air-dropped by the millions over occupied Europe. The text was forwarded in the diplomatic pouches of the neutral nations and widely reprinted in their newspapers. The statement included the following passages:

> In one of the blackest crimes of all history—begun by the Nazis in the day of peace and multiplied by them a hundred times in time of war—the wholesale systematic murder of the Jews of Europe goes on unabated every hour . . . That these innocent people, who have already survived a decade of Hitler's fury, should perish on the very eve of triumph over the barbarism which their persecution symbolizes, would be a major tragedy.
>
> It is therefore fitting that we should again proclaim our determination that none who participate in these acts of savagery shall go unpunished . . . That warning applies not only to the leaders but also to their functionaries and subordinates in Germany and in the satellite countries. All who knowingly take part in the deportation of Jews to their death in Poland or Norwegians and French to their death in Germany are equally guilty with the executioner. All who share the guilt shall share the punishment.
>
> Hitler is committing these crimes against humanity in the name of the German people. I ask every German and every man everywhere under Nazi domination to show the world by his action that in his heart he does not share

> these insane criminal desires. Let him hide these pursued victims, help them to get over their borders, and do what he can to save them from the Nazi hangman. I ask him also to keep watch, and to record the evidence that will one day be used to convict the guilty.

The British, in spite of their earlier reluctance, co-operated in disseminating the presidential statement. Through the State Department the War Refugee Board solicited Soviet support of the message for its potentially deterrent effects upon the Rumanians and Hungarians. But the Russians refused to go along, as indeed they had refused all such appeals in the past. Their argument was that all Russians, not only the Jews, faced extermination; therefore no special effort could be made on behalf of any one group. This, however, does not explain why, later on, the Soviet Union was unwilling to join the United States and Great Britain in bringing pressure to bear upon the Nazis to barter imprisoned Jews. As will be seen, the "trucks for Jews" scheme, originated by Eichmann, was not even explored because of a secret Soviet message demanding a stop to any negotiations.

Roosevelt's declaration of March 24, even though it lacked Soviet backing, was the Allies' most forthright accusation of Nazi guilt, and promised a despairing world that the criminals would be punished. It should have been made years earlier. The collective expression of Allied indignation over known Nazi brutality might have stimulated greater resistance to their German masters within the Axis satellites. It might also have strengthened what little internal opposition existed in Germany.

The cry of compassion from the governments of hundreds of millions of men and women fighting the Nazis would have reached the Jews in ghettos and death camps. The knowledge that they had not been forgotten might have clothed their naked deaths with dignity. Starved and without weapons, they might have summoned some final reservoir of defiance on the steps of the gas chamber. But by March 24, 1944, it was too late. Millions had perished. Only thousands could still be saved.

XIX
Free Ports and False Papers

FROM THE TIME OF ITS FORMATION, THE War Refugee Board grappled with the inconsistency of United States policy, which called for the rescue of the oppressed while denying them sanctuary within its borders. As Josiah DuBois expressed it in a note to Pehle:

"To Hitler the failure of the United States to afford shelter to those who might be able to escape persecution has served as an excuse to continue his mad plan to exterminate the Jews of Europe on the ground that the United Nations would be unwilling to receive these hapless people even if they were released. Among our friends this has caused our pronouncements of horror to be received with reserve and sometimes with outright skepticism, for they are well aware that neutral countries like Sweden and Switzerland have in proportion to their populations granted asylum on their soil to far more refugees than have we . . . The Gordian knot must be cut by the United States' assuming the leadership in the succoring of refugees, not because of the intrinsic merit of succoring the needy but for the even more important reason that it is a step toward victory . . . Unless we are prepared to receive refugees in the United States, our whole program of evacuation may founder on the British-Palestine position, the French reluctance to have North Africa as the only refugee haven, etc. Once we have taken the lead, however, our allies and friends must of necessity follow."

DuBois reminded Pehle that the nations of the world had noted the hypocrisy of the United States. The government of Nicaragua, replying to a War Refugee Board appeal to open its doors, had observed sarcastically that it would permit the entry of war refugees "under the same conditions as the United States and in a number proportionate to the population of both countries." DuBois thought that it would be preferable to treat refugees as prisoners of war than to allow them to perish in Europe. More than a hundred thousand Nazi prisoners were living in camps within the United States. They were well fed, adequately housed and humanely treated by a nation they had sought to destroy, but the refugees, who had harmed no one, could not even find temporary shelter. This led DuBois to suggest the establishment of refugee havens within the United States.

Pehle liked the idea and discussed it with Stettinius. The Undersecretary of State said that he shared Pehle's enthusiasm but told him that "the real hurdle would be to get the White House approval."

On April 5, 1944, New York *Post* columnist Samuel Grafton suggested the designation of "free ports for refugees" within the United States: "The need is for reservations of a few acres, here and there, where a man who has been running for ten years can sit down and catch his breath, and where somebody can tell a story to a frightened child, a few reservations where it would be possible for those who cannot satisfy the requirements of law to rest a bit, without violating the law. We do it, in commercial free ports, for cases of beans, so that we can make some storage and processing profit; it should not be impossible to do it for people."

Grafton's "free port" phrase caught the public's imagination and soon the White House was deluged with letters, telegrams and petitions supporting the plan. But Stettinius was right. "The real hurdle" *was* the White House. At a press conference the President said that it would not be necessary to establish havens in the United States because there were many countries to which the refugees could go.

The persistent prodding of his War Refugee Board eventually forced Franklin Roosevelt to accept a modest substitute for the "free port" concept. Then, with a fanfare of publicity, he announced the establishment of an emergency shelter in an abandoned Army camp in Oswego, New York. Fewer than one thousand refugees were brought to this camp. Though the sons of some were serving in the armed forces of the United States, they were kept under surveillance and permitted to leave camp for extended periods only in emergency circumstances. It was the only program of its kind authorized by the President.

The War Refugee Board was equally unsuccessful in locating sanctuaries within the nations of the British Commonwealth. Except for a brief period after the fall of France, England itself was most generous in its reception and treatment of refugees. Her Commonwealth colleagues were not. Australia, Canada, New Zealand and the Union of South Africa remained unyielding in their restrictionism.

Vast, underpopulated Australia had previously announced, at the Evian Conference, that "As we have no real racial problem, we are not desirous of importing one." Just before the war began, Australia had agreed to permit the entry of five thousand refugees a year, but hostilities prevented immigration for all but a few thousand Jews. The Australians remained inhospitable to refugees for the duration.

Canada shared this attitude. "Restrictive immigration policy," noted a message to the War Refugee Board, "was more rigidly enforced in the case of persons of Jewish extraction than in the case of any other race admitted to that country."

South Africa did not even reply to the War Refugee Board's inquiry about her willingness to welcome the homeless. Instead, its House of Assembly amended a bill calling for large-scale European immigration. The amendment specifically barred Jews.

Discouraged but not defeated by these setbacks, the War Refugee Board turned its attention to the nations of Latin America. From five to ten thousand unauthorized passports had been sold by profiteering Latin American consuls in Europe to endangered Jews. As a matter of policy the Germans did not deport Jews with Latin American passports but kept them in internment camps. Here the living conditions, unlike those of concentration camps, were tolerable. It was assumed that these Jews were being spared for possible exchange with several hundred thousand German nationals living in Latin America. As long as the Jews remained technically eligible for this exchange their safety seemed assured. Suddenly there were disquieting indications that the Germans had other plans. During 1944 they began to check the validity of the Jews' Latin American documents.

At the instigation of the War Refugee Board, a secret message was sent by courier from the State Department to all U.S. embassies in Latin America. The message notified the ambassadors that the Germans had begun to check the authenticity of the passports of the interned Jews and that their names would be submitted to the Latin American countries for verification. If the passports were declared invalid the Jews would be doomed, because they would then serve no useful purpose to the Nazis as hostages to be exchanged for Germans in South America.

"Although the Department does not condone the unauthorized use of passports," said the secret communication, "it does not follow that the Department should withhold its intercession in a situation in which the lives of so many persons are at stake." The Latin American nations should be asked to delay cancelling the false passports "until the holders shall have reached a place of safety, so that the act of cancellation shall not be, in essence, condemnation of the holder to a terrible death."

The ambassadors were then instructed to memorize the contents of the directive, burn it and communicate it orally to the respective Latin American governments. The War Refugee Board justified its unorthodox appeal on the ground that Nazi barbarism was equally unprecedented. Unfortunately the prior record of the Latin American nations did not inspire the board with confidence.

The Peruvian newspaper *Verdades* exemplified the Christian charity to be found in that country. In an article entitled "Latin America and European Refugees," it declared that hospitality should not be extended to "elements that might endanger the solid basis of our Ibero-American personality, our Catholic tradition, and the intangibility of our respective nationalities . . . under no circumstances should we accept the imposition of offering asylum to foreigners of contrary religious beliefs, of excessive liberal customs, and of moral norms different from our own."

The Peruvians soon demonstrated that their inhumanity was as good as their word. Since the neutral Swiss represented the diplomatic interests of most Latin American nations in Europe, the Germans handed them a list of forty-eight Jews interned in German camps who allegedly were Peruvian citizens. The Peruvian government denied their claim, and the Swiss were forced to relay this information to the Germans. That ended the lives of the forty-eight Jews. It was perhaps the first time that men, women and children, innocent of any crime, were murdered for lack of proof that they were citizens of Peru.

The Venezuelan attitude was not much better. As reported by the United States embassy in Caracas: "Upon applying for a visa the applicant is asked as to his race, religion and nationality, and if the person is Jewish, or of Jewish origin even though professing another religion, a visa is refused."

As for Cuba, the American embassy characterized its attitude toward refugees as "indifferent, if not slightly hostile, with little more than lip service being accorded to its humanitarian aspects."

Brazil was equally humanitarian. U.S. authorities reported that President Vargas "showed no inclination to commit Brazil to the reception of refugees of any kind."

It was in this moral climate that the War Refugee Board launched its drive to persuade Latin American governments to honor the Jews' passports until their danger had passed. The board first provided assurances that the Jews thus protected would not utilize the false documents to enter these countries. The Latin Americans were urged to insist that the Germans accept the validity of the identity papers or face retaliation against their own nationals in Latin America.

The program was first tested in an effort to rescue Jews interned in the German camp at Vittel in France. Several hundred of these internees were Poles who had purchased passports from representatives of Peru, Costa Rica, Ecuador, Honduras, Venezuela, Paraguay and Nicaragua. In December 1943 the Germans had forced them to hand over their passports. Since then the documents had been "under study," and apprehension was mounting in the camp.

Once again it would fall to the neutral Swiss to intercede with the German government. On February 21, 1944, the War Refugee Board sent the draft of a cable to the State Department, addressed to the American minister in Bern, who would instruct the Swiss to insist upon German protection of the Vittel internees. The State Department refused to send the message because it imposed excessive pressure upon the Swiss and represented a defense of fraudulent documents.

On March 16 the board submitted a more restrained version of the cable. This, too, was rejected by State.

On March 20, three months after their passports had been seized, 240 of the Jews at Vittel were rounded up and isolated from the others. It was clear that they would be sent to Poland.

The American minister to Switzerland informed the State Department on April 4 of the pending deportation and the following day John Pehle received a desperate plea from the Chief Rabbi of Palestine: "Have received news of imminent danger deportation to Poland of . . . most respected Jewish families now in Vittel . . . They left Poland over year ago furnished with citizenship Paraguay and other South American countries . . . Deportation means death . . . In Heaven's name pray take every step save them particularly through intervention neutral countries . . . Rest not may Almighty bless your efforts with success . . ."

Pehle and his staff tried frantically to budge the State Department. They deluged Stettinius and other officials with phone calls, memoranda and personal visits. On April 7 the department's Policy Committee finally agreed to communicate with the Swiss. After a three-week delay they sent the restrained draft of March 16. It was too late. Before the Swiss could approach the Germans, the first group of 173 Jews was sent from Vittel to the transit camp at Drancy. On April 29 about sixty of them—men, women and children—left Drancy for Auschwitz, never to return. At the instigation of the War Refugee Board, the Swiss made an earnest effort to intervene in behalf of the deportees, but German authorities claimed they did not know the whereabouts of the Vittel group.

In all, 238 Jews of Vittel died in Auschwitz. Among them were the distinguished Yiddish and Hebrew poet-playwright Itzhak Katznelson and his eighteen-year-old son. Earlier, Katznelson's wife and two younger sons had been arrested in the Warsaw ghetto and put to death at Treblinka; the poet and his son, Zvi, had escaped to a bunker dug deep beneath a hothouse outside the ghetto. In May 1943 they were given Honduran passports by a resistance fighter. Soon after, they were arrested in Poland by the Germans and sent to Vittel. During the next ten months Katznelson, wracked by the memory of his murdered wife and children, poured his agonizing lament into a diary, several plays and his epic poem, *The Song of the Murdered Jewish People*. Before he was taken from Vittel the poet placed his finely written, rolled-up manuscripts into bottles, which he buried beneath the sixth tree in a row of pines. He divulged this hiding place to several companions and one of the survivors later dug up the bottles. Other Katznelson writings were smuggled out of Vittel by a courageous French laundress who had sewn them into rags.

Twelve days after Itzhak and Zvi Katznelson were taken to Auschwitz, the Germans responded to the Swiss plea that they honor Latin American passports. On May 11, 1944, the Nazis agreed to stop deporting Jews with identity papers from Latin American countries. If the State Department had not held up its cable to Switzerland for three weeks, Katznelson and the Jews of Vittel might have survived.

The Ghetto Fighters' House, a kibbutz in Israel founded by survivors of the Warsaw ghetto, is dedicated to the memory of Itzhak Katznelson. It has published his powerful *Vittel Diary*, whose recurring theme is the apathy of the world in the face of Nazi murder:

"Sure enough, the nations did not interfere, nor did they protest, nor shake their heads, nor did they warn the murderers, never a murmur. It was as if the leaders of the nations were afraid that the killings might stop."

. . .

While the War Refugee Board was engaged in its fruitless efforts to save the 238 Jews of Vittel, its newest field representative reported to the U.S. legation in Stockholm. Iver Olsen had served with John Pehle in the Treasury Department, handling a variety of domestic and foreign assignments with an engaging blend of competence and conviviality.

Olsen's activities in Sweden illustrated the range of possibilities that existed for the rescue of diverse groups under attack by Hitler. Most of the people snatched from death were Jewish because the threat to their lives was immediate, but the board sought to rescue anyone in immediate danger regardless of his political or religious affiliation. From Stockholm, Iver Olsen organized the rescue of thousands of trade unionists, intellectuals and political leaders of all faiths. He was aided by the Swedish government and unanimous public support.

Sweden was neutral but its sympathies were clear. After the Swedes failed to dissuade the Germans from their intention to deport the Danish Jews in 1943, they offered sanctuary to all who reached Sweden's shores. Although their country was occupied by the Germans, the Danes, oblivious to personal danger, hid the Jews, then arranged for their escape by boat. In October eight thousand Danish Jews were welcomed to Sweden.

It was clear that Iver Olsen was in friendly territory. As he reported to John Pehle: "The purposes and aims of the War Refugee Board met with an instant response in Sweden, with offers of assistance and cooperation pouring in from all sides."

One of Olsen's first projects involved the escape of political and intellectual refugees from the Baltic States—Latvia, Lithuania and Estonia. He provided funds for the hiring of boats capable of outrunning German submarines and surface craft, and he planned the details of rescue operations with refugee Baltic leaders. More than 1,200 Estonians were liberated. A high-speed cabin cruiser hired by Olsen carried 275 to Sweden and the remainder were concealed in the holds of Estonian fishing vessels, with the blessing of Swedish authorities. Seven hundred Latvians, 135 Lithuanians and 150 Finnish Jews also entered Sweden during these operations.

If enemy ships threatened the unarmed rescue vessels, the Swedish navy appeared and carried out its neutral maneuvers in fortuitous proximity. When escape from the Baltic countries became too hazardous, Olsen's confederates brought food and supplies to the men and women in hiding. It is estimated that the communications network and underground liaison established by the American saved as many lives as the direct evacuation to Sweden.

But Olsen's most massive rescue efforts were directed toward Norway. Utilizing funds contributed to the War Refugee Board by the American Federation of Labor and Congress of Industrial Organizations, Olsen teamed up with escaped Norwegian labor leaders to liberate their endangered countrymen. With unofficial but extensive Swedish co-operation, more than ten thousand Norwegians were brought to Sweden. Some came by boat from southern Norway, others through the mountains in the north. At the same time, clandestine shipments of food and clothing supplied an additional ten thousand Norwegian youths in hiding.

Olsen was filled with admiration for the Norwegian resistance. "Even the Norwegian pastors," he reported to Washington, "were operating a lively underground with great skill—shading, if necessary, certain aspects of the Ten Commandments."

With Scandinavian rescue well organized, the War Refugee Board turned its attention to its greatest challenge—Hungary. At stake were the lives of two hundred thousand Budapest Jews threatened by Nazi massacre.

■ XX ■
Rescue from Hungary

BY 1944 HUNGARY'S PREWAR JEWISH POPULATION of over four hundred thousand had been almost doubled by refugees fleeing from Hitler. Although Hungary had allied herself with Germany and had adopted anti-Semitic laws, the government under the regency of Admiral Miklós von Horthy had managed to delay the deportation of Jews to the Nazi death camps. But in March, Hitler, infuriated by Hungarian indecision, intervened and forced Horthy's appointment of a more militantly anti-Semitic government. The new regime ordered the Jews to wear the Star of David and confiscated their property.

Chief Rabbi Ferenc Hevesi of Hungary consoled his people: "The yellow star will be removed from us, but a mark of humiliation will always show on the breasts of those who forced us to wear this star and those who by their indifference allowed this to happen."

The decree also caused great anguish to Justin Cardinal Serédi, the Prince Primate of Hungary, but for quite another reason. As the leading cleric in an overwhelmingly Catholic nation, he was pained by the realization that thousands of Jewish families which had converted to Catholicism would also be required to wear the insignia. On April 23 the cardinal handed his written protest to pro-Nazi Prime Minister Szotay:

"I herewith insistently request the Royal Hungarian Government of Christian Hungary . . . to consider the baptized Christians, even though they be of Jewish origin, and distinguish them from the Jews, as they, by the act of baptism, have already distinguished themselves."

Cardinal Serédi was concerned with saving property as well as souls. He reminded the Prime Minister that if the property of Jewish parents was confiscated, "children to whom the stipulations of the Jewish laws do not apply, are deprived of their fortune . . ." This action, said the pragmatic cardinal, might turn Hungarians against their government. There would be objections not merely from those directly involved "but also the public opinion of the entire Christian world, the Holy See and, most of all, God himself."

His Eminence gave no sign that God's wrath would be aroused by the plunder and brutalization of those who admitted to being Jews. Evidently, divine indignation could be provoked only by the mistreatment of converts to Christianity.

The Prime Minister yielded slightly to the Prince Primate's plea, in that baptized Jews could wear a cross *in addition* to the Star of David. In a pastoral letter the cardinal was able to write with a certain measure of satisfaction: "We have neither abandoned nor betrayed the true cause of our Catholic brethren but under the prevailing circumstances we could achieve no more."

The wearing of the yellow star was a mild prelude to the disaster that befell the Jews of Hungary. Beginning in April 1944, those living in the provinces were forcibly removed from their homes to makeshift camps in the open air or crammed into ghettos. There they awaited deportation to Auschwitz. The dragnet would first sweep the rural areas, tighten the ring toward Budapest and culminate in the capital with its prize of two hundred thousand Jews.

The roundups were conducted savagely by the Hungarian police. When the ominous freight trains rolled up to sidings at the improvised camps and ghettos, the police used rifle butts and whips to jam sixty to seventy people of all ages into each boxcar. There were two buckets—one for water, one for human waste. The cars were sealed before their departure, the heat intensifying the horror. As the trains passed through Hungarian cities, residents could hear the cries of women and children, many of whom died of suffocation before they reached their destination.

Hungarian newspapers reported the deportations and one article went so far as to describe the death of three Jewish women in a freight car. Their ages were reported as one hundred and four, one hundred and two and ninety-two.

In less than two months, between May 15 and July 7, 437,000 Jews were shipped to Auschwitz. Despite the German genius for the organized killing of civilians and the efficiency of the ovens built by Topf & Sons, the capacity of the crematoria proved inadequate. On Commandant Rudolf Hoess's orders, additional burning pits were dug. Within a forty-six-day period, between 250,000 and 300,000 of the Jews from Hungary were gassed or shot.

The Jews who had escaped the dragnet addressed leaflets to their Christian countrymen describing the details of the journey and the ultimate fate of the travelers. One closed with the words: "Should, however, this desperate appeal for our bare lives prove to be in vain, we have only one thing to ask: spare us the horrors of deportation and end our sufferings here, so that at least we can be buried in our native land."

The swift Hungarian-German action caught the world by surprise, for by this time the Axis faced certain defeat and a moderation of anti-Semitic acts was expected.

The War Refugee Board first reacted to the Hungarian deportations on April 26. A direct message to Pope Pius XII urged him to intervene personally and to threaten the Nazis' accomplices with excommunication:

"His Holiness, we deeply hope, may find it possible to remind the authorities and people of Hungary, among whom great numbers profess spiritual adherence to the Holy See, of the spiritual consequences of such acts and of the ecclesiastic sanctions which may be applied to the perpetrators thereof . . ."

The Pope would wait a full month before sending his personal plea to Admiral Horthy.

At the same time that the approach was made to His Holiness, the board urged American diplomatic missions in all neutral nations to request that these countries increase their staffs in Hungary. John Pehle assumed that Nazi-Hungarian brutality would be inhibited in the presence of international observers. As has been mentioned, the Red Cross at first refused to increase its staff in Budapest. Ambassador Hayes in Madrid remained true to his apathy by replying that it was useless to propose increased representation to the Spanish government. However, the board's proposal was well received in Sweden with results that would become apparent in July.

Meanwhile Ambassador Steinhardt in Turkey made the first reference to an event which later captured the imagination of the world. He ended his lengthy May 25 cable to the State Department:

"Two days ago an individual by the name of Joel Brand, documented as the representative of the Jewish Community of Budapest, arrived in Istanbul and submitted to Barlas of the Jewish Agency a proposal which it is said originated with the Commissioner for Jewish Affairs, Eichman [*sic*], to the effect that in exchange for two million cakes of soap, two hundred tons of cocoa, eight hundred tons of coffee, two hundred tons of tea and ten thousand trucks Eichman would agree to stop the deportation and extermination of Jews in all areas which the Germans occupy and including Rumania and he would further agree to permit the exit of Jewish limited numbers to Palestine and in unlimited numbers to Spain."

Steinhardt informed the board that André Antol Gyorgy, a man of many aliases and loyalties, had accompanied Brand. "It is said," observed Steinhardt, "that American and British intelligence regard him as a Gestapo agent and completely unreliable." Gyorgy, who was known to Brand as Bandi Grosz, had served both the Germans and the Hungarian secret service. Eichmann had assigned him to keep an eye on Brand, and his presence would further complicate the already complex mission.

As the Brand story developed, a number of points became clear. He had been an official of the Zionist Relief and Rescue Committee of Budapest, helping Jews escape to Hungary from Poland and Slovakia. After the German occupation of Hungary and the immediate threat of deportation, the committee had switched its tactics. It established contact with Eichmann's subordinate, Dieter Wisliceny, in an attempt to purchase the safety of the Hungarian Jews. On May 8 Eichmann himself had summoned Brand, announcing that he was prepared to sell one million Jews. As Eichmann put it, "Blood for money, money for blood." Brand was to go abroad and contact Jewish groups and representatives of the Allies to arrange the details.

At a later meeting Eichmann substituted trucks and merchandise for cash as the proposed payment for the Jews. It was agreed that Brand would go to Istanbul to meet with representatives of the Jewish Agency for Palestine. When Brand asked Eichmann what guarantees he could provide for the release of the Jews, the SS official answered, "If you return from Constantinople [Istanbul] and tell me that the offer has been accepted, I will close Oświęcim [Auschwitz] and bring ten percent of the promised million to the frontier." Eichmann further volunteered his pledge that the ten thousand trucks would be used only on the eastern front against the Russians.

At no time during the ensuing months did Brand believe that the Allies would agree to give trucks to the Nazis. Nevertheless, his firsthand experience with German corruption convinced him that time could be gained by negotiations, and a private bribe substituted for military equipment. Armed with an official authorization from the Central Council of Hungarian Jews, and accompanied by the ubiquitous Bandi Grosz, Brand departed for Istanbul in a German courier plane.

They were met on May 23 by the Istanbul representatives of the Jewish Agency. Brand described the Eichmann offer, including his promise that trucks would be used only against the Russians. When this information was relayed to British and American authorities, there was understandable alarm at this transparent attempt to split them from their Soviet ally. They feared that the Germans might leak the proposal to the Russians, who were always quick to doubt the fidelity of their comrades in arms.

Brand soon realized that his conversations in Istanbul were getting nowhere. It was apparent that the Jewish Agency representatives lacked the authority to take any action. Moshe Shertok, the influential head of the agency's political department in Jerusalem, had applied for travel papers to join Brand in Istanbul but, unaccountably, the British refused to authorize his trip. As the two-week deadline imposed by Eichmann neared without any developments, Brand decided to attempt a meeting with Shertok in Aleppo, Syria; if that failed he would continue to Palestine.

Brand was warned that in Syria and Palestine he would be subject to British arrest, a danger which did not exist in neutral Turkey. Nevertheless, he boarded the Taurus Express for Aleppo. As he debarked from the train he was arrested by British security agents.

Meanwhile the British government had informed the State Department of its reaction to the Brand mission:

"Assuming suggestion was put forward by Gestapo in form

conveyed to us, then it seems to be sheer case of blackmail or political warfare . . . Implied suggestion that we should accept responsibility for maintenance of additional million person is equivalent to asking the Allies to suspend essential military operations." Then followed the equally familiar British disclaimer that genuine proposals involving rescue would always be welcome, since the "whole record of United States Government and His Majesty's Government over refugees is a proof of their active sympathy with victims of Nazi terror."

With Brand now in custody, Moshe Shertok managed to wangle travel papers to visit Aleppo. The future Prime Minister of Israel waited for five days, then was permitted to interview Brand. Shertok described his impression of the Hungarian in a report to Jerusalem:

"Generally we were all—and this includes the British officers who spoke to him—very much impressed by his courage and spirit. Every minute of the day in Budapest he was risking his life in conspiring against the Germans. He is a very solid type: squarely built, broad-nosed, peasant-like, a bit slow and heavy, but with a very clear head and a firm grasp of facts. He breathes honesty."

Brand told Shertok that the Nazis hoped to divert the world's attention from the killing of six million Jews by offering to release those millions still alive. He had no illusions about Eichmann or Bandi Grosz, but he must be permitted to return to Budapest on the slim chance that deportations would stop. Shertok promised to do everything in his power to help him.

In Washington the War Refugee Board became suspicious of the continued British imprisonment of Brand. It happened that Ira Hirschmann was in the United States for consultation, so John Pehle cut short his visit and assigned him to investigate Brand's captivity.

Before he left, Hirschmann was invited to the White House. The President urged him to "cable back everything you hear.

While you talk these people still have a chance to live." Roosevelt handed him a letter which endowed the assignment with presidential authority.

Hirschmann finally caught up with Brand and his captors in Cairo. First he tried to arrange a meeting with Lord Moyne, the Deputy Minister of State and senior British official in the Middle East. Lord Moyne sent word that he thought it unnecessary for them to meet and preferred that Hirschmann not interview Brand either. It would be much better, suggested the Englishman, if Hirschmann flew to London and discussed the matter with Mr. Eden.

Hirschmann, not easily cowed, refused to leave Cairo and hammered his way into Lord Moyne's office. When the Deputy Minister of State repeated the invitation to London, Hirschmann replied, "I will agree to take my instructions from Mr. Eden if you will agree to take yours from Mr. Hull. I will go to London if you will go to Washington." At this point Hirschmann produced his presidential letter and Lord Moyne promptly arranged the meeting with Brand.

In his report to the War Refugee Board Hirschmann described the Hungarian: "Brand impressed me as honest, clear, incisive, blunt and completely frank . . . In short, Brand's disclosures are to be accepted in my view as truthful, without reservations." As for Grosz: "He is in a different category, an agent with a perfidious record."

Hirschmann recommended that Brand be sent back to Hungary at the earliest moment, with careful instructions "indicating that consideration is being given the proposals in connection with money and possible immunity." There would be no mention of the trucks.

Hirschmann could not know as he wrote his report that the decision had already been made by the United States and Britain to terminate any dealings with Brand or with Eichmann. The veto had been cast by the Soviet Union. The U.S. embassy in Moscow had notified the Soviet government of American plans to explore the Brand proposal in the hope of stalling the Nazi extermination schedule. The Russians had been reassured that the United States would not be fooled by attempts to split the Allies.

On June 19, 1944, Ambassador Harriman relayed Soviet reaction. He had received a secret message from Deputy Foreign Minister Andrei Vishinsky: "Vishinsky had been instructed by the Soviet Government to state that it does not consider it permissible or expedient to carry on any conversations whatsoever with the German Government on the questions which the note from the Embassy touched upon."

This callous Soviet attitude ended any efforts to utilize Joel Brand in a stalling operation which might have saved lives. Brand languished for months in British custody, convinced that he was responsible for the continuing slaughter of the Jews of Hungary. After the war he wandered the earth with his story, reaching a high point in his confrontation with Adolf Eichmann in the Jerusalem courtroom. In the final irony of a tormented life he died in Germany of a heart attack following an impassioned statement at a trial of Auschwitz officials.

To this day it is impossible to tell whether Eichmann's promise to sell the Jews would or could have been fulfilled. It would be irresponsible to claim that substantial numbers would have been spared. It would be equally irresponsible to attempt to justify the Anglo-American failure to send Joel Brand back to Budapest. We can only conjecture what might have happened if the Allies had accepted Ira Hirschmann's recommendation for Brand's return to Budapest.

There was still another setback in the War Refugee Board's efforts to save the Jews of Hungary. In late June the board's representative in Switzerland, Roswell McClelland, proposed that the Allies bomb the railway lines from Hungary to Auschwitz. The Czech underground had supplied routes, key bombing locations and train schedules.

"It is urged by all sources of this information in Slovakia and Hungary," McClelland cabled, "that vital sections of these lines especially bridges along . . . Csap-Kaschau-Prešov-Lubotin-Nowysącz in direction of Oświęcim . . . be bombed as the only possible means of slowing down or stopping future deportations . . . There is little doubt that many of these Hungarian Jews are being sent to the extermination camps of Auschwitz and Birkenau in western Upper Silesia where, according to recent reports, since early summer 1942, at least 1,500,000 Jews have been killed."

Pehle forwarded the information to Assistant Secretary of War John McCloy. On July 4 McCloy replied: "The War Department is of the opinion that the suggested air operation is impracticable. It could be executed only by the diversion of considerable air support essential to the success of our forces now engaged in decisive operations and would in any case be of such very doubtful efficacy that it would not amount to a practical project."

During the next few months there were repeated attempts by the War Refugee Board to interest the War Department in bombing the railways and the camps themselves. James Mann, who now represented the board in London, relayed a message from the Polish government-in-exile "that the War Refugee Board again explore with the Army the possibility of bombing the extermination chambers and German barracks at largest Polish concentration camps which, they state, are sufficiently detached from the concentration camps to permit precision bombing."

Once again McCloy rejected the suggestion. Some months later McClelland sent Pehle eyewitness descriptions and diagrams of Auschwitz and nearby Birkenau. This time Pehle was more insistent.

"If the elaborate murder installations at Birkenau were destroyed," he wrote to McCloy, "it seems clear that the Germans could not reconstruct them for some time . . . I am convinced that the point has now been reached where such action is justifiable if it is deemed feasible by competent military authorities. I strongly recommend that the War Department give serious consideration to the possibility of destroying the execution chambers and crematories in Birkenau through direct bombing action."

Pehle, attempting to illustrate the possibilities of precision bombing, enclosed a newspaper report which described an attack by Allied planes against a German prison in France. The French inmates had escaped unharmed while the pilots, who had studied detailed plans of the prison, bombed and machine-gunned their guards.

McCloy replied that the operations staff of the War Department had given careful consideration to Pehle's suggestion but had rejected it because the target was too distant for dive bombers and fighter-bombers. Auschwitz and Birkenau were within the range of heavy bombers, but they would be forced to fly a two-thousand-mile round trip over enemy territory without fighter escort. "The positive solution to this problem," concluded McCloy, "is the earliest possible victory over Germany . . ."

While Pehle was pressing McCloy unsuccessfully, representatives of the Jewish Agency for Palestine were attempting with equal futility to interest the British in a similar scheme. Dr. Chaim Weizmann had first discussed the proposed bombing with Mr. Eden in July 1944. Months later he was informed that the suggestion had been turned down "because of the great technical difficulties involved."

Some of "the great technical difficulties" may have been caused by the Soviet Union. The Russians were notified that the Americans and the English were considering bombing the camps. The Soviet reaction has never been revealed, but there may have been a hint of it in a terse note from Winston Churchill's private secretary, J. F. Martin. On October 30, 1944, in response to still another inquiry about the proposed bombing by the persistent Dr. Weizmann, he wrote: "We have discussed this matter with the Soviets, and that's it."

Repeated requests for the bombing of Auschwitz were made by the Czech and Polish governments-in-exile. All were turned down. The British rejected an even more daring suggestion in defense of the Jews of Hungary. It was later summarized by Chaim Weizmann:

"At the beginning of 1944 when more than 700,000 Jews were still alive in Hungary, the Jewish Agency proposed to the British authorities to take hundreds of Palestinian Jews and drop them by parachute into Hungary and this according to the considered judgment of Birtish military circles could have helped the Allies militarily and could have also been of value for the prevention of the extermination of many Hungarian Jews who were then alive. When this program was approved by all military authorized bodies and arrangements were made to carry out this plan, the Colonial and Foreign Offices intervened and because of political considerations ordered the military authorities to refrain from applying this program."

The British documents which might either substantiate or refute Dr. Weizmann's contention remain classified and unavailable. One can only presume that the British objected to a Palestinian parachute force in Hungary because of the enhanced recognition this would give the Jews in their drive for nationhood.

In any event, the refusal to sanction either the destruction of the camps or the physical defense of the Jews of Hungary appeared to have doomed the two hundred thousand who still remained in Budapest after the deportations of May–July 1944. But the War Refugee Board, which had been thwarted in its search for sanctuaries, frustrated in its efforts to influence a papal denunciation of the Hungarians, and rebuffed in its recommendations regarding Joel Brand, suddenly forced a mobilization of world opinion.

On June 25 the Pope finally sent his long-delayed message

to Regent Horthy. By that time more than 350,000 of the 437,000 deportees had been gassed. While the papal plea was characteristically evasive and lacked the threat of punishment suggested by the board, it nevertheless produced a useful effect.

The day after Pius XII's appeal Franklin D. Roosevelt, responding to continuing pressure by John Pehle, sent a sharp message to the Hungarian government threatening to bomb Hungary unless the deportations ceased. Lest the warning be ignored Cordell Hull reiterated it one day later. Now it was the turn of the International Committee of the Red Cross. The ICRC, belabored by the War Refugee Board for its failure to intercede in the deportations, at last appealed to Horthy, calling the cruelties "so utterly contrary to the chivalrous traditions of the great Hungarian people that it is difficult for us to credit even a tithe of the information we are receiving." But the most powerful force brought to bear upon the regent of Hungary was a thirty-two-year-old Swede named Raoul Wallenberg.

For generations the name Wallenberg has been identified with Swedish statesmen, bishops, diplomats, military and financial leaders. Raoul was the son of a young naval officer who had died three months before his son's birth. Reared by his beautiful, cultivated mother, he was a special favorite of his grandfather Gustav, who had served as Swedish minister to Japan and Turkey. Under Gustav's tutelage Raoul developed a world view, traveling extensively in Europe and the Middle East. Skilled in languages, he combined a subtle sense of humor with a highly developed sense of compassion. After earning an honors degree in architecture from the University of Michigan, Raoul reverted to the family interest in finance and went to work for a bank in Haifa, Palestine. Here he first glimpsed Jews in flight from Hitler. This recollection was reinforced by his experience in the early 1940's as foreign representative of a Stockholm export-import firm. His visits to German-occupied Europe and business trips to Budapest in 1942–43 evoked vivid impressions of Nazi brutality. These were heightened by his friendship with a Hungarian Jewish partner.

Wallenberg's combination of pragmatic and idealistic qualities were brought to the attention of Iver Olsen, the War Refugee Board's representative in Stockholm. At this time Olsen was seeking to implement the board's suggestion that Sweden increase its diplomatic delegation in Budapest. Simultaneously a movement had developed within Sweden for a program to aid the destitute Hungarian Jews. Enlisting the support of the Swedish Foreign Ministry, King Gustaf V and Jewish organizations within Sweden, Olsen played an essential if unobtrusive role in the most dramatic lifesaving operation of the war. There was no overt American involvement. Instead, Wallenberg was given full diplomatic accreditation as third secretary of the Swedish legation in Budapest. He was assigned to organize a special department responsible for the protection and relief of Jews. To finance this ambitious effort the War Refugee Board authorized Olsen to transmit to the "neutral" Wallenberg a first installment of $100,000 in Joint Distribution Committee funds. As a further extension of its unorthodox diplomacy the board provided Wallenberg with a list of corrupt Hungarian passport officials, undercover anti-Nazis, and others who could be of assistance. The board described one Hungarian contact as "a lawyer who for a number of years very skillfully played the role of an ardent Nazi and anti-Semite with the objective of helping distressed or endangered Jews and liberals."

Prior to Wallenberg's departure King Gustaf sent Admiral Horthy a personal message urging humanitarian treatment for the Jews. The deluge of telegrams from world leaders shook the regent, who expressed his apprehension to his German masters. Suddenly everyone seemed concerned about the Jews.

Wallenberg arrived in Budapest early in July. The Swedish minister, Carl Ivan Danielsson, had already begun the rescue effort by issuing six hundred provisional passports to Jews who had personal or commercial ties to Sweden. Wallenberg expanded this scheme radically. He printed a protective passport of his own elaborate design, complete with official seals and the triple-crown insignia of Sweden. It stated that the bearer awaited emigration to Sweden and, until his departure, enjoyed the protection of that government. Wallenberg persuaded the Hungarian authorities to respect five thousand of these homemade passports.

Although the appeal of the Pope, the President of the United States, the president of the International Red Cross and the King of Sweden had halted the deportations temporarily, the Jews of Budapest remained at the mercy of Hungarian gendarmes and the armed street fighters of the Fascist Arrow Cross organization. Their property and possessions had been confiscated, their apartments seized, and access to food and medicine had been cut off. They were daily subjected to humiliation and violence. Death in the streets of Budapest was a commonplace event.

In this grim setting Raoul Wallenberg wrought a man-made miracle. Working around the clock, he built a city-wide relief organization, establishing hospitals, nurseries and soup kitchens. He employed four hundred Jews to staff these institutions. With funds replenished by the JDC, Wallenberg purchased food, clothing and medicine. He dropped the requirement that the Jews have some direct connection with Sweden and distributed an additional five thousand protective passports. Neither the Germans nor their Hungarian ally wished to antagonize the neutral Swedes, and though Wallenberg was continually threatened, no direct action was taken against him.

Wallenberg's example was contagious. Soon the Swiss began providing similar protection to the Jews. Red Cross delegate Robert Schirmer, sent to Budapest after repeated entreaties by the War Refugee Board, began an energetic distribution of supplies, and the international insignia of mercy appeared everywhere.

Even the representatives of the Franco regime were inspired

by Wallenberg's courage and ingenuity. Together with the Portuguese they supported a small program for the sheltering of several hundred Sephardic Jews, whose ancestors had been banished from Spain and Portugal. Ambassador Hayes in Madrid, who had pleaded Spain's inability to assist in earlier rescue efforts, was responsible for this intercession.

A major effort was undertaken by the Papal Nuncio in Budapest, Monsignor Angelo Rotta. This, like the earlier rescue of the Jews of Sofia, can be traced to the man who later became Pope John XXIII. In this instance it was the War Refugee Board which linked the Apostolic Delegate to Turkey with the Nuncio in Budapest.

On August 1, 1944, as Raoul Wallenberg sought to enlarge the protection of the Jews of Budapest, Ira Hirschmann visited Angelo Roncalli at his summer residence on an island near Istanbul. Hirschmann described the desperate situation in Hungary and asked for Roncalli's help. The Apostolic Delegate had already seen Chief Rabbi Isaac Halevi Herzog of Palestine and had assured him of his support. Hirschmann knew of rumors that Roncalli had tried unsuccessfully to arrange a meeting between the rabbi and Pope Pius XII. There had also been unsubstantiated stories that on his own authority, Roncalli had asked leading Catholic prelates in eastern Europe to intercede on behalf of the Jews.

The Apostolic Delegate admitted to Hirschmann that at Rabbi Herzog's request he had written to the Papal Secretary of State urging him to do all in his power to save the Jews, but regretted that he could not divulge the texts of his letters regarding Rumania and Hungary. Contrary to rumor, said Roncalli, these appeals had been forwarded via the Papal Secretariat and could not be revealed without special permission from the Vatican.

Roncalli was visibly moved by Hirschmann's description of the disaster that had befallen the Jews of Hungary. He asked the American whether he thought the Jews would be willing to undergo baptism as an emergency measure (he had heard that such certificates guaranteed safety), and stressed that the ceremony would serve a lifesaving rather than proselytizing function. If Hirschmann thought the idea would not be offensive to the Jews, Roncalli would be happy to suggest it to the Papal Nuncio in Budapest. Hirschmann said wryly that he thought the Jews would welcome the opportunity to live.

On August 18 Monsignor Roncalli confirmed his actions in writing, informing Hirschmann that he had sent thousands of baptismal certificates to the Nuncio. He had also forwarded Palestine immigration papers which he had wangled from the British. In his letter to Hirschmann, Roncalli noted that he would be happy to do anything of a nonpolitical nature to assist him, that he would do whatever he could on behalf of individual Jews (he mentioned the case of a Rabbi Solomon Halberstam whom he had aided) and he summed it all up by saying: "I repeat that I am always ready to help you in your charitable work as far as in my power and as far as circumstances permit."

Within months of Hirschmann's visit to the Apostolic Delegate, thousands of Jews were baptized in the air-raid shelters of Budapest and thereby snatched from death at the hands of their German and Hungarian oppressors. Others escaped to Palestine thanks to the immigration certificates forwarded by Monsignor Roncalli, and still others survived because of "safe-conduct" passes issued by the Papal Nuncio in Budapest.

But if the number of rescuers had grown, so had the emergency. On October 15, 1944, as the Russian armies smashed through Rumania toward Hungary, a new and more dangerous crisis enveloped Budapest. While Hungary sought to conclude an armistice with the Allies, the Germans moved a panzer division into Budapest, kidnapped Horthy's son and installed a new government. At its head they placed the fanatically anti-Semitic Arrow Cross leader, Ferenc Szálasi. The day after he assumed power his men roamed the streets, murdering an estimated six hundred Jews and dumping their bodies into the Danube.

To meet this new threat Raoul Wallenberg begged, borrowed and rented thirty-two apartment houses to which he removed the five thousand holders of his unique document. The Swedish flag flew over these buildings, and Wallenberg and his colleagues guarded the entrances. With funds continually replenished by the JDC, Wallenberg bought food and medicine for his wards, who were forbidden to enter most retail stores. Growing more daring as the crisis mounted, Wallenberg issued an additional five thousand protective passports. Eventually he shielded twenty thousand Jews, thirteen thousand in the so-called "Swedish houses." Forty doctors recruited by Wallenberg inoculated the residents of the crowded ghetto against typhoid, paratyphoid and cholera.

The Swiss kept pace with the Swedes, providing housing for an estimated twenty thousand Jews to whom they had issued their own protective documents. Prime Minister Szálasi attempted by law to nullify the Jews' international protection but Wallenberg, playing upon the Arrow Cross leader's ambition for diplomatic recognition, persuaded him to retract the order. But Wallenberg could not prevent Szálasi from yielding to a new Nazi demand.

The reservoirs of German slave labor were running low and the vast underground armament factories of Austria were undermanned. As their new candidates for slow, subterranean death the Nazis turned to the more than one hundred thousand Jews of Budapest who still lacked the protection of the neutrals. Because of the shortage of rolling stock the Germans ordered the Hungarians to march the Jews to the Austrian border 144 miles away.

The neutrals were helpless to prevent the new disaster. In the bitter cold of late November, more than thirty thousand men, women and children began the death march to Austria. Without food, medical attention or shelter, they straggled down the highway in groups of one thousand, whipped on by Hungarian guards. Those who faltered or fell were shot. An observer noted that Bertha Schwartz, aged seventy-four, had reached toward a guard for support. She was killed before her hand touched his.

But even at this late hour Wallenberg was undeterred. With utter disregard for his personal safety, he picked up two thousand marchers who he declared were entitled to Swedish protection. He forced the return of several thousand laborers from Austria because of their alleged Swedish ties. And he was not alone in his rescue efforts.

Monsignor Rotta had given hundreds of "safe-conduct" certificates to Sándor Ujváry, a volunteer worker for the Red Cross. Ujváry roamed the line of marchers, with nuns carrying food and medicine for the Jews. They described the scene:

"Endless columns of deported persons were marched along: ragged and starving people, mortally tired, among them old and wizened creatures who could hardly crawl along. Gendarmes were driving them with the butt-end of their rifles, with sticks and with whips. They had to cover thirty kilometres a day until they came to a 'resting place.' This generally was the marketplace of a town. They were driven into the square and spent the nights in the open, huddled together and shivering with cold in the chill of a November or December night. On the morning following the 'rest' we saw the number of corpses, which would never again rise from the frosty ground of the market-square."

More than one-fifth of the Jews died en route, a toll so heavy that Szálasi canceled the marches.

The horrors they saw with their own eyes forced the neutral observers to take more direct rescue action. The delegates of the International Red Cross issued thirty thousand certificates of protection to the Jews. The papers lacked any basis in international law but they were effective. Red Cross kitchens fed twenty thousand people a day and Red Cross children's homes sheltered two thousand youngsters. The men from Geneva were no longer afraid to interfere in the internal affairs of a nation dedicated to the destruction of its own citizens.

Unlike Cardinal Serédi, Protestant Bishop László Ràvasz was outraged over the brutal treatment, whether of Jews or of Christians of Jewish origin. He persisted in his courageous but futile attempts to halt the persecution. Monsignor Rotta issued no less than fifteen thousand "safe-conducts" and encouraged a record-breaking number of baptisms as suggested by his old friend, the Apostolic Delegate to Turkey. Bishop William Apor of Györ, who objected to the indifference of his superior, Cardinal Serédi, was tireless in his efforts to aid the Jews, as were hundreds of priests and nuns.

Although mass deportation to Auschwitz by rail had ended, there were sporadic German efforts to round up trainloads of Jews. Inevitably Wallenberg, who had established a network of listening posts in Budapest, would receive word of the impending deportation and arrive at the railroad station with a great show of official papers and a barking of orders in Swedish and Hungarian. Once, with German guns leveled at him, he displayed his Swedish credentials and marched three hundred Jews away from the station. Another time his cohort Per Anger freed 150 Jews from a German transport, although only two had a remote connection with Sweden.

On one of the rare occasions when he failed to arrive at the station in time to halt a deportation, Wallenberg raced ahead of the train in his automobile and leaped aboard at a border station. By bluffing the German guards he was able to rescue those deportees who carried any papers at all, whether tax receipts or vaccination certificates.

Wallenberg and the neutrals were winning their race. The Nazis and the Arrow Cross had failed to murder the Jews and the Soviet invaders were at the gates of Budapest. Led by Marshal Rodion Malinovsky, they began their siege of the capital on December 8, 1944. They liberated the so-called international ghetto, which included the "Swedish houses," on January 16. Earlier, Wallenberg had told friends that he would not return to Sweden until the property of the Jews was restored to them. As a first step he planned to discuss the rehabilitation of the Jewish community with Marshal Malinovsky.

On January 17 Wallenberg, accompanied by several Russian soldiers, drove up to the Jewish relief office at 6 Tatra Street. He explained that he was being taken to Malinovsky's headquarters at Debrecen but he added ominously, "I don't know whether I'm going as a prisoner or a guest." He waved good-bye and began the 137-mile journey. It was the last time he was seen in Hungary.

It is now known that the Russians suspected Wallenberg of espionage. Perhaps they found it inconceivable that this representative of one of the world's leading capitalist families would dedicate himself to the rescue of the Jews without some ulterior motive. Adding to Soviet suspicions, Wallenberg had expended great sums of American money in creating an efficient, city-wide relief organization. The entire Swedish legation had participated in this effort. The Russians as a first step toward the communizing of Hungary, were systematically eliminating foreign influence. The Swedish-American collaboration may have seemed a threat to these plans.

Whatever their reasons the Russians took Wallenberg into custody and spirited him to a Moscow prison. Through the years the Stalin regime rebuffed repeated Swedish inquiries and protests, denying any knowledge of his whereabouts. In 1957, four years after Stalin's death, Soviet Foreign Minister Andrei Gromyko announced that a document had been uncovered in the archives of a Moscow prison certifying that Wallenberg died of a heart attack in 1947.

The Swedes have never accepted this explanation. To this day they continue their search for a man who is now considered a national hero. Against fearful odds they have penetrated the Soviet prison system. By interviewing released prisoners of many nationalities, Swedish investigators believe that they have traced Wallenberg *alive* at least fourteen years after his supposed death. They have obtained convincing evidence that in 1961 he lay seriously ill in a Moscow mental hospital. In spite of more than twenty Swedish government inquiries, the Russians have refused to give additional information, and the unsolved mystery of Raoul Wallenberg remains a continuing irritant in Swedish-Soviet relations.

Whatever his actual fate, Wallenberg left a rich legacy—the lives of more than a hundred thousand Jews. His gallantry bridged the chasm between the pretense and performance of the forces of international morality. All those who had thrown up their hands in despair could no longer plead the impossibility of rescue, for Raoul Wallenberg provided daily proof of its feasibility. The War Refugee Board gave him the resources to do the job but his actions gave meaning to the very existence of the board.

On the border between Switzerland and Austria a related drama was taking place. When Joel Brand failed to return from Istanbul in May 1944, his frantic colleagues of the Zionist Relief and Rescue Committee had pursued the negotiations with the Germans, in the hope that this continuing dialogue would prevent further deportations from Hungary. With the approval and support of the War Refugee Board, discussions continued in neutral territory between Nazi emissaries and a memorable old gentleman named Saly Mayer, a leading Swiss Jew who represented the Joint Distribution Committee. His task was to keep the Germans talking and tempt them with dreams of wealth without actually giving them anything. Occasionally the courtly, fastidious Mayer would depart from the text and deliver sermons on human decency to the Gestapo agents, who carried empty suitcases to be filled with the cash that somehow never materialized.

Mayer's silent partner was the War Refugee Board representative Roswell McClelland. His cables to Washington were filled with admiration for the dignity and skill of his associate, and he still recalls the philosophical discussions that followed the departure of the Nazi delegates.

To enhance his credibility, Mayer arranged to have the Joint Distribution Committee deposit $5,000,000 in his name in a Swiss bank. This transaction was accomplished with the secret connivance of the State, War and Treasury departments. The account was so designed that withdrawals could not be made without the signatures of both McClelland and Mayer, a provision which Mayer neglected to tell the Gestapo about. A man of austere bearing, Mayer's only ostentation was the frequent display of his bankbook to the representatives of the "master race."

Just when it appeared that further stalling was impossible, Mayer would invent a new list of complicated questions for the Germans or improvise a new justification for delay. As the months drifted by and the German military position worsened, Mayer maneuvered the talks further and further from ransom, appealing to growing Nazi fears of postwar retaliation. He proposed that in exchange for a German cessation of the killing of the Jews, he would arrange with the International Red Cross to provide all relief supplies necessary for their survival. The Germans rejected this offer, but there were other, tangible results from the talks. The scheduled deportation in late August of the total Jewish population in Budapest was canceled. There were two principal causes: Nazi interest in Saly Mayer's negotiations, and a strong protest by the neutrals, led by the Papal Nuncio in Budapest. Monsignor Rotta had been barraged by urgent pleas from the Apostolic Delegation in Washington, which in turn received constant entreaties from John Pehle. Now Rotta personally delivered the neutrals' note to the Hungarians:

"The Envoys of the neutral States represented in Budapest have been acquainted with the fact that the deportation of the

Jews is about to be accomplished. They all know what this means, even though it be described as 'labor service' . . . The representatives of the neutral powers herewith request the Hungarian Government to forbid these cruelties, which ought never to have been started."

Besides the successful outcome of this protest, the talks on the border led directly to the release of 1,673 Hungarian Jews from Bergen-Belsen. They were brought to safety in Switzerland as a demonstration of the German negotiators' power and influence.

From August 1944 until April 1945, one month before the German surrender, Mayer held the Nazis at bay. The lives of seventeen thousand Jews, originally headed for Auschwitz, were also saved because of Nazi greed for ransom. In Eichmann's words, they had been "put on ice" at a labor camp in Austria to await their future purchase. They remained unmolested throughout the negotiations. Saly Mayer's skillful bargaining also resulted in the German concessions which permitted the International Red Cross to shelter several thousand homeless Jewish children.

The team of Mayer, the Swiss Jew, and McClelland, the American Quaker, symbolized the diverse forces that combined to prevent the total annihilation of Hungarian Jewry. The War Refugee Board finally fulfilled its objectives, by linking neutrals, the Papal Nuncio and the International Red Cross in a powerful, unarmed alliance. The Nazis and the green-shirted Arrow Cross could not penetrate its defenses. When they attacked they were trapped not by weapons but by an international spotlight.

When the Jews emerged into the sunlight of a peaceful Budapest, they named a street in honor of Raoul Wallenberg. There was little more they could do to express their gratitude, for he had already disappeared in the vastness of the Soviet Union. But the Israelite Congregation of Pest, where the Swedish houses had been located, paid him a quiet tribute which included these words:

"The time of horror is still fresh in our memory, when the Jews of this country were like hunted animals, when thousands of Jewish prisoners were in the temples preparing for death. We recall all the atrocities of the concentration camps, the departure of trains crammed with people who were to die, the sufferings in the ghettos and the attacks against the houses which had been placed under international protection. But we also remember one of the greatest heroes of those terrible times: the Secretary of the Royal Swedish Legation, who defied the intruding government and its armed executioners. We witnessed the redemption of prisoners and the relief of sufferers when Mr. Wallenberg came among the persecuted to help. In a superhuman effort, not yielding to fatigue and exposing himself to all sorts of dangers, he brought home children who had been dragged away and he liberated aged parents. We saw him give food to the starving and medicine to the ailing.

"We shall never forget him and shall be forever grateful to him and to the Swedish nation, because it was the Swedish flag which warranted the undisturbed slumber of thousands of Jews in the protected houses.

"He was a righteous man. God bless him."

■ XXI ■

Crimes of War, Crimes of Peace

THE MASSACRE OF HUNDREDS OF THOUSANDS of Hungarian Jews failed to affect the languid ineptitude of the War Crimes Commission, which had been established by the United States and Great Britain in 1942. The inability of the commission to reach agreement about the punishment of war criminals reduced the effectiveness of the War Refugee Board in waging psychological warfare against the Nazis. Yet the individual members of the commission were not to blame. Instead their failure can be traced to the indecisiveness of the respective Allied governments, which refused to formulate clear-cut policies.

The State Department's disinterest was exemplified by the six-month lag between the appointment of an American member of the War Crimes Commission and his actual participation in its work. A two-line memorandum from President Roosevelt to Secretary Hull had led to the selection of the United States representative. "Do you think there is some place where we could use Herbert Pell?" wrote the President on April 19, 1943. "As you know, he is a very devoted friend of the Administration."

Pell, a New York congressman from 1919 to 1921, had also

served as chairman of the New York State Democratic Committee. Later he had been appointed minister to Portugal. The President's memorandum jogged Hull's memory, and in June 1943 he announced Pell's appointment to the War Crimes Commission.

In July, Ambassador Winant in London informed the State Department that the British government had appointed Sir Cecil Hurst to the commission but still awaited replies from the Chinese and Soviet governments regarding their participation. The British had told Winant that "Mr. Pell should not leave for London until the position is clearer."

Mr. Pell, although eager to get to work on his new assignment, deferred to the British and did not book steamship passage for his wife and himself until August 28. However, the State Department considered even this premature, and forced him to cancel his reservations. Furthermore, no one bothered to brief Mr. Pell on his duties or on United States policy concerning the treatment of war criminals. Possibly this reflected the dilemma facing Green Hackworth, the State Department's legal adviser. Hackworth's preliminary studies had revealed the embarrassing fact that there was no precedent in international law for punishing the officials of a defeated nation for annihilating their own citizens or those of their military allies.

In September the President asked Cordell Hull somewhat plaintively: "Why can't we get Herbert Pell off for London? Is there any reason for the continued delay?"

Hull explained about the British request, but he must have been somewhat embarrassed when the first meeting of the War Crimes Commission took place on October 20 without the American representative. Pell was still at home awaiting his instructions and his steamship ticket.

Once again the Chief Executive inquired of the State Department: "Just what is the present status of the war criminals' trials? What is Pell and his group doing?"

Acting Secretary of State Stettinius had to report that the commission had met without Russian or American representation. However, he explained that Pell, "who does not wish to fly or to travel without his wife, is now awaiting the first available steamship transportation for himself, Mrs. Pell and his secretary in order to proceed to London."

Mr. Pell, though still "a very devoted friend of the Administration," was becoming somewhat exasperated. In a meeting with Ralph Hill of the State Department on November 19 Pell "showed considerable irritation that he was still in this country and had not been sent to London some months ago. He complained that he had had no instructions from the Department and had received no information in regard to the work of the Commission." Actually, he had been shown various British proposals; all he lacked was an understanding of American policy.

Finally, on December 7, 1943, Herbert Pell attended his first meeting of the War Crimes Commission. During the next eight months he steeped himself in the documentation of Nazi crime and developed a passionate sense of indignation. In the absence of contrary instructions, he decided that crimes committed by the leaders of nations against their own citizens because of race, religion or politics should fall within the commission's jurisdiction. He became an articulate advocate of punishment for war criminals, quoting the declarations of his Commander in Chief, Franklin D. Roosevelt, to support his position. But Pell knew, and John Pehle knew, that declarations were one thing and national policy was another. The State Department remained silent.

On August 28, 1944, Pehle wrote to Acting Secretary Stettinius, reminding him of Pell's difficulties and the fact that the War Crimes Commission had refused to grapple with the unique judicial challenge created by Nazi mass murder. "Needless to say," he commented, "it would be a fearful miscarriage of justice if such war criminals were permitted to escape punishment for their inhuman crimes."

Pehle added that Pell disagreed with the limited jurisdiction adopted by other members of the commission, but had not yet received his instructions from Washington. Tactfully Pehle suggested that the State Department advise Pell to continue his vigorous efforts, "indicating clearly that the declared policy of the United States Government is to ensure the just punishment of all Axis war criminals."

To expedite action, Pehle enclosed a draft cable to Pell incorporating these ideas. All Stettinius had to do was add his signature. But the future Secretary of State was not willing to act so hastily. Some days later James Mann of the War Refugee Board cabled from London complaining that Pell had "as yet received no instructions directing him to urge the Commission to treat as war crimes those crimes committed by one Axis state against its own nationals or against the nationals of another Axis state . . . Time is most important and I strongly urge that every effort be made to have instructions on this point transmitted to Mr. Pell at once."

The plea was in vain. As Pell carried on his one-man campaign for vigorous action by the commission, the Washington *Post* observed: " . . . the prospects today are that if the United Nations War Crimes Commission in London has its way the immense majority of culprits will literally get away with murder. The Commission has been working at the pace of a rheumatic snail."

The War Refugee Board was anxious to publicize the commission's threat of postwar punishment for war criminals, in the hope that this would serve as a deterrent to a last-ditch Nazi orgy of murder. In the absence of any action by the commission, the board drafted a strong statement which General Eisenhower issued on November 7, 1944. Given massive distribution by radio and leaflet, it warned the Germans against molesting forced laborers or prisoners in concentration camps and threatened heavy punishment. "The Allies," said General Eisenhower, "expect, on their advance, to find these people alive and unharmed."

The statement was useful, but it was not enough. Pehle was so disenchanted with the War Crimes Commission that on December 23 he intervened personally. Stettinius was now Secretary of State and Pehle wrote him a forthright letter pressing for direct support.

"In view of the fact that an unfortunate impression has been created that the United Nations have no real intention of punishing those guilty of crimes against stateless persons, I think it would be an extremely propitious time for you, as the new Secretary of State, to reaffirm publicly this Government's intention to punish all war criminals, including those who have committed crimes against stateless and Axis nationals. Such a statement would be particularly effective if you were to declare specifically that in the eyes of this Government persons who commit crimes against Axis Jews are war criminals. I would appreciate an early response to this letter."

But before Pehle received Stettinius' negative reply, the State Department announced the resignation of Herbert Pell. According to Undersecretary Joseph Grew, this was due to congressional failure to appropriate funds for his salary and expenses. Pell, who had suffered in silence for many long months, described this excuse as "just damn nonsense." He further deflated the State Department's explanation by offering to serve without compensation. The department countered weakly that it was "illegal to accept gratuitous services."

The press response to Pell's "resignation" was unexpectedly acute and virtually unanimous. According to reporters who had followed the laborious sessions of the War Crimes Commission, Pell had displeased both the State Department and the British Foreign Office by his insistence that Hitler and the major Nazis be treated as war criminals rather than conventional political prisoners.

This interpretation was strengthened by the resignation of Sir Cecil Hurst, the chairman of the War Crimes Commission. Sir Cecil had experienced somewhat the same reluctance on the part of his superiors that Herbert Pell had with his. A third resignation—that of the Norwegian representative—struck a further blow at the commission's prestige.

United States and British newspapers hammered at the weak Allied policy toward war criminals. The London *Express* described Pell's resignation as a "severe shock" and called him "a forthright, plain-speaking, vigorous and valuable member of the Commission."

New York *Post* columnist William O. Player speculated "that somewhere down the line in the State Department, certain legalistic-minded Old School individuals have failed to find any precedent in international law for the punishment of a country's murder of its own citizens, and therefore have refused to approve this nation's participation in such a project."

The influential Washington *Post* carried an editorial entitled "The Pell Affair": ". . . Apparently the President did not make the point [about war crimes] clear enough to certain well-entrenched functionaries in the State Department . . . It was the same legalism that was responsible for the fiasco that attended the execution of the clause in the Versailles Treaty regarding the perpetrators of atrocities in the last war."

With its attitude toward war criminals exposed to public examination, the State Department announced a reversal of its position. It had suddenly developed a program for punishing Nazi leaders and others guilty of atrocities. The insurmountable legal obstacles had somehow been overcome. Thus Herbert Pell had not only managed to get to London, had not only succeeded in serving on an international commission without instructions from his government, but by being ousted, had accomplished a reversal of U.S. policy.

. . .

From the Pell affair until the German surrender in May, Allied psychological warfare stressed a united determination to hold war criminals accountable for their acts. Through all the communications media, Axis citizens were urged to protect and shelter war prisoners, slave laborers and inmates of concentration camps. The War Refugee Board was in the forefront of the campaign. It recruited prominent Americans, ranging from Governor Thomas E. Dewey to Archbishop Francis Spellman, to add their voices to a powerful chorus urging the enemy's last-minute reversion to civilized behavior. Behind this drive lay the board's fear of final Nazi vengeance against the hundreds of thousands of captives awaiting liberation.

During the last months of the war the board's principal effort concerned its arrangements with the Red Cross and the neutrals to stockpile and distribute vast supplies of food and clothing. Roswell McClelland rented some of the Red Cross trucks and carried food directly to the living skeletons in the concentration camps. Thousands close to death were thus saved.

In little more than a year the War Refugee Board was responsible for the direct rescue of several hundred thousand men, women and children, and the sustenance of additional thousands. It assisted in the wartime concealment and maintenance of tens of thousands of other potential victims of the Nazis. More than that, the board stirred the apathetic, encouraged the active and breathed new life into the forgotten American tradition to help the oppressed, in the name of humanity. For example, toward the very end of the war, when the International Red Cross was able to deliver food packages to some of the concentration camps, most of its funds for this purpose were provided by the American Jewish Joint Distribution Committee. There were thousands of Christians among the masses of Jews in the camps, and the International Red Cross received permission from the JDC to apportion packages among Christian prisoners as well as Jewish. Thus there are former non-Jewish prisoners of the Nazis alive today because of food, medicine and clothing parcels purchased by the contributions of Americans to the United Jewish Appeal.

Only Henry Morgenthau of the original Morgenthau-Hull-Stimson trio remained active in the affairs of the board. While the Treasury Secretary was not involved in the board's day-to-day affairs, he was always available in emergencies, and always ready with a "Dear Cordell" letter when State Department obstruction became critical.

During the final months of the war Morgenthau persuaded Pehle to resign from the board to oversee the Treasury Department's disposal of war-surplus property. He knew it would take a tough administrator to ward off the corruption and waste that would inevitably plague a postwar program of such vast dimension. Morgenthau had seen Pehle perform under pressure and when the war was over, he was further impressed by a rather startling statistic. The War Refugee Board had received an appropriation of $1,150,000 for its work and had returned $603,000 in unexpended funds. Its activities had been financed almost entirely by $20,000,000 in contributions from philanthropic organizations. Three-fourths of this total—$15,000,000—had been donated by the Joint Distribution Committee. The next largest contributors were the Union of Orthodox Rabbis, which provided more than $1,000,000, and the World Jewish Congress, which donated $300,000 (to say nothing of the incalculable services of Gerhart Riegner).

The final reports of the War Refugee Board's field representatives reflected their sorrow that the vast rescue actions had not been set in motion much earlier. From Turkey, Ira Hirschmann wrote:

"It bears repetition that it is regrettable that the Board, which has demonstrated its vitality and the success of its operations, was not created a year or two ago. There is no doubt from the evidence at hand that additional thousands of refugees could have been saved . . . the mere existence of the Board and its representatives in Turkey acted as a catalytic agent in spurring the morale of the destitute and terrorized citizens in the Balkans . . . it provided for the victims a ray of hope which resulted in lifting their own morale and an eleventh-hour self-sustaining effort on their own part."

Roswell McClelland, who had shipped medicines to the French underground, persuaded border guards to admit fleeing Jews and discussed philosophy with Saly Mayer, summarized these experiences nostalgically to John Pehle's successor, Brigadier General William O'Dwyer. His final report concluded:

"Such was the fight on one of the War Refugee Board's fronts, with its sorties and skirmishes, its trenches stormed and its ground gained—and lost—in the uneven struggle to succor and to save some of the victims of the Nazi assault on human decency. Its successes were slight in relation to the frightful casualties sustained; yet it is sincerely felt that its accomplishments constitute a victory, small in comparison to that far greater one carried by force of arms, but which nevertheless adds a measure of particularly precious strength to our cause."

The War Refugee Board represented a small gesture of atonement by a nation whose apathy and inaction were exploited by Adolf Hitler. As he moved systematically toward the total destruction of the Jews, the government and the people of the United States remained bystanders. Oblivious to the evidence which poured from official and unofficial sources, Americans went about their business unmoved and unconcerned. Those who tried to awaken the nation were dismissed as alarmists, cranks or Zionists. Many Jews were as disinterested as their Christian countrymen. The bystanders to cruelty became bystanders to genocide.

The holocaust has ended. The six million lie in nameless graves. But what of the future? Is genocide now unthinkable, or are potential victims somewhere in the world going about their business, devoted to their children, aspiring to a better life, unaware of a gathering threat?

Who are the potential victims? Who the bystanders?

Acknowledgments

The author is indebted to many individuals and institutions for their co-operation and assistance. In particular, a grant from the Ford Foundation's International Relations program made possible travel to several European archives and research trips throughout the United States, as well as lengthy stays in Washington.

A generous invitation from the Rockefeller Foundation enabled the author and his wife to spend two productive months at Villa Serbelloni on Lake Como, where a portion of this book was written.

The bulk of documentation was obtained from the diplomatic records on deposit in the National Archives in Washington. This material was made available by the Historical Office of the State Department's Bureau of Public Affairs. Much of it is published here for the first time. In spite of lengthy security and review procedures, the State Department is more generous in providing access to official records than its counterparts in other countries. A particular word of appreciation is due James L. Greenfield, who served as Assistant Secretary of State for Public Affairs while this volume was being researched. His devotion to the principles of free inquiry is known to every journalist who covered the State Department during his tenure, and his frequent interventions undoubtedly speeded access to this material.

The author is most grateful to Mrs. Patricia Dowling, archives assistant in the Security Room at the National Archives, where the diplomatic records are stored. Her knowledge and helpfulness were invaluable during the months the author spent at the Archives.

Librarians and archivists in many countries contributed to this research. Principal among them are the staffs of the Franklin D. Roosevelt Library, Hyde Park, New York; the Institute for Advanced Studies in Contemporary History (formerly the Wiener Library), London; the Foreign Office Library, Cornwall House, London; Yad Vashem, the Martyrs' and Heroes' Remembrance Authority, Jerusalem, Israel;

Centre de Documentation Juive Contemporaine, Paris; and Royal Ministry for Foreign Affairs, Stockholm.

Although officials of the International Committee of the Red Cross in Geneva had assured the author that their records would be made available, this promise was not fulfilled and only published materials, rather than the original documents, were provided. Information obtained from other sources and referred to in the narrative may explain the reluctance of the Red Cross to be as candid as the United States government.

Grateful acknowledgment is made for the translation of documents from French, Swedish, Spanish and Italian by, respectively, Joan Morse, Ann Morse, Anne Hombroeckx; Annette Forsström and Jonna Christianssen; Edith Kolton; Nina Beckwith. Joan Ogden researched newspaper files with skill and discernment. Dr. Frank Moskowitz made valuable comments during the development of the manuscript and also prepared the index.

Several hundred participants in the events recounted in these pages were interviewed by the author during the past three years, and their courtesy and frankness have been greatly appreciated.

Finally, a particular word of appreciation is due Mr. Robert D. Loomis of Random House, who as editor made many contributions to this volume, as did Mrs. Barbara Willson, a copyeditor of the highest professional competence.

A.D.M.

Source Notes

Documentation is arranged by chapter and page. Diplomatic records deposited in the National Archives of the United States are indicated by file numbers in parentheses after the entry, e.g.: (862.4016/2234). The titles of the most frequently used diplomatic files are:

150.01	Laws and Regulations, Immigration to the United States
150.626 J	Immigration into the United States of Jews from Germany
540.16	World Jewish Conferences
548.D1	Problem of German Refugees in Foreign Countries
548.G1	International Refugee Conference—Bermuda
740.00114 EW 1939	Prisoners of War—European War 1939
740.00116 EW 1939	Illegal and Inhumane Warfare—European War 1939
740.00119 EW 1939	Termination of European War 1939
811.111 Quota	Procedures, Policy and Regulations Pertaining to Quotas and the Establishment of Quota Controls
811.111 Regulations	Instructions and Regulations Pertaining to Visas
840.48	Calamities—Relief—Europe—Refugees
851.00	Political Affairs—France
862.00	Political Affairs—Germany
862.00 PR	Conditions in Germany—Weekly Reports
862.4016	Race Problems—Germany
862.4063	Olympic Games
FDRL	Documents on deposit in the Franklin D. Roosevelt Library, Hyde Park, New York (OF refers to Official File; PPF to the President's Personal File).
FRUS	*Foreign Relations of the United States,* issued annually in several volumes by the Department of State, Washington.
WRB	Papers from the extensive files of the War Refugee Board, which are stored at the Franklin D. Roosevelt Library, Hyde Park.

I A Plan for Murder

PAGE

5 Polish report on massacre of 700,000 Jews: summarized in *N.Y. Times*, July 2, 1942.

6 Zygielbojm's broadcast: qtd. in dispatch of Aug. 13, 1942, from U.S. embassy to Polish government-in-exile (740.00116 EW 1939/527).

6 Paris roundup of July 16: announced over Berlin radio on July 17, and latter qtd. in *N.Y. Times*, July 18, 1942.

6 Polish notification to U.S. and Britain that Nazis beginning extermination of last occupants of Warsaw ghetto: *N.Y. Times*, July 29, 1942.

8 Text of Riegner's cable to Rabbi Stephen Wise and Elting's memo of his meeting with Riegner: attached to State Dept. memo from Atherton to Reams, Aug. 26, 1942 (862.4016/2234). Text of Riegner cable also included in Aug. 28 telegram from Sydney Silverman, Liverpool, via War Dept. to State Dept. for transmittal to Rabbi Wise (740.00116 EW 1939/553).

9 Culbertson's comment re Rabbi Wise: memo of Aug. 13, 1942 (862.4016/2333).

9 Durbrow re "fantastic nature of the allegation": memo of Aug. 13, 1942 (862.4016/2235).

10 Frischer's memo forwarded by Amb. Biddle, Aug. 26, 1942 (740.-00116 EW 1939/536).

12 Myron Taylor writes to Cardinal Maglione: FRUS, 1942, Vol. III, pp. 775–6.

13 Leland Harrison's information from a Polish colleague and details of deportations from western Europe, forwarded in dispatches of Sept. 26 and Oct. 6, 1942 (740.00116 EW 1939/599 and /601).

13 Cardinal Maglione's "informal, unsigned response" and Tittmann's dissatisfaction with this reply: FRUS, 1942, Vol. III, pp. 777–8.

14 British statement re the Vatican's "policy of silence," included in Sept. 15, 1942, dispatch from U.S. representative, Vatican (740.-00116 EW 1939/590).

15 Monsignor Montini's statement: FRUS, 1942, Vol. III, pp. 776–7.

15 Information from an anti-Nazi German officer and coded letters from Warsaw, sent by Consul Squire to State Dept., Sept. 28, 1942 862.4016/2242).

17 Sumner Welles's cable to Leland Harrison for substantiation of extermination order, Oct. 5, 1942 (740.00116 EW 1939/600).

19 Prof. Guggenheim's affidavit and Squire's comments, attached to Squire's Political Dispatch #49 of Oct. 29, 1942, which was not sent to the State Dept. A copy of the affidavit was attached to

PAGE

Leland Harrison's personal letter of Oct. 31, 1942, to Sumner Welles. The original is now filed in the National Archives, Record Group 84, "Records of the U.S. Consulate in Geneva."

21 Squire's memo of his conversation with Burckhardt, enclosed in his personal letter of Nov. 9, 1940, to Leland Harrison.

22 Description of mass execution of Jews from Vatican source, Nov. 23, 1942 (740.00116 EW 1939/726).

II The Atrocity Stories

23 Rabbi Wise's fears confirmed by Sumner Welles: qtd. in *Challenging Years: The Autobiography of Stephen Wise,* pp. 275–6.

24 Winant's letter to President Roosevelt, Aug. 5, 1942: FRUS, 1942, Vol. I, p. 48.

25 Winant's telegram of Sept. 20, 1942: *ibid.,* pp. 54–5.

25 Hopkins' reply of Sept. 21, 1942: *ibid.,* p. 55.

25 Winant's personal telegram to Secy. Hull of Sept. 26, 1942: *ibid.,* p. 57.

26 Telegram of Oct. 5, 1942, to Winant confirming U.S. support of War Crimes Commission: *ibid.,* p. 59.

26 Roosevelt re small number of Nazi ringleaders to be punished: *ibid.,* p. 59.

26 Rabbi Wise's "Dear Boss" letter of Dec. 2, 1942, to President Roosevelt: FDRL OF 76–C.

31 Proposed text of Allied war crimes declaration and Secretary Hull's change in draft: FRUS, Vol. I, p. 68.

33 Reams's objections to the war crimes statement in his memo to John Hickerson and Ray Atherton, Dec. 9, 1942 (740.00116 EW 1939/694).

33 Reams's meeting with a British embassy representative, described in memo of Dec. 10, 1942: *ibid.*

34 Reams answers Rep. Hamilton Fish, memo of Dec. 10, 1942, from Reams to Hickerson and Atherton (740.00116 EW 1939/674).

34 Reams's reply to the American minister to Costa Rica, Dec. 12, 1942 (740.00116 EW 1939/672).

35 Sydney Silverman's question, Anthony Eden's reply and Viscount Samuel's statement, contained in *Hansard* (official record of proceedings of Houses of Parliament) and enclosed in U.S. embassy, London, dispatch of Dec. 31, 1942 (740.00116 EW 1939/752).

III Bermuda and Warsaw

PAGE

39 Long's surprise at his effectiveness; Diary #2 entry of Mar. 20, 1917; Breckinridge Long Papers, MS. Div., Library of Congress.

39 Italy as "the most interesting experiment," letter from Long to Joseph E. Davies, Sept. 6, 1933: *ibid.,* Box 102.

39 Long praises Mussolini, letter to Mrs. Almy Edmunds, July 27, 1933: *ibid.,* Box 102.

40 Italian trains run on time, letter from Long to President Roosevelt, June 27,1933: *ibid.,* Box 105.

40 No moral element in Ethiopian war, letter from Long to President Roosevelt, Oct. 30, 1935: *ibid.,* Box 114.

40 "Fruitful harvest of Mussolini's enterprise": qtd. in *Current Biography,* 1943, p. 455.

40 "You are a grand fellow" letter from President Roosevelt to Long, June 18, 1936: Breckinridge Long Papers, Box 117.

42 British proposal of Jan. 20, 1943: FRUS, 1943, Vol. I, pp. 134–7.

42 Richard Law statement of Feb. 20 qtd.: *ibid.,* pp. 138–40.

43 Secy. Hull's reply: *ibid.,* pp. 140–44.

43 Sir Ronald's comments and Sumner Welles's acrimonious reply, memo of conversation by Welles, Mar. 5, 1943 (548.G1). A milder version of the exchange appears in FRUS, 1943, Vol. I, pp. 144–46.

46 Description of "Stop Hitler Now" rally: *N.Y. Times,* Mar. 2, 1943.

48 Rabbi Wise's letter to Secy. Hull, Mar. 5, 1943 (740.00116 EW 1939/815).

48 Engineer Pruefer's test and the crematoria description: in Reitlinger, *The Final Solution,* p. 150–1, and Hilberg, *The Destruction of the European Jews,* p. 566.

48 Kurt Gerstein's description of Belzec gassing, cited by Eichmann prosecution (T/1309, p. 7) and Nuremberg Documents (ND 1533–PS): qtd. in Hausner, *Justice in Jerusalem,* p. 166–7.

50 Sergeant Major Moll: qtd. in Reitlinger, *op. cit.,* p. 151.

50 Auschwitz killing capacity: cited by Hausner, *op. cit.,* p. 170.

50 Sir Ronald's visit to Long: described in WRB review of Bermuda Conference.

51 Rabbi Wise-Breckinridge Long exchange: cited in Long diary entry, Apr. 13, 1943; Breckinridge Long Papers.

51 Myron Taylor's letter to Long with enclosures, Mar. 26, 1943 (740.00116 EW 1939/959).

52 Memorandum of instructions for U.S. delegates to Bermuda Conference, Apr. 13, 1943: cited in WRB review of the conference.

PAGE

52 Petition signed by 282 scholars: *N.Y. Times*, Mar. 23, 1943.
53 Opening statements at Bermuda: *N.Y. Times*, Apr. 20, 1943.
53 London *Observer*, on well-dressed gentlemen at Bermuda, Apr. 20, 1943.
54 *Manchester Guardian*, on Bermuda Conference's side-stepping of Jewish problem, Apr. 22, 1943.
54 Are we fighting the war for the Jews? Long diary entry, Apr. 20, 1943; Breckinridge Long Papers.
55 Bermuda deliberations: contained in WRB review of the conference.
57 Appeal from the Warsaw ghetto: qtd. in Friedman, *Their Brothers' Keepers*, pp. 122–3.
58 Message on ninth day of battle: qtd. in Friedman, *Martyrs and Fighters*, pp. 269–70.
58 Text of U.S.-British joint statement on Bermuda: *N.Y. Times*, Apr. 30, 1943.
59 Bermuda "confidential" recommendations: summarized in WRB, also in *N.Y. Times*, Apr. 28, 1943.
59 Report of status of Intergovernmental Committee bank account: FDRL OF 3186.
59 Reams's recollections: interviews with author.
60 Myron Taylor memo: in WRB review of Bermuda Conference.
60 Roosevelt-Hull exchange, Hull to Roosevelt, May 7, 1943; Roosevelt to Hull, May 14: FRUS, 1943, Vol. I, pp. 176–8.
63 Lord Coleraine quote: interview with author.
63 Descriptions of Zygielbojm: from Friedman, *Martyrs and Fighters*, and various *N.Y. Times* and English newspaper articles and obituaries.

IV The Reluctant Rescuers

66 Sweden's proposal to accept 20,000 Jewish children: WRB Projects and Documents, Box 31.
68 Protests by French clergy: Vichy newspaper quote. Rescue of children by Abbé Glasberg: in Lowrie, *The Hunted Children*.
69 Monsignor Rémond's quote: in statement by Moussa Abadi, Centre de Documentation Juive Contemporaine, Paris.
69 Donald Lowrie's telegram, Sept. 11, 1943 (740.00116 EW 1939/1090).
70 Abbé Glasberg statement that virtually all French Jews could have been saved: interview with author.
71 Plight of the Rumanian Jews in Transnistria: described by Levai, *Black Book on the Martyrdom of Hungarian Jewry*.

PAGE

73 Rabbi Wise's letter of Mar. 31, 1943, to Sumner Welles (862.-4016/2266).

73 Harrison's two messages of Apr. 20, 1943 (862.4016/2268 and /2269).

74 Reams's memo to Long: attached to 862.4016/2269.

74 Role of Herbert Feis: described by Henry Morgenthau, Jr., "The Morgenthau Diaries," Part VI, *Collier's* magazine, Nov. 1, 1947.

75 Riegner's meeting of June 4 with Daniel Reagan: described in files of Gerhart Riegner, World Jewish Congress, Geneva.

75 Harrison's cable of June 14, 1943 (862.4016/2274).

76 Harrison's telegram of July 3, 1943, informing State Dept. of International Red Cross message (862.4016/1276).

76 Riegner letter of July 6, 1943, to Daniel Reagan: in files of Gerhart Riegner, World Jewish Congress, Geneva.

76 Harrison's cable of July 10, 1943 (862.4016/2278).

76 Hull's invitation from Emergency Committee and quoted documents (740.00116 EW 1939/1008).

78 Visit of Polish ambassador and Hull's memo of their conversation (740.00116 EW 1939/1135).

79 Rabbi Wise's letter to Roosevelt: qtd. in memo of Aug. 2, 1943, from Bernard Meltzer to Herbert Feis and Asst. Secy. of State Dean Acheson (862.4016/2286).

79 Meltzer quote: from above memo.

81 Pehle's telegram of Sept. 28, 1943 (862.4016/2288).

81 Harrison expresses his doubts in Oct. 6, 1943, cable (862.4016/2292).

82 State Dept. telegram #2626 of Oct. 26, 1943, attached to which are Reams's memo, Long's reply, and memo of the Pehle-Long conversation (862.4016/2292).

84 Harrison's telegram about British Ministry of Economic Warfare objections, Nov. 14, 1943 (862.4016/2292).

84 Pehle quote at Treasury meeting: from Morgenthau, *op. cit.*

84 Morgenthau letter to Hull, Nov. 24, 1943 (862.4016/2297).

85 Ministry of Economic Warfare letter: qtd. in Amb. Winant's telegram #8717 of Dec. 15, 1943.

85 Hull's reply to above: in his telegram #7969 of Dec. 18, 1943.

86 Hull's quote about "people down the line": Morgenthau, *op. cit.*

V "Acquiescence of This Government . . ."

89 "Report to the Secretary on the Acquiescence of this Government in the Murder of the Jews," signed by Randolph E. Paul, Jan. 13, 1944: from a private file.

93 Breckinridge Long's testimony before House Committee on For-

PAGE

eign Affairs, Nov. 26, 1943: FDRL OF 3186, and *N.Y. Times,* Dec. 11, 12 and 31.

97 White House meeting of Jan. 16, 1944, and afternoon discussion with Stettinius: described in Morgenthau, *op. cit.;* author's interviews with Henry Morgenthau, Jr., and John Pehle.

98 Auschwitz orders its Zyklon B from Dessau: Hilberg, *op. cit.,* p. 570.

VI *"Wenn das Judenblut vom Messer spritzt . . ."*

104 Herbert Feis describes economic fear: in his *1933: Characters in Crisis,* p. 98.

105 Amb. Sackett on "Democracy in Germany": Mar. 9, 1933, dispatch from Berlin (862.00/2236).

106 Consul General Messersmith reports the discharge of Jewish employees: FRUS, 1933, Vol. II, pp. 323–6.

106 The boycott proclamation and Nazi brutality: cited by Messersmith, Mar. 13, 1933 (862.4016/314).

107 Dr. Best becomes head of the Hesse state police: reported by U.S. embassy, Berlin, Mar. 27, 1933 (862.00 PR/132).

107 U.S. complaints disturb German government: reports from U.S. consulate in Berlin, Mar. 14, 1933 (862.4016/164).

108 Eyewitness accounts of fleeing refugees: *N.Y. Times,* Mar. 20, 1933.

109 Hull cables to ascertain the facts: FRUS, 1933, Vol. II, p. 327.

110 Sackett's reply: *ibid.,* pp. 328–30.

110 Hull notifies the American embassy in Berlin about U.S. public opinion: *ibid.,* pp. 330–1.

111 George Gordon says situation is getting worse: *ibid.,* pp. 335–7.

111 Messersmith renews the warnings: *ibid.,* 338–41.

111 Hull's temporizing statement qtd. in transatlantic telephone conversation: *ibid.,* p. 342.

112 Consul General Kehl in Hamburg reports press exaggeration, Mar. 31, 1933 (862.4016/634).

115 Reports from U.S. consulates of Apr. 10 (862.01/90); May 4 (862.4016/1002); May 12 (862.00/3013); June 30 (862.00/3022); July 8: FRUS, 1933, Vol. II, pp. 354–6.

116 Samuel Untermyer forwards a resolution of protest, Apr. 19, 1933 (862.4016/668).

117 New York Bar Assn. message, May 20, 1933 (862.4016/1010).

117 Hull's memo of conversation with Amb. Luther: FRUS, 1933, Vol. II, pp. 352–4.

118 Asst. Secy. Carr's summary, May 15, 1933 (150.626/5).

119 Germany protests: FRUS, 1933, Vol. II, p. 357.

PAGE

119 Hull's Sept. talk with chargé Leitner: *ibid.*, p. 358.

120 Amb. Dodd's diary entry: qtd. in Feis, *op. cit.*, p. 158.

120 Vice-President Garner quoted at Cabinet meeting: Williams, *The Rise of the Vice-Presidency*, pp. 157–8.

121 Election at Dachau, reported by Amb. Dodd, Nov. 4, 1933 (862.-00/3131).

121 Dr. Wise's Town Hall statement: qtd. *N.Y. Times*, June 26, 1933.

122 Dorothy Thompson on the American Jewish Committee: "Hitler and the American Jew," *Scribner's Magazine*, Sept., 1933.

123 Documentation of U.S. intercession on behalf of citizens of other countries: contained in Adler and Margolith, *With Firmness in the Right;* "The United States and German Jewish Persecutions, Precedents for Popular and Governmental Action," *Bulletin of the Jewish Academy of Arts and Sciences*, No. 1, 1933; and various volumes of FRUS.

VII "Likely to Become a Public Charge"

136 Asst. Secy. Carr's testimony: qtd. in *N.Y. Times*, Mar. 30, 1933.

136 A. Dana Hodgdon prepares Carr for his appearance in memo of May 15, 1933 (150.626/5).

137 Legal Adviser Hackworth and police certificates for Jews, memo of Aug. 28, 1933, attached to letter from American Jewish Committee (150.626/J17).

138 Consul General Dominion describes Jewish applicants for immigration, Aug. 17, 1933 (150.626/J18).

139 Jan.–Aug., 1934 immigration report, Oct. 27, 1934 (811.111 Quota 62/468).

139 The American consul in Rotterdam protests the "public charge" provision, Jan. 15, 1937 (150.626/J257).

140 Case histories of applicants to Rotterdam consulate, Feb. 20, 1934 (150.626/J64).

144 Vice-Consul Burke's analysis of "public charge," Feb. 23, 1934 (150.626/J80).

145 Small number of Jews applying for visas explained by Consul General Messersmith, Apr. 7, 1933 (862.4016/627).

145 Jews allowed to take $4,000 from Germany reports American consul in Stuttgart, June 28, 1934 (150.626/J90).

145 Hitler statement about U.S. immigration policy: qtd. in *N.Y. Times*, Apr. 6, 1933.

146 *Völkischer Beobachter* observation about U.S. immigration and treatment of Negroes: qtd. *N.Y. Times*, July 15, 1933.

147 William Green letter to President Roosevelt, Sept. 22, 1933: FDRL OF 133.

PAGE

147 Legal Adviser Hackworth's commentary on Judge Proskauer's proposal in memo of Oct. 5, 1933 (150.01/1215½).

148 James G. McDonald says President Roosevelt could help refugees, letter of Oct. 29, 1935, to Felix M. Warburg: FDRL OF 133.

149 Roosevelt's press conference of Nov. 15, 1938: reported in *N.Y. Times,* Nov. 16.

VIII The New Germany

151 Cincinnati physician's letter of Apr. 19, 1933, and Pierrepont Moffat's reply (862.4016/610).

152 German towns and cities posting signs announcing the exclusion of Jews: named in James G. McDonald's letter of resignation as High Commissioner for Refugees (Jewish and Other) Coming from Germany, Dec. 27, 1935.

153 Humiliation of Jewish shopkeepers in Nuremberg, reported by Amb. Dodd, July 28, 1938 (862.4016/1226).

153 Roundup of members of Jewish Benevolent Association, Stuttgart, reported by U.S. consulate, Stuttgart, Aug. 17, 1933 (862.4016/1250).

153 Exclusion of Jews from Association of Blind University Men, their exclusion from municipal pools, and death of Dr. James Loeb, included in Dodd's dispatch of July 28, 1938 (862.4016/1226).

154 Incident of Willy Stein, described in dispatch from Stuttgart, Aug. 1, 1933 (862.4016/1232).

155 Dr. Gercke's confidential memo forwarded by U.S. consulate general, Berlin, Sept. 21, 1933 (862.4016/1280).

156 Consul General Messersmith writes to Undersecy. of State Phillips about German sadism, Oct. 28, 1933 (862.00/3128).

156 Frederick T. Birchall's article: *N.Y. Times,* Sept. 6, 1933.

160 James G. McDonald's radio broadcast about Dachau: reported in *N.Y. Times,* Sept. 11, 1933.

163 John Farr Simmons meets Cecilia Razovsky, described in memo from Simmons to Asst. Secy. of State Wilbur Carr, Apr. 9, 1934 (150.626/J94).

163 Wixon's fear of Miss Razovsky's plan, in memo from Simmons to Carr, July 17, 1934 (150.626/J93).

164 Simmons writes a memo for the file, Aug. 23, 1934 (150.626/J100).

165 Simmons writes another memo to Carr about his failure to dissuade Col. MacCormack, Oct. 8, 1934 (150.626/J101).

165 Simmons' note to Undersecy. Phillips: attached, *ibid.*

165 Asst. Secy. Carr draws a parallel between contending groups: his

PAGE

note attached to Visa Division memo from Simmons to Carr of Nov. 21, 1934 (150.626/J123).

170 Roosevelt fails to use his influence: Burns, *Roosevelt: The Lion and the Fox,* pp. 254–5.

IX The Olympic Spirit

174 List of places forbidden to Jews: in Amb. Dodd's dispatch of May 17, 1935 (862.4016/1457).

175 Minister of the Interior Frick's public announcement: *N.Y. Times,* Apr. 28, 1935.

175 Julius Streicher's summer-solstice speech: qtd. *N.Y. Times,* June 24, 1935.

177 Rudolf Schoenfeld prepares Acting Secy. of State Phillips for meeting with representatives of Jewish organizations, memo of July 25, 1935 (862.4016/1509).

177 Memo left by Jewish organizations, July 26, 1935; Phillips' reply and his note of July 29 to President Roosevelt (862.4016/1495).

179 Senator King explains his resolution to Acting Secy. of State Phillips: Phillips' memo of the conversation, Aug. 3, 1935 (862.4016/1506).

179 Brundage insists that Germany has not broken her Olympic pledge: qtd. *N.Y. Times,* Aug. 2, 1935.

181 Gen. Sherrill worries about anti-Semitism: qtd. in *N.Y. Times,* Oct. 22, 1935.

182 Gen. Sherrill praises Mussolini: qtd. *N.Y. Times,* Nov. 7, 1935.

182 Amb. Dodd reports the embassy's investigation of the status of Jewish athletes, Oct. 11, 1935 (862.4063/49).

184 Climactic AAU meeting: *N.Y. Times,* Dec. 7 and 9, 1935; and files of Jeremiah T. Mahoney.

X "I Cannot Remain Silent . . ."

187 McDonald's letter of resignation and annexes: printed in full in *The Christian Century,* Jan. 15, 1936.

189 McDonald's letter to Felix Warburg; Lehman's letter to President Roosevelt; Simmons' memo to Carr and Phillips; and State Dept.'s reply to Lehman, Nov. 1, 1935 (FW 150.626/J1744).

190 McDonald's visit to Phillips and comments by Schoenfeld and Simmons, attached to memo from Phillips to James Clement Dunn, Feb. 7, 1936 (150.626/J185).

191 Sir Neill Malcolm quote, "I have no policy": qtd. *N.Y. Times,* Feb. 20, 1936.

PAGE

191 Consul General Erhardt's warning about pressure from American Jews, May 15, 1936 (150.626/J205).

192 Sir Herbert Samuel's letter to Felix Warburg, May 27, 1936 (150.-626/J208).

193 Streicher says that extermination is the only solution to the Jewish problem: qtd. *N.Y. Times,* Sept. 16, 1936.

194 Prof. John Dewey urges President Roosevelt to re-establish principle of asylum, letter of Oct. 22, 1936: FDRL OF 2303.

195 All documents quoted, beginning with Huddle's report, attached to Visa Instructions from State to Diplomatic and Consular Officers, Jan. 12, 1937 (150.626/J242).

198 Consul Brett writes jubilantly from Rotterdam, Jan. 15, 1937 (150.626/J257).

XI 1938: Evian

203 Origins of Evian Conference, as revealed in Division of European Affairs undated memo on refugee problems, attached to Division of the American Republics memo of Nov. 15, 1938 (840.48/900½).

204 Hitler speech at Königsberg: qtd. *N.Y. Times,* Mar. 27, 1938.

204 Undersecy. Welles briefs the President in a note of Apr. 11, 1938: FDRL OF 3186.

206 Text of Julius Streicher's *First Reader:* qtd. *N.Y. Times,* Apr. 7, 1938.

207 Six Jewish congressmen meet Asst. Secy. Messersmith, memo from Messersmith to Hull of Apr. 17, 1938 (150.01 BILLS/34).

208 Suicide of Luise Wolf: *N.Y. Times,* May 26, 1938.

208 Presidential secy. McIntyre accepts 120,000 signatures and sends a "courteous but stereotyped answer": FDRL OF 3186.

208 245,325 more signatures are filed: *ibid.*

209 James McDonald speaks of Christian responsibility: qtd. *N.Y. Times,* June 16, 1938.

210 Myron Taylor meets with Sir Michael Palairet, described in telegram from Taylor to Secy. Hull, July 1, 1938 (840.48 REFUGEES/442).

211 Clarence K. Streit reports preliminary maneuvering at Evian: *N.Y. Times,* July 6, 1938.

212 Evian conferees' unwillingness to accept refugees, in materials contained in *Wiener Library Bulletin* (London), No. 3, 1961; also, memo from Sumner Welles to President Roosevelt, Nov. 28, 1938; FDRL PPF; and Norman Bentwich, "The Evian Conference and After," *The Fortnightly,* Sept. 1938.

PAGE

213 Taylor's draft proposal of July 7, 1938, and Secy. Hull's reply (840.48 REFUGEES/468).

215 British Medical Association threatens a "stay-in strike": E. Hearst, "A Brain Gain Rejected," *Wiener Library Bulletin*, Apr. 1965.

215 Complaints of Socialist doctors: *ibid.*

215 Lord Beaverbrook's *Sunday Express* publishes a fearsome editorial on June 19, 1938: qtd. *N.Y. Times*, June 20.

216 Dr. Olin D. West of the AMA writes to Secy. Hull, Sept. 7, 1938 (150.626/J).

216 Letter and galley proofs from *Medical Economics* sent to State Dept., Dec. 30, 1938 (840.48 REFUGEES/1211).

217 Dr. Lawrence Kubie writes to President Roosevelt about medical restrictionism, Nov. 29, 1938: FDRL OF 3186.

218 Description of George Rublee: in Acheson, *Morning and Noon*, pp. 127–8.

219 The Nazis decree "Jewish" names, Aug. 30, 1938 (862.00 PR/252).

219 Nuremberg Trial affidavit NG–1944–A: reported by Hilberg, *op. cit.*, p. 119.

XII 1938: The Night of Broken Glass

222 Grynszpan qtd. in *Current History*, 1939, "The Plight of the Jew in Germany."

223 Report of the American consul, Stuttgart, to Amb. Wilson in Berlin, enclosed in letter of Nov. 15, 1938, to Asst. Secy. of State Messersmith (862.4016/2002).

224 British Consul General Bell in Cologne is shocked by German behavior, Bell to Sir George Ogilvie-Forbes, Nov. 14, 1938: *Papers Concerning the Treatment of German Nationals in Germany* (CMD 6120), 1938–1939, His Majesty's Stationery Office.

224 Sir George cables the For. Secy., Nov. 16, 1938: *Documents on British Foreign Policy*, 1919–1939, H.M.S.O.

225 Deaths in Buchenwald reported to British Foreign Office in 1938: *Papers Concerning the Treatment of German Nationals in Germany* (CMD 6120), 1938–1939, H.M.S.O.

226 Dachau after the *Kristallnacht*, reported by British Consul General Carvel to Lord Halifax, Jan. 5, 1939: *ibid.*

226 Deaths at Dachau: *News Chronicle*, Sept. 6; London *Observer*, June 12; London *Times*, June 4, 1938.

226 Mr. Noel-Baker's speech, reported by U.S. embassy, London, Nov. 26, 1938 (840.48 REFUGEES/1089).

227 Father Coughlin qtd.: *Newsweek*, Dec. 5, 1938.

PAGE

227 George Rublee's description of Intergovernmental Committee crisis in telegram of Nov. 14, 1938, to Secy. Hull (862.4016/1822).

229 Messersmith's memo to Hull of Nov. 14, 1938: FRUS, 1938, Vol. II, pp. 396–8.

230 Hull tells Amb. Wilson to return from Germany: *ibid.*, pp. 398–9.

231 Thirty-six prominent writers urge an American protest, Nov. 16, 1938 (862.4016/1841).

232 Amb. Biddle presses for action, Nov. 15, 1938 (862.4016/1961).

233 Summary of refugee situation prepared by member of Division of European Affairs (n.d.), attached to Nov. 15, 1938 memo of Division of the American Republics (840.48/900½).

234 Sir Ronald Lindsay tells Sumner Welles that Britain is willing to relinquish part of its immigration quota, memo of conversation, Nov. 17, 1938 (840.48/911½).

236 President Roosevelt's confidential letter to Myron Taylor, Nov. 23, 1938: FDRL OF 3186.

237 President Roosevelt's correspondence with Isaiah Bowman, Oct. 14–Dec. 15, 1938: FDRL PPF 5575.

238 AP dispatch of Nov. 27, 1938; *N.Y. Times*. Nov. 28.

238 Amb. Dieckhoff pays final call on Secy. Hull, Nov. 22, 1938: FRUS, 1938, Vol. II, p. 405.

239 Dieckhoff's list of prominent American Jews in his memo of Oct. 9, 1941: qtd. in Friedlander, *Hitler et les États-Unis, 1939–41.*

239 *Das Schwarze Korps* predicts the solution of the Jewish problem as "complete extermination": qtd. *N.Y. Times,* Nov. 23, 1938; and dispatch from U.S. embassy, Berlin, Nov. 23, 1938 (862.4016/1893).

XIII The Attempt to Buy Lives

241 Details of Schacht's "package deal" for the Jews: Rublee's message of Dec. 15, 1938 (840.48 REFUGEES/1119).

242 Sumner Welles's reply of Dec. 19, 1938: attached to above.

243 Jewish newspaper (*Nachrichtenblatt*) comments on the United States' moral duty: qtd. in *N.Y. Times,* Jan. 28, 1939.

243 Wohlthat's unexpected announcement: summarized in *N.Y. Times,* Feb. 14, 1939, and detailed in FRUS, 1939, Vol. II, pp. 77–81.

245 Rublee's hopeful telegram to Hull: *ibid.*, pp. 82–4.

245 Hull's dampening reply: *ibid.*, pp. 84–7.

247 Pell puts Wohlthat's question to the State Dept.: *ibid.*, pp. 95–7.

247 State Dept. replies to Pell: *ibid.*, pp. 97–8.

248 Myron Taylor reports three stumbling blocks: *ibid.*, pp. 105–7.

248 The Gestapo permits Jewish representatives to visit London and

PAGE

Pell reports their meetings with the Intergovernmental Committee: *ibid.*, pp. 110–14.
249 Hull's objection to matching funds: *ibid.*, p. 124.
249 Pell and Achilles feel U.S. should "get full credit": *ibid.*, pp. 130–1.
250 The public and Congress have no direct interest: *ibid.*, pp. 135–6.
250 Sir Herbert Emerson finds the villain: *ibid.*, p. 134.
250 Robert Pell attempts to dissuade President Roosevelt: FRUS, 1940, Vol. II, pp. 215–8.
251 The President disagrees with Pell: *ibid.*, pp. 218–9.

XIV "Suffer Little Children . . ."

252 Quentin Reynolds' description of refugee children at Dovercourt: "Unwanted," *Collier's* magazine, Feb. 11, 1939.
254 Eddie Cantor's correspondence with Marvin McIntyre: FDRL PPF 1018.
255 Mrs. Roosevelt explains her husband's seeming indifference: in her autobiography, *This I Remember*, pp. 161–2.
256 Mrs. Roosevelt's telegram to the President, Feb. 22, 1939: FDRL PPF 2.
256 Roosevelt warns Myron Taylor of impending disasters, cable of Jan. 14, 1939 (840.48/1290B).
256 British reject Taylor's proposal, Feb. 9, 1939 (840.48/1399).
257 Hitler's speech of Jan. 30, 1939, predicting "the annihilation of the Jewish race in Europe": qtd. in Hausner, *op. cit.*, p. 48.
257 "Admission of German Refugee Children," transcript of hearings held by subcommittees of Committee on Immigration of House and Senate, 76th Cong., 1st sess., April 20, 21, 24, 1939.
265 "Admission of German Refugee Children," transcript of hearings held by Immigration Committee of House of Representatives, 76th Cong., 1st sess., May 24, 25, 31, June 1, 1939.
268 "Pa" Watson's memo of June 2, 1939, to President Roosevelt: FDRL OF 3186.

XV The Voyage of the *St. Louis*

Details of the voyage of the *St. Louis* were obtained from United States, British, German and Cuban newspapers; the files of the Joint Distribution Committee; published materials and files of the Institute for Advanced Studies in Contemporary History (Wiener Library), London; and interviews with Cecilia Razovsky and Lawrence Berenson.

XVI Prelude to the "Final Solution"

PAGE

290 Report of the first deportation of German Jews to Poland: telegram of Feb. 16, 1940, from U.S. embassy, Berlin (862.4016/2156).

290 Detailed descriptions of the "resettlement": *N.Y. Times,* Feb. 22, 1940.

291 Berle's memo of Feb. 17, 1940, to Long (862.4016/2172).

291 Berle's memo of Feb. 23, 1940, to Hull (862.4016/2162½).

291 Long replies to Berle and expresses sympathy "with the poor people involved," his memo attached to note of Feb. 26, 1940, from Asst. Chief, Division of European Affairs (862.4016/2198).

293 Alsop memo to the President: FDRL OF 3186.

294 Information about Rockefeller Foundation and University in Exile: from Wetzel, *The American Rescue of Refugee Scholars and Scientists from Europe, 1933–45.*

294 Varian Fry's feats: Fry, *Surrender on Demand.*

295 James G. McDonald's protest to the President, memo of Oct. 8, 1940: FDRL OF 3186.

296 Breckinridge Long's summary of visa activities to Secy. Hull of Jan. 6, 1944: FDRL OF 3186.

297 Roosevelt trades destroyers for bases and takes "the lion's role": Burns, *op. cit.,* p. 442.

297 Reporter Steinkopf tours the General Government of Poland: *N.Y. Times,* Oct. 13, 1940.

298 Minister Gunther reports a massacre in Rumania: FRUS, 1941, Vol. II, p. 860.

299 Minister Gunther lacks firm instructions from Washington: *ibid.,* pp. 864–5.

299 Minister Gunther quotes Marshal Antonescu on settling the Jewish problem "once and for all": *ibid.,* p. 871–4.

299 Cavendish Cannon discourages the Turkish minister's proposal to rescue Rumanian Jews: *ibid.,* pp. 875–6.

303 James G. McDonald tries to eliminate discrimination against refugees: recommendations of the President's Political Advisory Committee on Refugees, Sept. 4, 1941: FDRL OF 3186.

303 Albert Einstein's letter of July 26, 1941, to Mrs. Roosevelt: FDRL PPF 7177.

304 Göring's directive of July 31, 1941: qtd. in Shirer, *The Rise and Fall of the Third Reich,* p. 964.

304 Mandate of the *Einsatzgruppen:* qtd. in Hilberg, *op. cit.,* p. 183.

305 Children arrive on the *Serpa Pinta:* N.Y. *Herald Tribune,* Sept. 25, 1941.

PAGE

306 Dispatches describing deportation of German Jews to Poland, from U.S. embassy, Berlin, Oct. 18 and 20 and Nov. 16, 1941 (862.4016/2206, 2207, 2208).

307 A correspondent watches the embarkation of Jews in Berlin: *N.Y. Times,* Oct. 30, 1941.

307 Descriptions of Wannsee conference from Nuremberg documents: qtd. in Reitlinger, *op. cit.,* pp. 95–8; Hilberg, *op. cit.,* pp. 264–5; Shirer, *op. cit.,* pp. 965–6.

308 Sinking of the *Struma:* in Hirschmann, *Life Line to a Promised Land,* pp. 3–9; Reitlinger, *op. cit.,* pp. 405–6; L.B. Namier, "Refugee Boats," *Time and Tide,* Mar. 14, 1942.

309 President Roosevelt's letter to Madison Square Garden rally: qtd. *N.Y. Times,* July 22, 1942.

XVII The War Refugee Board

316 Hirschmann slashes red tape in issuing visas: WRB History, "Rescue to and through Turkey."

317 Hirschmann pressures Cretzianu to free the Jews from Transnistrian camps: Hirschmann, *Caution to the Winds,* pp. 155–60; WRB History, "Rescue from Rumania"; and messages from Hirschmann to Pehle, in WRB Projects and Documents, Box 31.

318 U.S. warning to the Rumanians, letter of Feb. 15, 1944, from Pehle to Stettinius, and Stettinius telegram of Feb. 25 to Amb. Steinhardt: WRB Projects and Documents, Box 42.

319 Balabanoff writes to Gilbert Simond, July 25, 1944: WRB Projects and Documents, Box 36.

319 Hirschmann meets Balabanoff early in Aug. 1944, memo from Hirschmann to Counselor Kelly, U.S. embassy, Ankara: WRB Projects and Documents, Box 36.

319 Balabanoff–Hirschmann correspondence: Hirschmann, *Life Line to a Promised Land,* pp. 158, 160–1.

320 Barlas meets Monsignor Roncalli: letter from Chaim Barlas to author, Feb. 14, 1967, enclosing Barlas' essay "Pope John XXIII and His Attitude to the Jews."

321 Intervention of Monsignor Roncalli: described in letter of Mar. 4, 1966, from Luigi Bresciani to Monsignor Loris Capovilla, former private secretary to Pope John XXVIII, and in author's interviews and correspondence with Mr. Bresciani and Monsignor Capovilla.

XVIII Obstruction and Rescue

323 WRB drafts a cable about Cyrenaica, entry of Mar. 20, 1944: WRB Liaison with State Department file.

PAGE

323 Mann reports Cyrenaica cable delay to Pehle, Mar. 24: *ibid.*

325 WRB message to Red Cross of Mar. 23, 1944: WRB History, "Relief Programs."

326 Red Cross president Huber's reply, May 17: *ibid.*

326 Huber reluctant to increase Red Cross delegation in Budapest, telegram from U.S. legation, Bern, Apr. 13, 1944: WRB Projects and Documents, Box 34, Folder 3.

326 The board snaps back in response, Secy. of State Hull to Minister Harrison and Roswell McClelland, Bern, May 25, 1944: *ibid.*

328 Red Cross delegate Dunand risks his life: Dunand, *Ne perdez pas leur trace!*

329 Hoeflinger incident: reported in *L'Activité du CICR en faveur des civils détenus dans les camps de concentration en Allemagne,* pp. 138–42.

329 Pehle notifies Morgenthau that board has broken the blockade, memo of June 16, 1944: WRB Projects and Documents. Box 29.

329 Red Cross defense of its position: *Report of the International Committee of the Red Cross on Its Activities during the Second World War,* Vol. III, p. 81.

330 McClelland's work with French resistance: Final Report of Roswell McClelland to WRB, July 1945.

332 Amb. Hayes's obstructionism: detailed in WRB History, "Rescue to and through Spain."

333 Pehle memo re Hayes: WRB Projects and Documents, Box 30.

333 An outline of grievances against Hayes in memo of J. B. Friedman: *ibid.*

334 Rep. Celler urges Amb. Hayes's recall, statement of June 21, 1944: WRB Projects and Documents, Box 24.

336 Pehle reacts to British opposition to war crimes declaration, letter of Feb. 11, 1944, to Stettinius: WRB History, "Psychological Warfare."

337 Mar. 24, 1944, presidential statement on war crimes: qtd. *N.Y. Times,* same date.

XIX Free Ports and False Papers

340 DuBois memos to Pehle of Mar. 6, 1944, and unspecified later date in March: WRB Temporary Haven file.

341 Pehle discusses the idea of temporary havens with Undersecy. of State Stettinius, Pehle note of Mar. 9, 1944: *ibid.*

342 President Roosevelt's press conference: N.Y. *Post,* May 31, 1944.

342 Establishment of emergency shelter at Oswego, N.Y.: WRB History, "Oswego Shelter."

PAGE

343 Canada's restrictive immigration policy: WRB History, "Cooperation with Other Countries."

343 South Africa fails to reply: *ibid.*

343 Secret message by courier to Latin America, secret circular airgram of Mar. 31, 1944: WRB History, "Latin American Passports."

344 Quotation from *Verdades:* WRB Projects and Documents, Box 32.

344 Peru denies the citizenship of forty-eight Jews, message of Apr. 10, 1944, from American embassy, Lima: WRB Projects and Documents, Box 45.

345 The Venezuelan attitude, report from U.S. embassy, Caracas, Feb. 4, 1944: *ibid.*

345 The Cuban attitude, Mar. 1944 report: WRB History, "Cooperation with Other Countries."

345 The Brazilian attitude: *ibid.*

345 Sequence of cables of Feb. 21, Mar. 16 and Apr. 7 detailed in letter of Apr. 14, 1944, drafted for Morgenthau by James Mann of WRB, addressed to Hull but not sent. Text of cable #1181 of Apr. 7: WRB Camp Vittel file.

346 The Chief Rabbi of Palestine cables John Pehle, Apr. 5, 1944; WRB Projects and Documents, Box 45.

346 Pehle and staff attempt to influence State Dept. action, Pehle memo to Morgenthau of Apr. 19, 1944, describing efforts: WRB Camp Vittel file.

347 Quotation: Katznelson, *Vittel Diary,* p. 204.

348 Iver Olsen's accomplishments: WRB History, "Rescue to and through Sweden."

XX Rescue from Hungary

350 Chief Rabbi Hervesi's sermon: qtd. in Levai, *op. cit.*

351 Cardinal Serédi's written statement to Prime Minister Szotay, Apr. 23, 1944: *ibid.*

351 Cardinal Serédi reports that baptized Jews can wear the cross, pastoral letter of May 17, 1944: *ibid.*

352 Death of three old women, qtd. from May 23, 1944 issue of *Uj Nemzedék: ibid.*

353 WRB message to Pope Pius XII, May 26, 1944: WRB Projects and Documents, Box 34, Folder 7.

353 Amb. Steinhardt's first ref. to Joel Brand, telegram of May 25, 1944: WRB Projects and Documents, Box 70.

354 Amb. Steinhardt describes Brand's traveling companion, Gyorgy, June 5, 1944: *ibid.*

354 Eichmann promises to close Auschwitz if his offer is accepted: Weissberg, *Desperate Mission,* p. 105.

PAGE

355 Britain reacts to the Brand mission, *aide-mémoire* delivered by Lord Halifax to State Dept., June 5, 1944: Weizmann Archives, Rehovoth, Israel.

356 Shertok describes Brand in report: *ibid.*

357 Hirschmann defies Lord Moyne: Hirschmann, *Caution to the Winds,* p. 115.

357 Hirschmann's analysis of Brand in report of June 22, attached to his letter to Pehle of July 3, 1944: WRB Projects and Documents, Box 70.

358 The Soviets cast a veto on the Joel Brand negotiations, telegram from Secy. of State to Amb. Steinhardt of June 20, 1944, incorporating June 19 message from Amb. Harriman in Moscow: *ibid.*

358 McClelland proposes the bombing of the railway lines to Auschwitz in telegram of June 24; Pehle's transmittal to McCloy of June 29; and McCloy's reply of July 4, 1944: WRB History, "Rescue from Hungary."

359 James Mann relays a message from the Polish government-in-exile, Sept. 29, 1944: WRB Projects and Documents, Box 34, Folder 5.

359 Pehle becomes more insistent about bombing proposal, in letter to John McCloy, Nov. 8, 1944; and McCloy's response of Nov. 18: WRB Projects and Documents, Box 5.

360 Weizmann's bombing proposal turned down, letter from Richard Law to Weizmann, Sept. 1, 1944: Weizmann Archives.

360 Winston Churchill's private secy. replies tersely, letter to Weizmann from J. F. Martin, Oct. 30, 1944: *ibid.*

361 Jewish Agency proposal to drop Palestinian parachutists into Hungary, *aide-mémoire* of Nov. 1945, prepared for Dr. Weizmann's possible use at Nuremberg trials: *ibid.*

362 The ICRC appeals to Adm. Horthy: *Report of the International Committee of the Red Cross on Its Activities during the Second World War,* Vol. I, p. 648.

362 ff. Raoul Wallenberg's achievements and capture by the Russians: WRB History, "Rescue from Hungary"; WRB Projects and Documents, Box 33 and Box 35; White Papers of the Royal Ministry for Foreign Affairs, Stockholm, on Raoul Wallenberg case, issued in 1957 and 1965; Philipp, *Raoul Wallenberg* and *Raoul Wallenberg: Fighter for Humanity;* author's interviews with Per Anger and members of Wallenberg family.

363 WRB provides Roaul Wallenberg with list of corrupt Hungarians: WRB History, "Miscellaneous Documents," Vol. II.

365 Ira Hirschmann meets with Monsignor Roncalli, Aug. 1, 1944; Hirschmann, *Caution to the Winds,* pp. 179–85; author's inter-

PAGE

views with Hirschmann; and WRB Projects and Documents, Box 34, Folder 7.

366 Monsignor Roncalli confirms his assistance to the Jews, letter of Aug. 18 to Hirschmann: *ibid.*

368 Ujváry group's description of the death march to Austria: qtd. in Levai, *op. cit.*

371 Achievements of Saly Mayer: WRB History, "Rescue—Special Negotiations"; WRB Projects and Documents, Box 70; Final Report of Roswell McClelland to WRB, July 1945; files of the Joint Distribution Committee; author's interview with Roswell McClelland.

372 Monsignor Rotta delivers the neutrals' note: text qtd. in Levai, *op. cit.*

374 Tribute to Wallenberg by the Israelite Congregation of Pest: qtd. in Philipp, *Raoul Wallenberg: Fighter for Humanity*, pp. 19–20.

XXI Crimes of War, Crimes of Peace

375 President Roosevelt reminds Secy. Hull of Herbert Pell, memo from Roosevelt to Hull, Apr. 19, 1943 (740.00116 EW 1939/994).

376 Amb. Winant informs State Dept. that Pell should not leave for London, telegram of July 13, 1943 (740.00116 EW 1939/991).

376 President Roosevelt inquires about the delay in sending Pell to London, memo of Sept. 2, 1943 (740.00116 EW 1939/1084).

376 The President asks again about Pell and the war criminals' trials, memo of Oct. 29, 1943, to Acting Secy. of State Stettinius (740.-00116 EW 1939/1143).

377 Pell becomes exasperated, Ralph W.S. Hill's memo of conversation with Pell, Nov. 19, 1943 (740.00116 EW 1939/1178).

377 John Pehle describes Pell's plight to the Acting Secy. of State, letter of Aug. 28, 1944: WRB History, "United Nations War Crimes Commission."

378 James Mann complains that no action has been taken on war crimes, telegram to Pehle, Oct. 6, 1944: WRB Projects and Documents, Box 18.

378 Criticism of War Crimes Commission: Washington *Post,* Jan. 31, 1945.

379 Pehle presses Stettinius for action, letter of Dec. 23, 1944: WRB Projects and Documents, Box 18.

380 Newspaper reaction to the resignation of Herbert Pell: London *Express,* Jan. 28; N.Y. *Post,* Jan. 27; and Washington *Post,* Jan. 31, 1945.

382 Amounts contributed to work of WRB: WRB History, "Relief Programs."

PAGE

383 Ira Hirschmann's final report to John Pehle, Oct. 4, 1944: WRB Projects and Documents, Box 31.

383 Roswell McClelland sums up: Final Report to WRB, July 1945.

Bibliography

Acheson, Dean, *Morning and Noon.* Boston, Houghton Mifflin, 1965.

Adler, Cyrus, and Margalith, Aaron M., *With Firmness in the Right.* New York, The American Jewish Committee, 1946.

Arendt, Hannah, *Eichmann in Jerusalem.* New York, Viking Press, 1963.

Bennett, Marion T., *American Immigration Policies.* Washington, D.C., Public Affairs Press, 1963.

Bentwich, Norman, *They Found Refuge.* London, The Cresset Press, 1956.

Bullock, Alan, *Hitler: A Study in Tyranny.* New York, Bantam Books, 1961.

Burns, James MacGregor, *Roosevelt: The Lion and the Fox.* New York, Harcourt, Brace and World, 1956.

Churchill, Sir Winston S., *The Second World War* (six volumes). Boston, Houghton Mifflin, 1948–1953.

Coursier, Henri, *The International Red Cross.* Geneva, International Committee of the Red Cross, 1961.

Deuel, Wallace R., *People under Hitler.* New York, Harcourt, Brace, 1942.

Documents on British Foreign Policy, 1919–1939. London, H. M. Stationery Office, 1947, 1956.

DuBois, Josiah E., Jr., *The Devil's Chemists.* Boston, Beacon Press, 1952.

Dunand, Georges, *Ne perdez pas leur trace!* Neuchâtel, Éditions de la Baconnière, 1950.

Eden, Anthony (Earl of Avon), *The Memoirs of Anthony Eden.* Boston, Houghton Mifflin, 1962.

Eisenhower, Dwight D., *Crusade in Europe.* New York, Doubleday, 1948.

Extermination and Resistance. Israel, Kibbutz Lohamei Haghettaot, 1958.

Feis, Herbert, *1933: Characters in Crisis.* Boston, Little, Brown, 1966.

Foreign Relations of the United States (volumes covering 1932–1944). Washington, D.C., Department of State.

Friedlander, Saul, *Hitler et les États-Unis, 1939–41.* Geneva, Droz, 1963.

Friedlander, Saul, *Pie XII et le IIIe Reich*. Paris, Éditions du Seuil, 1964.
Friedman, Philip, *Their Brothers' Keepers*. New York, Crown, 1957.
———, ed., *Martyrs and Fighters*. New York, Frederick A. Praeger, 1954.
Fry, Varian, *Surrender on Demand*. New York, Random House, 1945.
Goebbels, Josef, *The Goebbels Diaries 1942–1943*. Louis P. Lochner, ed. Garden City, Doubleday, 1948.
Gunther, John, *Roosevelt in Retrospect*. New York, Harper and Bros., 1950.
Handlin, Oscar, *A Continuing Task*. New York, Random House, 1964.
———, *Race and Nationality in American Life*. Boston, Little, Brown, 1957.
Hausner, Gideon, *Justice in Jerusalem*. New York, Harper & Row, 1966.
Hecht, Ben, *A Child of the Century*. New York, Simon & Schuster, 1954.
Hilberg, Raul, *The Destruction of the European Jews*. Chicago, Quadrangle Books, 1961.
Hirschmann, Ira A., *Caution to the Winds*. New York, David McKay, 1962.
———, *Life Line to a Promised Land*. New York, Vanguard Press, 1946.
Hochhuth, Rolf, *The Representative [The Deputy]*. London, Methuen, 1963.
Hull, Cordell, *The Memoirs of Cordell Hull* (two volumes). New York, Macmillan, 1948.
Ickes, Harold, *The Secret Diary of Harold L. Ickes*. New York, Simon & Schuster, 1954.
Inter Arma Caritas. Geneva, International Committee of the Red Cross, 1947.
Katznelson, Yitzhak, *Vittel Diary*. Israel, Kibbutz Lohamei Haghettaot, 1954.
L'Activité des organisations juives en France. Paris, Éditions du Centre de Documentation Juive Contemporaine, 1947.
L'Activité du CICR en faveur des civils détenus dans les camps de concentration en Allemagne (1939–1945). Geneva, Comité International de la Croix-Rouge, 1947.
Levai, Eugene, *Black Book on the Martyrdom of Hungarian Jewry*. Zurich, Central European Times Publishing Co., 1948.
———, *Raoul Wallenberg—hjälten i Budapest*. Stockholm, Saxon & Lindströms Förlag, 1948.
Lewy, Guenter, *The Roman Catholic Church and the Third Reich*. New York, McGraw-Hill, 1964.
Long, Breckinridge, *The War Diary of Breckinridge Long*, Fred L. Israel, ed. Lincoln, University of Nebraska Press, 1966.

MacDonald, Dwight, *Memoirs of a Revolutionist.* New York, Farrar, Straus & Cudahy, 1957.

Medlicott, W. N., *The Economic Blockade.* London, H. M. Stationery Office, 1952.

Papers Concerning the Treatment of German Nationals in Germany, (CMD 6120), 1938–1939. London, H. M. Stationery Office.

Philipp, Rudolp, *Raoul Wallenberg.* Stockholm, Fredborgs Förlag, 1946.

Poliakov, Leon, and Sabille, Jacques, *Jews Under the Italian Occupation.* Paris, Éditions du Centre de Documentation Juive Contemporaine, 1955.

Reitlinger, Gerald, *The Final Solution.* New York, A. S. Barnes, 1961.

Report of the International Committee of the Red Cross on Its Activities During the Second World War (three volumes). Geneva, International Committee of the Red Cross, 1948.

Robinson, Jacob, and Friedman, Philip, *Guide to Jewish History under Nazi Impact.* New York, and YIVO Institute for Jewish Research, and Jerusalem, Yad Vashem, 1960.

Roosevelt, Eleanor, *This I Remember.* New York, Harper and Bros., 1949.

Roosevelt, Franklin D., *The Public Papers and Addresses of Franklin D. Roosevelt,* compiled by Samuel I. Rosenman. New York, Random House, 1938–50.

Sabille, Jacques, *Lueurs dans la tourmente.* Paris, Éditions du Centre de Documentation Juive Contemporaine, 1956.

Sharf, Andrew, *The British Press and Jews under Nazi Rule.* London, Oxford University Press, 1964.

Sherwood, Robert E., *Roosevelt and Hopkins.* New York, Harper and Bros., 1948.

Shirer, William L., *Berlin Diary.* New York, Alfred A. Knopf, 1943.

———, *The Rise and Fall of the Third Reich.* New York, Simon & Schuster, 1960.

Tartakower, Arieh, and Grossman, Kurt R., *The Jewish Refugee.* New York, Institute of Jewish Affairs of the World Jewish Congress, 1944.

Unity in Dispersion. New York, Institute of Jewish Affairs of the World Jewish Congress, 1948.

Vrba, Rudolf, and Bestic, Alan, *I Cannot Forgive.* New York, Bantam Books, 1964.

Weissberg, Alex, and Brand, Joel, *Desperate Mission.* New York, Grove Press, 1958.

Wetzel, Charles John, *The American Rescue of Refugee Scholars and Scientists from Europe, 1933–1945.* Unpublished MS. thesis, University of Wisconsin, 1964.

Williams, Irving G., *The Rise of the Vice-Presidency*. Washington, D.C., Public Affairs Press, 1956.

Wise, Stephen S., *Challenging Years: The Autobiography of Stephen Wise*. New York, Putnam, 1949.

The Yellow Spot: The Extermination of the Jews in Germany. London, Victor Gollancz, 1936.

Zahn, Gordon, *German Catholics and Hitler's Wars*. New York, Sheed & Ward, 1962.

Index

ABOUT THE AUTHOR

ARTHUR D. MORSE began his career as a free-lance writer for national magazines. His awards in this field include Sigma Delta Chi's annual citation for "distinguished public service journalism." In 1953 he joined CBS News and became a reporter-director for Edward R. Murrow's *See It Now* television series. He was responsible for many of its most provocative broadcasts, including the network's first presentation of the cigarette-lung cancer controversy. After serving as a producer of *CBS Reports,* he succeeded Fred Friendly as executive producer of this pioneering group. His documentaries have won numerous honors, including the Robert E. Sherwood and George Foster Peabody awards. He is the author of *Schools of Tomorrow—Today*.

Mr. Morse resigned from CBS in 1965 to write this book. He and his wife and their two children live in Scarsdale, New York.

YS
for each day the book